Second Language Study Abroad

John L. Plews • Kim Misfeldt
Editors

Second Language Study Abroad

Programming, Pedagogy, and Participant Engagement

Editors
John L. Plews
Department of Modern
Languages & Classics
Saint Mary's University
Halifax, NS, Canada

Kim Misfeldt
Fine Arts and Humanities
Augustana Campus, University of Alberta
Camrose, AB, Canada

ISBN 978-3-319-77133-5   ISBN 978-3-319-77134-2   (eBook)
https://doi.org/10.1007/978-3-319-77134-2

Library of Congress Control Number: 2018937674

© The Editor(s) (if applicable) and The Author(s) 2018
This work is subject to copyright. All rights are solely and exclusively licensed by the Publisher, whether the whole or part of the material is concerned, specifically the rights of translation, reprinting, reuse of illustrations, recitation, broadcasting, reproduction on microfilms or in any other physical way, and transmission or information storage and retrieval, electronic adaptation, computer software, or by similar or dissimilar methodology now known or hereafter developed.
The use of general descriptive names, registered names, trademarks, service marks, etc. in this publication does not imply, even in the absence of a specific statement, that such names are exempt from the relevant protective laws and regulations and therefore free for general use.
The publisher, the authors, and the editors are safe to assume that the advice and information in this book are believed to be true and accurate at the date of publication. Neither the publisher nor the authors or the editors give a warranty, express or implied, with respect to the material contained herein or for any errors or omissions that may have been made. The publisher remains neutral with regard to jurisdictional claims in published maps and institutional affiliations.

Cover image © courtneyk / Getty Images

Printed on acid-free paper

This Palgrave Macmillan imprint is published by the registered company Springer International Publishing AG part of Springer Nature.
The registered company address is: Gewerbestrasse 11, 6330 Cham, Switzerland

Contents

Introduction: Shifting Attention to Second Language Study
Abroad Programming, Pedagogy, and Participant Engagement   1
John L. Plews and Kim Misfeldt

Part I   Curriculum and Design   23

Positioning Year-Long Study Abroad at the Centre
of the Modern Languages Curriculum: Supporting
and Assessing Learning   25
Penny Johnson and Simon McKinnon

Lessons from 25 Years of Experimenting with Arabic Study
Abroad: Programme Evaluation, Culture, Location,
and Curriculum   49
Matthew T. Bird and R. Kirk Belnap

Student-Centred Second Language Study Abroad for Non-
traditional Sojourners: An Anglophone Caribbean Example   83
Ian Craig

Part II Pedagogical Approaches   123

Student Awareness of Teaching and Learning Approaches in Second Language Study Abroad   125
John L. Plews, Kim Misfeldt, and Feisal Kirumira

Increasing Student Engagement During Study Abroad Through Service Learning: A View from Japan   165
Dawn Grimes-MacLellan

Part III Participant Experiences and Engagement   193

Exploring Intercultural Learning and Second Language Identities in the ERASMUS Context   195
Ana Beaven and Claudia Borghetti

'I Thought I Was Prepared.' ERASMUS Students' Voices on Their Transition from L2 Learners to L2 Users   223
Sònia Mas-Alcolea

Language Teachers on Study Abroad Programmes: The Characteristics and Strategies of Those Most Likely to Increase Their Intercultural Communicative Competence   257
Deborah Corder, Annelies Roskvist, Sharon Harvey, and Karen Stacey

Adopt a Class: Engagement and Reflection During the Year Abroad   299
Elizabeth A. Andersen and Sophie Stewart

Second Language Speaking and Intercultural Friendship Formation in Study Abroad: Experiences and Perspectives of International Students in the USA   327
Rebecca K. Smith

**Gender as a Cultural and Social Construct in Language
Learning During Study Abroad** 371
Mar Galindo

Index 403

Notes on Contributors

Elizabeth A. Andersen *Senior Lecturer in German, School of Modern Languages, Newcastle University, UK, and Director of the Routes into Languages North East Consortium.* Dr. Andersen is a Senior Lecturer in German at the School of Modern Languages at Newcastle University. She teaches and researches in German Medieval Studies and Film. Since September 2007, she has been the Director of the North East Consortium of the National Routes into Languages project, an outreach project designed to stimulate and foster interest in the teaching of foreign languages in secondary schools.

Ana Beaven *English Language Teacher, University Language Centre (C.I.L.T.A.), University of Bologna.* Dr. Beaven is an English Language teacher at the University Language Centre, University of Bologna, Italy. Her main areas of interest are intercultural (language) education, intercultural adaptation during study abroad, and foreign language teaching and learning. She was the coordinator of the European project IEREST (*Intercultural Education Resources for ERASMUS Students and their Teachers*).

R. Kirk Belnap *Professor of Arabic, Brigham Young University.* Dr. Belnap is a Professor of Arabic at Brigham Young University. He is also Director of the National Middle East Language Resource Center and of BYU's STARTALK summer Arabic high school camps. His research interests include language policy and planning, second language acquisition, study abroad, and the history of Arabic.

Matthew T. Bird *PhD Candidate, Instructional Psychology and Technology, Brigham Young University.* Mr. Bird is a PhD candidate at Brigham Young University. He is interested in the design of second language instruction, study abroad, and educational evaluation.

Claudia Borghetti *Research Fellow, Department of Modern Languages, Literature and Cultures, University of Bologna.* Dr. Borghetti is Research Fellow in Language Learning and Teaching at the Department of Modern Languages, Literature and Cultures, University of Bologna, Italy. She was the project manager of the IEREST Project. She researches on intercultural language learning and teaching, language education, and teaching Italian as a foreign/second language.

Deborah (Debbie) Corder *Senior Lecturer and Associate Head of the School of Language and Culture, Auckland University of Technology.* Ms. Corder is a Senior Lecturer and Associate Head of the School of Language and Culture at Auckland University of Technology. She has taught Japanese at secondary and tertiary levels and her teaching now focusses on intercultural competence in BA programmes. Her research interests include learner autonomy, ICT, intercultural competence, and study abroad.

Ian Craig *Senior Lecturer in Spanish, University of the West Indies, Cave Hill Campus (Barbados).* Dr. Craig is a Senior Lecturer in Spanish at the University of the West Indies. Since joining the Cave Hill Campus of UWI in 1999, he has led two student trips to Cuba and began research in study and residence abroad by Caribbean sojourners in 2007. He is currently developing summer programmes for UWI students in Costa Rica, Mexico, and Spain and hopes to continue to research and enhance the experience of sojourners from non-traditional study abroad source contexts such as the Caribbean.

Mar Galindo *Senior Lecturer in Linguistics, University of Alicante.* Dr. Galindo is a Senior Lecturer in Linguistics at the University of Alicante. She specialised in SLA and the Teaching of Modern Languages at the University of Pennsylvania and the University of Hawai'i at Manoa. She has been awarded with the ASELE prize for excellence in research of Spanish language teaching (2011) and the Young research prize of the Spanish Applied Linguistics Association (2013). She is interested in languages, feminism, sports, and study abroad. She is a member of the Institute for Research in Gender Studies of the University of Alicante.

Dawn Grimes-MacLellan *Assistant Professor, Meiji Gakuin University.* Dr. Grimes-MacLellan received her Ph.D. in Anthropology from the University of Illinois and is currently an Assistant Professor at Meiji Gakuin University in Tokyo. She is conducting research on student volunteerism and community partnership in post 3.11 Japan.

Sharon Harvey *Associate Professor and Head of the School of Language and Culture, Auckland University of Technology.* Dr. Harvey is an Associate Professor and Head of the School of Language and Culture, as well as Deputy Dean (Research) of Faculty of Culture and Society, at Auckland University of Technology. Her research interests cover critical language and migrant studies, discourse analysis, language learning and teaching, curriculum studies, language policy and planning, intercultural communication and competency, and language teacher development.

Penny Johnson *Teaching Fellow, School of Modern Languages and Cultures, Durham University.* Dr. Johnson teaches Spanish and Translation at Durham University and is Year Abroad Assessment Co-Ordinator in the School of Modern Languages and Cultures. Her research and scholarship activities are based on Bourdieusian concepts of field and capital and postcolonial theory in translation.

Feisal Kirumira *Sessional Instructor, Augustana Campus, University of Alberta.* Mr. Kirumira has a Master's degree in German Language and Literatures from the University of Saarland, Germany, and in Applied Linguistics from the University of Alberta. He is currently enrolled in a PhD programme in Secondary Education at the University of Alberta. His research interests include error analysis, social linguistics, critical pedagogy, and phenomenology.

Sònia Mas-Alcolea *Associate Professor of English as a Foreign Language, University of Lleida.* Dr. Mas-Alcolea is an Associate Professor of English as a Foreign Language in the Department of English and Linguistics at the University of Lleida. Her current research, which adopts a discourse-analytic approach, specialises in (European) student and academic mobility, identity and language learning/use abroad, and cross-cultural communication and interculturality.

Simon McKinnon *Teaching Fellow, School of Modern Languages and Cultures, Durham University.* Dr. McKinnon teaches French and Translation at Durham University and has responsibility for curriculum development in the School of Modern Languages and Cultures. His research interests include the intersection between translation and imagology, translation pedagogy, and language learning pedagogy.

Kim Misfeldt *Professor of German and Vice Dean, Augustana Campus, University of Alberta.* Dr. Misfeldt is Professor of German and Vice Dean at the Augustana Campus, University of Alberta. She directed the Canadian Summer School in Germany 2003–2016. Her excellence in university teaching and educational leadership has been recognised with four teaching awards, including a 3M

National Teaching Fellowship and the Charles Dunn COPLAC Award. She teaches courses in language, literature, translation, and gender studies. Her research interests include second language pedagogy, drama pedagogy, Heinrich von Kleist, and Mariella Mehr.

John L. Plews *Professor of German, Saint Mary's University, President of the Canadian Association of University Teachers of German, and DAAD Research Ambassador.* Dr. John L. Plews is Professor of German at Saint Mary's University in Nova Scotia, President of the Canadian Association of University Teachers of German, and DAAD Research Ambassador. He earned PhDs in German Literature, Languages, and Linguistics and in Secondary Education. He publishes in the area of second language curriculum and teaching, second language learner identities, and study abroad for language learners and teachers.

Annelies Roskvist *Senior Lecturer and Deputy Head of the School of Language and Culture, Auckland University of Technology.* Ms. Roskvist is a Senior Lecturer and Deputy Head of the School of Language and Culture at Auckland University of Technology, and has taught in Language Teacher Education programmes. Her research interests are study abroad, professional development for language teachers, and the development of intercultural communicative competence.

Rebecca K. Smith *English as a Second Language Instructor, Lone Star College, Tomball, Texas.* Ms. Smith teaches English as a Second Language near Houston, Texas. She earned an MA in Linguistic Studies from Syracuse University with concentrations in language acquisition and language teaching. Her research interests include the sociocultural factors of language acquisition in an immersion context.

Karen Stacey *Senior Lecturer, School of Language and Culture, Auckland University of Technology.* Ms. Stacey is a Senior Lecturer at the School of Language and Culture at Auckland University of Technology. Her research interests include study abroad as professional development for language teachers and the role of paraprofessionals in the teaching of English as an additional language.

Sophie C. Stewart *Project Manager of the Routes into Languages North East Consortium, Newcastle University.* Ms. Stewart is Project Manager of the Routes into Languages North East Consortium at Newcastle University. She coordinates activity in collaboration with colleagues at partner universities, aiming to inspire a new generation of language learners across the region with the help of a trusty team of Student Language Ambassadors.

List of Figures

Second Language Speaking and Intercultural Friendship Formation in Study Abroad: Experiences and Perspectives of International Students in the USA

Fig. 1   Reported number of days per week of speaking English outside of class. Note: *Pre* refers to the results from the initial survey, and *Post* to those from the final survey   338

Fig. 2   Reported percentages of English speaking on an average day. Note: *Pre* refers to the results from the initial survey, and *Post* to those from the final survey   341

List of Tables

Lessons from 25 Years of Experimenting with Arabic Study Abroad: Programme Evaluation, Culture, Location, and Curriculum
Table 1   Schedule for working with newspaper articles for week 3 of the reading course   56
Table 2   Distribution of students' pre- and post-programme OPI scores   65

Student Awareness of Teaching and Learning Approaches in Second Language Study Abroad
Table 1   Selected participants from the 2010–2012 study   138

Increasing Student Engagement During Study Abroad Through Service Learning: A View from Japan
Table 1   Differences between a course-based model of SL and the Volunteer Center programmes   174

'I Thought I Was Prepared.' ERASMUS Students' Voices on Their Transition from L2 Learners to L2 Users
Table 1   A longitudinal data collection   229
Table 2   Participant profiles   230
Table 3   Examples (adapted from Du Bois, 2007)   231

Adopt a Class: Engagement and Reflection During the Year Abroad

Table 1 Summary profile of the students' educational background and their engagement with the project ... 304

Second Language Speaking and Intercultural Friendship Formation in Study Abroad: Experiences and Perspectives of International Students in the USA

Table 1 Demographic information of participants ... 336
Table 2 Reported relationships with native speakers ... 344

Introduction: Shifting Attention to Second Language Study Abroad Programming, Pedagogy, and Participant Engagement

John L. Plews and Kim Misfeldt

Introduction

The chapters assembled in this edited volume are either derived from or inspired by original research presented at the 'Culture of Study Abroad for Second Languages' conference, held on July 14–17, 2015, in Halifax,

---

We would like to express our gratitude to Palgrave Macmillan for accepting the proposal of this edited volume as well as to the contributors for developing their ideas and data into scholarly chapters. We would like to acknowledge the support of the SSHRC in awarding a Connection Grant to enable the 'Culture of Study Abroad for Second Languages' conference that led to the initiation of this volume. We are especially grateful to Carla Pass for her ever reliable and diligent editorial assistance and to Destiny Kirumira for her valuable help with this book.

J. L. Plews (✉)
Department of Modern Languages & Classics, Saint Mary's University, Halifax, NS, Canada
e-mail: jplews@smu.ca

K. Misfeldt
Fine Arts and Humanities, University of Alberta, Camrose, AB, Canada
e-mail: kim.misfeldt@ualberta.ca

Nova Scotia. This conference was organised in association with the 'Research Network on Study Abroad and Language Learning', an investigative sub-group of the Association Internationale de Linguistique Appliquée, and financially supported by Saint Mary's University and a Connection Grant from the Social Sciences and Humanities Research Council of Canada (SSHRC). The conference brought together researchers and practitioners from across the world for presentations and discussions on various facets of residence and study abroad (SA) for second languages (L2). While concerned with the broadly defined topic of 'culture' in the SA context, the conference's call for papers emphasised five specific sub-themes: (1) participants'/stakeholders' culture; (2) cultural and intercultural learning (in relation to language acquisition); (3) the post-sojourn effect of cultural learning; (4) the cultural specificity of SA in and from Canada (especially regarding the French language); and (5) the cultural interests of L2 students moving to, from, or within Asia. These sub-themes were chosen specifically to inspire new directions in disciplinary discussion and were well addressed at the conference, resulting in three special issues of scholarly journals with expanded versions of papers presented (Plews, 2016a, 2016b; Plews & Jackson, 2017). The chapters gathered in this volume emerged from a realisation at the conference that a number of presenters, while still addressing one or more of the abovementioned sub-themes, also drew especial attention to critical issues in and empirical explorations of SA curriculum, programme design, and educational frameworks.

Context: The Case for Greater Attention on L2 SA Programming, Pedagogy, and Participant Engagement in SA Research

SA research has made considerable strides over the last two decades in generating important expert disciplinary knowledge across a range of linguistic, intercultural, developmental, sociocultural, and educational topics in a slowly increasing range of sending and receiving domains by means of both quantitative and qualitative methods. Isabelli-García, Bown, Plews, and Dewey (Forthcoming), Kinginger (2009b), and Sanz

(2014) are a few examples of surveys that capture the major outcomes. Comp, Gladding, Rhodes, Stephenson, and Vande Berg (2007) estimate over one thousand assorted publications on SA appeared in the first decade of this century. The growth of the field seems to be continuing at the same pace as it celebrates a new specialist journal (Howard, 2016) and attends to lesser-researched but important areas of interest, for example, Asian countries as sources or destinations of internationally mobile students (Plews & Jackson, 2017), critical perspectives (Diao & Trentman, 2016; Müller & Schmenk, 2016; Trentman & Diao, 2017), homestay (Di Silvio, Donovan, & Malone, 2015; Tan & Kinginger, 2013), the post-sojourn dimension (Plews, 2016b), racialisation (Anya, 2017; Diao, 2017; McGregor, 2017), and social networking (Dewey, Bown, & Eggett, 2012; Mitchell, Tracy-Ventura, & McManus, 2017).

Certainly, the emphasis has thus far been on endeavouring to ascertain and measure linguistic outcomes and gains in communicative competence or to interpret intercultural experiences and development, aspects both fundamental to the field and inherently wide-ranging in their scope. Academic research and scholarship have paid far less attention to topics in SA education. This gap between the predominant focus and lack of full attention in the field is clearly illustrated, for example, in both the title and general scope of the field's most seminal, thorough, and valuable survey, namely, Kinginger's (2009b) *Language Learning and Study Abroad*, where the summarised results of the then extent of the field's discussion of 'instruction' and reflection on SA and 'language education' span just 14 pages (over pp. 118–30 and 220–2, respectively) or an allocation of only 6.3 per cent of the whole text. Of course, such a circumstance is no fault of Kinginger, who concludes her meticulous book with the observation that 'there is a need for more careful description of program design, and the extent to which these programs actually promote and organize opportunities for language learning' (p. 217; see also Lafford & Collentine, 2006, p. 111).

Lewin's (2009) *The Handbook of Practice and Research in Study Abroad*, a comprehensive and informative collection dedicated to topics related to the promotion and organisation of SA education, fares only somewhat differently. Most chapters discuss (macro-level) aspects of institutional, national, or geo-regional missions, policy, and strategies for international education and—with the exception of Kolb (2009) and Wanner (2009)—tend not to concern L2 education specifically, although they are often applicable to it. This is acute for the presentation of actual SA programme models (see chapters in part four, Lewin, 2009, pp. 412–564) and the chapter (Cushner, 2009) on SA in teacher preparation. In the latter, Cushner (2009, p. 158) makes the questionable assumption that 'because the curriculum, instructional material, and approach to teaching that one encounters when placed in a school overseas *are all likely* to be different from what the student would experience in a local placement, the student has increased opportunities to examine alternative approaches to teaching' (emphasis added). One cannot help but wonder if such a sweeping statement would be avoidable if more attention were paid by the field to micro-level aspects of the lived experience of curriculum, teaching, and materials. What are those 'alternative' approaches? Are they useful? Is absolutely everything really different abroad (and the same at home)? And what about the foreign language? Such questions remain unanswered here. Again, only 6.4 per cent of a volume dedicated to the practice of SA explores specifically L2 SA programming. Meanwhile Vande Berg, Paige, and Lou's (2012) collection on student learning in SA is overall more inclined towards L2, but still only two (Engle & Engle, 2012; Paige, Harvey, & McCleary, 2012) of the six programme models presented are specifically L2 SA. At minimum, and in spite of their enthusiasm and insight, the abovementioned works are an indictment of the state of affairs in higher education (including international education) in North America, which continues to struggle with realising the full value of L2 education.

In light of the abovementioned recent and primarily US-focussed surveys, the rationale for compiling a volume on SA programming, pedagogy, and participant engagement specifically in relation to L2 education must surely be self-explanatory. The amount and scope of work aimed at discovering L2 SA linguistic and intercultural outcomes or at reviewing international education structures generally is not nearly matched by research on L2 SA education. This is rather concerning given how much decisions about programme components, the classroom, and the articulation of any cultural itinerary *are all likely* to affect the linguistic and intercultural learning outcomes and establishment of best practices. As indisputably important as the record of L2 SA learning outcomes and a passion for global citizenship education are, hardly any of the results, elaborations, or arguments of that research and scholarship are possible without there first having been not only general curriculum thinking and educational planning, but also thought for the classroom (or work placement) and consideration of learners in relation to teaching and educational experience, whether informally or informed. So why not account for it and study it more thoroughly and insightfully? This volume thus seeks to further encourage a shift in attention in the field of SA research and scholarship towards both focussed theorisations, investigations, and assessments of programming and the engagement of participation as well as accounting for the educational structures and teaching approaches, activities, and materials that support students' learning on SA. It is incumbent on SA researchers to be more broadly curious about the educational circumstances that lead to SA learning rather than reporting outcomes without attending to practitioner and teacher action.

Of course, beyond the abovementioned works, several aspects of SA education have been explored in SA research and scholarship. Most of this work underscores the role of thoughtful programming, pedagogy, and participant engagement in facilitating L2 SA learning. A primary concern has been categorising the forms and constituent parts of SA (Coleman, 2009; Engle & Engle, 2003), but as Twombly, Salisbury, Tumanut, and Klute (2012, p. 30) point out this has told us 'little about how a specific study abroad programme configuration might impact learning uniquely'. Just a few studies have explored the classroom in a foreign educational domain (e.g., Bacon, 2002; Brecht & Robinson, 1995; Churchill, 2006; Kinginger, 2004; Misfeldt, 2013; Pellegrino Aveni, 2005; Polanyi, 1995). Dewaele, Comanaru, and Faraco (2015) show the positive influence of an on-site pre-sessional class on subsequent residence and academic life abroad. Keen to combine the setting (or extracurriculum) with the classroom (or curriculum)—and so engage the students' desire and decision to experience another language and culture more intimately—many scholars have suggested more effective interventions (e.g., Beaven & Borghetti, 2015; Bown, Dewey, & Belnap, 2015; Brewer & Cunningham, 2009; Byram, Nichols, & Stevens 2001; Engle & Engle, 1999, 2002; Jackson, 2008, 2010; Kinginger, 2009a; Paige, Cohen, Kappler, Chi, & Lassegard,

2002; Plews, Breckenridge, & Cambre, 2010; Vande Berg, 2007; Vande Berg, Connor-Linton, & Paige, 2009; Vande Berg et al., 2012). Programmes that have implemented Paige et al.'s (2002) *Maximizing Study Abroad* have shown gains in linguistic and cultural competences (Brubaker, 2007; Cohen, Paige, Shively, Emert, & Hoff, 2005; Craig, the current volume; Goldoni, 2007). Brubaker (2007) also points out that when integrating extracurricular cultural activities with course work, students must be provided with the necessary language and theory to be able to describe and interpret their experiences; Misfeldt's (2013) pedagogical treatment of a novel and lived place in a German SA course enables students to build the vocabulary and confidence to engage intellectually with each other and their hosts on challenging topics. Other methods for integrating L2 students into the local culture on a personal level include tandem partnerships (Badstübner & Ecke, 2009; Bown et al., 2015; Engle & Engle, 1999; Wilkinson, 2012), pursuing hobbies (Engle & Engle, 1999; Fraser, 2002; Schmidt-Rinehart & Knight, 2004), and community service (Engle & Engle, 1999; Gorka & Niesenbaum, 2001; Grimes-MacLellan, the current volume; Kiely & Nielson, 2003; Lewis & Niesenbaum, 2005; Miller, Berkey, & Griffin, 2015; Parker & Dautoff, 2007; Stebleton, Soria, & Cherney, 2013). Journals and ethnographic studies are effective strategies for integrating the experience of the immersion setting into course learning. Paige et al. (2002) caution against journals as mere records of the extracurricular itinerary, suggesting students describe and evaluate impressions of people, places, events, experiences, and so forth (see also Bridges, 2007; Ingram, 2005; Lee, 2011; Raschio, 2001; Rollmann, 2007). Bown et al. (2015) and Plews and Misfeldt (2016) describe journals intended specifically to help students reflect on and plan oral interaction with locals. Brockington and Wiedenhoeft (2009), Jackson (2006a, 2006b, 2008, 2010), Plews, Misfeldt, and Kirumira (the current volume), Thompson (2002), and Tschirner (2007) have found that ethnography and ethnographic-like tasks require students to engage in purposeful and meaningful L2 interaction with local people as well as involve several components beneficial for language and intercultural development (namely, observation, note-taking, interaction, description, analysis, self-reflection, and presentation). Regarding social and emotional support, Engle and Engle (2012), Jackson (2009), and Vande Berg et al. (2009) have shown that ongoing mentoring is significant for language proficiency and intercultural development. Research and scholarship focussed especially on thoughtful pre-, per-, and post-programme structures and design shows how learning outcomes are as much dependant on such educational interventions as they are on students' predisposition to learning in SA or the immersion environment per se. Without more research in educational matters, how do scholars and practitioners know with confidence, for example, whether a particular linguistic uptake, or an adaptation of cultural beliefs, occurs thanks to interactions on the street in everyday service encounters or in the homestay conversations of the immersion experience, or *in class*, or a combination of both? Without this body of work, we risk putting too much responsibility or blame on students' willingness or ability (compare, DeKeyser, 2014) before knowing whether the pedagogical structures of a programme had or could have a role to play in their success or failure.

Chapters 2 Through 12

The aim of the current volume is thus to build on preceding work in SA research by presenting the voices of scholars and practitioners who are concerned especially with programming, pedagogy, and engaging participants. The contributing authors represent a range of academies, and the SA programmes, practitioners, and participants they discuss further expand that cultural and geographic reach and exchange. Altogether, they concern Canada, the Caribbean, China, Denmark, Egypt, England, France, Germany, Italy, Japan, Jordan, Morocco, New Zealand, Peru, Spain, the United States, and Wales. Their chapters critically and constructively review established and new programming, provide theoretical and research-informed support for curricular and/or pedagogical interventions and innovation, as well as explore and analyse participant experiences and language support and strategies. This book differs from others by emphasising the theoretical and practical curricular foundations and the pedagogical and experiential considerations and means of attaining SA learning objectives. All chapters focus on student engagement (including student-teacher engagement). They are concerned with the articulation of study/residence abroad with domestic curricula and participants as distinct persons. They explore learning activities and relationships in the target language and culture as well as teaching approaches or specially designed assignments undertaken in-sojourn. This book promotes diversity in approaches and experiences while drawing the common thread of learner- and learning-centredness through each chapter. Each chapter also includes recommendations for improving the SA experiences and engagement of students.

The book is divided into three sections, moving generally from more (though not purely) macro-level matters to more micro-level interests and, thus, from curriculum and design to pedagogical approaches, to participants, whether students or in-service teachers, and their experiences and engagement. To begin the first section, in the second chapter, Penny Johnson and Simon McKinnon of Durham University, UK, view SA as an opportunity for language learning and 'as a means of fostering international citizenship'. They describe their attempt to ensure quality learning and 'distinguish study abroad from tourism' through 'changes to the system of assessment and through the introduction of a programme of increased support for social and experiential learning before, during, and after the period of residence abroad'. Durham now has a customised programme characterised by teacher intervention, student-driven self-reflection, assessment, and integration into the curriculum across the modern languages degree. In the third chapter, Matthew T. Bird and R. Kirk Belnap of Brigham Young University, Provo, Utah, present an overview of important improvements in a SA programme (and especially its media course) spanning more than two decades in various sites across North Africa and the Middle East. The primary motivation of their programme was to improve speaking proficiency in Arabic. The improvements involve scaffolding learning experiences in collaboration with on-site language instruction and local instructors, trained conversational partners, and systematic teacher and student observations and evaluations. The authors argue especially for the importance of evaluating learning outcomes, leading to more engaging courses and improved classroom performance. In the fourth chapter, Ian Craig of the University of the West Indies, Cave Hill Campus, Barbados, examines the creation of an undergraduate course entitled 'Immersion for Languages' at the University of the West Indies, during which students participate in a month-long sojourn in Spain. This course development differs from traditional SA because the students are crossing a perceived critical border, moving from a 'developing' to a 'developed' country. The author argues strongly for a post-colonial approach, noting the necessary considerations involved when sojourners of African (or European) descent in a Caribbean nation move to a mostly 'white' city. Craig underlines the importance of giving students who might believe that such an experience is 'not for them' an opportunity to become global citizens and discover their own unique perspectives on the cultures they encounter.

To begin the second section, in the fifth chapter, John L. Plews of Saint Mary's University, Halifax, Nova Scotia, and Kim Misfeldt and Feisal Kirumira of Augustana Campus, University of Alberta, Camrose, Alberta, explore L2 students' awareness of teaching approaches used in SA. SA research rarely describes the pedagogy of a given programme, despite making claims about SA learning outcomes. The authors introduced drama-pedagogical and task-based approaches for teaching Canadian undergraduate students German in a short-term SA programme in Germany in order to place their developing sense of subjective, affective, and creative ownership of the L2 as a primary curriculum goal. The authors were interested in whether students notice a relationship between the instructional approaches used and their personal sense of and commitment to language development, or whether the immersion context alone featured in their narratives of learning. They find that students do indeed attribute learning to the SA classroom and not just the immersion setting. In the sixth chapter, Dawn Grimes-MacLellan of Meiji Gakuin University, Tokyo, Japan, discusses the pedagogical process and effects of authentic experiences in SA especially regarding increasing students' intercultural competence, language skills, and appreciation of difference. The author argues that skills such as cultural understanding are not experienced in theory but lived through volunteer opportunities provided by the host institution. The inclusion of service learning within a SA context is seen as a way for students to be transformed in a holistic sense. Using volunteering in an East Japan study tour as an example, Grimes-MacLellan describes how students are able to develop social networks with Japanese peers, facilitating intercultural friendships as well as exposure to formal and informal language and the societal norms of the host country.

To begin the third section, in the seventh chapter, Ana Beaven and Claudia Borghetti of the University of Bologna, Italy, investigate an activity from the European project intercultural education resources for ERASMUS students and their teachers, which is titled '24 h ERASMUS Life' and was conducted at the University of Bologna with 33 participants. Focussing on interculturality and analysing the data through the lens of Benson, Barkhuizen, Bodycott, and Brown's (2012, 2013) framework of L2-identity development, the authors suggest four measures to improve the effectiveness of student experience of international mobility. These include regular peer-to-peer interaction, theoretical input on intercultural awareness, reflection tasks and the time to reflect, and an awareness that students may have difficulty with a non-essentialist view of culture. In the eighth chapter, Sònia Mas-Alcolea of the University of Lleida, Catalonia, Spain, examines the experiences of nine ERASMUS students from Catalonia studying in Denmark, Italy, or Wales. Using interview and observational data, she focusses on their possible transition from being L2 learners to L2 users and how well prepared they were linguistically prior to their sojourn. The transition was often described as frustrating and difficult, in part because the students expected the language requirement from their home university to guarantee their linguistic well-being. Consequently, some restricted their social interactions to other co-nationals, which further limited their L2 learning and use. This chapter underscores the importance of customised pre-departure preparation on the part of students and the home university. In the ninth chapter, Deborah Corder, Annelies Roskvist, Sharon Harvey, and Karen Stacey of the School of Language and Culture, Auckland University of Technology, New Zealand, explore the experiences of three New Zealand in-service language teachers who participated in short- and long-term SA. The authors were interested in determining the characteristics and strategies of teachers most likely to increase their intercultural communicative competence (ICC) during SA. They note that each teacher made at least some gains in language and culture knowledge and demonstrated some characteristics of ICC, but also exhibited differences related to motivation, language teacher identity, attitudes about language learning and the immersion-language culture as well as language ability. In the tenth chapter, Elizabeth A. Andersen and Sophie Stewart of Newcastle

University, UK, show how participation in the Adopt a Class project provides students with an opportunity to reflect upon their own language learning in a new professional and personal context. This project is part of a larger initiative, the Routes into Languages programme, whose primary aim has been to bring universities and schools together in order to encourage young people to become more interested in studying languages. Through the Adopt a Class project, university-level Student Language Ambassadors (SLAs) are linked with local secondary classes before, during, and after the student's time studying abroad in order to bring the foreign language and culture to life for the school pupils. In turn, the students improve their communication, presentation, and organisational skills. The authors explore how and why the SLAs communicated with their classes in different ways and therefore had different experiences. In the eleventh chapter, Rebecca K. Smith of Lone Star University, Tomball, Texas, examines patterns of L2 usage among international students in the United States 'in order to better understand the underlying factors that could either inhibit or facilitate successful intercultural interaction in an immersive environment'. Some participants shared that they felt embarrassed because of a lack of social knowledge and language skills. This caused them to be hesitant to interact with L2 peers. For others, a lack of cultural knowledge and language skills hindered them in being truly immersed in the host culture. Smith argues that 'by understanding if and how intercultural connections are formed, as well as any potential barriers to interaction, it may be possible to better assist SA participants in obtaining the maximum benefits from their experiences in a host country'. In the twelfth chapter, Mar Galindo of the University of Alicante, Spain, focusses on gender and L2 learning in SA. This chapter differs from others in the current volume in that there is no particular SA programme on which it is based; rather, it takes on the issue of gender more generally in the field of SA research and programming. Galindo proposes a feminist post-structuralist approach towards the examination of the SA experience. She provides an invaluable review of both quantitative and qualitative studies on gender and SA and argues that because gendered practices shape both the residence abroad and the post-sojourn experience, gender must be considered as a factor in SA research as well as in the design and planning of SA programmes.

Conclusion and Recommendations

We hope that the findings, discussions, and recommendations of the chapters in the current volume will benefit students, instructors, programme directors, administrators, hosts, and researchers by being used to optimise positive SA effects in individual participants' lives. In compiling these chapters, we intend to inspire further enquiry into the organisation and experience of L2 SA education in light of the various linguistic, cognitive, affective, and sociocultural complexities, factors, and goals of SA contexts. Indeed, there is still much room for investigating which aspects of language or ICC are learned and used—or not—during immersion abroad. But there is also considerable need especially for research and scholarship focussed on how such learning is anticipated, encouraged, and built upon through curriculum and instruction, not only to provide a more solid and validating foundation for the outcomes of linguistic and intercultural enquiries, but also to enable improvement in SA programming overall in order to guarantee greater results and more widespread student success in a range of national or regional frames of reference.

Typical of the field, all the authors are SA practitioner-researchers (and likely former SA participants) and, while they are all personally aware of the benefits of SA, they are professionally and critically concerned about the current structural limitations they have observed and motivated to seek and examine ongoing improvement. Some of the discussions they have moved forward in the current volume and on which they, ourselves included, invite further exploration include (1) how best to integrate SA into domestic degree programmes; (2) the role of evaluation and assessment of curriculum and teaching (and especially empirical data) in student learning outcomes and ongoing programme planning and improvements; (3) the experiences of under-represented students, for example, those from less typically researched sending countries as well as those going to less typically researched host countries; (4) the potentially mutually enriching relationship between host community members and especially actively engaged SA participants; (5) expanding the learning support for students' critical awareness of personal developmental as well as professional goals; (6) the importance of the home campus in preparing, sustaining, and optimising both linguistic and intercultural aspects of the SA experience; (7) the potential long-term educational, linguistic, developmental, professional, institutional, economic, and sociocultural effects of SA, namely, how do students narrate and evaluate their SA experience after one year, after five years, and so forth; (8) SA as a matter for critical gender studies; and (9) best practice for each local sending and receiving SA immersion context. Certainly, we would like the current volume to inspire more research in L2 SA that focusses attention and integrates the full gamut of educational matters. Curriculum, theoretical frameworks, syllabus development, textbooks or course materials and readings, pedagogy and learning preferences, course activities and assignments, formative and summative learning assessment, instructional and learning support, programme review, educational or institutional policy and administration, and practitioners' and instructors' professional deliberations, intentions, and reflections all represent essential aspects of SA conceptualisation, delivery, management, and experience.

In this regard, we offer a series of recommendations for supporting SA programming, pedagogy, and participant engagement both practically and in research. First, recalling the current imbalance in the foci of SA research, and given the role of educational institutions and processes in SA as factors in shaping learning opportunities, research studies focussed on linguistic and intercultural outcomes should at minimum account for the programming and chosen pedagogical effects in those outcomes. Similarly, international education scholarship, especially in the Anglophone world, should pay greater attention to the role of L2s in the actual and theorised programming it discusses. Second, in terms of academic work directly investigating educational aspects of SA, an international group of programme designers, directors, and instructors (much like the contributors to the current volume) could collaborate as evaluators to assess SA programming, pedagogy, and the community engagement of participants across a series of contexts. Perhaps such collaboration could lead to compiling evidence-based best practices for SA programmes that might be both location-dependent or more universally applicable. Third, such collaboration should also involve former participants. SA participants need to be asked regularly and carefully (not just in a research project) about their expectations of and experiences in and out of the SA classroom. In this way, the lived insight of former and current participants can be utilised to improve programme design and teaching and learning strategies. Fourth, that being said, readers learn throughout the current volume that participant expectations need to be clearly articulated, contemplated, and likely also challenged. In order that participants attain deep learning goals, it is essential for educators to help them to think more critically about their expectations and their goals prior to their SA. Such deliberations and discussion serve as a foundation for in-sojourn and post-sojourn linguistic and intercultural development (see also Jackson, 2013; Plews et al., 2010). Fifth, readers also learn throughout the current volume that curricular, extracurricular, and pedagogical interventions improve participants' experiences. Clearly, considerably more published documentation of and scholarly research on such (successful) interventions is needed if they are to take full effect across of the field of practice. Perhaps in this regard, SA curriculum and extracurriculum can be regarded and articulated as one and the same and not so much as, on the one hand, a course syllabus that might connect in part with, on the other hand, an immersion itinerary. Finally, we would encourage a view of SA a holistic educational process in which all its components play their part (i.e., pre-, per-, and post-sojourn; linguistic, intercultural, psychological, and sociocultural goals; source and host; as well as institutional and national or regional discourses). By adopting such a stance, both programming and research will be more accountable and self-critical.

Summary of recommendations for supporting L2 programming, pedagogy, and participant engagement

- SA research should account for programming and pedagogy effects in linguistic and intercultural outcomes as well as L2 effects in international education.
- SA researchers should consider international collaboration to assess SA programming, pedagogy, and participant engagement across SA contexts.
- Such research should involve more former SA participants so as to integrate their lived insight into SA programme design.
- Participant expectations need to be articulated, contemplated, and challenged so that they can think more critically about their expectations and their goals prior to, during, and after their SA.
- Practitioners and researchers should document and explore successful SA interventions so that they can have a greater effect in the field of practice.
- Practitioners and researchers should view SA as a holistic educational process, thus enabling themselves to be more accountable and self-critical.

Bibliography

Anya, U. (2017). *Racialized identities in second language learning. Speaking blackness in Brazil.* New York: Routledge.

Bacon, S. (2002). Learning the rules: Language development and cultural adjustment during study abroad. *Foreign Language Annals, 35*(6), 637–646.

Badstübner, T., & Ecke, P. (2009). Student expectations, motivations, target language use, and perceived learning progress in a summer study abroad program in Germany. *Unterrichtspraxis, 42*(1), 41–49.

Beaven, A., & Borghetti, C. (Eds.). (2015). *IEREST. Intercultural education resources for ERASMUS students and their teachers.* Koper: Annales University Press. Retrieved from http://www.ierest-project.eu/sites/default/files/IEREST_manual_0.pdf

Benson, P., Barkhuizen, G., Bodycott, P., & Brown, J. (2012). Study abroad and the development of second language identities. *Applied Linguistics Review, 3*(1), 173–193.

Benson, P., Barkhuizen, G., Bodycott, P., & Brown, J. (2013). *Second language identity in narratives of study abroad.* New York: Palgrave Macmillan.

Bown, J., Dewey, D. P., & Belnap, R. K. (2015). Student interactions during study abroad in Jordan. In R. Mitchell, N. Tracy-Ventura, & K. McManus (Eds.), *Social interaction, identity and language learning during residence abroad* (pp. 199–222). EuroSLA Monographs Series, 4. Retrieved from http://www.eurosla.org/monographs/EM04/Bown_etal.pdf

Brecht, R., & Robinson, J. L. (1995). The value of formal instruction in study abroad: Student reactions in context. In B. Freed (Ed.), *Second language acquisition in a study abroad context* (pp. 317–334). Philadelphia: Benjamins.

Brewer, E., & Cunningham, K. (2009). Capturing study abroad's transformative potential. In E. Brewer & K. Cunningham (Eds.), *Integrating study abroad into the curriculum* (pp. 1–17). Sterling, VA: Stylus.

Bridges, S. (2007). Learner perceptions of a professional development immersion course. *Prospect, 22*(2), 39–60.

Brockington, J. L., & Wiedenhoeft, M. D. (2009). The liberal arts and global citizenship: Fostering intercultural engagement through integrative experiences and structured reflection. In R. Lewin (Ed.), *The handbook of practice and research in study abroad* (pp. 117–132). London: Routledge.

Brubaker, C. (2007). Six weeks in the Eifel: A case for culture learning during short-term study abroad. *Unterrichtspraxis, 40*(2), 118–123.

Byram, M., Nichols, A., & Stevens, D. (Eds.). (2001). *Developing intercultural competence in practice.* Clevedon, UK: Multilingual Matters.

Churchill, E. (2006). Variability in the study abroad classroom and learner competence. In M. A. DuFon & E. Churchill (Eds.), *Language learners in study abroad contexts* (pp. 203–227). Clevedon, UK: Multilingual Matters.

Cohen, A. D., Paige, R. M., Shively, R. L., Emert, H. A., & Hoff, J. G. (2005). *Maximizing study abroad through language and culture strategies: Research on students, study abroad program professionals, and language instructors*. Minneapolis, MN: Center for Advanced Research on Language Acquisition, University of Minnesota.

Coleman, J. A. (2009). Study abroad and SLA: Defining goals and variables. In K. Kleppin & A. Berndt (Eds.), *Sprachlehrforschung: Theorie und Empirie* (pp. 181–196). Frankfurt: Peter Lang.

Comp, D., Gladding, S., Rhodes, G., Stephenson, S., & Vande Berg, M. (2007). Literature and resources for education abroad outcomes assessment. In M. Bolan (Ed.), *A guide to outcomes assessment in education abroad* (pp. 97–135). Carlisle, PA: The Forum on Education Abroad.

Cushner, K. (2009). The role of study abroad in preparing globally responsible teachers. In R. Lewin (Ed.), *The handbook of practice and research in study abroad. Higher education and the quest for global citizenship* (pp. 151–169). New York: Routledge.

DeKeyser, R. M. (2014). Research on language development during study abroad: Methodological considerations and future perspectives. In C. Pérez-Vidal (Ed.), *Language acquisition in study abroad and formal instruction contexts* (pp. 313–325). Amsterdam: Benjamins.

Dewaele, J. M., Comanaru, R. S., & Faraco, M. (2015). The affective benefits of a pre-sessional course at the start of study abroad. In R. Mitchell, N. Tracy-Ventura, & K. McManus (Eds.), *Social interaction, identity and language learning during residence abroad* (pp. 95–114). EUROSLA Monograph Series, 4. Retrieved from http://www.eurosla.org/monographs/EM04/EM04tot.pdf

Dewey, D. P., Bown, J., & Eggett, D. (2012). Japanese language proficiency, social networking, and language use during study abroad: Learners' perspectives. *Canadian Modern Language Review, 68*(2), 111–137.

Di Silvio, F., Donovan, A., & Malone, M. (2015). Promoting oral proficiency gains in study abroad homestay placements. In R. Mitchell, N. Tracy-Ventura, & K. McManus (Eds.), *Social interaction, identity and language learning during residence abroad* (pp. 75–94). EUROSLA Monograph Series, 4. Retrieved from http://www.eurosla.org/monographs/EM04/DiSilvio_etal.pdf

Diao, W. (2017, February 10–11). *Doing anti-racism through Mandarin: A Muslim student in China*. Paper presented at the Conference on Study Abroad,

Center for Languages & Intercultural Communication, Rice University, Houston, TX.
Diao, W., & Trentman, E. (2016). Politicizing study abroad: Learning Arabic in Egypt and Mandarin in China. *L2 Journal, 8*(2), 31–50. Retrieved from https://escholarship.org/uc/item/90g8r79m
Engle, J., & Engle, L. (1999). Program intervention in the process of cultural integration: The example of French practicum. *Frontiers: The Interdisciplinary Journal of Study Abroad, 5*(2), 39–59.
Engle, J., & Engle, L. (2002). Neither international nor educative: Study abroad in the time of globalization. In W. Grünzweig & N. Rinehart (Eds.), *Rockin' in Red Square: Critical approaches to international education in the time of cyberculture* (pp. 25–40). Münster: Lit Verlag.
Engle, J., & Engle, L. (2012). Beyond immersion. The American University Center of Provence experiment in holistic intervention. In M. Vande Berg, R. M. Paige, & K. H. Lou (Eds.), *Student learning abroad: What our students are learning, what they're not, and what we can do about it* (pp. 284–307). Sterling, VA: Stylus.
Engle, L., & Engle, J. (2003). Study abroad levels: Toward a classification of program types. *Frontiers: The Interdisciplinary Journal of Study Abroad, 9*, 1–20.
Fraser, C. C. (2002). Study abroad: An attempt to measure the gains. *German as a Foreign Language Journal, 1*, 45–65.
Goldoni, F. (2007). The ethnography of study abroad: What is study abroad as a cultural event? *EMIGRA Working Papers, 8*, 1–18.
Gorka, B., & Niesenbaum, R. (2001). Beyond the language requirement: Interdisciplinary short-term study-abroad programs in Spanish. *Hispania, 84*(1), 100–109.
Howard, M. (2016). Message from the editor. *Study Abroad Research in Second Language Acquisition and International Education, 1*(1), 1–3.
Ingram, M. (2005). Recasting the foreign language requirement through study abroad: A cultural immersion program in Avignon, France. *Foreign Language Annals, 38*(2), 211–222.
Isabelli-García, C., Bown, J., Plews, J. L., & Dewey, D. P. (Forthcoming). Language learning and study abroad. *Language Teaching*.
Jackson, J. (2006a). Ethnographic pedagogy and evaluation in short-term study abroad. In M. Byram & A. Feng (Eds.), *Living and studying abroad: Research and practice* (pp. 132–185). Clevedon, UK: Multilingual Matters.
Jackson, J. (2006b). Ethnographic preparation for short-term study and residence in the target culture. *International Journal of Intercultural Relations, 30*, 77–98.

Jackson, J. (2008). *Language, identity and study abroad: Sociocultural perspectives.* London: Equinox.
Jackson, J. (2009). Intercultural learning on short-term sojourns. *Intercultural Education, 20*, 59–71.
Jackson, J. (2010). *Intercultural journeys: From study abroad to residence abroad.* London: Palgrave Macmillan.
Jackson, J. (2013). The transformation of 'a frog in the well': A path to a more intercultural, global mindset. In C. Kinginger (Ed.), *Social and cultural aspects of language learning in study abroad* (pp. 179–204). Amsterdam: Benjamins.
Kiely, R., & Nielson, D. (2003). International service learning: The importance of partnerships. *Community College Journal, 73*, 39–41.
Kinginger, C. (2004). Alice doesn't live here anymore: Foreign language learning and identity (re)construction. In A. Pavlenko & A. Blackledge (Eds.), *Negotiation of identities in multilingual contexts* (pp. 219–242). Clevedon, UK: Multilingual Matters.
Kinginger, C. (2009a). *Contemporary study abroad and foreign language learning: An activist's guidebook for language educators.* University Park, PA: CALPER Publications.
Kinginger, C. (2009b). *Language learning and study abroad. A critical reading of research.* Basingstoke, UK: Palgrave Macmillan.
Kolb, C. (2009). International studies and foreign languages: A critical American priority. In R. Lewin (Ed.), *The handbook of practice and research in study abroad. Higher education and the quest for global citizenship* (pp. 49–60). New York: Routledge.
Lafford, B., & Collentine, J. (2006). The effects of study abroad and classroom contexts on the acquisition of Spanish as a second language: From research to application. In R. Salaberry & B. A. Lafford (Eds.), *The art of teaching Spanish: Second language acquisition from research to praxis* (pp. 103–126). Washington, DC: Georgetown University Press.
Lee, L. (2011). Blogging: Promoting learner autonomy and intercultural competence through study abroad. *Language Learning & Technology, 15*(3), 87–109.
Lewin, R. (Ed.). (2009). *The handbook of practice and research in study abroad. Higher education and the quest for global citizenship.* New York: Routledge.
Lewis, T. L., & Niesenbaum, R. A. (2005). Extending the stay: Using community-based research and service learning to enhance short-term study abroad. *Journal of Studies in International Education, 9*, 251–264.
McGregor, J. (2017, February 10–11). *The researcher's experience in study abroad: An autoethnographic reconstruction.* Paper presented at the Conference on

Study Abroad, Center for Languages & Intercultural Communication, Rice University, Houston, TX.

Miller, J., Berkey, B., & Griffin, F. (2015). International students in American pathway programs: Learning English and culture through service-learning. *Journal of International Students, 5*(4), 334–352.

Misfeldt, K. F. (2013). Pedagogies of affect and lived place: Reading Der Vorleser on a short-term intensive immersion. In J. L. Plews & B. Schmenk (Eds.), *Traditions and transitions. Curricula for German studies* (pp. 191–208). Waterloo, ON: Wilfrid Laurier University Press.

Mitchell, R., Tracy-Ventura, N., & McManus, K. (2017). *Anglophone students abroad. Identity, social relationships and language learning*. London: Routledge.

Müller, M., & Schmenk, B. (2016). Conceptualizations, images, and evaluations of culture in study abroad students. *Canadian Journal of Applied Linguistics, 19*(2), 128–150. Retrieved from https://journals.lib.unb.ca/index.php/CJAL/article/view/24235/29565

Paige, R. M., Cohen, A. D., Kappler, B., Chi, J. C., & Lassegard, J. P. (2002). *Maximizing study abroad. A students' guide to strategies for language and culture learning and use*. Minneapolis, MN: Center for Advanced Research on Language Acquisition.

Paige, M. R., Harvey, T. A., & McCleary, K. S. (2012). The maximizing study abroad project. Toward a pedagogy of culture and language learning. In M. Vande Berg, R. M. Paige, & K. H. Lou (Eds.), *Student learning abroad: What our students are learning, what they're not, and what we can do about it* (pp. 308–334). Sterling, VA: Stylus.

Parker, B., & Dautoff, D. A. (2007). Service-learning and study abroad: Synergistic learning opportunities. *Michigan Journal of Community Service Learning, 13*(2), 40–53.

Pellegrino Aveni, V. (2005). *Study abroad and second language use: Constructing the self*. Cambridge: Cambridge University Press.

Plews, J. L. (Ed.). (2016a). The culture of study abroad. [Special issue of]. *Canadian Journal of Applied Linguistics, 19*(2). Retrieved from https://journals.lib.unb.ca/index.php/CJAL/issue/view/1891

Plews, J. L. (Ed.). (2016b). Language and culture after study abroad. [Special issue of]. *Comparative and International Education, 45*(2).

Plews, J. L., Breckenridge, Y., & Cambre, M. C. (2010). Mexican English teachers' experiences of international professional development in Canada: A narrative analysis. *e-FLT, 7*(1), 5–20. Retrieved from http://eflt.nus.edu.sg/v7n12010/plews.pdf

Plews, J. L., & Jackson, J. (Eds.). (2017). Study abroad to, from, and within Asia. [Special issue of]. *Study Abroad Research in Second Language Acquisition and International Education, 2*(2).

Plews, J. L., & Misfeldt, K. (2016, July 19–22). *Reviewing language learning journals in study abroad, or engaging students' language awareness.* 13th International Conference of the Association of Language Awareness, Vienna, Austria.

Polanyi, L. (1995). Language learning and living abroad: Stories from the field. In B. F. Freed (Ed.), *Second language acquisition in a study abroad context* (pp. 271–292). Philadelphia: Benjamins.

Raschio, R. A. (2001). Integrative activities for the study-abroad setting. *Hispania, 94*, 534–541.

Rollmann, M. (2007). Three German web courses with a study abroad component. In C. Lorey, J. L. Plews, & C. L. Rieger (Eds.), *Interkulturelle Kompetenzen im Fremdsprachenunterricht. Intercultural literacies and German in the classroom. Festschrift für Manfred Prokop zum 65sten Geburtstag* (pp. 161–181). Narr: Tübingen.

Sanz, C. (2014). Contributions of study abroad research to our understanding of SLA processes and outcomes: The SALA project, an appraisal. In C. Pérez-Vidal (Ed.), *Language acquisition in study abroad and formal instruction contexts* (pp. 1–13). Amsterdam: Benjamins.

Schmidt-Rinehart, B. C., & Knight, S. M. (2004). The homestay component of study abroad: Three perspectives. *Foreign Language Annals, 37*(2), 254–262.

Stebleton, M. J., Soria, K. M., & Cherney, B. T. (2013). The high impact of education abroad: College students' engagement in international experiences and the development of intercultural competences. *Frontiers: The Interdisciplinary Journal of Study Abroad, 22*, 1–24. Retrieved from https://frontiersjournal.org/wp-content/uploads/2015/09/STEBLETON-CHERNEY-SORIA-FrontiersXXII-GoingGlobal.pdf

Tan, D., & Kinginger, C. (2013). Exploring the potential of high school homestays as a context for local engagement and negotiation of difference: Americans in China. In C. Kinginger (Ed.), *Social and cultural aspects of language learning in study abroad* (pp. 155–177). Amsterdam: Benjamins.

Thompson, G. (2002, March 29–30). *Teachers studying abroad: An analysis of changes in linguistic and cultural knowledge, attitudes toward the Spanish culture and the effects of ethnographic interviews.* Paper presented at the TexFlec Conference, Austin, TX. *Texas Papers in Foreign Language Education*, 53–75. Retrieved from https://files.eric.ed.gov/fulltext/ED476263.pdf

Trentman, E., & Diao, W. (2017). The American gaze east: Discourses and destinations of US study abroad. *Study Abroad Research in Second Language Acquisition and International Education, 2*(2), 175–205.

Tschirner, E. (2007). The development of oral proficiency in a four-week intensive immersion program in Germany. *Unterrichtspraxis, 40*(2), 111–117.

Twombly, S. B., Salisbury, M. H., Tumanut, S. D., & Klute, P. (2012). Study abroad in a new global century: Renewing the promise, refining the purpose. *ASHE Higher Education Report, 38*(4), 1–152.

Vande Berg, M. (2007). Intervening in the learning of U.S. students abroad. *Journal of Studies in International Education, 11*(3/4), 392–399.

Vande Berg, M., Connor-Linton, J., & Paige, M. (2009). The Georgetown consortium project: Interventions for student learning abroad. *Frontiers: The Interdisciplinary Journal of Study Abroad, 18*, 1–75.

Vande Berg, M., Paige, R. M., & Lou, K. H. (Eds.). (2012). *Student learning abroad: What our students are learning, what they're not, and what we can do about it.* Sterling, VA: Stylus.

Wanner, D. (2009). Study abroad and language: From maximal to realistic models. In R. Lewin (Ed.), *The handbook of practice and research in study abroad. Higher education and the quest for global citizenship* (pp. 81–98). New York: Routledge.

Wilkinson, R. (2012). English-medium instruction at a Dutch university: Challenges and pitfalls. In A. Doiz, D. Lasagabaster, & J. M. Sierra (Eds.), *English-medium instruction at university worldwide: Challenges and ways forward*. Bristol: Multilingual Matters.

Part I

Curriculum and Design

Positioning Year-Long Study Abroad at the Centre of the Modern Languages Curriculum: Supporting and Assessing Learning

Penny Johnson and Simon McKinnon

Introduction

The opportunity to study abroad (SA) is a major attraction of the undergraduate degree in modern languages at Durham University. Questions about the year abroad always feature prominently in contact with prospective students and then from our own students when they first arrive in Durham. This enthusiasm for SA reflects broader trends nationally and, indeed, within Europe: in a 2015 survey of UK students, 34 per cent expressed an interest in SA (British Council, 2015), and European Commission (2015) data indicate that Europe-wide participation in ERASMUS+ study and training exchanges continues to grow steadily each year, with 272,497 students taking part in these exchanges in 2014–15. SA is actively promoted by government bodies, academic organisations, and student networks. The UK government funds a Strategy

---

P. Johnson (✉) • S. McKinnon
Durham University, Durham, UK
e-mail: penelope.johnson@durham.ac.uk; s.g.mckinnon@durham.ac.uk

for Outward Mobility with the aim of increasing the number of UK-domiciled students having an 'international experience as part of their UK higher education' (Go International, 2016, para. 1), while the European Union has a target for 2020 of 20 per cent of all graduates completing part of their university studies abroad (European Commission, 2015). In 2012, the British Academy and the University Council of Modern Languages (UCML), an organisation representing UK-university modern languages departments and related professional associations, published a joint report stressing 'the importance of the year abroad as part of a degree programme for UK students' (UCML, p. 1). This report sits within an established European tradition of presenting SA not only in terms of the development of subject-related knowledge and skills but also as a means of fostering international citizenship. It argues that:

> The international experience has been shown to contribute both to students' individual experience and employability and to their home country's national prosperity. In addition to academic learning and deeper cultural insights, students on a year abroad develop both essential skills which help them to observe without misinterpretation or ethnocentric judgement, and interpersonal skills which allow adaptation to complex cultural milieux. They learn to show respect for local values without abandoning their own. (UCML, 2012, pp. 2–3)

Recent years have also seen the growth of numerous student-led initiatives, such as the popular thirdyearabroad.com, offering first-hand information, practical guidance, and useful tips on every aspect of the wide range of often very different year abroad experiences.

Universities have understood the value of SA in terms of its contribution to the internationalisation of higher education. Many of them in the UK have made significant efforts to integrate opportunities for student mobility into their degree programmes. By offering placements in English-speaking as well as non-English-speaking countries and by promoting language study to students across all disciplines, they have extended the take-up for SA beyond just languages students. At Durham, for example, internationalisation features prominently in the University's 'Principles for the development of the taught curriculum': all students are 'strongly encouraged to undertake credit-bearing languages as optional modules within their programme of study' and 'curricula will be designed to provide students with the opportunity to develop as international citizens [...] so that students can make a positive contribution to an increasingly globalised society'; SA is encouraged in a number of ways, not least because 'the University will facilitate opportunities for programmes to permit students to undertake year-long placements, or placements within individual modules' (Durham University, 2016d, section 3).

However, this growth in interest in and access to SA, though pleasing, is also potentially problematic. As increasing numbers of students opt to complete some of their studying abroad, managing their expectations and, at the same time, ensuring the quality of experience and learning while abroad become more difficult. Students may have unrealistic expectations of SA, fed by a discourse that presents it as automatically and effortlessly transformative and necessarily the *best year of your life*. Faculty, on the other hand, have little direct control over the quality of learning and pastoral support available in the host country. This is especially problematic in an environment in which students in England now pay substantial tuition fees (though capped at 15 per cent of the full tuition fee during residence abroad) and increasingly see education in consumerist terms. Other problems arise through misperceptions about the nature of SA. Some UK students see it as an extended holiday or little different from the kind of gap year for travel often taken between secondary education and university. Here the priority is on having fun or participating in what, in a US context, Kinginger has described as 'globalized infotainment' (Kinginger, 2008a, p. 206; see also Kinginger, 2013, p. 7; Streitwieser, 2010). Such perceptions are too often encouraged by the way SA is sold to students, with text and images in official publicity or circulating on social media that would not look out of place in a glossy travel brochure. In an analysis of the marketing of SA in the USA, Zemach-Bersin (2009, p. 303) notes the way such 'institutionalized commercial rhetoric' has an impact on 'how students approach international education' and 'the quality of education in which they are prepared to engage'. This rhetoric also risks reinforcing a narrative in which SA is not taken seriously by faculty, is considered time away from *real* academic work, and is understood as something not unlike a modern Grand Tour (Gore, 2005).

Within this context, questions of how to ensure quality learning, how to distinguish SA from tourism or a holiday, and how to establish the specificity of SA within a modern languages degree in a particular institution all have an important impact on curriculum design and development. This chapter considers efforts to ensure the quality and distinctiveness of SA within the modern languages degree at Durham University through (1) changes to the system of assessment and (2) the introduction of a programme of increased support for social and experiential learning before, during, and after the period of residence abroad. Rather than being driven by expediency or a desire simply to please an ever growing number of eager prospective SA consumers, the approach taken to curriculum review at Durham was underpinned by relevant educational, curriculum design, and SA research. Overall, it was 'grounded in experiential/constructivist assumptions' and was 'holistic' in the sense used in Passarelli and Kolb (2012, p. 137) and Vande Berg, Paige, and Lou (2012, p. 19). In addition, the review of year abroad assessment, more specifically, was informed by Biggs (2003), Healey (2005), Jenkins and Healey (2009), as well as by Coleman (2005) and Coleman and Parker (2001) on SA learning objectives and by Dörnyei (2005), Ushioda (2003), and Willis Allen (2013) on motivation. Development of more targeted learning support drew on Meier (2010), and on Coleman (2013, 2015) and Meier and Daniels (2011) for social learning, Kolb and Kolb (2005), Kolb (1984), and Passarelli and Kolb (2012) for experiential learning, and Alred and Byram (2002), Bathurst and LaBrack (2012), Byram (1997), Byram and Zarate (1997), and Jackson (2010, 2013), as well as the Intercultural Educational Resources for ERASMUS students and their Teachers (IEREST) discussed by Beaven and Borghetti in this volume, for intercultural learning. We argue that the effective integration of formal academic learning abroad into the broader undergraduate curriculum, as well as appropriate support for and acknowledgement of other forms of informal learning, are all essential in the creation of a successful SA programme.

Institutional Context

The School of Modern Language and Cultures at Durham offers a four-year undergraduate degree in modern languages in which students can study one or two languages from Arabic, Chinese, French, German, Italian,

Japanese, Russian, and Spanish. Students take six modules in each year: one core-language module for each language studied with the remainder selected from a wide range of cultural options, covering literature, cultural history, cinema and visual culture, translation, and, in some languages, interpreting. Students on Combined Honours and Joint Honours degree courses (e.g., liberal arts, history and French, economics with French) also take modules in the School. There are roughly 240 to 270 students in each year of study, across the School. The students come with excellent secondary-level qualifications; they are all advanced language learners (though some begin one of their languages ab initio in first year) and tend to be independent, self-motivated, and ambitious, going on after Durham either to further study or to a variety of careers, from language-specific work in translation or teaching to work in the media, civil service, business, or finance. The year abroad is compulsory for students on the modern languages degree and is taken in the third year of study. It is considered to be central to the degree and to each student's development linguistically and intellectually as well as in terms of intercultural competence, enterprise skills, and employability (Durham University, 2016a).

A particular attraction of the programme at Durham is the freedom given to students as to what they can do during their year abroad. Although described as a *year abroad*, most students in fact spend 15 months in a country or countries in which the languages they are studying are used, from the July at the end of their second year to the October at the start of the final year. Those studying two languages divide their time abroad as they please, though they must spend a minimum of four months in each host culture. There are very few limitations on which countries can be visited: the majority go to France and Belgium, Germany and Austria, Italy, and Spain, but many also take up placements in Latin America, and a limited number go to Canada, the Caribbean, or Africa. These students either: (1) complete a study placement of one or two semesters in one of our partner universities; (2) work as an English language assistant in a school; (3) undertake a paid or unpaid work placement or internship in a company or non-profit organisation; or (4) choose a combination of these options. Some students visit three or even four different locations, with different placements in each one. Whereas study placements (such as ERASMUS or most other university placements) are arranged for students by the School and assistantships are organised by the British Council, students must find their own work placement should they decide this is what they want to do. For students of Arabic, Chinese, Japanese, and Russian, the options are slightly more limited with placements normally arranged at a specific language school or university. Nevertheless, with the exception of these languages, work placements are now by far the most popular choice, in spite of the fact that they require the most organisational effort on the part of the students. Over the past five years the percentage of students completing at least one work placement has consistently been above 80 per cent of the whole cohort. The trend towards work placements is possibly due to the level of flexibility they offer and also due to the importance students now attach to employability and building an impressive CV. This trend had to be taken into account in our review of assessment and learning provision in order to integrate learning on work placements into broader learning on the degree and to mitigate what might otherwise be an interruption in academic work for a significant period of time. Although the School is keen to offer freedom and flexibility in relation to the year abroad, faculty also want to stress that it should be understood as a period of ongoing *study* and not as a gap in the degree curriculum.

History and Development of Assessment

Given this diversity, in terms of location, languages studied, and type of placement completed (not uncommon in European or North American contexts (Coleman, 1997, 2013; Engle & Engle, 2003)), assessment of the Durham year abroad has always been problematic. The need for a single system of assessment for all students means that course credits gained in host universities abroad cannot contribute to the Durham degree. Indeed, the University insists that formal assessment of the year abroad should be in-house.

Until 2007, students produced a 2000-word target-language essay for each language studied based on an aspect of their experience abroad. Supervision of this project was minimal, effectively limited to approval of the topic and feedback on an essay plan, and there was little direct relationship between topics covered and the broader Durham curriculum. The mark for each essay was worth less than 5 per cent of the overall final degree mark and was not specifically mentioned on the degree transcript. Student and faculty dissatisfaction with this situation led to the setting up of a working party that drew on national initiatives such as the Learning and Residence Abroad (LARA) project to develop a new system of year abroad assessment in which students compiled a portfolio relating to their research into one of nine topics (e.g., 'changing places', 'local media', 'local food', 'local humour', and so forth (LARA, 2016)). The portfolio encourages students to follow an ethnographic approach to interpreting their experience and elicits reflection on the development of intercultural understanding and competence. However, the portfolio itself was not assessed; to comply with University regulations, the mark (now only 2.5 per cent per language of the final degree mark) was awarded strictly only according to performance in a 15-minute oral exam at the start of the final year where students presented their portfolio and answered questions on it. Success in this short, onetime exam was determined as much by oral language competence (on the day) as by evidence of intercultural sensitivity. Indeed, students felt, quite justifiably, that there was little relationship between the effort required to produce the portfolio and the place accorded to it in the exam and that the development of their written language skills was not being assessed at all. Moreover, collecting portfolios in hard copy from students and redistributing them to examiners proved to be a significant burden on administrative staff, with faculty also complaining that they had to spend considerable time reviewing work as preparation for the oral exams but which they could not, in fact, assess. The portfolio was eventually dropped and replaced by a 700-word reflection related to the same set of topics but, again, only forming the basis for discussion in an oral exam. Students and faculty still felt that there was insufficient relationship between these topics and learning elsewhere in the curriculum and some students even complained that the topics were simplistic, while faculty commented that because of the absence of a rigorous programme of preparation and support, the project could be unintentionally counterproductive by inviting an uncritical approach to stereotypes and generalisations.

It was in this context of general unease that a further working party was set up in 2013, this time with the specific objective of more closely aligning the year abroad with the learning aims and outcomes of the Durham modern languages degree as well as with the University's principles for curriculum development (Durham University, 2016a, 2016d). This essentially meant aligning the year abroad with the University's culture of research, understood in terms of learning and teaching as either: 'research-led' (the curriculum is focussed on content resulting from faculty research specialisms), 'research-oriented' (attention is given to research processes and the development of a researcher mentality), 'research-based' (with the focus on enquiry-based activities), or 'research-informed' (drawing on and contributing to research into teaching and learning), or a combination of these approaches (Durham University, 2016d; Healey, 2005; Jenkins & Healey, 2009). It was therefore decided that formal learning on the year abroad should involve work towards a substantial research project in the target language that would sit alongside a compulsory final-year dissertation, both of which forming the 'intellectual pinnacles' of the degree (Durham University, 2016c). The centrality of the year abroad was thus recognised and its full integration into the curriculum was achieved by closely aligning the students' year abroad research projects with study in the second and final year (Biggs, 2003). Thus, students would not only be engaged in their own research while abroad (developing their research skills and becoming part of a community of research practice), they would also be able to draw upon and engage with the research and expertise of staff in the School (Streitwieser, 2010). Moreover, since the project requires submission of an extended essay (2500 or 5000 words), students would be encouraged to develop their academic writing skills, an aspect of linguistic development that had been neglected in the past but which research suggests could benefit significantly from targeted input (Pérez-Vidal & Barquin, 2014; Pérez-Vidal & Juan-Garau, 2009; Sasaki, 2011). Finally, the assessment was designed so as to ensure ongoing contact between students abroad and their supervisors in Durham. As well as regular informal emails, there are five formal stages towards completion of the project, each involving submission of a piece of work on which feedback is given. Students take the lead in constructing their project, set their own goals, negotiate deadlines to fit in with their other commitments, and, through the learning support resources described below, reflect on this process, thereby improving motivation (Ushioda, 2003; Willis Allen, 2013). However, unlike with the previous forms of assessment, the current project does not now contribute directly to the final degree mark but must nevertheless be passed in order for the year abroad to be validated as a year of academic study.

This new system of assessment went live in June 2014, but, from the outset, there was a sense that the focus had shifted too much towards formal learning and that there was a danger that other, equally valuable forms of learning abroad—especially through interaction—would be neglected. As early as 2001, Coleman and Parker had identified six different types of SA learning objectives and more recent research looked more to social and experiential learning than to formal academic study. Consequently, a project to develop learning resources and support for informal learning abroad was set up to run alongside the new formal assessment.

Learning Support

In the context of students at Durham and their varied experiences abroad, social and experiential learning was understood as the whole range of things students learn simply by interacting with others and experiencing life. This included interactions with fellow year abroad students as well as with target-language-speaking peers and friends, co-workers, other students and teachers, and other members of the host culture encountered in day-to-day activities such as shopping for food or accessing basic services. The School's objective here was to equip students with effective strategies for maximising contact with others abroad (Coleman, 2013, 2015; Isabelli-García, 2006; Jackson, 2008; Kinginger, 2008b; Mitchell, Tracy-Ventura, & McManus, 2017), to promote realistic expectations and maintain motivation (Dörnyei, 2001; Ushioda, 2003; Willis Allen, 2013), and to encourage a reflective approach to interactions (Kolb, 1984; Kolb & Kolb, 2005; Passarelli & Kolb, 2012; Vande Berg et al., 2012) not just as fun but as opportunities to learn (Benson, Barkhuizen, Bodycott, & Brown, 2013, p. 36; Gardner, Gross, & Steglitz, 2008; Kinginger, 2013, p. 7). For students to experience deep learning, it has to be 'experiential, developmental, and holistic' (Vande Berg et al., 2012, p. 25).

Kolb's (1984) experiential learning cycle consists of four concepts: concrete experience, abstract conceptualization, reflective observation, and active experimentation; these correspond to four learning styles: experiencing, reflecting, thinking, and acting. That is, students learn by doing and then reflecting on the learning experience: 'When a concrete experience is enriched by reflection, given meaning by thinking and transformed by action, the new experience created becomes richer, broader and deeper' (Passarelli & Kolb, 2012, p. 146); the experience becomes deep learning when students develop 'meta-awareness' (Vande Berg et al., 2012, p. 21). However, research suggests that students often need to be taught how to reflect: 'Teaching reflection needs to be planned and integrated into students' individual courses of study' (Quinton & Smallbone, 2010, p. 125).

SA offers an opportunity for students to engage in the four modes of the experiential learning cycle and allows learners *to be in charge of their learning* and, therefore, motivated (Passarelli & Kolb, 2012, pp. 143–5; Ushioda, 2003; Willis Allen, 2013). Potentially, it allows students to shift from one learning style to another within the learning cycle depending on the learning situation. That is, it gives them 'learning flexibility' and promotes deep learning (Passarelli & Kolb, 2012, p. 143). In other words, deep learning is achieved by an increased integration of the four primary learning styles, which students may have the opportunity of achieving during their residence abroad supported by the guidance of an educator (Passarelli & Kolb, 2012, p. 147).

SA also offers the experience of dealing with life in a new and unfamiliar environment. This involves milestones, such as finding accommodation, signing a work contract, opening a bank account, or completing administrative formalities; but it also involves the mundane, such as shopping, using public transport, eating out, watching television, joining clubs, or playing sports (Barro, Jordan, & Roberts, 1998). This time the School's objective was to help students negotiate these experiences successfully, to raise awareness of their value, and, again, to get students to reflect on their learning (Kolb, 1984; Kolb & Kolb, 2005; Passarelli & Kolb, 2012; Vande Berg et al., 2012).

It was important to support and recognise social and experiential learning because this learning is fundamental not only to the development of cultural knowledge (Byram & Feng, 2004; Kinginger, 2013) and linguistic ability (Adams, 2006; Kinginger, 2008a, 2008b), but also to the development of intercultural competence (Alred & Byram, 2002; Byram, 2014; Holmes, Bavieri, Ganassin, & Murphy, 2016; Jackson, 2010), enterprise skills, and employability (Brooks, Waters, & Pimlott-Wilson, 2012; Busch, 2009; Gardner et al., 2008; Jones, 2013; UKCES, 2016). Visits to sites of historical or architectural significance, museums, theatres, and the cinema, participating in festivals and cultural events, experiencing local food, or just observing a particular way of life, all help provide first-hand knowledge of specific cultures. Moreover, social interaction and real-life experience can have an important positive impact on language learning by presenting students with opportunities for regular, purposeful communicative acts (Mitchell et al., 2017). All of this informal learning clearly feeds into the students' formal academic work, aligned to the curriculum and assessed either through the year abroad research project or in final year. However, the School also wanted to support and capture the soft skills SA so effectively promotes. During their year abroad, students face cultural otherness daily and, for some, this experience is repeated in a number of different locations (e.g., Argentina then rural France then Spain then Paris). Thus, students get the opportunity to develop the skills necessary for successful intercultural interaction in several cultural contexts (McKinnon, 2018). Following Byram's (1997) model, in order to gain intercultural communicative competence, students need to: (1) gain sociocultural knowledge of the other culture (*savoir*); (2) interpret and relate to documents and texts of the receiving culture (*savoir comprendre*); (3) develop the ability to gain new knowledge of a culture and cultural practices, to be used in social interaction, such as strategies of politeness (*savoir apprendre/faire*); (4) develop critical cultural awareness to be able to critically evaluate beliefs and practices in the receiving culture as well as their own (*savoir s'engager*); and (5) develop respect for others by questioning their own values and beliefs (*savoir être*).

While abroad students also have to independently and proactively find solutions to problems that can no longer be resolved by recourse to the usual sources of help, such as family or close friends. Even in the age of social networking and cheap mobile communications, contacts in the home culture may simply not have the skillset needed to be useful in target-culture contexts. Research has shown that, while abroad, most students do develop the attributes and skills that are attractive to employers: independence, adaptability, time management, decision-making, dependability, diplomacy, creativity, resourcefulness, as well as an ability to think ahead, assess risk, prioritise, and compromise (Gardner et al., 2008, p. 4). Indeed, it is precisely the development of such soft skills that makes those who have studied abroad so employable (Larzén-Östermark, 2011, p. 455), yet feedback from students consistently revealed that this aspect of their learning and development was something they found especially difficult to articulate (McKinnon, 2018).

The School's project aimed to provide a programme of targeted intervention before, during, and after the period of residence abroad, focussing on culture-specific and linguistic support, as well as intercultural competence, enterprise skills, and employability. Support was thus to be focussed on the whole cycle, not just the period of residence abroad and designed not just to *prepare* but to *educate* students about SA itself (Benson et al., 2013, p. 146). A guided, interventionist approach allows students to articulate, reflect, and re-examine their motives, expectations, and actual experiences during the whole cycle (Bathurst & LaBrack, 2012; Benson et al., 2013, pp. 150–5). The methodological approach drew on a number of pre-existing learning support programmes, some of which also provided materials that could be used directly or adapted. Projects such as the EU Online Linguistic Support (OLS, 2016) were already available to our students in receipt of an ERASMUS+ grant; and other EU projects such as the ERASMUS Mundus Intercultural Competence (EMIC, 2016) toolkit or the IEREST (2016) resources were both accessible and easily adaptable. By collaborating with other University departments, such as the International Office and the Careers Service, we were also able to draw on their expertise, avoid duplication, and offer a seamless experience to our students. Finally, the project was able to exploit resources that had been developed in previous iterations of the Durham year abroad, and a small grant from the University allowed us to create new materials in order to cater to our own current students' specific learning needs.

In developing this programme of learning support, we adhered to the same holistic approach and principles of curriculum alignment as for the assessment. The intention was to provide students with a 'meta-awareness' of their cultural self-positioning and to scaffold their learning with 'meaningful cultural mentoring and opportunities for reflection on meaning making' (Vande Berg et al., 2012, p. 21). Preparation activities were to be integrated into second-year classes (principally in core-language modules); year abroad activities would be delivered through ongoing contact with teachers and lecturers and through access to the Virtual Learning Environment (VLE) (e.g., Blackboard); final-year activities would again be integrated into core-language modules and through specially organised year abroad meetings. At each stage, students would be involved in the delivery of the programme, with returning students and incoming exchange students sharing their first-hand experience of SA with those preparing to go away. This was considered important not just as a means of cascading useful information and advice but also as a way of encouraging returning students to reflect on and value their own learning (Benson et al., 2013, p. 155; Kolb, 1984; Passarelli & Kolb, 2012, p. 146; Vande Berg et al., 2012, p. 21).

Pre-residence abroad activities and materials include practical, culture-specific preparation delivered either in class, via the VLE (e.g., video tutorials, student blogs, web links), or in meetings with a language-specific advisor, and include information about cultural norms, rules of behaviour, accommodation, and administrative formalities as well as information about the education system for British Council and ERASMUS placements, and help completing target-language applications for work placements. This is supplemented by a series of ten-minute, non-culture-specific activities to be integrated into classes in any language and designed to foster intercultural competence. For example, students are asked to reflect on the intercultural experiences they have already had since arriving at university (most are not from Durham, which has a strong local cultural identity) and to consider how they have negotiated these experiences; another activity asks students to list well-known stereotypes relating to their year abroad host culture, and then reflect on ideas of individual identity, the legitimacy of generalisations, and the power structures they frequently hide. A similar series of ten-minute linguistic exercises aims to encourage students to reflect on and develop their own strategies for language learning abroad.

While abroad, ongoing language learning is supported by work towards the assessed research project (vocabulary building; supervisor's feedback on samples) and by access to in-house online language-learning exercises (essentially grammar and vocabulary) aligned to prior learning and study in final year, as well as generic resources such as the ERASMUS+ OLS. Short video tutorials provide guidance on the compilation of a reflective portfolio, suggesting evidence to collect in relation to activities that help demonstrate the development of enterprise skills and intercultural competence (finding accommodation, administrative formalities, negotiating social structures and relationships, and so forth). Students are thus encouraged to become attentive to and actively conscious of their activities abroad, reflecting on their learning as it happens and then retrospectively (if they have a similar experience in a different country). The self-awareness afforded by this activity motivates students intrinsically but they are also motivated extrinsically because they know that the portfolio will form an important part of their language work in final year.

In final year, the emphasis shifts to consolidation of learning and to its recognition both by students and the institution. In the past, students had complained that they found it difficult to articulate what they had gained from SA, for example, in employment interviews. They also complained that the School did not do enough to acknowledge their learning. Under the former system of assessment, the 15-minute oral exam at the start of final year was often the only opportunity students had to discuss SA with their teachers; it was never mentioned again. An important part of the School's project was therefore to build ongoing reflection on the year abroad into final-year teaching. This was achieved through developing ten-minute activities to be used in core-language classes (as for second year), including writing tasks and oral presentations, and exploiting materials and reflection in the portfolios compiled abroad. The focus of these activities was mainly on enterprise and interculturality, but employability was addressed elsewhere through closer collaboration with the University Careers Service who organise a series of meetings to help students explore the match between knowledge and skills developed abroad and what employers are looking for in future employees. Finalists are also encouraged to deploy their own expertise as SA participants by producing blogs or information booklets and by participating in year abroad meetings, all intended for second-year students. Although none of this is currently officially credited by the University, the School is looking at forms of accreditation such as a separate year abroad certificate, participation in the Durham Award (a certificate recognising the skills Durham students develop beyond their academic studies (Durham University, 2016b)), or a scheme for digital certification such as Open Badges (Mozilla, 2016).

Conclusion and Recommendations

Many of our assumptions about what and how students learn during SA are open to question (Vande Berg et al., 2012, pp. 3–4). One of these assumptions is that students will learn simply by going abroad: they will enhance not only their linguistic and intercultural competences, but they will also develop enterprise skills and acquire employability without any institutional intervention or focussed effort of their own. However, as Vande Berg et al. (2012, p. 20) point out 'when viewed through an experiential/constructivist lens, we see that immersion in experience abroad will not, in and of itself, lead students to learn effectively'. That is, going abroad is not in itself a guarantee of learning. Indeed, research indicates that 'students learn and develop effectively and appropriately when educators intervene more intentionally through well-designed training programs that continue throughout the SA experience' (Vande Berg et al., 2012, p. 21).

Our experience of designing a SA package for our own institution leads us to a number of specific recommendations. Firstly, in modern languages, SA should be central to the degree in terms of both recognition and actual learning. This will ensure that both staff and students give this aspect of their studies the seriousness it merits. This is one of the recommendations also proposed by Meier (2010, p. 10) as well as by the UCML (2012, p. 9). It clearly has implications for staff training and development since to develop and run a SA programme successfully within an institution, it is essential to have ongoing staff development so that all participants can understand and value the role of SA within the degree as a whole (Coleman & Parker, 2001, pp. 143–4).

A second recommendation involves the different contexts in which SA takes place. That is, variation in terms of experience and the type of students and institutions involved must be taken into account because curriculum design will differ according to the specific learning objectives of both student and institution. Moreover, SA programmes and experiences may vary not only from country to country and institution to institution but also within the same institution (Coleman, 2013, pp. 26–7). In Durham University, for example, the year abroad programme in modern languages is very different from that available in some other departments.

A third recommendation is that for SA to be integrated within any one programme, a holistic approach needs to be adopted, ensuring that it is taken seriously and supports broader student learning. Even where it is a supplementary component to the degree, such as an additional or extracurricular year, it should support and develop upon the student's longer-term learning aims. As mentioned above, learning needs to be holistic in order to become deep learning (Vande Berg et al., 2012), and by holistic we mean that all types of learning should be recognised, not just formal, cultural learning and language acquisition; important as they are, these types of learning do not account for all of the full range of SA learning objectives (Coleman, 2015, p. 38). In other words, 'the whole person and the whole context' need to be taken into account when designing a programme of study (Coleman, 2013, p. 36).

As a fourth recommendation, we would propose full curriculum integration of SA with formal learning elsewhere in the degree. Without some form of formal learning clearly linked to the broader learning outcomes of the degree as a whole, the period of SA risks becoming at worst a holiday and at best a gap year. Indeed, 'the widespread image of study abroad as dressed-up vacation time will persist as long as we allow it' (Engle & Engle, 2003, p. 16). To combat this perception, there is a need to 're-educate students and their parents regarding the nobler ends and means of study abroad' (Engle & Engle, 2003, p. 17), as well as faculty and administrators. In addition, formal learning motivates students intrinsically and extrinsically because it fits in with their broader learning aims (i.e., to master their subject but also to successfully graduate) (Dörnyei, 2001; Ushioda, 2003; Willis Allen, 2013). It also validates SA within the institution and helps maintain contact between students and their teachers.

A fifth recommendation relates to social and experiential learning. Both social and experiential learning must be fully integrated into the specific learning objectives for SA. Both must also be adequately supported, for example, with preparatory sessions prior to departure, a reflective portfolio while abroad, and debriefing sessions on return. They must also be recognised: 'If our institutions are serious about reinforcing the international dimension of the experiences they offer, one would hope that they are open to implementing a system that would clearly acknowledge the kind of overseas-study experiences their students have had and reward those achievements' (Engle & Engle, 2003, p. 16). This might be achieved either by including social and experiential learning in the assessment or validation of the degree or by means of supplementary certification.

Finally, we recommend that the preparation for SA should be ongoing so that the experience is seen as institutional and not something the students do outside of the home institution (Kolb, 1984; Kolb & Kolb, 2005; Passarelli & Kolb, 2012; Vande Berg et al., 2012). As mentioned above, students need to be taught how to reflect throughout the programme, even from the first year (Bathurst & LaBrack, 2012; Benson et al., 2013; Jackson, 2013; Meier & Daniels, 2011; Quinton & Smallbone, 2010; Vande Berg, 2009).

SA can be a rewarding and enjoyable experience. It can also contribute to the development of the knowledge and skills necessary for students to achieve their learning aims and objectives, and to reach their personal and professional goals. A well-designed programme of SA needs to take all of the different kinds of learning abroad into account, supporting, capturing, and acknowledging this learning in appropriate ways. In order to be seen as at the centre of the curriculum, it needs to be fully integrated within it, reflecting the reasons students came to a particular institution and playing a role in their learning and success there. Developments in the Durham year abroad have been both challenging and rewarding to students and staff alike. The programme has evolved over a long period of time, and changes in one part of it often highlight the need to develop provision elsewhere. Much as our students learn from their experiences abroad, it is in our own experience of working towards enhancing student learning that we most effectively come to understand our students' learning needs, and can thereby continue to develop and improve our interventions.

Summary of recommendations for positioning SA at the centre of the modern languages curriculum
• SA should be central to learning and teaching on a degree in modern languages and its importance should be recognised institutionally. • Curriculum design must take student and institutional diversity into account. No two students or institutions are identical. • SA should be integrated into students' whole lives; learning should be understood broadly and holistically. • Learning abroad should support and be supported by formal learning elsewhere in the modern languages curriculum. • Learning support interventions should acknowledge the importance and value of social and experiential learning abroad. • SA should be seen by students as part of their learning for the home institution.

Bibliography

Adams, R. (2006). Language learning strategies in the study abroad context. In E. Churchill & M. A. DuFon (Eds.), *Language learners in study abroad contexts* (pp. 259–292). Clevedon, UK: Multilingual Matters.

Alred, G., & Byram, M. (2002). Becoming an intercultural mediator: A longitudinal study of residence abroad. *Journal of Multilingual and Multicultural Development, 23*(5), 339–352.

Barro, A., Jordan, S., & Roberts, C. (1998). Cultural practice in everyday life: The language learner as ethnographer. In M. Byram & M. Fleming (Eds.), *Language learning in intercultural perspective: Approaches through drama and ethnography* (pp. 76–97). Cambridge: Cambridge University Press.

Bathurst, L., & LaBrack, B. (2012). Shifting the locus of intercultural learning. Intervening prior to and after student experiences abroad. In M. Vande Berg, R. M. Paige, & K. H. Lou (Eds.), *Student learning abroad: What our students are learning, what they're not, and what we can do about it* (pp. 261–283). Sterling, VA: Stylus.

Benson, P., Barkhuizen, G., Bodycott, P., & Brown, J. (2013). *Second language identity in narratives of study abroad*. New York: Palgrave Macmillan.

Biggs, J. (2003). *Teaching for quality learning at university* (2nd ed.). Buckingham: Open University Press.

British Council. (2015). *Broadening horizons 2015: The value of the overseas experience*. Retrieved from https://ei.britishcouncil.org/

Brooks, R., Waters, J., & Pimlott-Wilson, H. (2012). International education and the employability of UK students. *British Educational Research Journal, 38*(2), 281–298.

Busch, D. (2009). What kind of intercultural competence will contribute to students' future job employability? *Intercultural Education, 20*(5), 429–438.

Byram, M. (1997). *Teaching and assessing intercultural communicative competence*. Clevedon: Multilingual Matters.

Byram, M. (2014). Twenty-five years on—From cultural studies to intercultural citizenship. *Language, Culture and Curriculum, 27*(3), 209–225.

Byram, M., & Feng, A. (2004). *Culture and language learning: Teaching research and scholarship*. Cambridge: Cambridge University Press.

Byram, M., & Zarate, G. (1997). Definitions, objectives and assessment of sociocultural competence. In *Council of Europe, sociocultural competence in language learning and teaching* (pp. 7–43). Strasbourg: Council of Europe.

Coleman, J. A. (1997). Residence abroad within language study. *Language Teaching, 30*, 1–20.

Coleman, J. A. (2005). Residence abroad. In J. A. Coleman & J. Klapper (Eds.), *Effective learning and teaching in modern languages* (pp. 126–132). London: Routledge.

Coleman, J. A. (2013). Reaching whole people and whole lives. In C. Kingeger (Ed.), *Social and cultural aspects of language learning in study abroad* (pp. 19–44). Amsterdam: Benjamins.

Coleman, J. A. (2015). Social circles during residence abroad: What students do, and who with. In R. Mitchell, N. Tracy-Ventura, & K. McManus (Eds.), *Social interaction, identity and language learning during residence abroad* (pp. 33–51). EuroSLA Monographs Series 2. Retrieved from http://www.eurosla.org/eurosla-monograph-series-2/social-interaction-identity-and-language-learning-during-residence-abroad/

Coleman, J. A., & Parker, L. (2001). Preparing for residence abroad: Staff development implications. In J. Klapper (Ed.), *Teaching languages in higher education: Issues in training and continuing professional development* (pp. 134–162). London: CILT.

Dörnyei, Z. (2001). *Teaching and researching motivation*. Harlow, UK: Longman.

Dörnyei, Z. (2005). *The psychology of the language learner: Individual differences in second language acquisition*. Mahwah, NJ: Lawrence Erlbaum.

Durham University. (2016a). BA in modern languages and cultures with year abroad: Learning and teaching. Retrieved from https://www.dur.ac.uk/mlac/undergraduate/modlangs/

Durham University. (2016b). Durham award. Retrieved from https://www.dur.ac.uk/careers/daward/
Durham University. (2016c). Ongoing induction, TLRP and Dissertation. Retrieved from https://www.dur.ac.uk/mlac/undergraduate/tlrp-diss/
Durham University. (2016d). Principles for the development of the taught curriculum. Retrieved from https://www.dur.ac.uk/learningandteaching.handbook/
EMIC. (2016). ERASMUS Mundus intercultural competence toolkit. Retrieved from http://www.emic-project.org/
Engle, L., & Engle, J. (2003). Study abroad levels: Towards a classification of program types. *Frontiers: The Interdisciplinary Journal of Study Abroad, 9,* 1–20.
European Commission. (2015). ERASMUS: Facts, figures and trends. Retrieved from http://ec.europa.eu/education/library/
Gardner, P., Gross, L., & Steglitz, I. (2008). Unpacking your study abroad experience: Critical reflection for workplace competence. *Collegiate Employment Research Institute Research Brief, 1*(1), 1–10. Retrieved from http://files.eric.ed.gov/fulltext/ED509854.pdf
Go International. (2016). About us. Retrieved from http://go.international.ac.uk/about-us
Gore, J. (2005). *Dominant beliefs and alternative voices: Discourse, belief and gender in American study abroad.* New York: Routledge.
Healey, M. (2005). Linking research and teaching: Exploring disciplinary spaces and the role of inquiry-based learning. In R. Barnett (Ed.), *Reshaping the university: New relationships between research, scholarship and teaching* (pp. 67–78). Maidenhead: McGraw-Hill.
Holmes, P., Bavieri, L., Ganassin, S., & Murphy, J. (2016). Interculturality and the study abroad experience: Students' learning from the IEREST materials. *Language and Intercultural Communication, 16*(3), 452–469.
IEREST. (2016). Intercultural education resources for ERASMUS students and their teachers. Retrieved from http://www.ierest-project.eu/
Isabelli-García, C. (2006). Study abroad social networks, motivation and attitudes: Implications for second language acquisition. In E. Churchill & M. A. DuFon (Eds.), *Language learners in study abroad contexts* (pp. 231–258). Clevedon, UK: Multilingual Matters.
Jackson, J. (2008). *Language, identity and study abroad: Sociocultural perspectives.* London: Equinox.
Jackson, J. (2010). *Intercultural journeys: From study to residence abroad.* Basingstoke, UK: Palgrave Macmillan.

Jackson, J. (2013). The transformation of 'a frog in the well': A path to a more intercultural, global mindset. In C. Kinginger (Ed.), *Social and cultural aspects of language learning in study abroad* (pp. 179–204). Amsterdam: Benjamins.

Jenkins, A., & Healey, M. (2009). Institutional strategies to link teaching and research. Retrieved from https://www.heacademy.ac.uk/sites/default/files/resources/id585_institutional_strategies_to_link_teaching_and_research_2.pdf

Jones, E. (2013). Internationalization and employability: The role of intercultural experiences in the development of transferable skills. *Public Money & Management, 33*(2), 95–104.

Kinginger, C. (2008a). *Language learning and study abroad. A critical reading of research.* Basingstoke: Palgrave Macmillan.

Kinginger, C. (2008b). Language learning in study abroad: Case histories of Americans in France. *Modern Language Journal, 92*, 1–124.

Kinginger, C. (2013). Introduction: Social and cultural aspects of language learning in study abroad. In C. Kinginger (Ed.), *Social and cultural aspects of language learning in study abroad* (pp. 3–15). Amsterdam: Benjamins.

Kolb, A., & Kolb, D. (2005). Learning styles and learning spaces: Enhancing experiential learning in higher education. *Academy of Management Learning and Education, 4*(2), 193–212.

Kolb, D. (1984). *Experiential learning: Experience as the source of learning and development.* London: Prentice-Hall.

LARA. (2016). The LARA project, archived. Retrieved from https://www.llas.ac.uk/lara/index.htm

Larzén-Östermark, E. (2011). Intercultural sojourns as educational experiences: A narrative study of the outcomes of Finnish student teachers' language-practice periods in Britain. *Scandinavian Journal of Educational Research, 55*(5), 455–473.

McKinnon, S. (2018). Foregrounding intercultural learning during study abroad as part of a modern language degree. In J. Jackson & S. Oguro (Eds.), *Intercultural interventions in study abroad* (pp. 103–118). London: Routledge.

Meier, G. (2010). Review of the assessment of the year abroad in the modern language degrees at Bath: Assessment for experiential and autonomous learning based on the continuity model. University of Bath. Retrieved from https://ore.exeter.ac.uk/repository/handle/10871/16146

Meier, G., & Daniels, H. (2011). 'Just not being able to make friends': Social interaction during the year abroad in modern foreign language degrees. *Research Papers in Education, 1*, 1–27.

Mitchell, R., Tracy-Ventura, N., & McManus, K. (2017). *Anglophone students abroad: Identity, social relationships, and language learning*. London: Routledge.

Mozilla. (2016). Mozilla open badges. Retrieved from http://openbadges.org/

OLS. (2016). ERASMUS+ online linguistic support. Retrieved from http://ERASMUSplusols.eu/

Passarelli, A. M., & Kolb, D. A. (2012). Using experiential learning theory to promote student learning and development in programs of education abroad. In M. Vande Berg, R. M. Paige, & K. H. Lou (Eds.), *Student learning abroad: What our students are learning, what they're not, and what we can do about it* (pp. 137–161). Sterling, VA: Stylus.

Pérez-Vidal, C., & Barquin, E. (2014). Comparing progress in academic writing after formal instruction and study abroad. In C. Pérez-Vidal (Ed.), *Language acquisition in study abroad and formal instruction contexts* (pp. 217–234). Amsterdam: Benjamins.

Pérez-Vidal, C., & Juan-Garau, M. (2009). The effect of study abroad on written performance. *EUROSLA Yearbook, 1*, 270–296.

Quinton, S., & Smallbone, T. (2010). Feeding forward: Using feedback to promote student reflection and learning—A teaching model. *Innovations in Education and Teaching International, 47*(1), 125–135.

Sasaki, M. (2011). Effects of varying lengths of study-abroad experiences on Japanese EFL students' L2 writing ability and motivation: A longitudinal study. *TESOL Quarterly, 45*, 85–105.

Streitwieser, B. T. (2010). Undergraduate research during study abroad. Scope, meaning, and potential. In R. Lewin (Ed.), *The handbook of practice and research in study abroad: Higher education and the quest for global citizenship* (pp. 399–419). London: Routledge.

UCML. (2012). Valuing the year abroad: The importance of the year abroad as part of a degree programme for UK students. Retrieved from http://www.ucml.ac.uk/

UKCES. (2016). Employer skills survey 2015: UK report. Retrieved from https://www.gov.uk/government/collections/ukces-employer-skills-survey-2015

Ushioda, E. (2003). Motivation as a socially mediated process. In D. Little, J. Ridley, & E. Ushioda (Eds.), *Learner autonomy in the foreign language classroom: Learner, teacher, curriculum and assessment* (pp. 90–103). Dublin: Authentik.

Vande Berg, M. (2009). Intervening in student learning abroad: A research-based inquiry. *Intercultural Education, 20*(1), 15–27.

Vande Berg, M., Paige, R. M., & Lou, K. H. (2012). Student learning abroad: Paradigms and assumptions. In M. Vande Berg, R. M. Paige, & K. H. Lou (Eds.), *Student learning abroad: What our students are learning, what they're not, and what we can do about it* (pp. 3–28). Sterling, VA: Stylus.

Willis Allen, H. (2013). Self-regulatory strategies of foreign language learners. From the classroom to study abroad and beyond. In C. Kinginger (Ed.), *Social and cultural aspects of language learning in study abroad* (pp. 47–73). Amsterdam: Benjamins.

Zemach-Bersin, T. (2009). Selling the world: Study abroad marketing and the privatization of global citizenship. In R. Lewin (Ed.), *The handbook of practice and research in study abroad: Higher education and the quest for global citizenship* (pp. 303–320). New York: Routledge.

Lessons from 25 Years of Experimenting with Arabic Study Abroad: Programme Evaluation, Culture, Location, and Curriculum

Matthew T. Bird and R. Kirk Belnap

Introduction

In 2003 Engle and Engle (p. 219) called for a 'structured, coordinated, profession-wide assessment effort' to discover study abroad (SA) programme characteristics that correlate with desirable learning outcomes. Research over the last decade has tried to answer that call and resulted in evidence that some variables are strongly associated with higher language and intercultural gains during SA (Isabelli-García, Bown, Plews, & Dewey, Forthcoming; Paige, Cohen, & Shively, 2004; Vande Berg, Connor-Linton, & Paige, 2009). The factors that have been studied so far may generalise to most SA programmes, but the field also stands in need of detailed descriptions of programme, curriculum, and material designs that demonstrate effective ways to apply research findings. Engle and Engle (2003) initiated a conversation about how to describe and organise SA programmes conceptually, and occasional

---

M. T. Bird (✉) • R. K. Belnap
Brigham Young University, Provo, UT, USA
e-mail: matthew.bird@byu.edu; belnap@byu.edu

publications have put individual SA designs on display (e.g., Archangeli, 1999; Misfeldt, 2013; Raschio, 2001), but the examples available are still relatively few and far apart.

The Arabic faculty at Brigham Young University (BYU) in Provo, Utah, have been conducting SA programmes in the Arab world since 1989. An active evaluation and improvement cycle, especially in the last decade, has resulted in programme improvements and interventions that research has since associated with better SA outcomes, such as content-based instruction and onsite coaching (Vande Berg et al., 2009). This chapter highlights lessons learned from BYU's Arabic SA programme from two perspectives. First, we present a general timeline of significant changes to the programme. Second, we review some of the lessons learned in greater detail for the purpose of possibly facilitating their adoption by other programmes with similar needs.

Context: History of the Programme's Development

The essential structure of the BYU SA programme has been in place since the beginning, but some aspects have evolved considerably as we have carried out more than 20 SA programmes in the Arab world. One useful approach to the programme's history is to divide it into the following developmental phases: (1) building interest and investment (1989–2002); (2) growing pains (2004); (3) taking advantage of local affordances (2006); (4) consolidating the reading course and implementing programme reviews (2009–2010); (5) strengthening institutional collaboration and adjusting the reading course (2011); (6) institutionalising speaking and writing appointments (2012); and (7) reaping the fruits of collaboration (2013–2015).

Building Interest and Investment in SA (1989–2002)

For the first 14 years, SA programmes were held every other year in order to put together large enough groups of interested students. As interest in the Arab world and therefore Arabic enrolments increased throughout the 1990s, faculty began to consider the possibility of an area studies major and an annual SA. Following the tragic events of 11 September 2001, and due to increased student interest in the region, the university approved a Middle East Studies/Arabic (MESA) major that was immediately embraced by scores of students wanting to learn more about the region and soon became the largest area studies major on campus. The two primary learning objectives of the major were that students would (1) speak Arabic at the Advanced level, as defined by the American Council on the Teaching of Foreign Languages (ACTFL, 2012), and (2) fluently read Arabic newspaper articles from the front, international, and Arab World pages. To facilitate reaching these learning outcomes, majors are required to participate in BYU's intensive Arabic SA programme, which accounts for 16 of the major's 61+ credits. In order to staff this programme, the faculty cancelled third-year Arabic courses on campus because they had observed that students who went abroad on BYU's SA programme reached a much higher level of language proficiency than those who completed third year on campus.[1] The first SA programme with students from the MESA major took place in Alexandria, Egypt, in 2004.

Growing Pains (2004 in Alexandria)

In all of the pre-MESA SA programmes students had participated in a media class that entailed reading carefully selected Arabic newspaper articles prior to classroom discussion of the content. As a result of the size of the 2004 programme, totalling 54 students, the director was not able to closely supervise or even be present during the teaching of all sections of the media class. However, he did recognise that local instructors rarely chose reading assignments appropriate for their students' level, which may be the result of differences in cross-cultural literacy expectations as discussed by Taillefer (2005). Students expressed frustration about the teachers' unrealistic expectations and most of them eventually gave up on doing the reading that would prepare them for class discussion. As a temporary fix, the director began finding recent articles for the students that recycled vocabulary and focussed on topics that were more familiar to the students. The director's role in selecting articles for the media class had been part of the first programme in 1989, but systematically tracking vocabulary became a regular feature in 2004 and continued to develop in later programmes.

Taking Advantage of Local Affordances (2006 in Jordan and Morocco)

The SA programme has been based in a variety of cities, including Alexandria, Amman, Cairo, Damascus, Fez, and Jerusalem. Many improvements to the programme have been the result of efforts to make the most of local affordances. This was especially the case in the summer of 2006 when the media course became a true content course taught by a dynamic Jordanian political scientist who wrote a weekly column on Jordanian politics for a major newspaper. Now called a 'current events' class, students read about and discussed social issues (e.g., gender roles) and political events (e.g., the Israel-Hezbollah War) that were relevant to the Arab world and Jordan in particular. Dr. Ahmad Majdoubeh, then Director of the Language Center at the University of Jordan, played a key role in making the SA director's vision for this course a reality, resulting in a highly engaging classroom experience. He was able to make newspaper articles about local and regional topics come alive, giving the backstory, for example, on various aspects of the Muslim Brotherhood's activities in Jordan. As the students' reading ability improved to the point where they were ready to handle opinion pieces, he would share and discuss pieces he had authored. Directors of subsequent SA programmes have not succeeded in recreating the same experience, but the level of student engagement with local issues set high expectations for future classroom experiences.

Eleven BYU students ended up studying in Morocco during the fall of 2006, because the BYU administration was uncomfortable with students going to Egypt or Jordan so soon after the Israel-Hezbollah War. This smaller programme did not have the benefit of a regular faculty member on site throughout the semester, but a PhD student, who knew Morocco well and had studied Arabic at BYU as an undergraduate and was therefore familiar with its SA expectations, was able to provide the students with opportunities for deep cultural learning, including rewarding homestay experiences with families who made the students a part of their daily lives and social groups. This resulted in many acquiring facility in Moroccan Arabic and cultural practices. Unfortunately, a subsequent experiment with homestays in Jordan in 2008 proved to be far less effective, given that: (1) host families did not typically integrate the students into their family life; and (2) most of the homestays were not near the University of Jordan where classes were held, making daily transportation frustrating, time-consuming, and expensive.

Consolidating the Reading Course and Implementing Programme Reviews (2009–2010 in Cairo)

Building on past experience, the faculty made several changes to the reading course in order to continue to provide students with an immersion experience with the Arab press while giving better scaffolding to facilitate their success. In 2009 the programme director split the current events class into two parts: an issues class for discussing prominent social topics with an instructor who is a native speaker (NS) and a newspaper class led by the programme director. The director selected recent, relevant, and linguistically appropriate articles for the students. Students were assigned each day to complete intensive reading assignments consisting of excerpts from two or three articles each day. They were instructed to 'struggle' to get the details and understand how the language 'hangs together' in front-page news articles, where topics ranged from economics and politics to war and natural disasters, as well as some human interest stories. On the other hand, extensive reading assignments of other articles helped students develop automaticity as they skimmed articles to answer specific comprehension questions. After completing the assignments, students spent approximately 30 minutes a day as a group working through challenging aspects of the intensive articles with the programme director and receiving reading strategy training. Such training, especially over an extended period of time, can make a significant difference in students' reading comprehension gains (Taylor, Stevens, & Asher, 2006).

In 2010, Kirk Belnap, Dan Dewey, and Madeline Ehrman, researchers associated with the National Middle East Language Resource Center (NMELRC) based at BYU, travelled to Cairo to observe the programme and try to better understand how to improve the student learning experience. The primary takeaway from their visit was that some students' anxiety levels were preventing them from learning effectively (see also Pellegrino Aveni, 2005). They suggested that the students needed time together each week to process their experience, to discuss what was working well for them and what was not. As a result, subsequent programmes have set aside 15–30 minutes or more of the Arabic newspaper class once a week for a group processing experience. Typically, the director starts this by mentioning a challenge that he has observed or heard about from students and invites them to talk about their own experiences freely. As students volunteer their own stories and discuss them, they typically find their way to solutions or acceptance of cultural practices they find difficult. Sometimes the director or another programme leader offers an example of a similar challenge overcome by previous students. For example, one student who dreaded approaching total strangers and asking them if she could talk with them, found that she could readily strike up conversations if she offered to take a picture of friends who were taking selfies together.

Despite efforts to provide scaffolding that would help the students succeed, the faculty found that every year one or two students lacked the preparation that would allow them to effectively participate in the programme and therefore required a disproportionate amount of attention to structure an experience that would work for their ability level. As a result of a conversation that took place during the 2010 site visit, the programme leadership decided to focus their efforts on students who are adequately prepared by setting a minimum standard for admittance to the programme. Starting in 2011, only students who receive at least a B-grade (80 per cent) in the second-year courses would be allowed to go on the SA. The grading system is criterion-referenced so, in principle, all can meet the standard.

The NMELRC research team travelled to Amman in 2011, with Jennifer Bown, for a week-long visit to the programme in order to review the implementation of their previous suggestions and follow up on research questions generated from the first visit. Besides providing feedback on the student experience, these visits allowed the team to contextualise data gathered that year and in previous and subsequent years. A number of articles have been published using data from the SA (Baker-Smemoe, Dewey, Bown, & Martinsen, 2014; Bown, Dewey, & Belnap, 2015; Dewey, Belnap, & Hillstrom, 2013; Dewey, Bird, Gardner, & Belnap, 2013; Dewey et al., 2014; Tare et al., 2016). While a review team has not returned since 2011, annual site visits by university administrators and research carried out by programme leadership have continued to provide useful evaluative feedback on the student experience (see Wilson, 2015). Concern about student anxiety resulted in Patrick Steffen (BYU

Department of Psychology and Behavioral Medicine Research Center) joining the research team and assisting in designing biofeedback training for students preparing to participate in the SA.

Strengthening Institutional Collaboration and Adjusting the Reading Course (2011 in Amman)

The Egyptian Revolution of 2011 and the subsequent deterioration of the security situation resulted in BYU and many other SA programmes relocating to Amman. This was the beginning of an ongoing highly productive partnership with a private language institute. While BYU had positive experiences with host institutions in the previous decade, the faculty had been unable to establish a long-term relationship due to regional instability, management changes, and some institutions' lack of receptivity to feedback. Fortunately, the SA has been able to deepen its collaboration with the Qasid Institute (QI) in Amman, Jordan, over multiple years, resulting in many mutual benefits. Rather than imposing a one-size-fits-all curriculum on BYU's programme, QI administrators worked to accommodate the programme's needs and incorporate feedback from the BYU faculty and students. For example, BYU's programme director in 2011, Dilworth Parkinson, worked on site at QI daily and regularly met with staff to explain student needs. When some students struggled to immerse themselves in the language outside of class, he was able to set up speaking partners mid-semester through QI. This cycle of providing feedback and making adjustments has continued ever since. After the programme's first semester of collaboration and recognising its potential, Khaled Abuamsha, QI Academic Director, came to BYU as a visiting professor to help launch BYU's Arabic major for advanced Arabic students (Belnap & Abuamsha, 2015).

Parkinson recalls 2011 as a critical moment for finding balance between the intensity of the reading course and the students' abilities. For the previous 3 years, he had asked students to learn *all* of the new vocabulary presented in both the intensive and extensive newspaper articles, but few succeeded. Based on feedback from the 2010 students and the review team, Parkinson decided early in the 2011 programme to adjust the load while still keeping the students focussed on activating vocabulary. Addressing

2011 students who complained early in the programme that they could not learn 50 new words a day (50 being an instance of hyperbole), he said, 'It probably *is* impossible for you to learn 50 words a day from a list, but it *is possible* for you to master *one* article a day, and learn that same vocabulary *in context*' (D. Parkinson, personal communication, 10 October 2015). From then on, he only assigned one article for intensive reading per day with typically no more than 10–20 completely new words.

Instead of giving the students one day to understand the article, assignments moved through a four-day rotation that specified what students were to do with the article on each day. Since new articles were assigned every day and students had to thoroughly understand each article by its fourth day, students were expected to be working on four intensive articles on any given day. So as not to confuse the article numbers with the number of days it had been assigned, on the first day of any given article it was called an A article, the next day a B article, then a C article, and finally a D article. Table 1 demonstrates the progression of a week's worth of articles (seen as numbers) through the four days (A, B, C, and D) in which students were expected to work on each one.

Students were expected to do the following reading homework on a daily basis:

1. 'struggle' for no more than 20 minutes to read and understand the A article;
2. review the B and C articles for no more than 15 minutes each;
3. review the D article, then finish by translating as much of it as possible in 10 minutes;
4. spend approximately 15 minutes with each of three to four extensive readings.

Table 1 Schedule for working with newspaper articles for week 3 of the reading course

Treatment	Sunday	Monday	Tuesday	Wednesday	Thursday
A	11	12	13	14	15
B	10	11	12	13	14
C	9	10	11	12	13
D	8	9	10	11	12

The goal of the reading course is for students to understand a sizeable corpus of authentic readings systematically through repeated reading and self-testing. The instructions that students were given later in 2015 for the intensive and extensive articles are included in Appendix A. The midterm and final exam include excerpts from the intensive readings, which helps to encourage students to regularly review past intensives. Timed reading of both intensive and extensive articles and rereading helps students to make considerable gains in reading fluency, as has been documented in other contexts (Chung & Nation, 2006; Grabe, 2010; Huffman, 2014). Students who embraced Parkinson's highly structured approach found it challenging, but also doable and rewarding, as they regularly report in anonymous end-of-programme surveys.[2]

In the same spirit of scaffolding learning experiences and in response to student feedback submitted through weekly speaking journals, the director of the 2011 SA also worked with administrators at QI to find, employ, and train speaking partners. Given that even some students with strong speaking ability were stressed about finding meaningful speaking opportunities on their own every day, this offer was well received by many students. Approximately one third of the students participated in the partnerships, typically meeting with their trained speaking partners who were hired to work with them for 1 hour twice a week.

Institutionalising Speaking and Writing Appointments (2012)

Weekly speaking journals and comments made to the faculty in 2011 indicated that providing trained speaking partners made a significant difference for students who availed themselves of the opportunity. For example, one student who struggled to find speaking opportunities and develop friendships outside of classes noted: 'I had my most meaningful conversations with my assigned speaking partner because I can direct the conversation and decide what words I want to learn.' Feedback like this led the faculty to make speaking partners a regular part of the programme. Beginning in 2012, all students met with an assigned partner for 3 hours a week in order to facilitate deeper conversations in an informal, extensive way, as documented in Bown et al. (2015). At the same time, faculty balanced these appointments with 5-minute spoken presentations with a NS tutor, who then gave the students feedback on their formal, intensive performance. Like the reading course, the approach to speaking tries to balance intensive and extensive learning experiences.

Writing has always been a part of the SA, but reading and speaking received the most attention up to this point. Recognising the value of writing, which helps activate vocabulary and in turn improves students' reading ability (Dewey, 2006; Hu & Nation, 2000), the faculty set up two weekly appointments in which each student met one-on-one with a tutor and presented a short writing piece in response to short prompts (e.g., tell the plot of a popular movie or book). The instructor would then provide feedback on the participant's word usage, spelling, paragraph structure, and overall appeal. After the first appointment, the student was expected to revise their writing and apply their instructor's suggestions before presenting their revised work during the second appointment for more feedback.

Reaping the Fruits of Collaboration (2013–2015)

Faculty continue to find ways to fine-tune various aspects of the SA with the full support of QI. For instance, whereas the 2012 programme began by providing participants with 60–90 minute appointments with speaking partners 2 or 3 days a week, the 2015 programme provided 30-minute speaking appointments 5 days a week. This change provided students daily feedback and more opportunity to implement suggestions.

Students also received regular training throughout the SA on how to make the most of these speaking appointments and input from the students was used to improve the process. The training involved 5-minute activities at the beginning of the article review class each day in which a programme assistant or the director would share strategies and discuss students' experience with speaking appointments and other speaking opportunities. For example, after encouraging the students to practise a specific task (e.g., describing how to make a favourite dish), the assistant might then ask the students to practise with each other in pairs, first in English and then again in Arabic. Then, after a minute of students realising what language was really necessary for the task, the assistant might give a brief demonstration, which they could personalise for their own practice in speaking appointments.

Prior to 2013, evaluation of the programme's content course had typically taken the form of occasional visits to classes and communicating concerns raised by students to the host institution's administrators, teachers, and tutors. At the beginning of each new programme, some instructors, speaking partners, and tutors were unfamiliar with the BYU leadership's expectations. Such gaps in understanding, even if they were observed or reported to the BYU leadership immediately, could take days to communicate to the QI administrators and weeks to adequately remedy. As the partnership between BYU and QI continued and as aspects of running the SA, such as the reading course, became more efficient routines, the opportunity for observing and providing more consistent and timely feedback to QI became available. Matthew Bird, a programme teaching assistant in 2013, set up a daily rotation of programme leaders observing each section of the content course (i.e., the issues class). Observers documented if teachers were speaking more than students and counted how many times each student spoke in class. Since these observations were as much about keeping an eye on student progress as they were about monitoring the quality of instruction, instructors took well to the observations without feeling intimidated into conformity. These systematic observations nevertheless communicated to instructors that the BYU leadership was serious about the quality of every class and accelerated the process of clarifying institutional expectations. Faculty were also able to challenge students who were not paying attention or not actively participating to set specific goals for what they would do each class. Additionally, students completed mid-semester and end-of-programme evaluations of QI staff, which revealed those who failed to implement feedback, those who needed additional guidance, and those who were actively implementing it as requested. QI then followed up with each instructor or tutor as needed.

From the beginning of our collaboration in 2011 on, the QI leadership showed a high degree of commitment to improving instruction. The systematic feedback from the issues class and student appointments has resulted in all concerned becoming more personally invested in improving the quality of the student learning experience. For example, teachers make sure to involve each student and, as much as possible, tailor this to the interest of each individual. Because of their genuine concern and thoughtful instruction, it is not uncommon for instructors to develop friendships with the students to the point that they keep in contact after the programme ends. The same is true of speaking partners and tutors who show their interest by giving consistent, direct feedback—no small feat given that QI staff consider students to be their guests in Jordan and cultural norms discourage pointing out a guest's weaknesses. On the other hand, students also are realising that they can get far more out of their classes and appointments by planning ahead and preparing and they see that by providing feedback to the programme leadership about their experience they can further influence the quality of their experience. In 2015, QI assigned a lead teacher to take responsibility for training BYU's speaking partners and tutors, further accelerating the process of feedback and instruction improvement.

Discussion of Lessons Learned

Every foreign language programme and every SA programme differs in financing, staffing, enrolment, curriculum, and other aspects. Few programmes enjoy the institutional support that BYU has provided its Arabic programme. Nevertheless, because of its longevity and its many iterations, our experience may benefit other programmes looking to make improvements. We especially see value in four lessons learned from reviewing the developmental history of our programme: (1) building the programme by developing a culture of SA; (2) continuing improvement by evaluating outcomes; (3) accelerating improvement by capitalising on local affordances; and (4) advancing student gains through thoughtful curriculum design, especially regarding the reading course.

Building the Programme by Developing a Culture of SA

One of the highest priorities of American students beginning to study Arabic is travelling to the Arab world and using the skills that they are developing (Belnap & Nassif, 2011). The BYU SA programme capitalises on this and creates a strong motivational current that draws students further into the language, resulting in many pursuing advanced studies and careers where they use Arabic (Dörnyei, Henry, & Muir, 2015). This aligns with Ryan's (2016) analysis of 2013 Italian enrolments in US higher education that revealed that US Italian programmes associated with a SA programme was a predictor of programmes whose enrolment remained stable or increased while others declined.

Students are also typically hopeful of developing some measure of fluency as a result of their overseas study. BYU's Arabic SA programme has a reputation for challenging students and a track record of their acquiring Advanced levels of proficiency. This has led over time to the development of a SA culture where students expect to work hard and be stretched. The Arabic faculty have made two programme design decisions to amplify this motivational current. First, the curriculum of the first four semesters of Arabic focusses on preparing students for SA. The SA is advertised as an 'intensive Arabic SA', which runs counter to the perceptions of SA held by many students and the public at large (Gore, 2005). This label does not bring to mind images of sandy beaches, hanging out at internet cafes, or speaking one's native tongue. Starting in Arabic 101, students are immediately made aware of the SA as their instructors are often students or faculty who have recently been on the programme. Additionally, the first- and second-year courses focus on developing oral proficiency in a specific dialect of Arabic (depending on the SA location), further pointing students towards the programme. The programme's high expectations are repeatedly made clear to students in their coursework and in a mandatory SA preparation course, which helps students develop the confidence in the programme that they need to commit themselves, prepare effectively, and complete the programme.

Students are made aware of the debilitating effect of anxiety and coached on how to deal with it. For example, on the first day of Arabic 101 an instructor noticed signs of stress in a student hearing Arabic addressed to her for the first time, and asked her what she was feeling at that moment. Minutes later, this student was able to spontaneously and creatively use basic phrases the instructor was using to introduce himself, upon which the entire class erupted in applause. Students are regularly exposed to examples of student experiences in Jordan, including footage of them interacting in classes and ice cream parlours and restaurants. In their fourth semester, students experience a limited version of the SA reading course (discussed below), reading short Arabic news articles. Especially effective in this regard are the activities of the mandatory preparation course which have included:

- outlining programme expectations and assignments,
- explaining programme decisions (e.g., class assignments based on student ability)
- training in stress management strategies (e.g., healthy living habits, breathing exercises),
- sharing prior experiences with different cultural norms and managing culture shock,
- presenting recent research related to identity, motivation, and language learning,
- and an assignment to reflect on one's language learning abilities and experiences, identifying weaknesses and leveraging strengths.

These activities give students the information they need to start making mental and emotional preparations for the programme months in advance. Frankly discussing the difficulties that they will likely face abroad empowers them to develop determination early on.

Strong initial confidence and commitment is far from sufficient. Faculty have found that they must work in a variety of ways to maintain high student engagement throughout the SA experience. The reading course, issues classes, speaking appointments, and a requirement for students to spend an additional seven hours per week speaking with Arabs have provided structured opportunities for students to continuously engage with the language and culture.

The second important aspect of the Arabic programme's design to amplify motivation is personnel decisions. BYU has leveraged the experience of returned programme participants in several ways to provide near-peer role models for students preparing for SA (Bandura, 1994; Murphey, 1998). The faculty have employed undergraduate and graduate students who have completed the SA to serve as teaching assistants in first- and second-year-level courses. They demonstrate to students in those courses that they can set and achieve high goals since they see a student only a year or two ahead of them can comfortably speak and read Arabic.

Faculty also regularly bring past SA participants to work as teaching assistants (TAs) in the overseas programme, not only to help carry some of the programme's workload but to serve as an example and help current participants navigate some of the difficulties that they themselves had faced only a year or two before. These former students describe to the current students the various types of avoidance behaviour they engaged in even though they had arrived in Jordan fully committed to making the most of their in-country experience. Many students struggle to balance their reading homework with their speaking assignment, and when faced with the daily choice they begin to neglect whichever assignment takes more effort. Former students empathise with these challenges and can offer moral support and ideas to overcome avoidance behaviour. Some common suggestions include trying out different schedules (e.g., going out to speak earlier, rather than waiting until the evening), meeting with programme leaders regularly to stay accountable for time spent, and learning relaxation techniques (e.g., regular exercise, breathing exercises, planned personal time, and so forth). Whenever possible, female TAs have also worked closely with female participants to identify culturally appropriate speaking opportunities and navigate other challenges specific to the female student experience on this SA (see Wilson, 2015).

Regularly reminding students about these behaviours in personal interviews and during weekly group processing sessions has helped many to identify their own avoidance behaviours, take responsibility for their SA experience, and embrace the programme's structured activities and opportunities in the community. Students learn from former participants that the SA requires hard work, and that it can be emotionally challenging but also highly rewarding linguistically and culturally.

Countering student tendencies to retreat into avoidance behaviour instead of seizing the day requires careful thought and preparation on the part of the faculty, but it is necessary for building and maintaining a SA culture of engagement. In the context of this SA, Belnap, Bown, Dewey, Belnap, and Steffen (2016) noted that coaching from programme staff, weekly speaking journals, group processing sessions, speaking partners, and providing biofeedback training has helped some participants to deal better with the stresses of SA and remain focussed on learning. These interventions have resulted in the development of a culture of *intensive* Arabic SA on the home campus and overseas. Students see the SA programme as a meaningful investment of resources to learn a language in a way that might not be possible otherwise.

As discussed above, housing has also been an influential part of previous designs. BYU successfully used homestays in Morocco to immerse students in Arabic language and culture. Other institutions, such as Cornell University and Middlebury College, have benefitted their students by arranging for them to room with NSs while on SA (Belnap & Nassif, 2011). Housing participants with NSs can provide an immediate environment in which to engage with the language and culture, but can also prove socially or linguistically overwhelming for some. While BYU's current housing situation in Jordan requires interventions to provide consistent immersion experiences, different interventions might be needed to scaffold a homestay experience. While housing currently does not show up as a major aspect of the programme's design, it has in the past and may do so again in the future.

Continuing Improvement by Evaluating Outcomes

To some degree with earlier programmes but especially since the start of the MESA major in 2001, the BYU Arabic faculty have carried out regular internal evaluations and created a culture of programme evaluation that has been critical for making targeted programme improvements. As described by Davis, Sinicrope, and Watanabe (2009), a *culture* of programme evaluation suggests more than simply conducting a regular regimen of evaluation activities, although exit surveys, language assessments, and other formal feedback are typically administered. It indicates a prioritisation of time and resources towards finding out how the programme can better serve its participants. These efforts won the confidence of the BYU administration, resulting in another full-time position which made possible BYU's Arabic major. The faculty began with standardised measures of reading, listening, and speaking proficiency, then end-of-programme surveys. These led to actively researching the student experience through various data collection methods, for example, interviews, daily and weekly reports, focus groups, and classroom observations. As numerous and more useful data were collected and analysed over the years, ideas for better evaluation tools and methods arose and were implemented in future programmes.

One of the most challenging trends that programme faculty have noted and tackled is the difficulty faced by students who enter the programme with lower language proficiency to reach the programme goal of Advanced-level speaking. While most students finish the programme with an Advanced rating on the Oral Proficiency Interview (OPI), the floor of the programme's OPI scores remained firmly in the Intermediate range until recent years. Leaders working with individuals who had struggled with Arabic before were surprised with the progress they made during the programme, prompting a closer look at proficiency measures over the years. Looking at programmes for which reliable OPI scores from both before and after the programme are available, faculty have reason to believe that the programme's floor has risen much closer to its stated goal in the last few years compared to the first year of collaboration with QI in 2011. Table 2 illustrates that while about 90 per cent of students start out below the Advanced level each year, more than 30 per cent *more* students reached Advanced speaking proficiency by programme end in 2015 than in 2011.[3]

After tentatively confirming this trend by appealing to available data, faculty have sought to understand what might have made the difference for struggling students who make unpredictable gains. One idea made apparent in language journals and interviews is the institution of the speaking partner programme at QI. In 2011 a minority of students began

Table 2 Distribution of students' pre- and post-programme OPI scores

OPI score	2011		2014		2015	
Advanced high	0	0	0	0	0	5
Advanced mid	0	5	2	11	1	13
Advanced low	3	14	1	12	6	15
Intermediate high	7	22	8	9	14	12
Intermediate mid	23	11	9	2	17	0
Intermediate low	18	0	11	0	7	0
Novice high	1	0	2	0	0	0
Novice mid	0	0	1	0	0	0
Total	52		34		45	

meeting with partners midway through the semester for two 1-hour appointments each week, in 2012 all students began meeting with speaking partners in three 1-hour appointments each week, and in 2015 students had 30-minute appointments every day. These changes were made in response to participant suggestions and leadership observations, providing critical scaffolding for students who would have struggled to engage meaningfully with Arabic speakers on their own to participate in conversations that facilitated the practice of Advanced-level skills such as description and narration (Bown et al., 2015).

Accelerating Improvement by Adjusting to Local Affordances

As the Arabic SA was compelled to change locations, faculty learned that identifying local resources and customising the programme design to take advantage of those resources can accelerate achievement of programme goals. Just as Engle and Engle (1999, p. 41), the BYU faculty have looked at local affordances with an eye to 'link a program of rigorous, culturally relevant course work to mechanisms that would incite rapid, authentic contact with the host culture […] for the full range of program participants'. This has led to very distinct programmes in different locations, from Morocco to the Levant.

The affordances of one site differ greatly from another. For instance, Egypt gave students access to a well-established dialect with many pedagogical resources for learners, whereas Jordan has given students the opportunity to experience greater linguistic and human diversity, including visitors and refugees from the Gulf, Iraq, Libya, Palestine, and Syria. Turbulent conditions in the Arab world have made faculty remain flexible and adapt the programme according to the restrictions and resources of each site.

When designing a SA experience, Trentman (2013) suggests that programme leaders should make connections between their participants and local affordances in order to best ensure their engagement with the host language and culture. This has happened for BYU's programme largely due to the faculty's intimate involvement in directing the programme on site. For example, after seeing many students struggle to find comfortable speaking opportunities that went beyond pleasantries, the programme leadership in Cairo included a sports club membership in the programme to ensure that students would have access to a social network of NSs. This decision especially benefitted female participants who previously struggled to find culturally appropriate and comfortable venues for meeting and getting to know NSs. Similarly, programme leadership in Jordan arranged speaking partners for each participant in order to provide consistent, high-quality speaking opportunities. While some speaking partner relationships probably do remain superficial even when discussing in-depth topics, student feedback in interviews and language journals suggest that many partners become friends. For some students, these connections serve as their first meaningful interaction with a Jordanian one-on-one. The hope, then, is for students to seek to develop other similar relationships outside of QI after gaining some experience with their speaking partner.

One of the most important connections in a new location is the host institution, such as a university or language institute, where students will participate in classes or other language learning activities. While the quality of language instruction and the degree to which teaching philosophies align between institutions should be considered, it is the experience of the Arabic faculty that a willingness to build a mutually beneficial programme may be more important in the long term. This willingness leads to a collaboration where feedback from both sides is welcome, where new ideas are shared and both institutions take pride in student successes. Finding a partnership in which responsibility for instruction and student well-being are balanced between the parties involved can lead to significant mutual benefits.

This SA programme has been fortunate to call QI home since 2011, where strong relationships have developed between programme leaders, students, and instructors. For example, QI and BYU leadership work together on a daily basis during the programme to coordinate instruction of the issues classes (taught by QI instructors), so that the student experience builds on recent events and news articles assigned in the reading course. In regard to implementing feedback, both BYU and QI ask students to complete formal evaluations of the instructors and classes, and the results are discussed together so that changes can be made for the next programme. This sometimes means a curricular change, such as adding writing and speaking presentation appointments, or it could involve a personnel question, such as deciding which instructors would work better with students of different ability levels. Additionally, daily interactions between leaders and students allow for the sharing of student concerns throughout the programme. For discussion in their issues class, the BYU leadership can immediately speak with the lead QI teacher and discuss ways that the respective instructor can balance participation among the students in a class.

Another result of a strong collaboration, conditions allowing, is the development of interinstitutional and intercultural familiarity. Returning to the same institution repeatedly can free up time and resources that otherwise would be used starting a new programme, and also allows the host institution's staff to become familiar with the participants' culture, values, and interests, as well as the training they receive prior to arrival. This has been the case with QI instructors, allowing them to build on what BYU students already know, develop meaningful relationships, and avoid cultural missteps that might disenchant a more sensitive student.

The BYU and QI programmes have invested in each other to the point that benefits extend outside of the SA. When the BYU programme director worked with QI to provide speaking partners to students, QI decided to extend this opportunity to other students at the institute as a regular part of their curricula. In addition, BYU has welcomed QI staff members as visiting professors on the BYU campus, enriching advanced Arabic instruction and creating continuity between the SA experience and post-programme studies for returning students. Indeed, enumerating all of the contributions that each side has made and the ensuing benefits could probably stand as a chapter unto itself.

The Reading Course

While it can seem natural to focus on speaking and listening skills while abroad, SA participants can also make impressive gains in their reading ability, better preparing them for post-programme studies that require Advanced-level skills in multiple modalities. Dewey (2006) found that even students of orthographically complex languages can make considerable reading improvement while abroad, though sometimes in different ways than students in intensive domestic programmes.

The faculty were confident from the start of the 1989 SA that students could make significant reading gains during SA, and their approach to reading was motivated in part by their own experience as students at the Center for Arabic Study Abroad (CASA) (Badawi, 2002) and in part by the fact that most authentic texts in Arabic are beyond the reading ability of even Advanced-level students, given that 'adequate reading comprehension' typically requires 95 per cent to 98 per cent understanding of the vocabulary of such reading material (Hu & Nation, 2000; Laufer & Ravenhorst-Kalovski, 2010; Salah, 2008). NSs of English might have difficulty learning to read novels in a cognate language, but learning to read such texts—or even simpler ones—in a non-cognate language requires more knowledge, time, and skill than many students possess at an equivalent point in their studies. The faculty recalled from their own experiences learning Arabic that some CASA students from acclaimed US Arabic graduate programmes feigned understanding of their reading homework during class discussion until enough of the story had been revealed that they could contribute what little they had gathered from their own reading. Faculty thus decided to focus instruction on a genre more suited to the students' level of reading proficiency: front-page news articles. Arabic news articles follow typical news conventions, using formulaic, predictable sentence and paragraph structures with which students can quickly become familiar. For example, most Arabic front-page news sentences begin with a common news verb such as 'to announce' or 'to report' and are followed at some point by the subject. Faculty found that giving students articles on a limited number of topics that regularly occur in front-page news articles provides the scaffolding needed to begin to advance to higher-level reading proficiency. We call this the 'beachhead approach', in that students gain traction in a restricted domain (e.g., front-page articles about a familiar current event) before moving on to additional topics (e.g., front-page articles about local sports) and then more challenging genres (op-ed articles, political columnists, and so forth). This approach was first implemented on campus in Utah in the early 1980s, and in 1989 a similar course became part of the first BYU Arabic SA programme.

From a linguistic perspective, the beachhead approach has benefitted students in two ways. First, a focus on developing reading ability in specific content areas has enabled students to understand and reproduce language in different modalities. The topics are chosen especially to enable the students to understand and participate in conversations important to locals, such as the ongoing Syrian conflict, American-Jordanian relations, the Israeli-Palestinian conflict, or local political elections. In short, the reading course provides content knowledge and pertinent vocabulary for students to engage in conversations about important contemporary and cultural topics. Articles are also chosen that repeat topics and vocabulary with which students are already familiar, providing mastery experiences that boost student morale and prepare them for new challenges (Bandura, 1994; Belnap et al., 2016).

Second, developing strong literacy skills while abroad results in better retention of language skills, both spoken and written, after returning to the USA (see Hansen & Chantrill, 1999; Hansen & Shewell, 2002). Instructors working with students in advanced Arabic classes in Utah after their return from SA have used this to inform course syllabi. They have found that students get a stronger start in their post-programme classes when the content begins with genres that students dealt with on SA, especially news topics. For example, the first assignment for an advanced writing course asks students to write a front-page article on a topic of their choice, and then assignments progress into less familiar forms such as editorials, short stories, and research essays. The strategy applies to classes focussed on other modalities as well.

Conclusion and Recommendations

SA can be a highly rewarding experience in terms of personal growth as well as progressing in linguistic and cultural proficiencies. Such growth is rarely if ever effortless. Indeed, many students experience intense negative emotions during SA, resulting in challenges to their very identity (Pellegrino Aveni, 2005). Recent research points to the necessity and value of various types of interventions to assist students in making more of their overseas experience (Belnap et al., 2016; Trentman, 2013; Vande Berg et al., 2009; Vande Berg, Paige, & Lou, 2012, part 3). The BYU Arabic faculty have been working for over 25 years to shape their SA programme to assist participants to engage effectively with the Arabic language and local Arabs and thus make the most of their overseas experience. Important breakthroughs include: (1) creating a culture of SA on campus that attracts committed participants, (2) developing a culture of evaluation within the Arabic programme dedicated to constantly improving the participant learning experience, (3) utilising the affordances of the SA location to encourage participant engagement with the target language and culture, and (4) designing a reading curriculum programme to facilitate participant performance at the Advanced level.

Prior to the creation of the MESA major at BYU, the Arabic SA programme could only be held every other year, as enrolment permitted. Placing the SA at the centre of the major in 2001 and cultivating a culture of high expectations attracted a large number of students, many from other majors, who were drawn to Arabic and the Middle East because of its high profile in the media. While not every language can rely on such publicity to increase student interest, faculty hoping to build a new or existing SA could propose and support a degree programme structure that at least encourages students to SA. Once that structure is in place, the SA can be tailored to the needs of students from the degree programme, further connecting the two.

Developing an effective system and culture of evaluation requires time. Evaluation instruments such as student reports, interviews, and exit surveys usually require repeated adjustments over several programme iterations to yield highly valuable student feedback and data relevant to the student experience. For BYU's Arabic faculty, this has happened naturally as faculty members' interests connected directly to the needs of the programme. As data from evaluations accrue and changes are made to improve the programme, faculty are able to more easily justify their SA empirically. We encourage SA directors to find ways to improve SA and contribute to its face validity by organising evaluation efforts from an early stage of a SA's lifespan in order to accelerate its growth.

Facilitating participant engagement on SA requires a familiarity with the host culture and with institutions that enable learning. In many cases this means finding language institutes or other partnering institutions significantly invested in their students' success, but generally, programme leaders must find resources (e.g., housing situations, cultural outreach organisations, social networks, internship opportunities, and so forth) that help students engage with locals in the target language and develop meaningful relationships. In order to connect students with these resources, we suggest that programme directors become familiar not only with the affordances of a given location, but also with the abilities, personalities, and daily concerns of participants. While many programmes can scarcely afford to send faculty abroad for the duration of a semester programme, technology now enables daily contact with on-site staff or even direct communication with students via email, language journals, or other reporting mechanisms.

Content courses have been recognised as a predictor of higher language gains while on SA, and as such BYU's faculty have given much of their time and energy to developing and fine-tuning the issues class and the news course. While work still remains to be done to better integrate the content of these two courses together, the reading course's philosophy (i.e., the beachhead approach) has proven effective in providing learners an access point to Advanced- and Superior-level reading abilities. Developing literacy on SA has in turn enabled them to continue learning Arabic in all modalities after the programme ends. Although it sometimes feels counter-intuitive to some students to place a focus on reading while abroad—after all, students can read just as easily back on campus—we encourage directors to consider how a linguistically accessible reading course might benefit participants both during and immediately after the SA. A well-designed reading curriculum will augment, rather than derail, the speaking and listening gains made while abroad.

Few institutions with smaller enrolments will have the personnel or the good fortune that we have to field a SA programme on the scale of ours, but a consortium of institutions could. Even if institutions were unable to coordinate at this level, they could achieve considerable benefit through collaborating on some aspects of their SA programme. For example, the selection and preparation of newspaper articles (including tracking vocabulary) for our students is a time-consuming process. A number of SA programmes targeting students at the same level could jointly fund one well-trained graduate student to produce these. Electronic tools that could assist in identifying articles that closely match the topic and vocabulary familiar to the students could substantially reduce the preparation time. We welcome such opportunities for collaboration.

Additionally, the cost of standardised tests, such as the OPI, results in some SA programmes choosing not to use them. We have found that such measures have great value for both programme evaluation as well as helping students to focus. Students are prone to think that just speaking a good deal will result in their acquiring Advanced-level proficiency. However, we have found that making students aware of the criteria for evaluating oral proficiency helps them to more effectively reflect on various aspects of language and communicative competence and plan how to use their time to better prepare for and make the most of their speaking opportunities. We typically spend a few minutes each day training the students on some aspect of Advanced-level performance, such as encouraging them to practise using rhetorical devices that will result in more native-like discourse. The 'Can-Do Statements' recently published by the National Council of State Supervisors for Languages (NCSSFL) and ACTFL are especially helpful to students in mapping out potential concrete steps to higher levels of proficiency (NCSSFL-ACTFL, 2013). Whether programme directors choose to use widely accepted measures of proficiency or not, we encourage the clear explication of programme goals to students by training them to recognise opportunities for higher-level performance and providing them with the tools to perform.

Summary of recommendations based on lessons learned from 25 years of Arabic SA

- Build enduring SA programmes with sufficient enrolment by proposing and supporting degree programme structures that point students towards SA.
- Improve SA outcomes and contribute to SA's face validity by organising evaluation efforts from an early stage.
- Recognise connections between participant interests and local resources by actively developing familiarity with both.
- Augment and enable Advanced-level speaking by including pertinent reading instruction in SA curriculum.
- Make intensive, well-designed SA available to more students by collaborating with other universities and institutions.
- Set and explicate clear programme goals towards which participants can work consistently.

Appendix A

2015 Jordan Study Abroad Reading Assignment Instructions

Quantity of Articles

Each class day you will receive an assignment with a set total number of articles to read (the total will usually include one listening passage in place of one of the articles). For the first 2 weeks, that total number will be four articles a day. One article will be added to that total at 2-week intervals after that point, so that by the end of the programme you will be reading nine to ten articles per day.

Intensive and Extensive Articles

Each day, out of that total number of articles, you will have exactly one *intensive* article and the rest will be considered *extensive* articles. The *intensive* article is to be mastered, completely. The *extensive* articles will come with activities or assignments, either a set of questions, or an instruction to summarise or gist, or some other activity. The extensive articles are not meant to be mastered in the sense that you would be expected to know every word and structure. Rather they are there to help you learn to read fluently and extract useful information even when you do NOT know every word or recognise every structure.

Extensive Article Instructions

Since the point of these articles is to help you learn to read fluently, you should NOT look up every word, or work through these articles very slowly and meticulously. Rather, you should read them fairly rapidly, and then try to do the assignment or activity associated with the article. It is important to *engage* and pay attention, but it is not important that you feel you have the article mastered. Learn to *float on a sea of uncertainty* and try to grasp anything you can without being debilitated by the fact that you cannot grasp everything.

You will need to strictly limit the time you spend on any one article in order to help yourself push towards fluency. We are not interested in what you can get out of an article given that you have an endless amount of time to work on it. We are interested in what you can get out of the article in a reasonable, limited time frame. In general, you should not be spending more than 15 minutes on any one extensive article. Push yourself to get through as much of the article and of the associated assignment as possible in the time you set for yourself to do it in.

You should start noticing that you have an easier time with these articles as the semester progresses, as your knowledge of basic news vocabulary increases, and as you get more experience dealing with this kind of language.

Intensive Article Instructions

Although you will receive exactly one *intensive* article every class day, you will work on these articles for 4 days in a row each. This means that after the first few days of class, you will always be working on four intensive articles at once: the one you received today, the one you received yesterday, the one you received the day before yesterday, and the one you received the day before that.

In order to talk about these articles, we are labelling them A, B, C, and D. The A article is the one you just received. The B article is the one you received yesterday. And so forth. Every day as part of your reading assignment you should be doing something with each of the four articles, A, B, C, and D. At the end of the fourth day, you then take a quiz on the D article, the one you have been working on for 4 days.

A Day (or *A* Article) (15–25 Minutes)

1. Read through the article quickly without looking up any words, and summarise anything that you were able to extract from it.
2. Read through it again, this time with the help of the provided vocabulary list, and looking up a few words if desired. Write out a translation of as much of it as you can. Leave blanks when there are things you cannot figure out.

We call this day *the struggle* since it is just you and the article, and you are likely to go very slowly, to miss a lot of the content, and to feel frustrated. It is likely that you will not get all the way through the article in the time allotted. In general, our attitude is that struggle is good for the soul, just not too much struggle. So give it all you've got, and go ahead and feel the frustration for a few minutes, but then, when the time is up or when you can't take it any more, simply move on. Do NOT continue to struggle and insist on getting through the whole thing no matter how frustrated you get, no matter how little sense it makes, no matter how many hours it takes. Go ahead and struggle for 10–20 minutes, and that is enough.

B Day (or *B* Article) (15–20 Minutes)

The main difference between A and B day is that an English translation of the article will be posted at the beginning of B day. Download and print out this translation, read through it once or twice, and have it with you when you work on the day's B article. It is also a good idea to make a few clean copies of the article for use in the B, C, and D day activities. You should also have several pens or pencils of different colours available.

1. NEVER write English glosses on the paper on which the article appears. If you feel you must write glosses, do so on a separate piece of paper.
2. Turn the translation of the B Article upside down so you cannot see it, and then read through the B Article (either in whole, or a paragraph or two at a time). Read relatively fluently (this is not *the struggle*). Underline with a pen any word or phrase that you cannot remember as you read. Don't spend a lot of time doing this. Either you remember it or you don't. Just be honest, and mark what you don't know or remember and move on to the end of the article (or paragraph).
3. Turn the translation over, and check the things you missed (the things you marked). Don't write them down, just note them in your head, and try to put them in enough context that you will remember them next time.
4. If you are doing it a couple of paragraphs at a time instead of the whole article at once, turn the translation back over, and do the next

few paragraphs, using the same procedure. Continue until you have finished the article.
5. Now, repeat the whole procedure outlined in #2 and #3 above, but this time with a different coloured pen. You will be able to see on the paper the words and phrases you didn't remember the last time through. Try hard to remember some of these the second time through. See if you can have less of the second colour on the paper than the first colour.
6. This whole procedure (a minimum of two times through the B Article) should go fairly rapidly, no more than 20 minutes. If you are taking more than that, you are changing it into a struggle. Every time through the article you are giving yourself a little test, but it is a kind of timed test, a test not only of what you know and can drag up, but of what you know right now, instantly, as you read fluently. The only way to make this assignment go fast enough is to quickly admit to yourself the things you don't know and move on.

C Day (or *C* Article) (15–20 Minutes)

C day is exactly like B day. Again you must read through the article at least twice with the translation upside down, marking the things you can't remember, and then checking with the translation after each reading. You should start with a fresh copy of the article, and again use two different coloured pens. The number of things you mark as not remembered should decrease dramatically by the end of the third day. You should also be making sure (not only) that you understand the words, but that you understand how they hang together (are there hidden structures like indefinite relative clauses, etc.?). The translation should help you with this, but if you have questions, don't hesitate to ask the instructors.

D Day (or *D* Article) (15–20 Minutes)

On D day, with the translation upside down, you take a fresh copy of the article and do one more read through. Again mark things you don't remember (hopefully very few), and check them. Then you must put both the translation and the article away for a minimum of 15 minutes (go ahead and work on other articles during this time).

After 15 minutes have passed, take a fresh copy of the article and the Rubric provided, find a fellow student, hand him the Rubric, and do a quick oral translation of the article. You will be marked for lexical and grammatical accuracy and fluency.

Periodically

Periodically throughout the rest of the semester, look at your old D day articles and read them through to keep them relatively fresh. By the end of the semester you will have a fairly large amount of Arabic text (50–75 articles) mastered. This will be a solid foundation that will serve you well throughout your Arabic career.

Notes

1. From 1989 to 2001 the SA programme had taken place from January to mid-June and required only three semesters of Arabic for enrolment. With the establishment of the MESA major, SAs have taken place later in the year, are one semester in length, and require a minimum of four semesters of Arabic. Students rarely begin the SA programme with more Arabic than this.
2. Official reading proficiency scores are not available, but the 2011 students did take the online Arabic reading test that NMELRC developed with ACTFL. Of the 43 students who completed the reading test, six scored 75 per cent or better on the Advanced-level items (one scored 100 per cent); 27 scored at least 50 per cent; ten scored less than 50 per cent. Based on results from the paper-and-pencil test that students take at the end of each SA programme and their performance in later courses in Utah, we are confident in estimating that the 2015 cohort would have done better than the 2011 students had they been tested. Unfortunately, they were not able to complete the NMELRC/ACTFL reading test due to a technical problem during the test administration in Jordan.
3. Participants typically completed their OPIs over the telephone. Students in 2012 used the OPIc, a computer-administered version with pre-recorded

prompts. Students in 2015 were interviewed face to face by certified Jordanian testers. No official scores are available for 2013. The lower scores in 2011 are in part likely due to the fact that at least some interviewers pushed the students to speak in a more formal register than they were accustomed to doing. Three of the five students scoring Advanced High in 2015 had significant Arabic speaking experience prior to the SA.

Bibliography

ACTFL. (2012). *ACTFL proficiency guidelines 2012*. Retrieved from http://www.actfl.org/publications/guidelines-and-manuals/actfl-proficiency-guidelines-2012/english/speaking

Archangeli, M. (1999). Study abroad and experiential learning in Salzburg, Austria. *Foreign Language Annals, 32*(1), 115–122.

Badawi, E. (2002). In the quest for the level 4+ in Arabic: Training level 2–3 learners in independent reading. In B. L. Leaver & B. Shekhtman (Eds.), *Developing professional-level language proficiency* (pp. 156–176). Cambridge: Cambridge University Press.

Baker-Smemoe, W., Dewey, D. P., Bown, J., & Martinsen, R. A. (2014). Variables affecting L2 gains during study abroad. *Foreign Language Annals, 47*(3), 464–486.

Bandura, A. (1994). Self-efficacy. In V. S. Ramachaudran (Ed.), *Encyclopedia of human behavior* (Vol. 4, pp. 71–81). New York: Academic Press.

Belnap, R. K., & Abuamsha, K. (2015). Taking on the 'ceiling effect' in Arabic. In T. Brown & J. Bown (Eds.), *To advanced proficiency and beyond: Theory and methods for developing superior second-language ability* (pp. 105–116). Washington, DC: Georgetown University Press.

Belnap, R. K., Bown, J., Dewey, D. P., Belnap, L., & Steffen, P. (2016). Project perseverance: Helping students become self-regulating learners. In T. Gregersen, P. MacIntyre, & S. Mercer (Eds.), *Positive psychology in SLA* (pp. 282–301). Bristol: Multilingual Matters.

Belnap, R. K., & Nassif, M. N. (2011). *Middle East language learning in US higher education*. National Middle East Language Resource Center. Retrieved from http://nmelrc.org/documents/Misc%20Docs/MELangFinal.pdf

Bown, J., Dewey, D. P., & Belnap, R. K. (2015). Student interactions during study abroad in Jordan. In R. Mitchell, N. Tracy-Ventura, & K. McManus (Eds.), *Social interaction, identity and language learning during residence abroad* (pp. 199–222). EuroSLA Monographs Series, 4. Retrieved from http://www.eurosla.org/monographs/EM04/Bown_etal.pdf

Chung, M., & Nation, P. (2006). The effect of a speed reading course. *English Teaching, 61*, 181–204.

Davis, J. M., Sinicrope, C., & Watanabe, Y. (2009). College foreign language program evaluation: Current practice, future directions. In J. M. Norris, J. M. E. Davis, C. Sinicrope, & Y. Watanabe (Eds.), *Toward useful program evaluation in college foreign language education* (pp. 209–226). Honolulu: University of Hawai'i, National Foreign Language Resource Center.

Dewey, D. P. (2006). Reading comprehension and vocabulary development in orthographically complex languages during study abroad. In S. Wilkinson (Ed.), *Insights from study abroad language programs* (pp. 72–84). Boston: Heinle and Heinle.

Dewey, D. P., Belnap, R. K., & Hillstrom, R. (2013). Social network development, language use, and language acquisition during study abroad: Arabic language learners' perspectives. *Frontiers: The Interdisciplinary Journal of Study Abroad, 22*, 84–110.

Dewey, D. P., Bird, S., Gardner, D., & Belnap, R. K. (2013). Social network formation and development during study abroad in the Middle East. *System, 41*(2), 269–282.

Dewey, D. P., Bown, J., Baker, W., Martinsen, R. A., Gold, C., & Eggett, D. (2014). Language use in six study abroad programs: An exploratory analysis of possible predictors. *Language Learning, 64*(1), 36–71.

Dörnyei, Z., Henry, A., & Muir, C. (2015). *Motivational currents in language learning: Frameworks for focused interventions.* New York: Routledge.

Engle, J., & Engle, L. (1999). Program Intervention in the Process of Cultural Integration: The Example of French Practicum. *Frontiers: The Interdisciplinary Journal of Study Abroad, 5*(2), 39–59.

Engle, L., & Engle, J. (2003). Study abroad levels: Toward a classification of program types. *Frontiers: The Interdisciplinary Journal of Study Abroad, 9*(1), 1–20.

Gore, J. E. (2005). *Dominant beliefs and alternative voices: Discourse, belief, and gender in American study abroad.* New York: Routledge.

Grabe, W. (2010). Fluency in reading—Thirty-five years later. *Reading in a Foreign Language, 22*(1), 71–83.

Hansen, L., & Chantrill, C. (1999). Literacy as a second language anchor: Evidence from L2 Japanese and L2 Chinese. In P. Robinson (Ed.), *Representation and process: Proceedings of the 3rd Pacific Second Language Research Forum, 1* (pp. 279–286). Tokyo: Aoyama Gakuin University.

Hansen, L., & Shewell, J. (2002). Keeping a second language: The influence of literacy and motivation. *Korean Journal of Applied Linguistics, 18*, 61–82.

Hu, M., & Nation, I. S. P. (2000). Unknown vocabulary density and reading comprehension. *Reading in a Foreign Language, 13*, 403–430.

Huffman, J. (2014). Reading rate gains during a one-semester extensive reading course. *Reading in a Foreign Language, 26*, 17–33.

Isabelli-García, C., Bown, J., Plews, J. L., & Dewey, D. P. (Forthcoming). *Language Learning and Study Abroad.* Language Teaching.

Laufer, B., & Ravenhorst-Kalovski, G. C. (2010). Lexical threshold revisited: Lexical text coverage, learners' vocabulary size and reading comprehension. *Reading in a Foreign Language, 22*(1), 15–30.

Misfeldt, K. (2013). Pedagogies of affect and lived place: *Der Vorleser* on a short-term intensive immersion. In J. L. Plews & B. Schmenk (Eds.), *Traditions and transitions. Curricula for German studies* (pp. 191–208). Waterloo: Wilfrid Laurier University Press.

Murphey, T. (1998). Motivating with near peer role models. In B. Visgatis (Ed.), *On JALT '97: Trends and transitions: Proceedings of the JALT 1997 international conference on teaching and learning* (pp. 205–209). Tokyo: JALT.

NCSSFL-ACTFL. (2013). *NCSSFL-ACTFL can-do statements: Progress indicators for language learners.* Retrieved from https://www.actfl.org/sites/default/files/pdfs/CanDo_Statements.pdf

Paige, R. M., Cohen, A. D., & Shively, R. L. (2004). Assessing the impact of a strategies-based curriculum on language and culture learning abroad. *Frontiers: The Interdisciplinary Journal of Study Abroad, 10*, 253–276.

Pellegrino Aveni, V. P. (2005). *Study abroad and second language use: Constructing the self.* Cambridge: Cambridge University Press.

Raschio, R. A. (2001). Integrative activities for the study-abroad setting. *Hispania, 84*(3), 534–541.

Ryan, C. (2016). *Enrollments in languages other than English.* Paper presented at the Modern Language Association Convention, Austin, TX. Abstract. Retrieved from https://apps.mla.org/conv_listings_detail?prog_id=73&year=2016

Salah, S. M. (2008). *The relationship between vocabulary knowledge and reading comprehension of authentic Arabic.* Unpublished Master's Thesis, Brigham Young University.

Taillefer, G. F. (2005). Foreign language reading and study abroad: Cross-cultural and cross-linguistic questions. *Modern Language Journal, 89*(4), 503–528.

Tare, M., Lancaster, A., Bonilla, C., Golonka, E., Jackson, S., & Belnap, K. (2016). *Relationships between cognitive aptitude and proficiency gains during study abroad.* Paper presented at the American Association of Applied Linguistics Conference, Orlando, FL. Abstract. Retrieved from http://c.ymcdn.com/sites/www.aaal.org/resource/resmgr/Conference/2016/AAAL_Summary_Book_2016_Abstr.pdf

Taylor, A., Stevens, J. R., & Asher, J. W. (2006). The effects of explicit reading strategy training on L2 reading comprehension: A meta-analysis. In J. M. Norris & L. Ortega (Eds.), *Synthesizing research on language learning and teaching* (pp. 213–244). Amsterdam: Benjamins.

Trentman, E. (2013). Arabic and English during study abroad in Cairo, Egypt: Issues of access and use. *Modern Language Journal, 97*(2), 457–473.

Vande Berg, M., Connor-Linton, J., & Paige, R. M. (2009). The Georgetown consortium project: Interventions for student learning abroad. *Frontiers: The Interdisciplinary Journal of Study Abroad, 18,* 1–75.

Vande Berg, M., Paige, R. M., & Lou, K. H. (2012). *Student learning abroad: What our students are learning, what they're not, and what we can do about it.* Sterling, VA: Stylus Publishing, LLC.

Wilson, J. (2015). *Access, gender, and agency on study abroad: Four case studies of female students in Jordan.* Unpublished Master's Thesis, Brigham Young University.

Student-Centred Second Language Study Abroad for Non-traditional Sojourners: An Anglophone Caribbean Example

Ian Craig

Introduction

This chapter charts the development of a credit-bearing undergraduate course entitled 'Immersion for Languages', available to Majors and Minors in a modern language at the University of the West Indies (UWI), a public regional university with residential campuses in Jamaica, Trinidad and Tobago, and Barbados, and a virtual or Open Campus. Since the course was conceived at the Cave Hill Campus in Barbados and its detailed development coincided with planning for a month-long sojourn at the Universidad Internacional Menéndez Pelayo (UIMP) in Santander, Spain, to be undertaken by a small group of Cave Hill Spanish students in the summer of 2016 (hereafter 'UWI in Spain 2016'), preparations for inaugural delivery around this particular experience are used to provide some specificity for the analysis of factors taken into consideration during the

---

I. Craig (✉)
University of the West Indies, Cave Hill Campus, St. Michael, Barbados
e-mail: ian.craig@cavehill.uwi.edu

developmental process. However, as will become apparent, both the broader contours of the course design process and its delivery with this particular home/host pairing raise questions that are salient to any study abroad (SA) programme involving students from non-traditional sending countries, particularly if they are crossing a perceived border between the *developing* and the *developed* world, as in this instance. The discussion below thus seeks to contribute to redressing the oft-noted dearth of SA research involving such less common source contexts (Block, 2007; Coleman, 2013, p. 17; Kinginger, 2013, p. 6; Plews, 2015, p. 286), particularly for short-term sojourns, and to offer a complementary analysis to existing work on students moving in the opposite direction, that is, from a developed to a developing context (Fobes, 2005; Ogden, 2007; Wells, 2006).

As such, this is a story of course and programme development prior to first implementation. While refinement based on actual experience is doubtless a crucial aspect of development, at some point SA course and programme designers all confront the blank page and lurking doubts as to whether they are really ready to offer something new and usually some way outside their normal field of expertise. These doubts are naturally magnified in the case of a course designed to articulate with an overseas programme that in itself entails a formidable *mise en scène* and numerous intangibles. This chapter thus attempts to offer a more than usually contemporaneous sense of how that blank page is being filled in the specific context in question, namely a public university serving postcolonial microstates, with exiguous resources and a minimal culture of short-term SA for language and culture learning, but nonetheless with a burgeoning interest in experiential learning (Craig, 2016). The aim is to describe the thinking behind decisions made, together with the consultations, programme arrangements, pedagogical explorations and leveraging of existing resources that have been undertaken as a result of these decisions, while still facing a number of less than ideal circumstances, such as uncertainty as to whether any students would ultimately be in a position to actually enrol in the programme or course, the difficulty of access to formal intercultural training for the tutors involved, or the absence of a fully articulated institutional strategy for integrating SA into the curriculum.

It is hoped that this will prove particularly useful for other neophytes in similarly challenging contexts, for whom better supported models can seem daunting or simply out of reach.

The first two sections below detail the overall configuration of the 'Immersion for Languages' course itself and factors motivating the first choice of destination (Santander, Spain) and the host-country SA programme, the UIMP's Spanish Language and Culture Course. The third section discusses pedagogical and theoretical approaches considered relevant to the development of 'Immersion for Languages', bearing in mind the non-traditional source context of the students involved. The fourth section describes in-country engagements and the rationale behind them for this particular destination, while the fifth section addresses in greater detail the process of adaptation for the Anglophone Caribbean of the core course texts, which are published by the University of Minnesota (UMN). The conclusion offers a set of recommendations on factors to bear in mind when designing an intercultural development course and a SA programme for students from non-traditional contexts, from an Anglophone Caribbean perspective. Appendix A offers an overview of 'UWI in Spain 2016' and 'Immersion for Languages' based on Coleman's (2013, p. 23) 'faceted classification', in an attempt to characterise it as fully as possible given limitations of space.

Context

Although the Caribbean region is multilingual, the citizens of the Anglophone region typically fit this description because they shuttle back and forth along a discursive spectrum with a national vernacular or Creole at one end and an official Standard form at the other, not because they have command of another of the official languages inherited from colonialism (Dutch, French, Spanish). In the context of globalisation and regional integration, the limitations imposed by this reality in the educational sphere have long been recognised, as asserted by the now Vice-Chancellor of UWI, Professor Sir Hilary Beckles, and his co-authors Perry and Whiteley (2002):

By necessity, any relevant inter-institutional student culture should transcend the Anglophone space and focus on the common identity and interest of the entire region. Exploiting fully the many collaborative agreements in existence with universities throughout the region, in order to normalize "free" movement within the multilingual teaching and learning environment, must be a pressing objective. In this regard, a quality education calls for the promotion of foreign-language skills as a student right rather than a privilege. (p. 21)

As a result, both increased pan-regional co-operation and broader internationalisation are key priorities of the UWI's current Strategic Plan (University Office of Planning and Development, 2012, pp. 2, 16). At the same time, socially and professionally engaged forms of pedagogy, such as service learning and internships, are being vigorously promoted as the institution transitions from a more traditional academic model towards a more avowedly activist and vocationally aligned one. The consonance in approach between service-learning and internship pedagogies and experiential/constructivist SA programmes is conspicuous (Craig, 2016, p. 285). Given the current convergence of these strategic and pedagogical tendencies, the institutional context would seem to be highly favourable for the introduction of a course such as 'Immersion for Languages', a perception vindicated by its positive reception when passing through the quality assurance and approval process. For a full discussion of the context around SA at the UWI, see Craig (2016).

The 'Immersion for Languages' Course

The general Course Description states:

This course for foreign-language Majors and Minors is designed to be structured around any approved immersion experience with a minimum duration of three weeks in a country where the language of study is spoken. The aim of the course is to maximize the benefits of such an experience in terms of both linguistic and intercultural competence. The course is structured across three modules: 1. Pre-departure, 2. In-country and 3. Return. Throughout the course, students will engage in practical activities and guided reflection with a view to developing their linguistic skills and their capacity to interact across cultures in a variety of scenarios. On return, they will engage in activities designed to enhance their ability to communicate the value of their immersion experience to potential employers or professional collaborators.

Participants must thus enrol separately in a host-country language course or attest involvement in an approved professional or voluntary activity (internship, placement) for at least 15 days during the sojourn. In the case of 'UWI in Spain 2016', the UIMP's Spanish Language and Culture course fits inside the 'Immersion for Languages' course, supplying the required language-learning component and in-country structure, while 'Immersion for Languages' focusses principally on optimising intercultural development outside the classroom. This explains the relatively modest second language (L2) writing requirement and assessed workload in general (see Assessment in Appendix A), an attempt to avoid overload given the demands of the UIMP's 100-hour Spanish Language and Culture course.

A number of features identify the course straight away as drawing on the experiential/constructivist model of SA pedagogy most commonly associated with the UMN and other institutions that have collaborated on the Minnesota Model,[1] built around the *Maximizing Study Abroad* project and the printed guides of that name (Kappler Mikk et al., 2009; Paige, Cohen, Kappler, Chi, & Lassegard, 2006): the tripartite structure in which the sojourn is the centre-piece, but pre-departure and return phases constitute substantive and compulsory components; the combination of 'practical activities and guided reflection' in line with Kolb's (1984) Experiential Learning Cycle, which in turn draws on Dewey (1938); the emphasis placed on the ability to articulate the value of the sojourn in meaningful ways for personal advancement upon return (Paige, Harvey, & McCleary, 2012). This approach, involving supported engagement and guided reflection throughout a three-stage cycle, also chimes with the recommendations of Mitchell, Tracy-Ventura and McManus (2017) arising from their studies of Anglophone sojourners in Europe:

> It is clearly challenging, but not impossible, for educators concerned with developing their students as 'intercultural speakers' to make the sojourn a central learning opportunity. We believe that LARA-style training (Roberts et al., 2001) presojourn, plus encouragement and support for reflection both insojourn and especially afterwards, provide the necessary framework for this. (p. 251)

The *Maximizing* project and its two key texts thus constitute the pedagogical core of this course, with the *Instructional Guide* (Kappler Mikk et al., 2009) as the main teacher text and the *Student's Guide* (Paige et al., 2006) as a required student text. The choice of this existing framework was guided by two main factors, one practical, the other pedagogical: (1) the comprehensive and ready-made character of the *Maximizing* materials, which provide a detailed conceptual and pedagogical framework, including an explanatory definition of intercultural communication competence (Kappler Mikk et al., 2009, pp. 86–8) based on Kim (1988, 2001), together with numerous specific activities across an integrated pairing of instructor and student texts; (2) the convergence of the experiential/constructionist approach with the UWI's current *Strategic Plan*, which under 'Weaknesses' attests that 'some employers have indicated that the University should, inter alia, enhance co-curricular activities and introduce more internships to develop work-ready graduates' (University Office of Planning and Development, 2012, p. 17).

The in-country phase of the course can in principle be taken online without the presence in the host country of a faculty member from the UWI, to facilitate students wishing to take the course outside the context of a faculty-led programme (such as during a semester-exchange programme). However, for this first iteration, as course designer and instructor, I arranged to be in Santander for the first 2 weeks of the month-long sojourn, although the current Cave Hill Spanish *lectora* (language assistant sponsored by the Spanish state) is a current employee of both the UWI Cave Hill Campus (during Fall and Winter/Spring semesters) and the UIMP (in the summer session) and thus already offers continuity across home and host environments and across pre-departure and in-country phases. (I rejoin the students for the return phase.) My presence as course developer is required because, as mentioned, a reconnoitring visit to Santander has not proved feasible—my last visit to the city was some 20 years ago—so that practical, in-country elements of the course will be designed to some extent at the same time as it is being offered for the first time. The participating students will thus be recruited as exploratory fieldworkers and course co-developers, reporting on the efficacy of various mooted forms of engagement with the host culture, with the specific remit that their reports will be used as a guide for future students and for refinement of the course by me as instructor. Though this apparently somewhat improvisational approach may cut against the high degree of prior orchestration preferred by contemporary quality assurance doctrine in higher education, it is in keeping both with the sense of adventure generated by the prospect of a journey to Europe and to Spain by Caribbean students, as discussed below, and with expert testimony on the value of a 'purposeful but intentionally flexible curriculum' (Mullens & Cuper, 2012, p. 158). This approach also chimes with the real-world, task-based approach advocated by Situated Learning Theory, and with Critical Pedagogy, in which 'the students—no longer docile listeners—are now critical co-investigators in dialogue with the teacher' (Freire, 2000, p. 68), both pedagogical approaches that informed the course design philosophy, as discussed below.

Clearly, there is risk attached to adopting democratising practices such as co-development:

> many [students] may have developed 'authority-dependence' to the extent that they 'assume education means listening to teachers tell them what to do and what things mean. Freire points out that if a liberating teacher asks students to co-develop the class with her or him, the students often doubt that this is "real" education' (Shor, 1987, p. 29). (Lutterman-Aguila & Gingerich, 2002, p. 72)

However, region-specific research from the field of cross-cultural management corroborates the transformative potential of taking this risk:

> In the Caribbean context, it seems that a tradition of nondelegation and nonparticipation makes it difficult for managers and their subordinates to accept and implement delegation and participation. To do so effectively involves changing perceptions, attitudes and behaviors. At the same time, where managers are willing to delegate and encourage participation, and where subordinates are appropriately trained and coached, it seems to have a positive effect on motivation and performance. (Punnett, 2004, p. 154)

'UWI in Spain 2016'

In addressing the choice of destination, it is important firstly to note that the programme in Santander, Spain, was chosen by majority preference over an alternative in Mérida, Mexico, by the small group of students who reported having saved sufficient funds to contemplate participation in 'UWI in Spain 2016' (Department of Language, Linguistics and Literature, 2015), despite being 30% more expensive. Though this makes the attempt to conduct a transatlantic short-term SA programme from a developing-region source context even more quixotic than it might already appear, the compelling reasons for this preference arose at a focus group with five students who had expressed an active interest in taking 'Immersion for Languages' as part of 'UWI in Spain 2016' (one male, four females; two Barbadians, two Saint Lucians, one Vincentian). Unsurprisingly, Caribbean students have a complex relationship with Europe in general, with the students offering the following range of opinions in response to an invitation to complete the sentence 'Europe is…': 'culturally diverse, refined, romantic', 'expensive', 'a dream come true', 'race- and class-oriented', 'a very wealthy continent that has extracted its wealth from Africa and the Caribbean'. All of the students present agreed that the characterisations offered by the other members of the group were neither surprising nor objectionable, and thus concurred that for Anglophone Caribbean students, Europe is simultaneously 'a dream come true' and 'a very wealthy continent that has extracted its wealth from Africa and the Caribbean'. Similarly, while they all included Spain at the top or very high on a shortlist of ideal destinations because it is 'rich in history' and 'the mother country, where it all began', they also agreed with the respondent who reported a perception that Spain might be somewhat 'backward' regarding attitudes to racial difference.

One respondent used a telling phrase to explain how he saw himself reconciling these contradictory resonances: 'I try to be naive to that [the possibility of experiencing racism], in a sense. I can't really understand the level of discrimination in that regard, so I try to just put it out of my head and concentrate on the good of the country.' This optimistic philosophy aligns with research findings in psychology regarding the correlation between so-called positivity bias and psychological well-being, an important factor in confronting the affective challenge of SA, particularly in the case of non-traditional sojourners (Mezulis, Abramson, Hyde, & Hankin, 2004; Savicki, 2013; Willis, 2015). Notwithstanding this student's strategic disengagement with discrimination, however, and while the lives of Anglophone Caribbean students are doubtless 'shaped by racialized consciousness and identities' (Anya, 2017, p. 4) in different ways from those of African Americans, the philosophy behind 'Immersion for Languages' coheres with the approach of Anya (2017), who asserts from a US perspective the necessary centrality of race in both interpreting and guiding the experiences of non-White sojourners, in light of their traditional under-representation in SA. Even if Caribbean sojourners do not typically declare a motivation to 'live a sense of global blackness' (Anya, 2017, p. 16) in their SA choices, failing to engage openly with race when orienting African-descended students about to sojourn in Europe would perpetuate the reactionary coyness or naïve liberal *colour-blindness* that has typified the treatment of such issues in applied linguistics (Anya, 2017, p. 13).

As indicated above, the language component of this programme is almost entirely outsourced to the host-country partner institution. That is to say, students are required to enrol in the UIMP Spanish Language and Culture Course at whichever language level is deemed appropriate by the UIMP Placement Test (Universidad Internacional Menéndez Pelayo, 2016). Whether this takes them into a level above the one already nominally achieved at the UWI or has them repeating a lower level, the UWI will not attempt to intervene in the streaming process, nor indeed offer any mechanism for direct transfer of credit for language learning alone after the sojourn (i.e. the UIMP Spanish Language and Culture course alone cannot count for credit back at the UWI). 'Immersion for Languages' counts for three elective credits in the UWI level following the sojourn, thereby relieving the student immediately after the sojourn of one elective out of five courses normally taken by full-time students per semester.

Two main factors motivated this approach to enrolment, streaming and credits. Firstly, if a student were to be streamed at the UIMP in a level of Spanish Language and Culture that took them beyond their point of departure at the UWI and were then exempted from the equivalent UWI language course on return, resource constraints on offering courses outside a single-track sequential progression, at least at the Cave Hill Campus, would mean that such students would have no course at their exact level to enrol in, and would thus spend a semester without doing a dedicated Spanish language course before advancing further in the programme. Diminishing their exposure to the language in this way immediately after immersion seemed inimical to its longer-term aims. For the purposes of 'Immersion for Languages', students are thus required simply to enrol in and take at least 15 days' worth of whichever level of the Spanish Language and Culture course they are placed in by UIMP; the linguistic benefits accrued are viewed principally in terms of reinforcement and enhanced confidence.

Secondly, in 2012, before 'Immersion for Languages' was conceived, six students from the Cave Hill Campus in Barbados did the 1-month Spanish Language and Culture Course at UIMP. Though they enquired about the possibility of credit transfer, they reported that the classroom ethos and pedagogical culture at the UIMP was so different from that of the UWI that they were frankly unsure as to whether they had repeated a level or had done a new one. They all agreed that the experience was linguistically and culturally enriching and had given impetus to their subsequent progress through the degree programme at UWI, particularly in the area of self-confidence in oral expression.

In turn, the UIMP was the destination for this pilot experience chiefly for a single important reason mentioned above: at the time, the UWI Cave Hill Campus's Spanish *lectora*, or language and culture assistant, was also a summer-session employee of the UIMP. Her presence at the Cave Hill Campus as a ready source of information on the host institution in Spain, where she would also again be employed during the students' sojourn, was key to reducing anxiety relating to the uncertainty of heading to an unknown university, country and, for most, continent. Her much more recent and deeper familiarity with Santander also provides vital knowledge of the destination to help offset my own limitations in this area, mentioned above (Mullens & Cuper, 2012, pp. 80–1). Though state budget cuts in Spain caused the *lectorados* in many countries, including Barbados, to be cancelled shortly afterwards, the same *lectora* was reemployed in the academic year 2015–2016; her presence was explicitly mentioned at the student focus group as a reason for choosing Spain as a preferred destination in 2016. Similarly, the direct testimony of two Barbadian students who participated in this 2012 pilot sojourn, offered at an information session to promote the 2016 iteration— including anecdotes inflected with creolised linguistic forms and point of view—were mentioned in the focus group as an important motivating factor. Both closely involving the *lectora* and bringing in returnees are strategies that cohere with advice in the *Student's Guide* (Paige et al., 2006) on 'Some Strategies for Culture-Specific Learning' to engage with 'People from the country and culture you are visiting', including 'visit[ing] with other students who have studied abroad in your host country' (p. 55); both strategies also reflect the importance in small states especially of face-to-face relationships and direct in-group testimony in overcoming latent anxieties related to challenging experiences such as a SA sojourn (Bray, 2011, pp. 47–9).

Although the factors that make short-term SA programmes for language and intercultural learning both precarious and attractive in the Anglophone Caribbean context are too complex to be fully addressed here (Craig, 2016), suffice to say that the 2014 introduction at the Cave Hill Campus of the requirement that students make a major contribution to their own tertiary education costs and the generally depressed state of Anglophone Caribbean economies do not generate a propitious context for this kind of endeavour (Cox, 2015; Wigglesworth, 2013). Various aspects of the integrative architecture of the 'Immersion for Languages' course and the host programme thus reflect a conviction that this kind of experience in this context will come into its own at an indeterminate time in the future and that the responsibility for now is to put in place a structure and a system that are scalable, flexible and robust enough to minimise wasted effort when no sojourn at all materialises and to accommodate either very low or rather higher numbers according to the prevailing circumstances. Both the UIMP programme and the equivalent offered by the Universidad Autónoma de Yucatán in Mexico (the alternative short-term programme for UWI Spanish students) are thus ongoing programmes that do not require the presence of UWI students for them to function. This removes an important source of pressure inherent in a number of alternative programme options that were considered, namely the need to ensure a significant minimum number of UWI participants to make the enterprise worthwhile for both the home tutors and the host providers and partners. A minimum of just two UWI participants has thus been established, in order to offer a degree of home-culture comfort and to allow for peer observation and reinforcement. For now, this strategy of anchoring to an existing host-country programme is necessary to avoid undue wastage of invested effort in fully customised experiences in the event of cancellation, as we steadily move to implement at least some of the strategies of the Minnesota Model of SA curriculum integration that might make these efforts less precarious.

A Pedagogical Framework for Caribbean Sojourners

As indicated above, the model of intercultural pedagogy presupposed by the chosen course texts is the experiential/constructivist approach, appropriate in this case for both practical and institutionally strategic reasons. However, due note was taken of Wong's (2015) critique of this approach, in which he suggests that it perhaps risks becoming something of an orthodoxy in itself, even as it continues to be advanced as a relatively recent antidote to the obduracy of the 'immersion assumption'. Whether one finds Wong's critiques compelling or not, his suggestion of Social Learning Theory and Situated Learning Theory as complementary frameworks certainly bears consideration in the Caribbean context. A recent study using a Social Learning analytical framework found that

> participants in the study abroad programmes gained significantly in internal locus of control compared to their typical peers who did not participate in the experience abroad. Possessing an increased internal LOC means that students are more likely to act in ways that will lead them to be more effective problem solvers. (McLeod et al., 2015, p. 35)

Given the likelihood that the history of the Anglophone Caribbean has predisposed its current inhabitants towards a more external locus of control, taking some account of this approach when designing SA for the region's students seems highly appropriate (Arneaud & Aibada, 2013; Boodhoo, 1988, p. 43). In the case of Situated Learning, as mentioned above, student engagement will be encouraged by asking our sojourners to perform a reconnaissance role at the destination, making the first face-to-face contact with partner organisations on the ground and assessing the fecundity of an ongoing relationship involving more truly host-centred involvement for their peers in future. While sojourners are likely to refer to these tasks in their evaluated journal or blog, there is no academic credit or evaluation specifically attached to the tasks themselves. Rather, they will be presented as an experiential service to the SA programme and to UWI that only they can effectively perform, as participants with comparable characteristics and outlook to their peers. Across both Social Learning and Situated Learning Theories, the emphasis on applied tasks, real-world experience and the development of self-efficacy corresponds closely to the current needs of the UWI as it seeks to 'fundamentally enhance the employability skills/attributes of students, which is a necessary ingredient in transforming the skilled workforce to be more innovative and entrepreneurial among other things that are critical to social and economic transformation', by devising an Employability Strategy that includes both 'work placements and internships' and 'opportunities for volunteering and placement overseas' (Dass, 2015, p. 107). Furthermore, the value of developing local investments and attachments is identified by Mitchell et al. (2017, pp. 230, 242) as predictive of greater linguistic gain, and also as crucial in contextualising overall sojourner development by Anya (2017, pp. 224–5), who situates a service-learning orientation in SA experiences within a compelling broader vindication of a social justice approach to foreign language learning in general (Anya, pp. 8, 229–30).

As Wong (2015) states, both Social Theory and Situated Learning Theory might be seen as complementary to the experiential/constructivist framework and all three are doubtless valid and insightful conceptual frameworks for constructing a pedagogy around SA. They also all originated in the global North and specifically the educational culture of the United States. In a region such as the Caribbean, both historically subject to epistemological imposition and prone to uncritical adoption of externally valorised models, it is as well to note their provenance in this external educational ethos and pedagogical tradition (George & Lewis, 2011; Kamugisha, 2007; Louisy, 2004). Furthermore, if the Caribbean is viewed, ideologically speaking, as a fulcrum across which the twin burdens of weighty North American and Latin American neighbours must be continually made to balance, an explicit global-South counterweight would seem to do no harm when seeking to build a SA pedagogy most appropriate for Caribbean students. Bringing to bear the weight of alternative epistemologies in order to counteract the historic density and insistence of Northern hegemonic discourses is of course the province of postcolonialist critique, which thus naturally provides a key impetus driving the pedagogical philosophy behind 'Immersion for Languages' (Young, 2001, pp. 57–8).

It should be noted, however, that the role of postcolonial critiques in the design of 'Immersion for Languages' is as a set of contestatory principles to be used by the instructor to anchor discussions on a variety of topics; with the possible exception of Hall (2001), students will not be required to read original postcolonial source texts in their entirety, as it was felt that this might be a prematurely destabilising means of eliciting self-reflection on their sociocultural investments immediately prior to the challenge of an overseas sojourn. The critique articulated by Postcolonial Theory is helpful in making an explicit virtue of the most important distinguishing feature of the sojourn, noted above: unlike most SA students, these sojourners are nationals of a developing nation crossing a threshold into a developed one. This would seem to require at least some historicising and discussion of the deeper implications of African-descended students—or indeed European-descended students from a Caribbean nation—sojourning in an overwhelmingly White city, whose current 'aristocratic' air does after all owe a great deal to its favoured position as a trading post with the Spanish American empire (Turespaña, 2016). It seems right that Caribbean students seeking to immerse themselves in the culture of the last mainland Spanish city to remove a statue of General Franco should at least be aware that enslaved Africans were employed as house servants in the late eighteenth and early nineteenth centuries in Santander (Maruri Villanueva, 1987, pp. 338–9; Tremlett, 2008).

Another reason for incorporating the postcolonial approach obliquely rather than directly is a sense of the risk that, upon discovering it perhaps for the first time in applied form, some students might become so invested in its cause that they become predisposed against adaptive in-country strategies that would otherwise optimise not only their linguistic and intercultural development, but also their enjoyment, doubtless a key component of the SA experience's enduring influence on attitudes and decision-making in later life. It is not the intention that our students set off looking for a good time only to return as militant anti-imperialists on the strength of taking 'Immersion for Languages' (though some might regard this as a positive outcome). The goal is more nuanced: to raise their awareness of the kinds of historical erasures that the European narrative of itself persists in perpetrating and thereby give them keener sight on the ground, but without spoiling their capacity to marvel at all that is marvellous about Europe. This nuanced awareness seemed a plausible goal, given the already complex student sense of Europe that arose in the focus group, described above.

For similar reasons, the Critical Pedagogy associated with Paulo Freire comprised another informing approach rather than a direct template for course and programme design. Since Critical Pedagogy might be seen as the educational first cousin of Postcolonial Theory, its advantages in the context of a Caribbean-origin SA programme and course are not hard to surmise: it implies a sociopolitically and historically aware critique that coheres with that of postcolonialism; it encourages participatory engagement in a specific sociospatial context; it requires that the educator reflect critically on the bases on which s/he is directing the flow of knowledge and engagement. This last criterion, while doubtless valuable in all faculty-led or guided SA endeavours, is likely more so than usual in this case, given the cultural distance between the tutors and the students involved: both the Spanish *lectora* and I are European, White, and were acquainted with the host city before we first travelled to the Caribbean, as against the prospective first cohort of 'Immersion for Languages', all of whom are of African descent and none of whom have visited Europe before. Merely at the level of expectations, assumptions and desires, these very distinct respective profiles configure quite different understandings of the host location, and likely very different lived experiences in it.

As elucidated by Lutterman-Aguila and Gingerich (2002), Critical Pedagogy foregrounds the inescapably political nature and socially transformative possibilities of educational experiences such as SA, an orientation that coheres with the postcolonial context of the Anglophone Caribbean and the need for a strong developmental vision and high level of 'global awareness' among its university graduates (Dass, 2015, p. 107; University Office of Planning and Development, 2012, p. 25). Due note was also taken of the marrying of Critical Pedagogy with more explicitly spatialised pedagogies invoking social geographic, radical multiculturalist and ecological imperatives (Gruenewald, 2003; Haymes, 1995). The explicit attention to engagement with both *race* and the natural environment in these 'critical pedagogies of place' is doubtless suited to the Anglophone Caribbean's current predicament, in which both the persistence of racial and ethnic division and accelerating ecological threats loom large (Allahar, 2005; Boruff & Cutter, 2007).

Pedagogy in Practice

What actual student engagements on the ground might allow these multifarious perspectives to cohere into experiences that would promote the kinds of nuanced reflection that they imply? A set of guided engagements under the heading 'Discovering Santander' was developed, divided into Finding New Partners and Free Explorations. For Finding New Partners, students will be asked to participate in fieldwork for course/programme development, comprising, in increasingly challenging sequence:

- Accompany and observe a tutor making two on-the-ground, face-to-face contacts with a community-based organisation with a view to establishing an ongoing relationship that would allow future UWI students to contribute in some way.
- Make and develop such a contact in pairs, without the presence of a tutor.
- Make and develop such a contact independently.

After prior initial email contact by the tutor to establish an institutional context, this exercise thus involves the sojourner setting up a meeting by phone or email, then an encounter at the organisation's premises or other mutually agreed location, comprising an information exchange regarding the interests of the respective parties, then a negotiation on possible collaboration. In accordance with the current sociocultural and environmental concerns of the Caribbean mentioned above, several areas and organisations initially identified were:

- Ecology/Sustainable Tourism: Jóvenes Ecologistas de Cantabria; Jóvenes por la Ecología de Cantabria; Turismo Sostenible Cantabria.
- Solidarity with Migrants: Cantabria Acoge; Plataforma Cántabra de Solidaridad con los Inmigrantes.
- Youth Groups: Espacio Joven-Juventud Santander.

In the observational phase, students will thus take note of both the environment of the host organisation and the interaction between tutor and host, noting aspects such as use of the physical space, norms of appearance and social engagement, formality or lack thereof in verbal interactions, personal space, negotiation strategies, and so forth.

Together with these three course development fieldwork assignments, students will also be given 'Specific Journal Prompts' (Mullens & Cuper, 2012, p. 167), based on their Free Explorations, requiring them to include accounts of: interactions with host-country nationals through the UIMP's *Café de las Lenguas* and *Hablamos* activities (Universidad Internacional Menéndez Pelayo, 2016); a visit to a church; a shopping trip; a tourist experience; or an approved alternative. The church assignment is designed to leverage the importance of attendance at church for many Anglophone Caribbean youth, as reflected in the consensus at the focus group that church might be a likely source of interaction with host nationals. While the shopping and tourism experiences self-evidently have a less socially engaged value than the encounters with community groups, their inclusion was guided by the sense that having these sojourners, especially, reflect on the experience of being a consumer in a large European country would likely generate productive reflection, since in their home territories the implicit dyad of White=consumer/tourist, non-White=service provider/local is often strongly inscribed. It seems important for students to reflect on the experience of being on the other side of this often racially inflected transactional arrangement, to feel and reflect on their new location in an economy of desire. Mutual observation was also built into this exercise, with a view to detecting any sociologically noteworthy behaviours among employees of retail spaces confronted with African-descended consumers.

Church, shopping and tourist activities are also a means of generating learning around many of the students' own declared proclivities and understandings of the likely environments their sojourn will lead them to, emerging from the student focus group and many years of class discussions, an important path-of-least-resistance consideration to set against the arguably more earnest service engagements, which are likely to appeal to some temperaments more than others. While noting well-founded critiques by Engle and Engle (2002), Kinginer (2013, p. 7), and Ogden (2007) regarding the deleterious effects of consumerism and commodification in SA contexts involving traditional sending nations, we might on the other hand view a *mindful consumerism of enquiry* by postcolonial students as combining both a defensible pleasure in experiencing a level of sheer material abundance harder to find in the marketplaces of the postcolonial microstates, perennially constrained by their consignment to the periphery, with an opportunity to explore the destination sociologically by testing the egalitarian claims of contemporary consumerist capitalism. Clearly, viewing consumerist experiences solely through the prism of race would be tendentious and other variables will naturally be factored into analysis of consumerist observations: other identity categories such as gender, class, age or local/foreign; intercultural factors such as maintenance of eye contact—an issue that arises in diasporic Caribbean educational settings (Nero, 2006, p. 508)—management of speech turns, volume or personal space; or more individual and interpersonal issues such as introversion/extroversion. Nonetheless, the often hypocritical erasure of racial difference in the iconography of contemporary consumerism means, somewhat subversively in both a SA and a broader sociopolitical sense, that a direct invitation to these particular sojourners to assume the role of conspicuous consumers with a view to conducting sociological research might be seen as cohering with 'black opposition to fundamental tenets of neoliberalism, calling attention to the vacuity of calls for "color-blindness," which rely unfailingly on the very logics of race they claim to dispossess' (Mukherjee, 2011, p. 189).

Adapting the Core Texts for the Caribbean

Since the *Instructional Guide* (Kappler Mikk et al., 2009) and the *Student's Guide* (Paige et al., 2006) are closely integrated, this section will focus on the latter, in keeping with the student-centred approach of the course and the UWI in Spain programme; 'the text' in this section thus refers to the

Student's Guide. Assessment of the text involved two phases: (1) an evaluation of its likely overall suitability based on the testimony of student respondents; (2) strategies of supplementation and adaptation where required. The text is divided into 'Pre-departure', 'In-country' and 'Post-SA' units, with each unit subdivided into 'Language-Learning' and 'Culture-Learning' sections. For the evaluation, the pre-departure, culture-learning section was chosen for two reasons: (1) the pre-departure section only, to avoid exposing students prematurely to sections best absorbed as the sojourn proceeds; (2) the culture-learning section, as this seemed more likely than the language-learning section to generate any dissonance between the implied US/traditional sending-country readership and Caribbean students. The evaluation thus involved a classificatory review of this section of the text, with each section being marked 'retain', 'supplement', 'adapt', 'replace' or 'skip'. The first two categorisations would tend to validate fully the choice of text, justifying its use as a course text and purchase by participants, while a predominance of the final three (and certainly the last two) would argue in favour of undertaking a thoroughgoing adaptation that would likely result in the in-house compilation of a separate, fully indigenous set of materials to be given to students. Appendix B shows the results of this evaluation, with the final column serving to elucidate the meaning of the action labels and the rationale governing the decision in each case.

As shown, of the nineteen sections reviewed, only two were considered to require outright replacement (with none attracting a 'skip' recommendation). On the basis of this co-evaluation, it was decided that the text was both sufficiently engaging and general in its applicability to be a suitable accompaniment to a SA experience for Anglophone Caribbean students: a majority of sections could be retained or supplemented and most of the adaptations were of the order of simple verbal amendments when addressing the text together, rather than entailing entirely new versions. The overall average student rating across all sections of 3.94 (78.8%, an A minus in the UWI system) was deemed to be a strong endorsement of the text and qualitative assessments reinforced this: 'it seems like a really good intro to study abroad'; 'contains very valuable information'; 'very informative and interesting; I like that they really didn't use a lot of complicated terms and it explained everything'.

Notwithstanding this positive overall response, the degree of supplementation and adaptation required should not be understated, probably suggesting that a fully Caribbean adaptation of the text would ultimately be the ideal tool, both pedagogically in eliminating distracting references to a third (US) culture not at stake for these students, and ideologically in avoiding yet another instance of implicit consignment of Caribbean learners to a cultural periphery. In certain instances, this US-centric viewpoint of the *Student's Guide* is relatively unproblematic, while in others it inevitably impedes pedagogical clarity. For example, in the former category, the Welcome to Study Abroad section's observation that 'there are numerous examples of "ugly travelers" (and not just Americans), whose lack of cultural sensitivity makes them instantly recognisable in an unpleasant sort of way' (pp. 1–3) opens the door for an engaging discussion of both *ugly Americans* in the Caribbean (and whether they do in fact behave any *uglier* than, say, British visitors), as well as Caribbean travellers' habits and behaviours. On the other hand, the Activity focussing on 'Core US American cultural values: What the experts say' and 'International Perspectives on US Americans' (pp. 68–73) are both irrelevant to the sojourn and somewhat distracting, since expert opinion on core US values is likely to pique the general curiosity of at least some Caribbean students culturally curious enough to be engaging in a SA sojourn, perhaps thereby causing them to read these sections even though instructed to skip them.

It should also be noted that the process of supplementation to create a cogent pre-sojourn orientation package around the *Student's Guide* involved productive collaboration and creative importation of materials from a variety of external sources. My own prior research on Caribbean sojourners' experiences thus directly entered the pedagogical realm for the first time in the form of postsojourn research interviews and summarised sections of a published article arising from these (Craig, 2010), used to augment the testimony on reentry in the 'Dimensions of Culture Learning' section of the *Student's Guide* (pp. 40–2). Also in the realm of published research, the task of gathering all relevant materials led me to track down work by others on cultural values in Barbados and the Anglophone Caribbean, which will ultimately need reducing down to the kind of summary offered in the 'Core US American cultural values: What the experts say' section of the *Student's Guide* mentioned above (Marshall et al., 2017; Punnett, Dick-Forde, & Robinson, 2014). Finally, for the section on 'Working with Stereotypes and Testing Hypotheses', a colleague in Gender Studies provided a 'micro-aggression tree' resulting from an exercise during an orientation for new students, designed to raise awareness of casual stereotyping between nationals of different Caribbean territories, who live in close proximity on the campus's communal student accommodation.

In sum, the process of bringing together these disparate resources can be seen as helping to gauge and consolidate the intercultural capacity of the campus at large, as well as providing an articulated network of materials for future projects, including further SA research and the production of an Anglophone Caribbean-specific version of the *Student's Guide*, ultimately a necessity, as mentioned above, given the importance of adopting an 'ethnoracially inclusive orientation' towards materials (Anya, 2017, p. 228).

Conclusion and Recommendations

Many of the prerequisites for launching a SA programme and course in a postcolonial context overlap with those of a traditional sending context. It is crucial, for example, to conduct an environmental scan to ascertain the internal and external factors likely to facilitate or hinder the endeavour. As noted above, in assessing relevant existing curricular connections at the home institution, this can prove highly productive. In this case, consultations with colleagues in cultural studies, social work, sociology, gender studies and cross-cultural management not only generated new activities and bibliography for the course, but also a strongly enhanced sense of how much work was already being done at the Cave Hill Campus involving student self-reflections around identity issues and cross-cultural analysis.[2] Since the interest generated is reciprocal, as the course tutor and programme director I feel increasingly motivated by a sense of a burgeoning community of practice around these issues that reinforces the institutional value of SA programmes in general and, in seeking to integrate these into the curriculum through 'Immersion for Languages', those of the modern languages section in particular.

The following further recommendations for prospective programme creators focus on those that are of particular salience to a postcolonial context. It is worth acquiring a thorough understanding of the dominant episteme of SA in traditional sending countries, since all students regardless of origin enter a transnational system in which the very terms 'study abroad' and 'SA student' are freighted with preconceptions, which in the case of postcolonial sojourners will also intersect in complex ways with the distinct *othering* implied by this latter status (Coleman, 2013, pp. 19–22; Gore, 2005). Similarly, the lessons learned in establishing and refining effective systems in contexts with a long SA tradition should be mined for transferable strategies. While factors arising from overall institutional culture may be intractable or require immense patience, smaller interventions such as creating a much more prominent profile for SA in orientation and student-advising scenarios should be much more achievable and can be decisive: all three students who paid the commitment fee and planned to take 'Immersion for Languages' were level-two students who had been saving since a promotional orientation shortly after they entered in level one (two ultimately travelled and took the course). In smaller population settings, it seems plausible that incorporating SA testimony and video footage into marketing materials for tertiary language programmes directed at secondary/high schools might have a major impact in both helping to situate SA as an integral part of tertiary language study and give students as long a period as possible to save sufficient funds to participate. These secondary/high school-level interventions are still a work in progress in the UWI case, but have been successfully used at the University of York (Beth Alaksa, Coordinator, International Mobility Programs, in discussion with the author, September 2013) and at the University of California Riverside, where their efficacy in increasing SA enrolment among lower-income and non-White students, particularly, has also been noted (Claassen Thrush & Victorino, 2016, p. 126).

The cultural values and mores of the source context (ascertained through scholarly sources, personal experience and direct consultation with sojourners and others) should be strategically factored into the matrix of home-host variables that can impact on the experience, being harnessed or resisted depending on their likelihood of enhancing or hindering optimal intercultural engagement. An example of resistance would be the critical pedagogical subversion of the marked teacher-student hierarchy of many Caribbean classrooms, elaborated in the pedagogical section above. It seems plausible that the SA environment, with its self-evident strangeness and removal from habitual scenarios of judgement—especially for sojourners moving from *tighter* to *looser* social environments—is the ideal setting to call into question certain cultural values that are in any case predominantly colonial in origin and a probable hindrance to learner autonomy and sojourner self-efficacy.[3] An element that might be harnessed is the already markedly intercultural character of the source context, exemplified by the fact that the three remaining prospective students for 'Immersion for Languages' as part of 'UWI in Spain 2016' comprise a tri-national group: a Barbadian, a Saint Lucian and a Vincentian. While this maximal diversity may not be typical (only one of six was non-Barbadian for the pilot experience), the Caribbean landscape of regional commonality amid international diversity offers a useful backdrop for intercultural enquiry around language learning. The linguistic complexity generated by the processes of creolisation that have configured the Caribbean should also be foregrounded in order to emphasise the essentially plurilingual or translingual character of any SA sojourn in the context of globalisation (Anya, 2017, pp. 26, 220–2; Mitchell et al., 2017, pp. 20–1).

The situated meanings of travel and study overseas in the given postcolonial source context, both contemporary and historic, should be thoroughly explored, as they will also likely configure a set of source-specific assumptions and expectations around SA in its various forms, and around choice of destination, especially. Generational differences will likely add complexity to this factor. The desires of students should be incorporated into the perception of the optimum pathway to intercultural engagement that undergirds course and programme decision-making, perhaps rather more than in the case of traditional sending-country students, whose desires are more likely to be met already by dint of the preeminence in the world order of their source context, though clearly with important exceptions generated by inequities in both contexts (there will clearly be instances in which a postcolonial student enjoys more privilege at home than a traditional student). SA as an arena of desire is only rendered dubious when that desire is untrammelled in the context of programmes that are unreflectively commodified, rather than harnessed as an energy propelling the exploration of its own origins. In the case of postcolonial students, their designs and desires on the destination will likely be different in revelatory ways from those of their counterparts from traditional sending sources.

Above all, the opportunity to usher postcolonial students into the joys and challenges of SA for intercultural learning should be relished. As well as offering them the chance to savour the fabled intensity of an experience long considered simply *not for people like them* and to foster their development as critical global citizens in contexts where the presence of such is likely disproportionately impactful (Craig, 2016), their unique perspective on that experience will doubtless enrich our understandings of SA as an ever more diverse global phenomenon.

Summary of recommendations for student-centred SA for non-traditional sojourners

- Know your specific context first: thoroughly assess affordances and constraints in the institutional and broader sociocultural context before crafting your SA programme and courses.
- Know the field: however different your context from that of traditional SA sending nations, not all factors are culturally determined, so the accumulated wisdom of your predecessors will be of use.
- Aim to get the message across early: introduce sensitisation materials and interventions as early in the education system as feasible to foster inclusivity and give time to save funds.
- When moulding a context-specific pedagogy, understand students' desires in order to steer a carefully calibrated pathway between alignment with these desires and the necessary degree of challenge entailed by all profound intercultural engagement.
- When facing challenges, be heartened by the potentially very powerful developmental effects of SA pedagogy in postcolonial and non-traditional SA contexts.

Appendix A

'UWI in Spain 2016' Faceted Classification

Facet	'UWI in Spain 2016'
Within programme/Whole programme	Within programme. One-month summer programme entailing enrolment in UIMP Spanish Language and Culture Course in Santander, Spain; those who have completed level two of the UWI Major or Minor in Spanish may also take level-three (final-year) UWI three-credit elective course 'Immersion for Languages' while undertaking the UIMP course.
Learning objectives and outcomes	For 'Immersion for Languages': 1. Follow the gist of most general conversations between native speakers conducted at normal speed. 2. Communicate effectively, orally and in writing, their needs, opinions and interests and make arrangements in the language in real-life situations in a native-speaker environment, or significantly advance towards this goal. 3. Diagnose and resolve communication difficulties resulting from linguistic or cultural misunderstandings, or seek appropriate assistance in doing so. 4. Explain the concepts of intercultural competence and cultural difference and begin to make informed decisions on how to negotiate an intercultural environment. 5. Reflect upon and analyse their own cultural-social standing and cultural influences. 6. Describe intercultural communication processes and the ways in which they are connected to issues of identity, social class, gender, sexuality and race. 7. Apply an array of skills necessary to communicate effectively in intercultural interactions. 8. Communicate to a potential employer or collaborator the value of their experience and the transferability of the skills acquired and developed.

(continued)

(continued)

Facet	'UWI in Spain 2016'
Age	Approximate average age of participants, 24 years.
Programme at home university	Must be enrolled in UWI BA in Spanish or Minor in Spanish. Three prospective participants at time of writing: one Major in Management with Minor in Spanish; one Major in Spanish with Minor in Linguistics; one Major in Spanish with Minor in Management.
Home country and L1	In principal, students are most likely to be from any Caribbean Community (CARICOM) country that contributes to the regional UWI, as this comprises the vast majority of the regularly enrolled UWI student population. At the Cave Hill Campus, most students in the Spanish programme are from Barbados, with a significant minority from other Eastern Caribbean territories such as Saint Lucia or Saint Vincent and the Grenadines. Students therefore typically speak a Creole or *nation language* as L1 and standard English as L2.
Previous language-learning/ Pre-departure proficiency	Though students from a variety of levels may travel with the group and take the multilevel UIMP Spanish Language and Culture course, those eligible to take UWI elective 'Immersion for Languages' are required to have reached level B2i according to the Common European Frame of Reference (the 'i' in fact designates an intermediate point within the B2 level, determined by the *Aula Internacional* textbook series, which so divides that level and is used in the Cave Hill Campus's Bachelor of Arts in Spanish).
Preparation, institutional support, debriefing, follow-up.	'Immersion for Languages' entails two 12-hour face-to-face workshops, one prior to departure and the other on return to maximise intercultural learning. Throughout the sojourn, students submit journal entries and receive feedback online (face-to-face discussion with the UWI tutor is included if, as with 'UWI in Spain 2016', s/he travels with the group). The UWI and the UIMP have a common member of staff, giving the UWI group at UIMP a familiar point of institutional contact in-sojourn.

Assessment	**Module One:** **Pre-departure Class participation, 5%:** class discussions, group activity, role-playing. **Online participation, 5%:** two evaluated posts to forums in the following areas: 1. Intercultural concepts 2. Online press and media for my destination—expectations and surprises. **Reading quizzes, 5%:** formative online quizzes to evaluate understanding of readings. **Module Two: In-country Online portfolio, 40%:** min. 1200 words per week of sojourn; min. 800 words in English, 400 in foreign language (can be adjusted to accommodate different levels of language competence). For example: 3-week sojourn = total journal 3600 words, 2400 in English, 1200 in Spanish To include report and reflection on the following intercultural activities: 1. Finding New Partners: total of four in-country encounters with potential partners for future collaboration with UWI students. 2. Free Explorations: total of four in-country experiences to include: interactions with host nationals through UIMP *Café de las Lenguas* or *Hablamos* intercultural spaces; going to church; a shopping trip; a tourist experience; or approved alternatives. Audiovisual material and relevant links may also be added to the portfolio, which can be used to make the learning experience visible to potential employers and collaborators. **Module Three: Return Class participation, 5%:** presentation, discussion, reflection on intercultural component of sojourn. **Final oral interview in foreign language, 40%:** 10- to 15-minute summative interview simulating interview for post at source-country Latin American embassy.
Type of group (if any)	N/A

(continued)

(continued)

Facet	'UWI in Spain 2016'
Host country and L2 • Institutional L2 • Societal L2 (s)	Spain, Spanish • Spanish and English. UIMP has a predominantly international summer student body. • Spanish, English in interaction with tourists and other temporary sojourners.
Accommodation type, shared with…	The UIMP course offers on-campus shared or single rooms, or homestay. While the latter offers greater intercultural challenge and therefore potential for learning, higher cost is likely to be a decisive inhibiting factor in uptake (personal preference for greater autonomy was also cited at the focus group) and in turn will likely determine that shared rooms will be the preferred (because the cheapest) option (as in the pilot in 2012, though not all students shared with co-national/regional fellow travellers).
Host university courses (if any) • language courses • non-language courses • courses taught by…	UIMP Spanish Language and Culture course. 100 hours over 1 month, intensive (5 hours per day), small group (eight to ten maximum) classes and cultural excursions, taught by Spanish university lecturers from a variety of origins (Universidad Internacional Menéndez Pelayo, 2016).

Appendix B

Adaptation of the *Student's Guide for Maximizing Study Abroad* (Paige et al., 2006) for Use by Anglophone Caribbean Sojourners

Section	Pp	Qu.1[a]	Qu.2[a]	Action	Description/Rationale for action
Welcome to Study Abroad	1–3	4.8	4.8	Supplement	General welcome to the text; note 'there are numerous examples of "ugly travelers" (and not just Americans), whose lack of cultural sensitivity makes them instantly recognisable in an unpleasant sort of way'. Discuss examples of both insensitive Caribbean travellers elsewhere and insensitive travellers in the Caribbean.
General Departure Tips	4–7	4.0	4.4	Supplement	Address dietary needs specifically, bearing in mind tutor knowledge of Spanish/Cantabrian diet, availability of specific products (e.g. 'you may wish to take a couple of bottles of pepper sauce'). 'Visibility and Invisibility' (p. 6) addressed at Student Focus Group.
Terms Used in this Guide	8	2.6	2.8	Retain	Short glossary, necessary for navigating the *Guide*.
Introduction: Culture-Learning Strategies	39	3.8	4.0	Retain	Posits culture-general advice on steering a course between spontaneity and caution.
The Dimensions of Culture Learning	40–42	3.6	3.4	Supplement	Use Caribbean reentry testimony from Craig (2010), and video interview sources of same, to supplement US reentry account on pp. 41–42.
Pre-Departure Culture Strategies Part I: What is culture, anyway?	43	3.2	3.2	Retain	General introduction to broader concept of culture used in intercultural development.

(continued)

(continued)

Section	Pp	Qu.1[a]	Qu.2[a]	Action	Description/Rationale for action
You as a Culturally Diverse Person	43–46	4.0	4.0	Adapt	Substitute '(a) US American' and 'the roles you play in the USA' with 'a Caribbean/[nationality] person', 'the roles you play in your home country or the country where you study'.
Becoming Familiar with Culture: The Iceberg Analogy	46–51	4.4	3.8	Supplement	Use student diaries from Colombia and France to find Caribbean sojourner account of resolving a challenge to supplement analysis of Joshua's story used to illustrate the iceberg analogy of cultural difference (Craig, 2010).
Differentiating Cultural from Personal and Universal	52–54	3.8	3.5	Retain	This section works through how to distinguish between these important categories of preference and behaviour, primarily using a narrative example involving a US student in Mexico.
Some Strategies for Culture-Specific Learning	54–56	4.6	4.2	Supplement	Note: 'Many find themselves intimidated by the knowledge people from other countries have not only about their own politics, history and culture, but also about US American politics and culture.' This assertion might introduce, by way of contrast, the concept of the 'anonymity' of Caribbean sojourners overseas (Craig, 2010).
Working with Stereotypes and Testing Hypotheses	57–60	4.8	4.2	Supplement	Use region-specific materials such as Cave Hill student-orientation micro-aggression exercise to address intra-regional stereotyping. This exercise used at an orientation for incoming students in 2015 generated a 'micro-aggression tree' harvesting such remarks as 'all Guyanese is steal', 'you speak like you "from foreign"' and 'You sure you from the Bahamas? You too bright…'

Topic	Pages			Action	Notes
Using Generalisations to Respond to Stereotypes about You	60–61	3.8	3.0	Replace	Use Craig (2010) to explore extra-regional responses to Caribbean SA sojourners. Also use TripAdvisor analysis exercise to infer expectations of visitors to Caribbean tourist destinations regarding the behaviour of 'locals'.
Pre-Departure Culture Strategies Part II: Understanding the Ways Cultures Can Differ in Values	63	4.0	4.0	Adapt	Short section on the sojourn as an opportunity to see yourself the way others see you. Substitute 'US American cultural values' with 'your own country's cultural values'.
Core Cultural Values: The Key to Understanding Culture	63–67	4.6	4.8	Retain	Asks students to identify their own self-perceived cultural values across nine spectra, such as Individualism-Collectivism, Meritocracy-Ascription and so forth.
Activity: Culture mapping	67–68	3.8	4.0	Adapt	Asks students to reflect on their own country's cultural values. Substitute 'US American values' and 'US Americans' with 'your country's values' and 'your co-nationals'. Use Spanish *lectora* as consultant for 'Assessing Host Culture Values for Further Comparison'.
Activity: Core US American cultural values: What the experts say	68–70	3.4	2.0	Replace	Extract from and craft discussion around Anglophone Caribbean cultural values bibliography (Punnett et al., 2014).

(continued)

(continued)

Section	Pp	Qu.1[a]	Qu.2[a]	Action	Description/Rationale for action
International Perspectives on US Americans	71–73	2.6	2.6	Replace	1. Have prospective students conduct research interviews with English as a Second Language students sojourning at Cave Hill (for 2016, from Ecuador and Panama) on their experiences and perceptions of Eastern Caribbean nationals and Barbadian society. 2. Use Craig (2010) to address 'anonymity' of Caribbean sojourners in many settings; use original video testimony of subjects of this study, having secured their permission.
Experiencing Value Differences	73–74	4.4	4.6	Retain	Short section exemplifying value orientations across areas such as privacy, independence, gender and sexual orientation, family commitment.
A few key points to wrap up the chapter	74–75	4.6	4.0	Retain	Short recap of chapter

[a]Figures in the columns labelled 'Qu.1' and 'Qu.2' refer to the average rating out of five given to the section by the five student testers in answer to the following two questions: 'Qu.1. How interesting and engaging do you find this section?' 'Qu.2. How directly does it speak to you personally as a student?'; with 5 = maximum: 'the section was very interesting and engaging/seems to be speaking to a student just like me'; 1 = minimum: 'the section was pretty dull/seems to be speaking to someone quite different from me'

Notes

1. The Minnesota Model of curriculum integration for SA entails a process of institutional interventions designed to optimise access to and quality of SA programmes, developed by the UMN. The process includes embedding SA into academic advising mechanisms, comprehensive institutional education and information dissemination strategies, dismantling of misconceptions regarding whom SA is for and an actively inclusive approach to increasing diversity among SA participants (Anderson, 2005). Its application at other US universities is assessed in Parcells (2011). One obvious structural deviation from the pedagogical model advocated by UMN in the case of Immersion for Languages is the current lack of a pre- and post-test for intercultural sensitivity or competence. While the public-access approach adopted by Shadowen, Chieffo and Guerra (2015) makes their Global Engagement Measurement Scale more appealing in the current circumstances than Hammer's (2009) better known Intercultural Development Inventory, a solely qualitative approach initially prevails in the case of Immersion for Languages. Longitudinal tracking of sojourners will be a significant component of ongoing efforts, the relative ease and impact of which is an advantage of the small-state context (Craig, 2016).
2. My sincere gratitude goes to the following colleagues, from the UWI and beyond, who offered their time and expertise to assist in enhancing Immersion for Languages: Paula González, Shari Inniss-Grant, Therese James, Aaron Kamugisha, Latoya Lazarus, Betty-Jane Punnett, Angela Trotman and Michael Vande Berg.
3. As Punnett, Dick-Forde and Robinson (Punnett et al., 2014) point out, the tendency towards authoritarian modes of organisational behaviour in Anglophone Caribbean societies may in fact be at odds with a countervailing democratic and inclusive impulse that seems to be increasingly widespread. Viewed in this nuanced way, authority dependency and hierarchical dominance can be seen merely as ultimately superficial colonial remnants, rather than cultural values as such. The emancipatory potential of this aspect of the sojourn might be seen as parallel to the recreations of self by Japanese women in *looser* Anglophone environments in Piller and Takahashi (2006) and Skarin (2001), or by some Canadians in Germany in Plews (2015, p. 299).

Bibliography

Allahar, A. (2005). Situating ethnic nationalism in the Caribbean. In A. Allahar (Ed.), *Ethnicity, class, and nationalism: Caribbean and extra-Caribbean dimensions* (pp. 1–22). Lanham, MD: Lexington Books.

Anderson, L. C. (Ed.). (2005). *Internationalizing undergraduate education: Integrating study abroad into the curriculum*. Minneapolis, MN: Learning Abroad Center, Office for International Programs, University of Minnesota.

Anya, U. (2017). *Racialized identities in second language learning: speaking Blackness in Brazil*. New York: Routledge.

Arneaud, M. J., & Aibada, N. A. (2013). Identity development in the Caribbean: Measuring socio-historic structures with psychological variables. *Revista Interamericana de Psicología, 47*(2), 339–346.

Beckles, H., Perry, A. M., & Whiteley, P. (2002). *The brain train: Quality higher education and Caribbean development*. Kingston, Jamaica: The University of the West Indies.

Block, D. (2007). The rise of identity in SLA research, post Firth and Wagner (1997). *Modern Language Journal, 91*, 863–876. https://doi.org/10.1111/j.1540-4781.2007.00674.x

Boodhoo, Y. R. (1988). *Career maturity and locus of control orientation in Jamaican high school students*. Gainesville, FL: University of Florida. Retrieved from http://archive.org/details/careermaturitylo00bood

Boruff, B. J., & Cutter, S. L. (2007). The environmental vulnerability of Caribbean Island Nations. *Geographical Review, 97*(1), 24–45. https://doi.org/10.1111/j.19310846.2007.tb00278.x

Bray, M. (2011). The small states paradigm and its evolution. In M. Martin & M. Bray (Eds.), *Tertiary education in small states: Planning in the context of globalization* (pp. 37–72). Paris: UNESCO Publishing; International Institute for Educational Planning.

Claassen Thrush, E., & Victorino, C. (2016). Providing study abroad opportunities for underrepresented populations: Lessons from the University of California, Riverside. In D. M. Velliaris & D. Coleman-George (Eds.), *Handbook of research on study abroad programs and outbound mobility* (pp. 115–136). Hershey, PA: Information Science Reference.

Coleman, J. A. (2013). Researching whole people and whole lives. In C. Kinginger (Ed.), *Social and cultural aspects of language learning in study abroad* (pp. 17–44). Amsterdam: John Benjamins. Retrieved from https://benjamins.com/catalog/lllt.37.02col

Cox, A. (2015, April 9). Enrolment woes for UWI Cave Hill. *The Barbados Advocate*, sec. Local. Retrieved from http://www.barbadosadvocate.com/newsitem.asp?more=local&NewsID=42724

Craig, I. (2010). Anonymous sojourners: Mapping the territory of Caribbean experiences of immersion for language learning. *Frontiers: The Interdisciplinary Journal of Study Abroad, 19*, 125–149.

Craig, I. (2016). Overseas sojourning as a socioeconomic and cultural development strategy: A context study of the University of the West Indies. *Study Abroad Research for Second Language Acquisition and International Education, 1*(1), 277–304.

Dass, A. (2015). Report on recent UWI first degree graduate experience beyond graduation—A comparative analysis of four tracer surveys conducted in 2009, 2010, 2011 and 2013 for UWI campuses (Draft Report—Revised August 2013). Kingston, Jamaica: The University of the West Indies.

Department of Language, Linguistics and Literature. (2015). Spanish Immersion Programme. Retrieved from http://www.cavehill.uwi.edu/fhe/LLL/spanish-immersionprogramme.aspx

Dewey, J. (1938). *Experience and education*. New York: Macmillan.

Engle, J., & Engle, L. (2002). Neither international nor educative: Study abroad in the time of globalization. In W. Grünzweig & N. Rinehart (Eds.), *Rockin' in Red Square: Critical approaches to international education in the age of cyberculture* (pp. 25–40). Münster: Lit. Verlag.

Fobes, C. (2005). Taking a critical pedagogical look at travel-study abroad: A classroom with a view in Cusco, Peru. *Teaching Sociology, 33*(2), 181–194. https://doi.org/10.1177/0092055X0503300205

Freire, P. (2000). *Pedagogy of the oppressed*. New York: Continuum.

George, J., & Lewis, T. (2011). Exploring the global/local boundary in education in developing countries: The case of the Caribbean. *Compare: A Journal of Comparative and International Education, 41*(6), 721–734. https://doi.org/10.1080/03057925.2011.579712

Gore, J. E. (2005). *Dominant beliefs and alternative voices: Discourse, belief, and gender in American study abroad*. New York: Routledge.

Gruenewald, D. A. (2003). The best of both worlds: A critical pedagogy of place. *Educational Researcher, 32*(4), 3–12. https://doi.org/10.3102/0013189X032004003

Hall, S. (2001). Negotiating Caribbean identities. In B. Meeks & F. Lindahl (Eds.), *New Caribbean thought: A reader* (pp. 24–39). Kingston, Jamaica: University of the West Indies Press.

Hammer, M. R. (2009). The intercultural development inventory: An approach for assessing and building intercultural competence. In M. A. Moodian (Ed.), *Contemporary leadership and intercultural competence: Exploring the cross-cultural dynamics within organizations* (pp. 203–217). Los Angeles: Sage.

Haymes, S. N. (1995). *Race, culture, and the city: A pedagogy for Black urban struggle*. Albany, NY: State University of New York Press.

Kamugisha, A. (2007). The coloniality of citizenship in the contemporary anglophone Caribbean. *Race & Class, 49*(2), 20–40. https://doi.org/10.1177/0306396807082856

Kappler Mikk, B., Cohen, A. D., Paige, R. M., Meagher, M., Weaver, S. J., Chi, J. C., et al. (2009). *Maximizing study abroad: An instructional guide to strategies for language and culture learning and use*. Minneapolis, MN: Center for Advanced Research on Language Acquisition, University of Minnesota.

Kim, Y. Y. (1988). *Communication and cross-cultural adaptation: An integrative theory*. Clevedon, UK: Multilingual Matters.

Kim, Y. Y. (2001). *Becoming intercultural: An integrative theory of communication and cross-cultural adaptation*. Thousand Oaks, CA: Sage.

Kinginger, C. (Ed.). (2013). *Social and cultural aspects of language learning in study abroad*. Amsterdam: Benjamins.

Kolb, D. A. (1984). *Experiential learning: Experience as the source of learning and development*. Englewood Cliffs, NJ: Prentice-Hall.

Louisy, D. P. (2004). Whose context for what quality? Informing education strategies for the Caribbean. *Compare: A Journal of Comparative Education, 34*(3), 285–292. https://doi.org/10.1080/0305792042000257121

Lutterman-Aguila, A., & Gingerich, O. (2002). Experiential pedagogy for study abroad: Educating for global citizenship. *Frontiers: The Interdisciplinary Journal of Study Abroad, 8*, 41–82.

Marshall, D., Bailey, C., Lashley, J., Lazarus, L., Lord, K., & Smith, J. (2017). *Barbados at 50: National values assessment 2016*. Bridgetown: Sir Arthur Lewis Institute of Social and Economic Studies, University of the West Indies, Cave Hill Campus.

Maruri Villanueva, R. (1987). Santander a finales del Antiguo Régimen: Cambio social y cambio de mentalidades. La burguesía mercantil, 1770–1850. Santander, Spain: Universidad de Cantabria. Retrieved from https://dialnet.unirioja.es/servlet/tesis?codigo=22432

McLeod, M., Carter, V., Nowicki, S., Tottenham, D., Wainwright, P., & Wyner, D. (2015). Evaluating the study abroad experience using the framework of Rotter's social learning theory. *Frontiers: The Interdisciplinary Journal of Study Abroad, 26*, 30–38.

Mezulis, A. H., Abramson, L. Y., Hyde, J. S., & Hankin, B. L. (2004). Is there a universal positivity bias in attributions? A meta-analytic review of individual, developmental, and cultural differences in the self-serving attributional bias. *Psychological Bulletin, 130*(5), 711–747. https://doi.org/10.1037/0033-2909.130.5.711

Mitchell, R., Tracy-Ventura, N., & McManus, K. (2017). *Anglophone students abroad: Identity, social relationships and language learning.* New York: Routledge.

Mukherjee, R. (2011). Bling fling: Commodity consumption and the politics of the 'Post-Racial'. In M. G. Lacy & K. A. Ono (Eds.), *Critical rhetorics of race* (pp. 178–94). New York: New York University Press. Retrieved from http://www.jstor.org/stable/j.ctt9qg0mg

Mullens, J. B., & Cuper, P. H. (2012). *Fostering global citizenship through faculty-led international programs.* Charlotte, NC: Information Age Pub.

Nero, S. (2006). Language, identity, and education of Caribbean English speakers. *World Englishes, 25*(3–4), 501–511. https://doi.org/10.1111/j.1467-971X.2006.00470.x

Ogden, A. (2007). The view from the veranda: Understanding today's colonial student. *Frontiers, 15,* 35–55.

Paige, R. M., Cohen, A. D., Kappler, B., Chi, J. C., & Lassegard, J. P. (2006). *Maximizing study abroad: A student's guide to strategies for language and culture learning and use.* Minneapolis, MN: Center for Advanced Research on Language Acquisition, University of Minnesota.

Paige, R. M., Harvey, T. A., & McCleary, K. S. (2012). The maximizing study abroad project: Towards a pedagogy for culture and language learning. In M. Vande Berg, R. M. Paige, & K. H. Lou (Eds.), *Student learning abroad: What our students are learning, what they're not, and what we can do about it* (pp. 281–303). Sterling, VA: Stylus Publishing, LLC.

Parcells, C. (2011). Institutional case studies of curriculum integration practices based upon the University of Minnesota model. Retrieved from http://global.umn.edu/icc/documents/institutional_case_studies.pdf

Piller, I., & Takahashi, K. (2006). A passion for English: Desire and the language market. In A. Pavelenko (Ed.), *Bilingual minds: Emotional experience, expression, and representation* (pp. 59–83). Clevedon, UK: Multilingual Matters.

Plews, J. L. (2015). Intercultural identity-alignment in second language study abroad, or the more-or-less Canadians. In R. Mitchell, N. Tracy-Ventura, & K. McManus (Eds.), *Social interaction, identity and language learning during residence abroad* (pp. 281–304). EuroSLA Monographs 4. Retrieved from http://www.eurosla.org/eurosla-monograph-series-2/social-interaction-identity-and-language-learning-during-residence-abroad/

Punnett, B. J. (2004). *International perspectives on organizational behavior and human resource management*. Armonk, NY: M. E. Sharpe.

Punnett, B. J., Dick-Forde, E., & Robinson, J. (2014). *Cultural values and the CSME*. St. Augustine, Trinidad and Tobago: Sir Arthur Lewis Institute of Social and Economic Studies. Retrieved from http://sta.uwi.edu/salises/workshop/papers/bpunnett.pdf

Savicki, V. (2013). The effects of affect on study abroad students. *Frontiers: The Interdisciplinary Journal of Study Abroad, 22*, 131–147.

Shadowen, N. L., Chieffo, L. P., & Guerra, N. G. (2015). The global engagement measurement scale (GEMS): A new scale for assessing the impact of education abroad and campus internationalization. *Frontiers: The Interdisciplinary Journal of Study Abroad, 26*, 231–247.

Shor, I. (1987). *Freire for the classroom: A sourcebook for liberatory teaching*. Portsmouth, NH: Boynton/Cook.

Skarin, R. (2001). Gender, ethnicity, class and social identity: A case study of two Japanese women in US universities. In E. Churchill & J. McLaughlin (Eds.), *Qualitative research in applied linguistics: Japanese learners and contexts* (pp. 26–55). Tokyo: Temple University.

Tremlett, G. (2008, December 18). Spain removes last Franco statue from mainland. *The Guardian*, sec. World news. Retrieved from http://www.theguardian.com/world/2008/dec/18/franco-statue-spain

Turespaña. (2016). Visit Santander: Walk around the City. Spain.info in English. *Spain.info*. Retrieved from http://www.spain.info/en/reportajes/santander_tranquila_y_senorial.html

Universidad Internacional Menéndez Pelayo. (2016). Spanish language and culture—UIMP. Retrieved from http://www.uimp.es/en/academic-activities/spanish-courses/spanish-language-and-culture-courses/spanish-language-and-culture.html

University Office of Planning and Development. (2012). *The University of the West Indies strategic plan 2012–2017*. University of the West Indies. Retrieved from http://www.uwi.edu/Libraries/PlanningDocs/UWI_Strategic_Plan_20122017_Final.sflb.ashx

Wells, R. (2006). Nontraditional study abroad destinations: Analysis of a trend. *Frontiers: The Interdisciplinary Journal of Study Abroad, 13*, 113–133.

Wigglesworth, R. (2013, December 16). Caribbean blown by winds of financial crisis. *Financial Times*. Retrieved from http://www.ft.com/intl/cms/s/2/ead62cda-60ec-11e3-b7f1-00144feabdc0.html#axzz3fV7ZHtGP

Willis, T. Y. (2015). 'And still we rise ...': Micro-aggressions and intersectionality in the study abroad experiences of Black women. *Frontiers: The Interdisciplinary Journal of Study Abroad, 26*, 209–230.

Wong, E. D. (2015). Beyond 'It was great'? Not so fast! A response to the argument that study abroad results are disappointing and that intervention is necessary to promote students' intercultural competence. *Frontiers: The Interdisciplinary Journal of Study Abroad, 26*, 121–135.

Young, R. (2001). *Postcolonialism: An historical introduction.* Oxford: Blackwell Publishers.

Part II

Pedagogical Approaches

Student Awareness of Teaching and Learning Approaches in Second Language Study Abroad

John L. Plews, Kim Misfeldt, and Feisal Kirumira

Introduction

We explore second language (L2) students' awareness of various teaching and learning approaches used in study abroad (SA). Considered most fundamentally, L2 SA aims to provide students with an opportunity to acquire a given target language in an environment where it is spoken as a first language (L1). This learning opportunity, especially from a North American perspective, often includes both residence abroad and classes

---

J. L. Plews (✉)
Saint Mary's University, Halifax, NS, Canada
e-mail: jplews@smu.ca

K. Misfeldt
Fine Arts and Humanities, University of Alberta, Camrose, AB, Canada
e-mail: kim.misfeldt@ualberta.ca

F. Kirumira
University of Alberta, Camrose, AB, Canada
e-mail: kirumira@ualberta.ca

© The Author(s) 2018
J. L. Plews, K. Misfeldt (eds.), *Second Language Study Abroad*,
https://doi.org/10.1007/978-3-319-77134-2_5

taught by accompanying and/or local instructors. Thus, language teaching—and not only being abroad—is at the heart of SA.

Various aspects of SA education have received some attention in SA research and scholarship (see Isabelli-García, Bown, Plews, & Dewey, Forthcoming; Plews & Misfeldt, the current volume), including classroom teaching. For example, it has been observed that host cultural norms are likely present in the classroom in a foreign educational domain, creating a perhaps unanticipated difference for students (Bacon, 2002; Brecht & Robinson, 1995; Churchill, 2006; Kinginger, 2004; Pellegrino Aveni, 2005; Polanyi, 1995). Yet despite such good work, topics related to the SA classroom and especially teaching in SA continue to receive comparatively short shrift. As Lafford and Collentine (2006, p. 111) remark, 'The lack of information on the type of instruction that takes place in the SA contexts constitutes the weakest aspect of the study of study-abroad research. For the most part, researchers have not examined the effects of different types of teaching methodologies on acquisition abroad'. Indeed, most often when describing linguistic, intercultural, and other outcomes in the immersion context, SA research does so regardless of teaching and pedagogy (for N. American examples, see Chieffo & Griffiths, 2004; Franklin, 2010; Kinginger, 2010; Pitts, 2009). Sometimes, it even compares the results of at-home (AH), formal language learning with SA linguistic outcomes, still with few or no details of the pedagogical approach in either location (e.g., Collentine, 2004; Cubillos, Chieffo, & Fan, 2008; Dekeyser, 2007; Freed, So, & Lazar, 2003; Sasaki, 2007; Segalowitz & Freed, 2004; Segalowitz et al., 2004; and chapters in part II of Pérez-Vidal, 2014a). Given the lack of detail about teaching and pedagogy in SA research, one can only assume that L2 SA courses, especially those in the common 'island programmes', resemble AH language classes except for being in an immersion environment (Freed, Segalowitz, & Dewey, 2004; Selby, 2008; Talburt & Stewart, 1999; Wilkinson, 2002). This might mean the continuation of form-based approaches (Andon & Wingate, 2013; Byrnes, 1998; Plews, 2013), with language use and authentic meaning-making reserved for the immersion context outside the classroom; Tschirner's (2007) task-, genre-, and project-based immersion course for American teachers of German is a notable exception. Pérez-Vidal (2014b, pp. 21-6) and Sanz (2014, p. 5) acknowledge that programme design is an influential factor in SA L2 acquisition, but also list a series of individual human qualities and individual, social, and programme factors without mentioning what is happening in the SA classroom or teaching specifically. DeKeyser (2014, p. 314) repeatedly highlights students' individual responsibility for their own learning in SA, referring to whether they are 'able and willing to engage in the right learning behaviors while overseas', their 'aptitude, [and] learning behavior', and 'their preparation', which he categorises as 'extremely limited'; in considering the effectiveness of the hosting environment, DeKeyser (2014, p. 317) again places the responsibility for learning, or not learning, on students and their 'initial ability [...] to engage native speakers in the target language, an ability that depends in turn not only on the [students'] personality, but also on initial levels of knowledge and skill in the second language'. DeKeyser, too, does not consider how SA programme directors and instructors can and do intervene in the students' learning processes in these situations by means of teaching as planned and performed. However, without knowing what is taking place pedagogically in the SA classroom (whether at a specialist language programme or a content course at a local, foreign educational institution), how students respond emotionally and cognitively to the instruction, or the relationship between classroom teaching and learning and the lived experience of SA beyond the classroom, we know at best only half the story about language learning in SA.

Thus, in the current chapter, we turn our attention to teaching in SA. Specifically, we are interested in whether students notice a relationship between the instructional approaches used in a SA programme and their personal sense of, and commitment to, language learning and development, or whether the immersion context alone features in their narratives of learning. That is, we are interested in whether the SA classroom teaching works in engaging the students to the extent that they can use it to leverage learning in the immersion environment, vice versa, or both. If students credit the immersion environment alone for their learning, then certainly all extant SA research outcomes are more than justified (and SA teaching would be rather futile). If they attend to and respond (favourably) to teaching in the SA, then teaching clearly plays a role and the field likely requires research methods with broader credibility—such as would include greater details about the SA classroom—in order to make claims about learning outcomes. We thus explore student awareness, appraisal, and buy-in or embrace of two specific approaches that we introduced in L2 SA courses as they express their lived experience of them; these were drama pedagogy and task-based language teaching (TBLT).

Much like the SA classroom, student awareness of teaching approaches per se is much under-researched; this, in spite of Block's (2000, p. 98) call for greater attention to what he terms 'meta-pedagogical awareness' or when language learners '[act] as educational theorists analysing and evaluating what they have experienced as an instance of pedagogy'. Schmidt (1990, 1993, 2010) examines the role of noticing regarding language-learning input and grammar structures but does not mention learners' awareness of teaching approaches. Garrett and Young (2009) investigate learners' experience of and affective responses to language learning; they describe one or two activities, but there is no intentional focus on awareness of methods or approaches despite their conclusion that 'in particular, [foreign language learners'] responses to events in the classroom are an under-researched area' (p. 224). Muñoz (2014) explores young learners' awareness of foreign language learning and learning conditions, but also does not focus on approaches. Cook (2001) focusses on the awareness of teaching styles and second language acquisition research on those teaching styles from the teacher's perspective, but not from the student's. Andon and Eckerth (2009) study four English as a second language (ESL) teachers and their use of TLBT, or lack thereof, reviewing what teachers believe they are doing, what they think they are doing, and also what they are observed to be doing. Hawkey (2006) researches whether learners' perceptions of the frequency of various classroom activities are the same as those of teachers. He found differences in the rankings of activities such as pair discussions and grammar exercises, but his scope does not extend to approaches or the perception of an activity's contribution to learning. Cotterall (2004) follows a student (Harry) through a university-level beginner Spanish course to examine the points at which the learner took control of his learning process. Her interviews with Harry provide the unfortunate evidence 'that the [Spanish] course carried with it a powerful set of assumptions about the respective roles of teachers and learners, which indicated that goal setting was not the domain of learners' (Cotterall, 2004, p. 117); Harry's personal learning goals diminished and the course goals took precedence. Cotterall concludes that 'learners' contribution to the curriculum—in terms of goals, interest, and effort—must be not only acknowledged but also utilised in order for the classroom experience to be meaningful' (p. 118). Barkhuizen (1998) reports on high school ESL learners' perceptions of language teaching/learning activities. He discovers that the activities that teachers think students like and want are not the ones that students say they like and want. Once again the focus is on the judgement of the activity and not on the awareness of the teaching approach or its relation to individual language development. Our study differs from the aforementioned since our focus is on students' awareness of teaching approaches and how they relate them to their own learning, for, as Block (2000, p. 117) maintains, 'if the learner is to be truly self-regulatory, he/she will have to develop not only meta-cognitive knowledge, but also meta-social knowledge [which subsumes] meta-pedagogical awareness'. We thus take up Block's (2000) and Barkhuizen's (1998, p. 85) challenge and attempt to make amends for the fact 'that language learners are hardly ever asked in any overt systematic way about their language learning experiences'.

In the following, we describe the context of our enquiry and the nature of drama-pedagogical and task-based approaches for teaching Canadian undergraduate students L2 German in a SA programme in Germany. We then outline our qualitative enquiry of the Canadian Summer School in Germany (CSSG) and present findings that we believe capture the breadth and depth of student awareness of the instructional approaches used in the SA classroom as well as the personal conclusions or implications they draw from this awareness. We conclude the chapter with recommendations concerning optimal approaches for L2 SA based on student awareness of teaching.

Context: The CSSG

The context of the current enquiry is a short-term SA programme. Since 1973, the Canadian Association of University Teachers of German has offered an undergraduate German language immersion programme in Kassel, Germany. Now known as the CSSG, this programme takes place for six and a half weeks in May and June every year. The programme blends a 3-day in-country orientation, intensive language and culture instruction by Canadian and German professors and instructors, homestay with experienced host families, cultural, social, and sporting events, and day-long and overnight study trips to cultural and historical sites. The CSSG routinely offers three levels of instruction: 'Intermediate German' (considered equivalent to a second-year North American undergraduate course, or A2–B1), 'Lower Advanced German' (a third-year course, or B1+–B2), and 'Upper Advanced German' (a fourth-year course, or B2+–C1). In recent years, a Community Service Learning course has also been offered to former participants only. Students have four hours of instruction every morning from Monday to Friday plus consultation hours for assistance in the afternoons. The curriculum is based in part on the findings of three surveys (Fordham, 2004, 2008; Misfeldt, personal communication, Jan. 17, 2016) regarding course content, requirements, and teaching materials in all Canadian universities offering German. As CSSG students come from universities across Canada, it is crucial that they achieve the level of language proficiency to allow them to continue their study of German upon returning to their home university.

The CSSG is an *island programme* in that the students all study at Canadian universities—that is, usually 20 or more—and the majority of students are Canadian, though each year there are also participants who are enrolled as international students at Canadian universities. Similarly, the teaching team is also mostly faculty and graduate students from Canadian universities. Certainly, among the potential risks to the legitimacy of such a programme as genuinely SA are (1) that the Canadian faculty members would simply import traditional Canadian university classroom teaching into the foreign setting and (2) that the students would remain unto themselves. Conscious of these possible weaknesses, the leadership team have implemented structural elements to guarantee a different educational experience and to integrate students more fully into the German host culture. There is a diverse teaching team in terms of cultural and ethnic backgrounds, language speaker identities (e.g., German L1 speakers, German L2 speakers, German heritage speakers, and German-other language bilinguals), and professional training histories. Before departure, the students sign a German-only language policy agreement not only for instruction but also for all cultural, social, and administrative aspects of the programme; this is accompanied by a reward system by which students vote each week for the class peer who has spoken German outside the classroom most consistently. The orientation—which necessarily takes place in Germany because the students come from all parts of Canada—is conducted entirely in German in order to habituate the students immediately to learning and living in the L2. Assignments across all levels regularly involve conscious and reflective interaction with the host families and other members of the local community. The programme uses only German-authored and published language textbooks with significant local cultural contextualisation and, whenever possible, not commonly used by colleagues in Canada. The CSSG students are paired with local German university students as part of a tandem partner project. This project was initiated bilaterally to give the Canadian and German students the opportunity to practise their respective L2 outside the classroom as well as to provide the Canadian students a view into German university life. As the current chapter will explore, the teaching approaches also play a key role in encouraging the students to engage with the language and culture differently from how they typically do in their AH foreign language classes (as well as not to interact with and rely on their compatriots exclusively).

The majority of CSSG students have not spent significant time in another country before arriving at the programme in Germany. Indeed, many have never previously left Canada before taking the programme. Not only do they learn German and come to know what it is like to live in a L2, but through the cultural aspects of the classes, homestay, and excursions their eyes are also opened to an array of cultural issues concerning Germany's past and present; this often allows them to see Canadian issues more clearly too and develop understandings of self and others. Throughout the 45 years of the CSSG, the directors, teachers, and host families have worked together to make the programme a constructive and meaningful learning experience for the students. In that time, the CSSG has contributed to a deeper understanding of German language and culture among over 2400 Canadian and international students; many students and host families stay in touch long after the sojourn, and lifelong friendships develop among students, faculty, and host families.

Innovative Teaching Approaches

As mentioned above, we introduced drama pedagogy and TBLT in various courses at the CSSG. Briefly, these approaches were chosen over traditional form-based, structural-analytical instruction in order to place students' developing sense of subjective, affective, and creative ownership of the L2 and their learning process as a primary curriculum goal. It is widely accepted that these genuinely communicative and functional-notional approaches lead optimally to L2 development and advancedness (Belliveau & Kim, 2013; Van den Branden, Bygate, & Norris, 2009).

Drama Pedagogy

Drama pedagogy, or performative teaching, effectively challenges students to become engaged in language learning through embodied experience, which involves students on intellectual, emotional, and physical levels. According to Even (2011), drama pedagogy makes extensive use of one of the most fundamental elements of drama: the dialogue. Students act and react spontaneously in staged situations, using both intellectual faculties as well as kinaesthetics and body language, namely, facial expressions, gestures, modulations of voice, movement, and so forth. Schewe (1993), an early proponent of drama pedagogy for the L2 classroom, values highly the holistic nature of this approach, for as he notes, 'We teach and learn a language with head, heart, hands, and feet!' (pp. 7–8; our translation). In collaboration with each other, students construct characters, develop situations, and change the course of action. The unforeseen nature of dramatic improvisations holds their attention, gives them ownership, and promotes intense engagement with the unfolding plot. The classroom becomes a forum for language learners to develop their own voices, invent their own personae, and adopt their own attitudes towards given situations. This differs substantially from the traditional role play of language classrooms in that a progression of activities allows the students to develop a deeper interest in the situations and personae than, for example, if they are simply told *now you are in a store and these are the things you want to buy*. Kinaesthetic, social, and empathic learning moments make for intensive and lasting language-learning experiences that go far beyond the stilted dialogues of traditional textbooks (Even, 2011).

Even (2011) posits that drama grammar is both content- and skill-oriented. Through performing arts techniques, grammar is put onto the classroom stage, and the fictionality of the dramatic context serves as a secure environment for learners to try out combinations of words, gestures, and movements in a collaborative effort to drive the action forward. Learners' cognitive, social, practical, and kinaesthetic potentials are brought to the fore, and the freedom to be someone else affords new perspectives and can be an effective outlet for creativity and imagination. According to Even (2011), drama-based teaching and learning involves five stages: the awareness-raising, context-finding, linguistic, dramatic play, and presentation phases. Drama pedagogy strips away the abstract conceptualisation of language learning as a purely cognitive process and exposes the pre-existing yet emergent nature of language. Students experience language learning as a juxtaposition of vulnerability, adventure, joy, and connectedness. During drama-pedagogical simulations students encounter the feelings and moods of others in themselves and can re-enter multiple identities from different vantage points, thereby rediscovering their identity as juxtaposed with others' and creating the foundation for real-life bonding with others. This continuous revisiting of languages, identities, and lifeworlds facilitates a deeper awareness of self/otherness. Consequently, by using drama pedagogy, instructors prepare L2 learners in the immersion setting to become equally bilingual speakers and bicultural actors. In their analysis of British German textbooks, Andon and Wingate (2013, pp. 200–1) note the danger of pupils being under-challenged by textbook exercises and conclude that 'learning to use a language communicatively requires opportunities to produce language in ways that are natural, authentic and personally meaningful'. As our data will show, a drama-pedagogical approach provides such opportunities and thereby fosters motivation and learning.

The following is a sample progression used at the CSSG. While reading a literary text, often for homework, students identify key sentences or sections within the text. They compare their findings with their colleagues in pairs or small groups to reach consensus as to which sentences are important or especially interesting; this is all conducted in German. They then work to dramatise their key sentences, first, as a tableau or sculpture and without any dialogue. They then answer a set of questions to deepen their connection to the character(s) before they try to imagine what the character(s) might say. Subsequent to the above steps, the students are prepared to create a more personally meaningful scene about, or diary entry for, the character(s). For a detailed description of how drama pedagogy has been used in this SA programme and for a list of relevant resources, see Misfeldt (2013).

Task-Based Language Teaching

Informed by L2 learning and teaching theories and research (Ellis, 2003; Samuda & Bygate, 2008), TBLT is a methodological frame and instructional approach in which teachers set students problem-oriented, real-world, outcome-driven tasks for the sake of purposeful and meaningful communication that also provide authentic contexts for language study (Willis, 1996). Following Willis' (1996) framework, tasks are preceded by pre-task language activities (e.g., brainstorming, comparing, scanning a text, sequencing, watching a video) and clear directions. They are followed by planning and presenting a report on the task outcome, often with peer-audience and instructor feedback, and post-task focus-on-form activities based on the grammar items that emerge as new or difficult for learners during task completion (and report planning), again with instructor feedback.

The pre-task language activities provide learners with the authentic language of speakers of the target language and the kind of language that they want and need for their own interests or purposes. The communication in the task is meaningful because the students have a stake in completing the task and are not practising preselected language or skills in isolation. When striving to complete the task, students draw freely on whatever language they see fit, have noticed in peer interaction or authentic (pre- or per-task) input, or elicit from peers and the instructor. The objective and outcome of the task is not singularly accurate language manipulation but rather the expression, attainment, or exchange of some thing or some knowledge by using context-driven and more-or-less appropriate language. Tasks thus provide opportunities for unrehearsed language use where students take informed risks, make choices, and negotiate meaning while seeking solutions to genuine queries. During the report planning and especially the focus-on-form activities, the teacher encourages students to recall, notice, and analyse the difficulties, uncertainties, and gaps in their per-task output (as compared with more proficient or authentic examples). Teachers thus (explicitly) instruct form only in the context of learners doing or having just done activities where meaning is primary. Teachers must therefore set learners task activities that consider their interlanguage and will *push* their language abilities, help them notice language forms and elicit self-correction, and enable personalised feedback per- or post-task.

Skehan (2003) defines 'strong' and 'weak' variations of TBLT. A strong task cycle does not require language learners to use a particular language structure in order to complete the task. After completing strong tasks, they focus on forms from their linguistic performance that they found to be absent, inaccurate, or more appropriate when interacting and negotiating with others or paying attention to more proficient speakers undertaking the same task. The design and process of a weak task cycle anticipate teaching specific language structures necessary for task completion (whether students use them or not). Students are still directed to focus on forms after completing the task, but now the teacher chooses these forms at the outset. Both variations can be adapted by teachers to match students' needs and proficiency levels, curriculum goals, or local circumstances (Ellis, 2003; Samuda & Bygate, 2008).

At the CSSG, TBLT has been used in the advanced German course. The tasks are all related to reading a contemporary novel by a Turkish-German author and come in various guises. These include drawing family trees, cataloguing cultural clichés, telling migration stories, visiting a Turkish restaurant, mapping the local Turkish and Islamic communities, investigating the (intercultural) rules of romantic dating, designing posters and advertising brochures, enquiring about vacationing in Turkey, composing love poetry, inventing a talk show skit, writing newspaper announcements, and so forth. Likewise, the themes of the course capping project, individual ethnographic studies, derive from the novel and are developed in class over a series of workshop-like tasks corresponding with each part of the process: generating a research question, identifying preconceptions, discussing observations, conducting interviews, reporting data as findings, and critical reflection and self-reflection.

Research Project and the Current Study

The study presented in the current chapter is part of a larger qualitative research project investigating Canadian students' experiences at the CSSG. That project asked the following general questions: (1) What is it like to speak German (or English) on SA? (2) What is the curriculum like? (3) What is it like to be a Canadian studying German in Germany? We used an interpretive method to research these questions since such an approach is especially insightful regarding the social or participatory and personal or psychological dimensions of L2 learning (Pavlenko & Lantolf, 2000). Sixty-eight programme participants were recruited in Germany in June 2010, 2011, and 2012 from a total of 180 students enrolled in the programme over the 3 years. They each signed a letter of consent and were assigned a pseudonym. The research participants are representative of all students enrolled in the programme: 50 are female and 18 are male (three individuals are each included twice since they took part in the programme in two separate years and each time participated in the research project); all were aged between 19 and 25 years; they came from a range of sending universities from across Canada; and they had declared majors in various academic disciplines (from the arts and humanities to social sciences, natural sciences, engineering, business, and medicine). The ratio of international students registered at Canadian universities taking part in the programme to Canadian citizens and permanent residents was approximately five per cent in a given year; since there were no international students involved in the research project, there is an under-representation in this demographic compared to their representation in programme enrolment per se. Data were collected in situ in the form of digital recordings of one-to-one semi-structured interviews (on average lasting 45 minutes), photocopies of language-learning journals, and select assignments. Research assistants transcribed all the recordings and conducted an initial coding based on six fundamental themes related to the general research questions.

In the current chapter, we have focussed on one aspect of the second research question, namely, what the participants said about their experiences of the SA classroom pedagogy. We were primarily interested in whether students noticed a relationship between the instructional approaches used in the programme and their personal sense of and commitment to language development, or whether the immersion context alone featured in their narratives of learning. To pursue this interest, we drew on the interview data from across all three years. We read the transcripts several times, paying particular attention to sections coded for discussions of teaching, learning, and the classroom. We highlighted especially relevant and insightful expressions and made individual notes for comparison and contemplation. We then selected exemplary excerpts from a total of 14 participants for further analysis by close reading, as presented below.

Participants in the Current Study

The participants selected for the current discussion are a homogeneous group, although they come from nine different home universities: all 14 received at least their high school education in Canada; 12 were English L1 speakers, one was raised French-English bilingual, and one immigrated to Canada as a child speaking a Romance language as her mother tongue. Table 1 provides an overview of the participants cited in the current discussion, indicating their gender, course level by undergraduate year, the calendar year in which they participated in the SA programme, and the teaching approach used in their course. We have chosen these participants because their expression of their lived experiences of teaching and learning either reflect comments that were typical across the research participants or represent instances especially pertinent to our interest in whether students attribute their learning in SA also to what happens in the classroom. We did not select these participants based on course level. In fact, this selection represents three levels, taught by one or more of seven teachers.

Table 1 Selected participants from the 2010–2012 study

Name	Gender	Course level by year	Calendar year	Teaching approach
Alice	Female	Fourth	2010	Task-based
Bobby	Male	Third	2012	Drama pedagogy
Dacia	Female	Fourth	2011	Task-based
Greg	Male	Third	2011	Drama pedagogy
Heather	Female	Fourth	2010	Task-based
Karen	Female	Fourth	2012	Task-based
Kieran	Male	Third	2011	Drama pedagogy
Lara	Female	Third	2012	Drama pedagogy
Liza	Female	Second	2012	Drama pedagogy
Mira	Female	Third	2011	Drama pedagogy
		Fourth	2012	Task-based
Ramona	Female	Fourth	2012	Task-based
Roger	Male	Fourth	2012	Task-based
Sophie	Female	Third	2010	Drama pedagogy
Tina	Female	Fourth	2012	Task-based

Findings and Discussion

First, it must be acknowledged that all study participants mention how living in the immersion setting and going on extra-curricular excursions provided opportunities for learning through interaction (both with locals and tourists), engaging with local culture, and reading signage and other written media in the local environment. This is not surprising since our interview questions about general experiences in Germany were followed by others seeking any linguistic and intercultural learning in this regard. In talking about the immersion context, the participants use a broad range of adjectives, metaphors, and narrative episodes that describe their experience varyingly as beneficial, enjoyable, exciting, difficult, intimidating, tiring, informative, transforming, and so forth. Likewise, as we will explore, all participants positively appraised the classroom experience as contributing to their language development. The crux of the students' collective narrative about the teaching and learning approaches is: *we see that this works by meeting our linguistic and social needs and taking us further.*

When asked, most students can recall the teaching approaches as genuinely communicative and engaging and in doing so express a general positive evaluation of their effectiveness. For example, Kieran provides a detailed recall of singing, acting, and interactive autobiographical pair work, even indicating their social and kinaesthetic nature and their purpose for developing speaking ability. He regards this as 'good' and 'com[ing] together nicely'.

KIERAN: Singing I guess. [...] Well, we do lots of [singing with the instructor]; we do also drama, we act plays out from our book or we do singing as a group of [third-year students] together. So it kinda it loosens us up a bit so we're not as uptight and like, er, let's do work all the time. [...] There's other like socialising activities that [the instructor] does too. Just like you get together, [...] you get a partner, and then you tell them about your weekend or ... The first one we did you tell them about yourself and then [the instructor] picks your partner and then they sit on a chair and they have to act as you, so people, you have to talk about as if you're your partner and what their story was. [Second-year German at home] was kind of more like the only time we really stood up or anything was for presentations and then other than that we always sat down and did work. [There] wasn't really any socialising or playing games, it was just sitting down and learning German.
JOHN: Okay, and what do you, what do you prefer?
KIERAN: Definitely the [SA programme] way. It's more overall good. All the stuff that we do is just like it comes together nicely and then in Canada it's just more like sitting down, doing work and projects.

Kieran is typical of those study participants who recall various aspects of teaching and learning mostly in a descriptive manner and stating basic preferences rather than linking these activities with any personal linguistic outcomes. Nonetheless, he does reveal the socio-affective effectiveness of song, drama, and peer interaction: 'It loosens us up a bit so we're not as like uptight'. Curiously, although Kieran evaluates such authentic communicative approaches positively, he expresses this evaluation in a manner that contrasts his SA classroom learning—not the SA context per se— with the sedentary and seemingly mundane 'work' of the AH classroom.

While Liza also evaluates the SA classroom activities, such as acting and singing, as fun, in contrast to Kieran, she is more typical of the participant who realises the connection between the classroom approaches and linguistic goals, including facilitating living in the immersion environment.

LIZA: I'd say here it's more fun and we probably learn things that are more practical because what we learn we have to go out and use the next day. For us in Canada: stuff that I don't ever have to use; the courses that I took in Canada, we've never really spoken German. It was just writing and reading. [...] It's easier to learn something when you need to learn it as opposed to just learning it for fun. Singing is good. [...] Because it gets you actively involved in vocabulary and I find that if I sing something I remember it.

Liza recognises not only the fun but also the 'practical' and 'need'-oriented nature of active approaches, as well as embraces the realisation and recall of vocabulary through the authentic task of learning (memorising) and performing a pop song. Liza indicates that classroom teaching and learning plays an intrinsic role in the SA immersion environment to produce L2 acquisition results. The immersion setting supplies a motivating 'need' for L2 learning, while the SA classroom can support the 'practical' daily reality. The enormous potential of this perspective is only rarely explored by SA scholars (e.g., Bacon, 2002; Bird & Belnap, the current volume), who normally do not examine the articulation of the linguistic content of a SA course with the necessities of the immersion context, perhaps because we still too often take for granted that the linguistic demands of the setting motivate a particular attention by students in the SA L2 classroom. Meanwhile, SA research (e.g., Isabelli-García, 2006; Pellegrino Aveni, 2005) has shown that the demands of the setting can be intimidating and demotivating, without delving into how the SA classroom could have mitigated this experience. Liza also contrasts her SA class with her (first-year) AH course, which had mostly avoided the development of L2 speaking skills.

Bobby provides considerable recall specifically of the drama-pedagogical approaches. He immediately draws attention to how creative, diverse, and interactive they are and how the participation and engagement this elicits is effective for learning.

BOBBY: I really enjoy when we talk about our novel. They give us interactive activities we do such as … drawing pictures [story board] or doing a play. Small play acting […] Just like posters on the wall, we make, or comparison charts. It's just very interactive! It's one of those things where you go in for the second half [of class] and, all of a sudden, it's over. […] You're learning and you're also, you know, having fun at the same time! […] And the rule of only speaking German here I think is very good. Because in Canada in the German language courses the teacher explains everything in English. A lot of, I'd say 95 per cent, 90 per cent of the class is in English. You know, just doing simple things but you're actually learning at the same time. […] Such as there's, I don't know what it's called, you freeze. You do frames. And then one person explains what happens and the class has to explain. We act out dialogues. We make posters and explain what happened in the posters.

In Bobby's words, the communicative approaches applied in this SA programme enable the students to actively take part in the L2 for many purposes. This 'interactive' and focussed or engaging ('all of a sudden, it's over') SA classroom contrasts with his AH experience where the instructor constrains and reduces the students' participation in L2 German by using most of the classroom time for (grammar) explanation in the L1; they seem to use a traditional presentation-practice-production approach and also model the L1 instead of the L2 as the primary means of classroom communication in a L2 course. It is apparent that Bobby has a growing yet possibly still biased understanding of effective teaching: while he identified the 'learning' he and his peers are achieving in SA via drama pedagogy, he also views the component activities as 'simple'. Although students think games, acting, and story-board posters are *simple* while explanations and drills are *work*, they actually require more planning and preparation on the instructor's part to create situations for engaged learning; they also require the learners to attend to and maybe take risks with the L2 in order to communicate meaningfully and successfully instead of knowing or guessing a grammatical form following the teacher's explanations.

Lara's detailed description of teaching approaches and activities also emphasises their creative and varied nature. While Bobby referred to the drama-pedagogical components as effective for learning generally, Lara identifies the creativity and variety of this teaching approach as the cause of setting appropriate conditions to help her personally develop the linguistic skills and confidence to analyse and discuss a German novel.

LARA: [The] novel was okay; I think it was an okay level. It was kind of hard for some things but then it was okay. I kind of understand the general idea. It was interesting that we actually discussed themes and like deeper meanings behind things instead of just trying to understand the words that were on the page. We went a little deeper, which I wasn't really expecting because I didn't think I could comprehend enough to go that far behind it and want to get talking about it and it works better. And it's good that they do all the different creative stuff with people. We're always doing something different.

Drama pedagogy helped Lara shift her learner self-concept in that previously she had not imagined herself being able to read and discuss a novel in another language. She credits the teaching approach with enabling her to move beyond understanding language acquisition as merely lexical comprehension ('just trying to understand the words') to seeing it as a process and experience for interpreting and discussing 'deeper' ideas. Her words—reflecting some other students too—show that drama pedagogy responds to her desire for higher-level cognitive engagement in L2 learning. Lara clearly indicates that the SA classroom is contributing to her L2 acquisition.

Likewise, Sophie's detailed description highlights the socio-cognitive elements of drama pedagogy and their effectiveness for learning as well as test preparation and success. Using the word 'games' broadly to describe interaction, acting, role play, and theatre games, Sophie links the embodied teaching approach to facilitating memory and retention and creating the proximal social circumstance for contextual learning.

SOPHIE: It's worked so well, playing the games, matching some of the verbs with their prepositions: we'd just get two teams, and you'd get a bag, and there's a whole bunch of verbs, and a whole bunch of prepositions, and that way you remember it. You pick it up easier than memorising a list. […] Everyone has had experience with German in Canada, but we're also here, and we're learning together, even though it is difficult for some of us and not others, we can help each other as well. Which I find amazing. […] Yeah, you remember easier with games. It's like when you get together for your exam tomorrow, you get together with some friends, and a joke is made or something funny happens, you're going to remember that tomorrow in the test. […] You're going to remember playing the game when it comes to writing the test. […] You think of the fun things, the enjoyment that you get out of learning something, rather than sitting down and reading a book, or sitting down listening to someone go on for 50 minutes. […] Yeah, I know there are a lot of professors who say: 'You play games with children, you're in university now. You're not going to be spoon-fed anymore'. Well guess what, the ones who are playing games are the ones who know more, and the ones who can grasp what's going on.

Similar to Lara, Sophie attributes the drama pedagogy games for greater acquisition of linguistic knowledge and ability. She also moves beyond seeing language learning as comprised of lexical accumulation through memorising vocabulary, solo study, or being lectured to for long stretches of time to understanding it as a participatory process in which attention to language is developed through socialisation and use. Sophie comes to an important realisation about how language is learned: she describes how meaning ('a joke is made') precedes lexical-grammatical accuracy ('you're going to remember that tomorrow in the test'). Sophie even goes so far as to challenge the bias we observed in Kieran and Bobby by talking back to an imagined AH professor. She has unlocked her personal sense of how best to learn and how learning can be enjoyable thanks to a lived awareness and embrace of various L2 classroom approaches.

Just as Lara says she is learning in her SA class by drama-pedagogical ways that go beyond *just trying to understand the words*, so does Alice note the effectiveness of the TBLT approaches of her SA classroom in contrast to her more typical classroom experience of 'drills' and 'repetition'.

ALICE: In terms of classroom activity, um … very good. I think we are learning things in a way that helps us actually remember them, and I think that a lot of time, er, a lot of situations of language learning, you kind of have these drills with a lot of repetition and that's just not how you learn it. It's really not, and that's one of the things with this teaching quality that I've noticed.

Not only does Alice assess the task-based approach as being more effective, but she does so by referring to both a breadth of course content ('things') and the special learning outcome of supporting memory ('actually remember'). Also, through her explicit positioning as someone who has invested time and had various experiences of (AH) language teaching and learning, she indicates she is qualified to make a judgement as to what works for her and others ('we are learning', 'helps us', 'how you learn'), acknowledging or stressing the social aspect of TBLT. Like Sophie and drama pedagogy, Alice expresses a lived awareness ('I've noticed') of the 'quality' of what is going on in her SA classroom and seems to both embrace this approach and thoroughly reject those she has typically experienced ('I think […] helps us' v. 'that's just not how you learn it. It's really not').

As has been the case with drama pedagogy, Dacia notices in TBLT both the variety of activities and how the task—for example, the performance of an original role play as a reworking of a chapter from a novel—leads the students beyond a basic reading and grammar comprehension—a rudimentary learning goal for an advanced class—to using the L2 creatively to interpret and hypothesise the lives and circumstances of the novel's characters.

DACIA: We do a lot of things in class that's very varied [...] Sometimes I feel that they're too simple? Like we'll end up doing drawing posters [for oral presentation] ... and other times we'll have to do a ... report or invent an ad [advertising brochure] or something like that, which is, yeah, a little bit more complicated. [...] I was surprised too at the ... rate we learned and how fast we learned? I really like [...] the grammar part like when [the instructor] reads our work things and he's ... I personally have problems with *Dativ*, and then somebody else might have problems with, I dunno ... *Akkusativ*? He WON'T all make us learn *Dativ* and *Akkusativ*, he'll just make a very personalised grammar and I think that helps a lot ... so ... yeah ... I like that it's more personal. [...] We do more interactive things here than in Canada. In Canada [...] all [the instructor] did was just take the grammar book out and read from the book and make us do the exercises from the book [...] There were times when I would just ... I didn't want to go to class [in Canada] because I had absolutely no interest in hearing her read from the book for an hour .... here ... it's more like we talk way more than [the instructor] does, which is a good thing [...] it's nice for once to actually have to do other projects and get to class not knowing what you're going to do every day. It's ... kind of surprising, and [...] we had such a fun day just making up a dialogue between um ... Mustafa, some guy in the book, and [...] two other people and just making up what he would say and what he would do, and all those things. And we laughed for like an hour and a half straight! And it was nice. That would never happen in Canada.

Dacia mentions many components and effects of TBLT when recalling her classroom experiences: variety, 'simple' tasks, 'more complicated' tasks, projects, a task cycle (composing and performing the genre-switch role-play dialogue), interaction, student-talk (oral preparation and production), individualised grammar focus, creativity, enjoyment while staying on task, motivation, and speed of learning. While, at first, Dacia reveals, as in previous examples, a discomfort with so-called simple task components such as drawing posters (for oral presentation) and might appear begrudging ('a little bit more complicated') about the effectiveness of others, she nonetheless shifts in her teaching and learning awareness to how the full task cycle is *pushing* her and her classmates by being so student-focussed. Not only does she repeatedly express her approval of the approach she has experienced, but she also states how 'surprised' she is by her and her classmates' increased rate of acquisition and how 'surprising' it is that the student is at the centre of learning. Indeed, Dacia values how the—strong—TBLT approach creates student-authored texts that are more meaningful and relevant than the usual demotivating textbook exercises as well as how the instructor and student can use these texts to co-develop an individualised focus-on-form study plan from what emerges in the student's output. This individualised approach follows Nunan's (1989, p. 177) suggestion that no curriculum can claim to be truly learner-centred unless the learner's subjective needs and perceptions related to the process of learning are taken into account. There could hardly be a clearer expression of Dacia's awareness-turned-embrace of the teaching approach as leveraging her L2 learning as when she contrasts her SA classroom experience to when she 'didn't want to go to class' at home.

Heather also shows a distinct awareness of TBLT in that her description of it breaks the task cycle down clearly into its sequenced components leading to an overall process that has a personal impact. Heather traces how the cycle of pre-task language activity, task, preparation of report, report, and form focus have *pushed* her to develop a stronger speaking ability and contextualised attention to grammar.

HEATHER: We read the book outside the class, and then [the instructor] will assign us into small groups and give us something that we have to do, and then we'll go to the next group and present it, or we'll present it to the class. And I don't always think that the things we're talking about in class is important, 'cause it's about the book … but standing in front of people talking or just having the casual conversation with the next group and them asking questions and responding ... that's actually making us talk and doing these things ... and we work on grammar. Because other students ... which I think is really good [...] is that they'll correct our grammar and help us ... and ... it's really good. [...] but everything that like ... talking before the class, as much as I don't like to do that, I'm better with that now. I'm more comfortable. [...] But actually using it and talking ... and not even just a one-way conversation where I can memorise everything! [Laughs] I think that's what I personally need ... it really helped me. [...] I only took one German course last semester, and we didn't really speak that much German in it ... I don't know why. [...] It's completely different here than back home. At home I feel like [German]'s almost like any other class. We learn this, we memorise it, we do the test and then [makes a whooshing sound].

Heather's previous academic success in the AH (teacher-centred) classroom was due to memorising the 'pseudo-communicative' (Plews, 2013) responses required to pass tests. This enabled her to reach a fourth-year German SA class without 'actually using [German] and talking [German]' and without leaving much lasting practical linguistic effect ('[makes a whooshing sound]'). But her participation in the full sequence of communicative components of the TBLT cycle provide her with the appropriate scaffolding or structured pedagogical and linguistic support (including preparing, two-way peer editing of content and of grammar, low-risk rehearsing, presenting, and contextualised focus-on-form all in the L2) to face an emerging self-evident personal and high-risk need, namely, speaking the L2 in groups and to groups. This linguistic outcome would only be possible in a student-centred class, whether AH or in SA. Indeed, Heather, like Dacia, not only praises her SA classroom experiences but contrasts them with the unenduring linguistic effects of her AH German course; she thereby expresses not only her awareness of the teaching approach and its effects ('actually making us talk'), but also her embrace of it as leveraging her L2 acquisition ('that's what I personally need').

Karen also contrasts the 'traditional classroom' and her experiences of learning by TBLT. Again, she provides the example of a genre-switch task to highlight the effectiveness of the creativity and socio-cognitive aspects of the approach.

KAREN: Well, it's completely different totally in German because the other classes I took this year were German courses but they were mostly done in English ... It doesn't really feel like a traditional classroom. While we analyse our book, but we're encouraged to do a lot of group work. We create little skits or summaries. Like this week, we did ... we created a TV show, a talk show based on the characters involved. And we're always working with different people, so you get a chance to know other people while you're working. [...] And like whenever we do these things it's not like [the instructor]'s there correcting every single mistake we make. You know, we get to speak freely and have fun ... We got to, you know, get creative. It's also good in a way because it got to appeal to the talents of different people.

As apparent in previous excerpts on drama pedagogy or TBLT, Karen highlights how the genuinely communicative approaches require the students and instructors to remain in the L2. For Karen, there is a significant shift from not understanding why she should speak English to learn German to enjoying 'speak[ing] freely' in German in the SA class. She is also aware of how these approaches accommodate students with a variety of learning styles and preferences, enabling them both to focus on their individual language development goals and to contribute to each other's learning.

For Mira, such student-centredness in the instructors' teaching approaches is key to her and her peers' success:

MIRA: None of them are teacher-centred actually. Which is good because it's not just ... like obviously the instructors are kind of, well they're in charge and they are the centre of the classroom … are not the centre of the classroom. It's not what I mean, like that they're facilitating, they're not the centre of the classroom. Not to reduce the role of an instructor … they're super important and we don't have the knowledge to begin with but, if the students aren't talking to each other or writing together or singing or doing something then it's kind of all for nothing because a person in isolation isn't going to be able to talk or write.

In trying to analyse how and why her student-centred SA class is so effective, Mira struggles with understanding the different leadership and management role of the teacher. The back-and-forth in her expression show that, on the one hand, she is used to teachers being leaders and imparting their knowledge to students, that is, in 'teacher-centred' classes, but that she is coming to recognise the value of teachers who lead and impart their knowledge instead by 'facilitating' students working together to co-create that knowledge, in student-centred classes. The result of her own analysis of the different kinds of classroom is a rejection of the teacher-centred approach: 'it's kind of all for nothing' because it puts the learners 'in isolation [unable] to talk or write' even among peers. Mira thus reiterates Heather's differentiation between the SA programme's 'actually using it and talking' and the traditional class' 'we memorise it, we do the test and [makes a whooshing sound]'.

Mira addresses not only the general effectiveness of different approaches for language learning but also their utility in terms of specific linguistic needs. She draws attention to the variety of activities and the importance of participation.

MIRA: You can't really learn a language just looking at your book […] there's a lot of participation, there's lots of different styles of activities, … I like that yesterday we were asked to memorise a poem if we could and present it to the class. A poem, that was fun. Um … we did get to read and act out scenes from [*Der Vorleser*] and I think that's been a really good part about being here, is reading that book. … or we do exercises where we sit back to back and we have to … it's usually for grammatical …

thing. SO we're asking questions about something, and so that it's, you're training your ears ... to hear. Because that is the hardest ... like looking at people you know what they're talking about ... or they can see when you don't understand [...] but when you're just listening, it's more fun than just listening to something off a CD ... which is OFTEN how it happens.

Here, Mira explains how a simple shift in seating arrangements turns a grammatical exercise into a purposeful communicative situation. Mira realises that this more motivating requirement to pay more attention to a peer's speech is better for developing listening comprehension than the usual method of using a CD. Not only does she value the exercise because it is 'more fun', but she also recognises while doing it exactly its purpose for L2 acquisition ('training your ears ... to hear') and effectiveness ('they can[not] see when you don't understand'), giving the grammatical activity greater salience. Mira, too, expresses her embrace of the drama-pedagogical teaching leveraging her learning in that she indicates how their success differs from less effective means ('just looking at your book', 'just listening to something off a CD').

As with previously cited participants, Tina's detailed description emphasises a variety of ways to use the TBLT approach. Like Mira, she also identifies personally relevant language development goals, in her case, L2 speaking and pronunciation.

TINA: So, I thought that part for me was gonna be really hard and then, yeah, actually speaking in German a lot, just because I haven't really had a lot of experience in that regard, like in my classes back home. I really enjoy doing, even though I don't like singing, I enjoy having a song and being able to kind of practice my pronunciation more. And that's kind of a way to kind of help me do that. And I enjoy with [the instructor] we've been doing a lot of drawing things or, um, we were writing poems [...] and writing fairy tales and doing really creative things and I really like doing those kinds of things, so that's been really good. But we've also ... we do those kind of in-class assignments, we've been using the novel. So, I think that too is, um, really great just because then I can take things out of the novel, I can read more in-depth that way, so I can get the answer that I'm looking for whatever the assignment is. [...] Yeah, it's kind of nice not to focus so much on grammar, um, just because in my other German courses it's very much grammar focused. Whereas here it's definitely more, um, I feel like I practice more of my, um, *Aussprache* and, yeah, for me that's a big thing, so I think that's definitely been really great.

While Tina ascribes singing performance tasks to having helped her practise her pronunciation, taking a multicycle TBLT approach ('drawing things', 'writing poems', 'writing fairy tales', 'doing really creative things', 'in-class assignments') to reading a German novel has enabled her to work 'more in depth' with it, seeking the meanings she wishes to find, rather than only doing a surface study. Because strong TBLT does not necessarily begin with a specific grammar objective, but rather treats grammar contextually as emergent, it enables Tina to choose and pursue her own focus in language learning. For her, while doubtless still studying some grammar, she has rather had the chance to focus on pronunciation and interpretation. The significance of creating her own learning journey within the syllabus is underlined by her use of emphatic and emotively strong adverbs and adjectives ('really', 'really good', 'really great', 'definitely', 'big') as well as the terminological code-switch to German ('*Aussprache*').

Roger describes the TBLT approach he has experienced by evoking especially the necessary socio-cognitive aspect of L2 learning over isolation, also using a terminological code-switch:

ROGER: There's a whole lot of group work and I love doing group work with people and it's more fun than just sitting there at the table by yourself just writing ... None of the grammar is really new but I find that I can actually understand it now! So, like the *Konjunktiv II*, I knew how to write it and everything, but I never really knew kind of what it was used for, but I never actually used it in terms of speaking or anything. But now I kind of use it a bit more and I can understand it exactly how it works and I find that the way that it was taught in like a few weeks, it's been, it's just really clear and simplified … And it's really really fun. But the difference between there and here is like it's much more intensive but it's also much more interactive and it's more fun and I found I have learned a lot more than I have in this little while and over the span of the year. […] Where at home it was like we have to do like *übersetzen* all the time and they were just brutal!

The example of Roger demonstrates how a different teaching approach enables students to perceive not only accurate form but also the appropriate function and use. Roger had previously learned the form of '*Konjunktiv II*' (subjunctive II/conditional) by practising it at the word- or sentence-level without necessarily understanding through endless and uninspiring '*übersetzen*' (translation), thus likely for the sake of accuracy and assessment. But in this SA course he realises that the 'interactive' approach requires the appropriate use for meaningful communication and so enables him to both understand the function of the grammar form more easily and, most importantly for acquisition, become a motivated user of the L2. Imagine, *Konjunktiv II* should be 'really, really fun'!? Joking aside, it is important to note that Roger finally fully understands this form in the SA classroom and not exclusively from the SA setting, thus any study measuring SA outcomes by tests without examining the SA classroom would likely interpret this grammar accuracy inaccurately.

One would hope that the following student, Ramona, would become aware of the teaching approaches especially because she is also a senior-level education student at home. Indeed, she does:

RAMONA: I find that [classes] go by really quickly, honestly. You don't really notice. It's like [the instructor] says, 'Oh it's break now'. And I'm like, 'What really? We've already been through that long?' But, um, I'm studying education and I've only taken a couple of classes, but I find that [the instructor] is definitely one of the expert teachers that like my educational psychology professor tells us about. He's like, 'Expert teachers do such and such and such and such'. And okay my teacher does that, that's good. But it's nice, because he, at the beginning of the course after he got all of our evaluations back from our [placement] tests and whatever [pre-course written assignment] at the beginning, he kind of designed the course around, okay, what were the six major things that everyone had problems with, and I really appreciated it, because it really benefited me in some regards, because there were definitely things that, even though you learn them in [third] or [second year], they don't really stick. [...] And so, it's nice to review those again. And the activities are good, because it's a lot of working in groups, which sometimes I think it takes a little bit longer than what [the instructor] might anticipate, but then he realises and he's like, 'Okay, we're going to cut it a little bit shorter or we'll work on it again tomorrow'. But I think that it's good to, um, the integration of our novel with all of the activities and with the grammar as well, so he, um, found lots of, like today we did passive voice, so he said, 'Okay, so this sentence on such and such a page, can someone still read that for us, read that for me?' And he would say, 'Okay, so why is that sentence passive? Or can you identify the structure?' And so, we went from there and so that I find really good. It's helpful. [...]

FEISAL: And what about the assignments?

RAMONA: Um, I think they're good. I like that the grammar is kind of self-led. [...] I like the *Sprachlernbio* [language learning journal]. I like writing in that every day and I think that it will be interesting to going back in a year, and reading it again. To be like, 'Oh wow! I didn't know that word?' or 'I learned that when?' Just stuff like that, but I find them helpful and it's interesting. It's a good way to reflect too on what you're learning every day.

Ramona sees her SA course teacher doing what her education professor has described as 'expert' teaching. That is, specifically, he works to the individual students' needs, uses group activities, and adapts the time-on-task in class flexibly according to class progress. She then describes how the teaching approach works—for example, by integrating activities with literary and grammar study, using inductive learning, a functional-notional emphasis, and contextualised language, being student-centred, and encouraging reflection—to help that student language need ('passive voice') come to the fore. Ramona not only becomes aware of the teaching approach and its effectiveness but, similar to Mira, she also understands the purpose of and values specific assignments. In this instance, she appreciates the language-learning journal both for its current pedagogical role in demanding critical reflection on language-learning needs and successes as a habitual practice ('every day') and for its ongoing potential for her personal language-learning journey as a record of her progress ('in a year').

We close the findings section with an excerpt that succinctly describes the ultimate outcome of much of what we have discussed thus far. Namely, while several students certainly experienced learning in the traditional AH German class, many became aware of, and found, how the purposeful and reflective teaching approaches of this SA programme facilitated a shift from knowledge for academic sake, which included only limited skills and excluded ownership of the language, to an embodied L2 user.

GREG: I thought I'm pretty comfortable in North America with my reading and writing in German but I've never spoken very much, I've never had an opportunity to practice that … You think, 'Oh man I gotta sing' or 'I gotta act', I'm not much of either of those. But it was good, it really made everyone really comfortable with each other and I think that's the purpose.

What strikes us here is Greg's delimiting comfort with passive language skills from his home university education and his initial shock and discomfort with learning active and interactive language skills once in his SA class. Yet, not only was he able, through different teaching approaches, to overcome his skills gap resulting from a lack of 'opportunity to practice', but he acknowledges the role of the SA classroom teaching to offer exactly the kinds of social learning for all students to become 'really comfortable' with the need to interact 'with each other' and doubtless members of the host community. Indeed, he consciously shifts to embrace the teaching approach as leveraging (social) L2 learning: 'I'm not much of either of those. *But* it was good' (emphasis added). Surely, 'that's the purpose' of instructed SA programmes: classroom instruction can contribute profoundly to students' personal sense of confidence in their learning as well as actual language development in SA not by leaving acquisition merely to chance in the immersion setting (or doing what seems to be done in many AH language programmes), but by enhancing students' ability to access and take optimum advantage of the different linguistic opportunities SA presents.

Conclusion and Recommendations

Our findings provide clear evidence of student awareness of teaching approaches in the SA classroom. The overall results show that all study participants at least signal, and describe the nature of, the drama pedagogy or TBLT activities as well as the language skills they are to develop. Many also provide details on the processes of the teaching approaches used in the SA classroom and their linguistic, intercultural, and psychological/developmental learning effects. They perceive the components of the approaches, variation and fun, interaction, more student-talk than teacher-talk, student-centredness, learning in social context, authentic, meaningful learning, and being intellectually challenged; they indicate a sense of learning not just as L2 knowledge outcomes, but also as lived (social) process and an increased rate of learning. The approaches are seen to lead to increased motivation, retention, satisfaction of personal language learning needs, linguistic and performative self-confidence in the L2, and deeper intercultural and critical competences. In fact, many participants in this study even express a commitment to learning in the manner of the teaching approach they experienced. That is, they indicate buy-in, or shift in their pedagogical beliefs through their 'meta-pedagogical awareness' (Block, 2000), which likely further motivated their learning. This is not only good news for drama pedagogy and TBLT. Since the participants' narratives of learning are not determined only by the immersion context but, rather, reveal a relationship between the SA classroom instructional approaches and their personal sense of language learning and development during the SA programme, this study is significant for future SA programming and research. Teaching is certainly part of the story of L2 SA learning.

Most surprising in our findings are the students' frequent positive/negative differentiation between the approaches used in the SA programme and those used in AH classes (in Canada). This is especially so since we designed our study expressly to avoid repeating the apples-and-oranges comparison between learning in the SA setting and learning in AH classes that is common in SA research in order to focus on the SA classroom. However, this comparison emerged as part of a recurring discourse pattern in the research interviews with the Canadian students (which we then took up in the natural conversation of the interview): they (1) recall a specific activity and/or approach in the SA classroom, (2) make (positive) value judgements, (3) connect this to individual and/or group learning, and (4) differentiate their SA (communicative) class experiences from AH (structural-analytical) class experiences while repeating the (positive) value judgement. Put mildly, such differentiation reveals a potential crisis in pedagogy in post-secondary modern languages in Canada in that students often evaluate the AH teaching as less effective or ineffective and offer low or no buy-in. Put more optimistically, student awareness of and buy-in regarding the drama-pedagogical and task-based teaching approaches used in this SA programme—which benefit from, but are not necessarily dependent on an immersion context—strongly indicate a path out of that domestic crisis. Furthermore, this differentiation indicating communicative and meaningful SA teaching approaches in our programme compared with less effective instruction otherwise also underlines the truism that a classroom in SA is effective when it is first and foremost an effective classroom no matter where it is; our data would surely not have been as strong if typical structural-analytical teaching approaches had been used in the SA classroom. This point again raises the spectre of the reliability of SA research that does not fully address the nature of teaching and the classroom in SA when making claims about linguistic, intercultural, and other outcomes.

Based on the current study, we offer the following recommendations. All planning should begin from the students' perspective, not the discipline's. While it is crucial to have clear and harmonised learning objectives—especially in a national programme such as ours that serves students from and returning to multiple universities—the curriculum must be flexible enough to adapt to student interests, needs, and personal learning goals. This means using a variety of activities and tasks relating to different student learning preferences and topics and genres so that students have access to the language structures they want, need, and are ready to learn given the specific situation.

Students indicate that the most motivating way to achieve retention of practical and transferrable vocabulary and grammar is for instructors to design meaningful, purposeful, creative, interactive assignments that require students to work together and engage with the host culture. Assignments could include role play, games, and tasks with directed interaction with each other, the host family, tandem partners, or other community members. Indeed, L2 socialisation should be integral to SA (Kinginger, 2009, 2013). Such interactive engagement requires thoughtful preparation on the instructor's part, by frequently changing the social forms, inputs, media, and skills needed, so that students can prepare and review in the lower stakes environment of the classroom.

University students are used to discussing intellectual issues on a daily basis in their L1 and can feel frustrated by their slow L2 development when wanting the same discussions in the L2. They might give up such goals thinking that they first need to learn more vocabulary and grammar. But linguistic goals do not have to be seen as separate from deeper intellectual enquiry into the host culture (compare, Brubaker, 2007). Instructors can help students overcome any resignation by making possible embodied L2 learning that connects students to their experiences through both their senses and their intellect. When learning is both emotionally anchored and intellectual, it is more memorable. Likewise, instructors should not shy away from creative tasks that may seem simple and fun since they too can scaffold expression and facilitate analytical thinking.

Student-centred teaching approaches necessarily require classroom activity, course assignments, and aspects of the itinerary to serve as context for subsequent individualised, focussed study and reviewing and resetting of individual learning goals. Thus, regular opportunities for guided reflection on L2 and intercultural learning can be provided through mandatory consultation hours and/or language learning journals (Bown, Dewey, & Belnap, 2015; Bridges, 2007; Plews & Misfeldt, 2016). Such requirements help students to realise that they are independent learners who can take responsibility for their own learning.

As Block (2000, p. 116) states, 'if we accept that learners come to the task of language learning with a great deal of knowledge about pedagogical practice, then it seems a logical recommendation that teachers should make use of this knowledge at every stage of the teaching process'. It is advisable to pay close attention to SA language learners' educational analyses in their consultations and journals, as well as formal evaluations, as perhaps the most insightful sources of optimising SA learning outcomes; our recommendations thus come full circle in that programme directors and instructors can plan from this student insight.

Summary of recommendations for optimal L2 SA programming based on student awareness of teaching approaches

- Plan from the students' perspective, including their interests, needs, goals, and awareness of teaching.
- Use a variety of activities, tasks, topics, and genres to enable different learning preferences and give access to the language that learners want to learn.
- Design meaningful and purposeful assignments that require students to interact and engage socially with each other and members of the host culture.
- Anticipate higher stakes interaction in the community with interactive preparation and review in the lower stakes classroom.
- Do not regard the discrete linguistic goals as separate from deeper intellectual enquiry into the host culture.
- Include forms of contextualised, individualised language study and linguistic and intercultural reflection.

Bibliography

Andon, N., & Eckerth, J. (2009). Chacun à son gout? Task-based L2 pedagogy from the teacher's point of view. *International Journal of Applied Linguistics, 19*(3), 286–310.

Andon, N., & Wingate, U. (2013). Motivation, authenticity and challenge in German textbooks for key stage 3. In J. Gray (Ed.), *Critical perspectives on language teaching materials* (pp. 182–203). Basingstoke, UK: Palgrave Macmillan.

Bacon, S. (2002). Learning the rules: Language development and cultural adjustment during study abroad. *Foreign Language Annals, 35*(6), 637–646.

Barkhuizen, G. (1998). Discovering learners' perceptions of ESL classroom teaching/learning activities in a South African context. *TESOL Quarterly, 32*(1), 85–108.

Belliveau, G., & Kim, W. (2013). Drama in L2 learning: A research synthesis. *Scenario, 7*(2), 7–27. Retrieved from http://research.ucc.ie/scenario/2013/02/BelliveauKim/02/en

Block, D. (2000). Learners and their meta-pedagogical awareness. *International Journal of Applied Linguistics, 10*(1), 97–123.

Bown, J., Dewey, D. P., & Belnap, R. K. (2015). Student interactions during study abroad in Jordan. In R. Mitchell, N. Tracy-Ventura, & K. McManus (Eds.), *Social interaction, identity and language learning during residence abroad* (pp. 199–222). EuroSLA Monographs Series, 4. Retrieved from http://www.eurosla.org/monographs/EM04/Bown_etal.pdf

Brecht, R., & Robinson, J. L. (1995). The value of formal instruction in study abroad: Student reactions in context. In B. Freed (Ed.), *Second language acquisition in a study abroad context* (pp. 317–334). Philadelphia: Benjamins.

Bridges, S. (2007). Learner perceptions of a professional development immersion course. *Prospect, 22*(2), 39–60.

Brubaker, C. (2007). Six weeks in the Eifel: A case for culture learning during short-term study abroad. *Unterrichtspraxis, 40*(2), 118–123.

Byrnes, H. (1998). Constructing curricula in collegiate foreign language departments. In H. Byrnes (Ed.), *Learning foreign and second languages. Perspectives in research and scholarship* (pp. 262–295). New York: The Modern Language Association of America.

Chieffo, L., & Griffiths, L. (2004). Large-scale assessment of student attitudes after short term study abroad program. *Frontiers: The Interdisciplinary Journal of Study Abroad, 10*, 165–177.

Churchill, E. (2006). Variability in the study abroad classroom and learner competence. In M. A. DuFon & E. Churchill (Eds.), *Language learners in study abroad contexts* (pp. 203–227). Clevedon, UK: Multilingual Matters.

Collentine, J. (2004). The effects of learning contexts on morphosyntactic and lexical development. *Studies in Second Language Acquisition, 26*(2), 227–248.

Cook, V. (2001). *Second language learning and language teaching* (3rd ed.). London: Routledge.

Cotterall, S. (2004). It's just rules ... that's all it is at this stage .... In P. Benson & D. Nunan (Eds.), *Learners' stories: Difference and diversity in language learning* (pp. 101–118). Cambridge: Cambridge University Press.

Cubillos, J. H., Chieffo, L., & Fan, C. (2008). The impact of short-term study abroad programs on L2 listening comprehension skills. *Foreign Languages Annals, 41*(1), 157–185.

DeKeyser, R. M. (2007). Introduction: Situating the concept of practice. In R. M. DeKeyser (Ed.), *Practicing a second language: Perspectives from applied linguistics and cognitive psychology* (pp. 1–18). New York: Cambridge University Press.

DeKeyser, R. M. (2014). Research on language development during study abroad: Methodological considerations and future perspectives. In C. Pérez-Vidal (Ed.), *Language acquisition in study abroad and formal instruction contexts* (pp. 313–325). Amsterdam: Benjamins.

Ellis, R. (2003). *Task-based language teaching and learning*. Oxford: Oxford University Press.

Even, S. (2011). Drama grammar: Towards a performative post-method pedagogy. *Language Learning Journal, 39*(3), 299–312.

Fordham, K. (2004, November 21). CSSG [Canadian Summer School in Germany] textbook report. Message posted to CAUTG [Canadian Association of University Teachers of German] electronic mailing list, archived at http://www.mailman.srv.ualberta.ca/mailman/private/cautg/2004-November/000021.html

Fordham, K. (2008, March 3). CSSG [Canadian Summer School in Germany] textbook survey. Message posted to CAUTG [Canadian Association of University Teachers of German] electronic mailing list, archived at http://www.mailman.srv.ualberta.ca/mailman/private/cautg/2008-March/000003.html

Franklin, K. (2010). Long-term career impact and professional applicability of the study abroad experience. *Frontiers: The Interdisciplinary Journal of Study Abroad, 19*, 169–190.

Freed, B. F., Segalowitz, N., & Dewey, D. P. (2004). Context of learning and second language fluency in French: Comparing regular classroom, study abroad, and intensive domestic immersion programs. *Studies in Second Language Acquisition, 26*(2), 275–301.

Freed, B., So, S., & Lazar, N. A. (2003). Language learning abroad: How do gains in written fluency compare with gains in oral fluency in French as a second language. *ADFL Bulletin, 34*(3), 34–40.

Garrett, P., & Young, R. (2009). Theorizing affect in foreign language learning: An analysis of one learner's responses to a communicative Portuguese course. *Modern Language Journal, 93*(2), 209–226.

Hawkey, R. (2006). Teacher and learner perceptions of language learning activity. *ELT Journal, 60*(3), 242–252.

Isabelli-García, C. (2006). Study abroad social networks, motivation and attitudes: Implications for second language acquisition. In E. Churchill & M. A. DuFon (Eds.), *Language learners in study abroad contexts* (pp. 231–258). Clevedon, UK: Multilingual Matters.

Isabelli-García, C., Bown, J., Plews, J. L., & Dewey, D. P. (Forthcoming). Language learning and study abroad. *Language Teaching*.

Kinginger, C. (2004). Alice doesn't live here anymore: Foreign language learning and identity (re)construction. In A. Pavlenko & A. Blackledge (Eds.), *Negotiation of identities in multilingual contexts* (pp. 219–242). Clevedon, UK: Multilingual Matters.

Kinginger, C. (2009). *Language learning and study abroad. A critical reading of research*. Basingstoke, UK: Palgrave Macmillan.

Kinginger, C. (2010). American students abroad: Negotiation of difference? *Language Teaching, 43*(2), 216–227.

Kinginger, C. (2013). Introduction. Social and cultural aspects of language learning in study abroad. In C. Kinginger (Ed.), *Social and cultural aspects of language learning in study abroad* (pp. 3–15). Amsterdam: Benjamins.

Lafford, B., & Collentine, J. (2006). The effects of study abroad and classroom contexts on the acquisition of Spanish as a second language: From research to application. In R. Salaberry & B. A. Lafford (Eds.), *The art of teaching Spanish: Second language acquisition from research to praxis* (pp. 103–126). Washington, DC: Georgetown University Press.

Misfeldt, K. (2013). Pedagogies of affect and lived place: *Der Vorleser* on a short-term intensive immersion. In J. L. Plews & B. Schmenk (Eds.), *Traditions and transitions: Curricula for German studies* (pp. 191–208). Waterloo, ON: Wilfrid Laurier University Press.

Muñoz, C. (2014). Exploring young learners' foreign language learning awareness. *Language Awareness, 23*(1–2), 24–40.

Nunan, D. (1989). Hidden agendas: The role of the learner in programme implementation. In R. K. Johnson (Ed.), *The second language curriculum* (pp. 176–186). Cambridge: Cambridge University Press.

Pavlenko, A., & Lantolf, J. P. (2000). Second language learning as participation and the (re)construction of selves. In J. P. Lantolf (Ed.), *Sociocultural theory and second language learning* (pp. 155–177). Oxford: Oxford University Press.

Pellegrino Aveni, V. (2005). *Study abroad and second language use: Constructing the self.* Cambridge: Cambridge University Press.

Pérez-Vidal, C. (Ed.). (2014a). *Language acquisition in study abroad and formal instruction contexts.* Amsterdam: Benjamins.

Pérez-Vidal, C. (2014b). Study abroad and formal instruction contrasted: The SALA project. In C. Pérez-Vidal (Ed.), *Language acquisition in study abroad and formal instruction contexts* (pp. 17–57). Amsterdam: Benjamins.

Pitts, M. (2009). Identity and the role of expectations, stress, and talk in short-term student sojourner adjustment: An application of the integrative theory of communication and cross-cultural adaptation. *International Journal of Intercultural Relations, 33*, 450–462.

Plews, J. L. (2013). 'Can anyone recommend a good German grammar?': An analysis of a popular North American German grammar. *Forum Deutsch, 21*(1). 40 pp. Retrieved from http://forumdeutsch.ca/f/nf85catg

Plews, J. L., & Misfeldt, K. (2016). *Reviewing language learning journals in study abroad, or engaging students' language awareness.* Association of Language Awareness 13th Conference, 19–22 July, Wirtschaftsuniversität Wien, Austria.

Polanyi, L. (1995). Language learning and living abroad: Stories from the field. In B. F. Freed (Ed.), *Second language acquisition in a study abroad context* (pp. 271–292). Philadelphia: Benjamins.

Samuda, V., & Bygate, M. (2008). *Tasks in second language learning.* Basingstoke, UK: Palgrave Macmillan.

Sanz, C. (2014). Contributions of study abroad research to our understanding of SLA processes and outcomes: The SALA project, an appraisal. In C. Pérez-Vidal (Ed.), *Language acquisition in study abroad and formal instruction contexts* (pp. 1–13). Amsterdam: Benjamins.

Sasaki, M. (2007). Effects of study abroad experiences on EFL writers: A multiple data analysis. *Modern Language Journal, 91*(4), 602–620.

Schewe, M. (1993). *Fremdsprache inszenieren. Zur Fundierung einer dramapädagogischen Lehr und Lernpraxis.* Oldenburg: Didaktisches Zentrum.

Schmidt, R. (1990). The role of consciousness in second language learning. *Applied Linguistics, 11*(2), 129–158.

Schmidt, R. (1993). Awareness and second language acquisition. *Annual Review of Applied Linguistics, 13*, 206–226.

Schmidt, R. (2010). Attention, awareness and individual differences in language learning. In W. M. Chan, S. Chi, K. N. Cin, J. Istanto, M. Nagami, J. W. Sew, T. Suthiwan, & I. Walker (Eds.), *Proceedings of CLaSIC 2010, Singapore, December 2–4* (pp. 721–737). Singapore: National University of Singapore, Centre for Language Studies.

Segalowitz, N., & Freed, B. (2004). Context, contact, and cognition in oral fluency acquisition. *Studies in Second Language Acquisition, 26*(2), 173–199.

Segalowitz, N., Freed, B., Collentine, J., Lafford, B., Lazar, N., & Díaz-Camos, M. (2004). A comparison of Spanish second language acquisition in two different learning contexts: Study abroad and the domestic classroom. *Frontiers: The Interdisciplinary Journal of Study Abroad, 10*, 1–18. Retrieved from https://frontiersjournal.org/wpcontent/uploads/2015/09/SEGALOWITZetal-FrontiersXAComparisonofSpanishSecondLanguageAcquisitioninTwoDifferentLearningContexts.pdf

Selby, R. (2008). Designing transformation in international education. In V. Savicki (Ed.), *Developing intercultural competence and transformation: Theory, research, and application in international education* (pp. 1–10). Sterling, VA: Stylus.

Skehan, P. (2003). Task-based instruction. *Language Teaching, 36*, 1–14.

Talburt, S., & Stewart, M. (1999). What's the subject of study abroad? Race, gender, and 'living culture'. *Modern Language Journal, 83*, 163–175.

Tschirner, E. (2007). The development of oral proficiency in a four-week intensive immersion program in Germany. *Unterrichtspraxis, 40*(2), 111–117.

Van den Branden, K., Bygate, M., & Norris, J. M. (Eds.). (2009). *Task-based language teaching. A reader*. Amsterdam: Benjamins.

Wilkinson, S. (2002). The omnipresent classroom during summer study abroad: American students in conversation with their French hosts. *Modern Language Journal, 86*(2), 157–173.

Willis, J. (1996). *A framework for task-based learning*. Harlow, UK: Longman.

Increasing Student Engagement During Study Abroad Through Service Learning: A View from Japan

Dawn Grimes-MacLellan

Introduction

Study abroad (SA) has increasingly become an important component of a university education. It provides international experiences that can raise awareness about life outside one's home country, develop intercultural understanding, improve foreign language fluency, foster a global perspective, and help prepare students to live and contribute productively in our increasingly globally interdependent world. As students and parents now increasingly demand these international experiences as a value-added component of undergraduate studies, universities are building programmes to serve this need, providing international experiences for students that also help to internationalise the university upon their return.

One of the major reasons why universities, educators, parents, and students look to SA is the belief that an experience abroad will be an

---

D. Grimes-MacLellan (✉)
Meiji Gakuin University, Yokohama, Japan
e-mail: maclelln@gen.meijigakuin.ac.jp

unforgettable, transformative learning experience that will positively impact their lives, possibly forever. While much attention has been placed on promoting SA as a life-changing event that will re-shape students' visions of the world and their place in it, less attention has been paid to assessment that demonstrates that SA is indeed providing learning experiences to students that lead to these outcomes. While there is no question that SA is rich in its possibilities for learning and may be transformative, educators might be so convinced of its potential that they neglect to view it with a sufficiently critical lens to ascertain whether students actually take advantage of the possibilities and do the thoughtful work needed to achieve this transformation. Ramírez (2013), citing the commonly-held expectation of SA as a passive educational endeavour, notes that there is a fundamental difference between 'learning abroad' and 'just going abroad'. From the international educational programmes between the USA and Mexico that he leads, he finds that time spent in a foreign culture does not guarantee meaningful learning outcomes, much less life-changing ones. In my own experiences working with SA students in the USA, Canada, and Japan, I have also found a great diversity in what students learn from the experience and, while I am convinced that many have gained deep knowledge from SA, few can be said to be transformed (see Grimes-MacLellan, 2012, 2016).

With the maturation of SA as a mainstream educational component of a North American university programme, it is not unreasonable to wish now to move beyond the standard narrative of SA as an international 'adventure' (Doerr, 2012) with all the attendant connotations of fun, excitement, and exploration, and ask what we truly hope to achieve from SA. Is transformation an appropriate goal and, if so, is it occurring? How can we increase the likelihood that SA will be transformational for our students? This chapter provides an international host institution perspective on SA, elaborating the possibilities available for those sending institutions that actively seek them. The chapter begins by problematising the assumption of SA as a transformational experience, arguing that it is more likely to occur if students are embedded in an authentic activity in the host country that promotes deep and extended engagement with host country nationals. The chapter then describes a community service-learning (CSL) experience in Japan in which international SA students participated in an authentic volunteer programme designed and organized locally. I discuss the programme's origin, mission, and model of CSL and then describe one of its projects, providing a glimpse of a study tour to an earthquake-ravaged area of northeastern Japan. Following this, I discuss the educational benefits of such an experience for SA students and the advantages of tapping into an existing event or ongoing activity. Finally, I present several recommendations as to how interested educators might best seek out similar opportunities abroad.

Context: Is Study Abroad an Inherently Transformational Experience?

The first questions educators should ask themselves about SA are what is its aim and how can that aim be achieved. A common assumption among educators, parents, and students is that SA aims to be a transformational, life-changing event. However, a growing body of research in the SA literature questions this standard view. Jackson (2015) recently noted that 'while educational international experience is widely assumed to be transformative, leading to significant gain in intercultural competence, [second language] proficiency, and global-mindedness, researchers are discovering that a range of complex internal and external factors can lead to quite disparate outcomes'. Though SA has the potential to be transformative, as it surely was for its early advocates such as SA practitioners and scholars, for this very reason some such advocates may now find themselves too ready to accept uncritically that it will also be so for students. Vande Berg, Paige, and Lou (p. 17) point out that SA practitioners often simply take students at their word: 'We know this to be true because our students themselves confirm it: When they return home, many of them tell us that SA has indeed "transformed" them or has "changed their lives".' Kiely (2004), a veteran educator who brings students to Nicaragua on a social justice international service-learning (ISL) programme, also accepted the 'automatic transformation' hypothesis until he decided to examine the project more critically as a case study:

Because post-trip evaluation of student journals and final reflection papers tended to indicate that profound transformational learning had occurred, I assumed transformation was largely unproblematic and would provide students with the intercultural knowledge and passion to adjust their lifestyles and engage in social justice work. As a result of the present case study, I found that my previous understanding of the meaning and long-term effects of students' 'transformation' on their daily lives had been sorely missing. (p. 6)

While reflection essays after returning home can be a valuable educational tool to help students to subsequently process their SA experiences (Plater, Jones, Bringle, & Clayton, 2009), it is important not to rely solely on them to evaluate whether learning goals have been achieved. Self-reports as a stand-alone measure can be suspect as data collection instruments in research (Vande Berg et al., 2012) and, as evidence of learning, are better triangulated by other measures such as first-hand observations and interviews. Further, while a transformative experience implies a change in outlook, it is important to be clear about the extent of the qualitative criteria—how deeply are students transformed? It is one thing for students to write about their transformed outlook in a reflection essay, but quite another for them to demonstrate that transformation in their subsequent actions. Kiely (2004) reports that while each of his students was 'transformed' to some extent on at least one of six dimensions of their worldview (political, moral, intellectual, personal, spiritual, and cultural), they nonetheless experienced what he calls the 'chameleon complex', a continuing struggle to change their lifestyles in accordance with that transformed worldview over the long term. In terms of Krathwohl, Bloom, and Masia's (1964) affective taxonomy of development, should it be required that students' transformation reach the level of 'characterization', whereby the transformed values are internalised to such an extent that they are expressed consistently in subsequent actions? Or are they merely expected to transform to the levels of 'receiving' or 'responding', with students demonstrating an awareness, sensitivity to, and tolerance of new ideas or a minimal level of commitment that might arise by writing positively about them in reflection journals? The answers to these questions will reside within each educator and institution, as would the consideration of a graded rubric, with higher demands on students according to the number, duration, and depth of SA experiences they have undertaken.

A related common misconception about SA is that the experience will be wholly positive, which is likely to be inconsistent with reality and perhaps not even entirely desirable, especially if the aim is an experience that is transformative. Kiely (2004, p. 8) notes that the ISL programme he leads is intentionally designed to disrupt students' sense of the world in which they live: 'The central premise underlying the programme's service-learning theory is that the experiential dissonance combined with critical reflection and deeper connections with community through service-learning activities will lead to a profound change in students' worldview.' Yet, in spite of such aims, de Wit (2013) points out that, as universities integrate international experiences into their educational programmes and as processes become standardised, the experience itself has changed. Many programmes increasingly try to provide students with a 'soft landing' in a new culture. In so doing, however, they run of the risk of cultivating 'student-tourists' (Engle & Engle, 1999, p. 50), or worse, 'student clients' (Engle & Engle, 2003, p. 6). In many current SA programmes, students are met at the destination airport on arrival, made comfortable while waiting to transfer as a group to local lodgings, given internet access to contact home and friends, and perhaps sequestered during their initial days for a group orientation that provides for their basic needs including food, shelter, and social and emotional refuge among peers, before finally being released to explore the new culture. Engle and Engle (2003, p. 6) write, 'Treating students as paying customers with needs is to deprive them of unfamiliarity and ambiguity, the troubling interaction with which is the heart of a successful sojourn.' If programmes offer students the comforts of home upon arrival abroad in a perhaps well-intended effort to ease their transition, educators should not be surprised if students approach the SA experience passively, somehow hoping that a transformation will magically occur.

Parents, students, and institutions invest a considerable amount of time and money in SA and surely do not want to learn that the experience has been little more than what could have been obtained from a visit to the library, a Wikipedia search, or a 'grand tour' of the area arranged by a commercial travel agency. If the SA experience aims to be transformative and life-changing for students, programmes should help prepare them for the realisation that it is not likely to be entirely positive and may involve some discomfort. They need to be instructed that they will be confronted with new experiences and new ways of thinking that will challenge them to re-think the world and their role in it. There has been a growing interrogation in the SA literature of the assumption that the SA experience will be wholly positive (e.g., Abbott & Lear, 2010; Langseth & Troppe, 1997; Leeds, 1999), and Kiely (2004, p. 8) goes further in calling out SA research as being complicit in perpetuating this stereotype of positive long-term transformation:

> Studies also assume that transformation is uniquely positive. They neglect to consider the challenges that result from questioning the status quo and fail to offer any empirical insight regarding the internal struggles that might result from re-evaluating cherished assumptions. By focussing on the short-term, positive nature of individual perspective transformation, prior research has indirectly fueled a romanticized and uncritical acceptance that the students' intent to act on perspective transformation will often lead to persistent engagement in social action.

One means of helping students realistically imagine their potential transformation and achieve the maximum benefit from their SA experience is a required course to prepare students for their sojourn. As Plater et al. (2009, pp. 492–93) note,

> When students learn at least basic information about the host community (e.g., history, political and economic context, demographics composition, language, social norms), it can help them feel more confident living in the host community and can generate important questions for them to think about and investigate further both before departure and in-country. When they give careful thought to who they are interacting with as well as how and why, and about how they will themselves be served, it helps them define an appropriate role for themselves in-country, avoiding both a 'tourist' approach and a 'technocratic' attitude [...]

The content of this advance preparation is important in shaping the SA experience and providing students with the tools to benefit most from it. Long, Akande, Purdy, and Nakano (2010, p. 92), in the preparation for their study tour of Japan, advocate using an anthropological 'emic' framework, that is, giving priority to local or native concepts, categories, and worldviews: 'In an emic methodology, the categories used and the process of analysis of people of another culture are elicited by relativizing one's own cultural assumptions and through careful observation and questioning of local people.' They further argue that this emic host country model helps to combine SA, personal growth, and deepened engagement with Japanese culture. By preparing students for their upcoming SA experience through this emic approach, the 'benefits were immediately apparent' as it allowed students 'deeper engagement with Japanese culture by participating in a Japanese-style learning process' that helps to 'undermine simple assumptions of globalism [...]. Students can begin to feel cultural differences even before they arrive in Japan' (Long et al., 2010, p. 95).

Pre-departure educational programmes extending beyond a short orientation can help to better prepare students for their upcoming SA experience and, further, the emic methodology can equip students for the interactions they will have when they arrive in the country by preparing them for meeting others with different worldviews, social systems, and cultural practices. However, this approach is only a necessary first step in orienting students for their experience. SA is not primarily an intellectual activity, and an SA experience would never become transformative if it remained only in the realm of cognition, but actual engagement is more difficult to achieve than is commonly assumed. While SA foregrounds the importance of understanding other cultures and worldviews as well as the learning of a foreign language, a means of achieving engagement that makes such understanding and learning more likely must be purposely built into the programme. The addition of CSL enhances this likelihood by adding a practical lived feature with both purpose and connection: 'Combining service learning with overseas study is a unique and powerful pedagogical innovation for increasing adult students' intercultural competence, language skills, appreciation of difference, tolerance of ambiguity, and experiential understanding of complex global problems related to their academic programme of study' (Kiely & Nielsen, 2002, p. 39). Plater et al. (2009, p. 487) add that 'service learning has—with varying degrees of emphasis—the advantage of integrating teaching, research, and service within a coherent educational experience. It thus offers benefits such as great flexibility and utility, which enhance its efficiency and effectiveness.' ISL, meanwhile, is 'one proven pedagogy of engaged learning [that] stands out as an effective means of increasing global awareness and knowledge, of deepening cross-cultural understanding and appreciation of diversity, and of experiencing some other part of the world first hand' (Plater et al., 2009, p. 485).

I would further argue that ISL also provides a mechanism to help SA students navigate barriers that can challenge their engagement in the host country by encouraging intercultural learning as they interact with others tasked with solving meaningful problems. Intercultural learning in ISL thus occurs not merely on a theoretical or intellectual level or through passive observation, but through the daily practice of volunteering and providing meaningful service learning (SL) in authentic activities. ISL also improves students' cultural understanding and language fluency through one-to-one interactions. On the other hand, while the service activity achieves this primarily through activity, pre-departure and post-departure discussions move it from the experiential into the intellectual realm. The following section provides an extended example of a host country ISL programme within which SA students and I became embedded through my collaboration with a volunteer centre at a university in Japan. It is important to note that the organisation and activities described below are not aimed at SA but are established programmes designed for domestic Japanese students and the local communities they support.

Promoting Engagement Through Service Learning at a Japanese University

Meiji Gakuin University Volunteer Center

The Meiji Gakuin University (MGU) Volunteer Center is founded on the Christian principles and educational philosophy of 'Do for Others', which was espoused by the university's American founder, Dr. James Curtis Hepburn. Established in 1998 following an outpouring of MGU student desire to provide support through relief work after the 1995 Great Hanshin-Awaji Earthquake in the western region of Japan, its mission is to 'promote humane education and support Meiji Gakuin students' participation in a variety of fields in which students' volunteer activities can be involved' (MGU Volunteer Center, 2015, p. 1). The Center offers a wide range of programmes open to student participation, including the short-term '1 Day for Others' programme offering single day activities in cooperation with people and organisations close to campus, a longer-term 'Do for Smile@East Japan' project (discussed below) to support a community devastated by the 2011 Great East Japan Earthquake and Tsunami, and an internship programme with Japan-based international organisations that offer first-hand experiences with international exchange and cooperation. In addition, the Volunteer Center serves as a clearinghouse for volunteering opportunities throughout Japan.

It is noteworthy that the MGU Volunteer Center is the first independent office within a university to make a social commitment to volunteer activities and SL in Japan. Its approach to SL is strongly student-centred, and students are actively involved in programme development and the management of the Center. None of its programmes are credit-bearing, however, nor do they fulfil graduation requirements in any way, and this is grounded in the philosophy that volunteering should fundamentally be an intrinsically-motivated activity in the service of others. Nonetheless, interest among students is high, and at any given time more than 100 students are registered with the Volunteer Center to participate in its wide-ranging activities. 'Their role is to learn how to enjoy volunteerism, to spread volunteerism and to build connections between the local area, the university and their fellow students' (MGU, 2015, p. 37), and students who are keenly interested eventually become student leaders who devote many hours of work towards promoting, leading, and developing activities.

While the non-credit-bearing SL model adopted by the MGU Volunteer Center differs from Zlotkowski's (1998, p. 3) widely accepted definition of CSL as 'meaningful community service that is linked to students' academic experience through related course materials and reflective activities', it nonetheless clearly embodies broader principles of experiential learning as outlined by Itin (1999, p. 93) that involve 'carefully chosen experiences supported by reflection, critical analysis, and synthesis [that] are structured to require the learner to take initiative, make decisions, and be accountable for the results'. The Volunteer Center programmes are

Table 1 Differences between a course-based model of SL and the Volunteer Center programmes

Differences of SL models		
	Typical	MGU
Curriculum	Within	Without
Instructor	Professor	Coordinator
Period	Limited (intersession)	Unlimited
Attitude	Less autonomous	Autonomous
Leadership	Fewer chances to occur	More chances to occur (due to on-going & multiple activities)

Source: From Saito and Ichikawa (2013)

carefully organised to provide students with pre-participation background information, volunteering activities on site, and post-participation reflection along with additional opportunities to put their own ideas into subsequent activities and projects. Table 1 outlines some of the ways in which the Volunteer Center model differs from the conventional course-based model. Operating outside the curriculum, Volunteer Center programmes are organised through a central office and supervised by a full-time coordinator and staff, rather than constructed and conducted by a professor. Programmes are on-going throughout the year, including when school is not in session, and students may participate in any activities that interest them as their schedules allow. Educational aims and outcomes are not necessarily determined a priori as would be the case within the structure of a course but are allowed to emerge more organically from within the experience itself. In addition, while a single course carried out during a term is frequently limited to short-term activities and a select group of participants, the Volunteer Center provides the entire campus community with on-going activities in which students can deepen their engagement, gain increased responsibilities, and hone leadership skills whenever they desire.

Another feature of the Volunteer Center model that has emerged due to the on-going nature of activities is the regular participation of some students in the programmes throughout their four years of university. Hence, they are able to become very knowledgeable about the communities and people they work with, forming deep relationships and making meaningful contributions based on long-term engagements with and assessments of their volunteer work.

The Do for Smile@East Japan Project

The Do for Smile@East Japan Project was created in response to the Great East Japan Earthquake and Tsunami that occurred on March 11, 2011 in northeastern Japan. Having had the experience of providing support during the previous 1995 Great Hanshin-Awaji Earthquake, within a few weeks after this latest disaster, the Volunteer Center quickly mobilised fundraising and dispatched teams of student volunteers to the northern region to assist in emergency relief efforts. Japanese MGU students initially assisted at evacuation centres distributing food and taking inventories of supplies and, later, by cleaning lost photographs found in the debris and supporting the resumption of local schools by cleaning classrooms and moving furniture. Their activities were focussed largely in the town of Otsuchi in Iwate Prefecture, which suffered not only extensive physical devastation but also the loss of the town mayor and nearly all of its administration executives, severely hampering recovery efforts in the succeeding months. When the immediate emergency relief work ended, MGU students then worked closely with community members to first understand their on-going needs and then create the following five programmes:

1. Tutoring and Mentoring: offers study support to junior high school students;
2. Social Activities: promotes events to relieve stress and foster communication among local people;
3. Seaside Forest Revitalisation: aids forest reconstruction and revitalisation in collaboration with a local non-profit organisation (NPO);
4. Local Culture Preservation: archives local culture, including language, history, and the process of reconstruction through digitalisation and publication; and
5. *Wanpaku-Hiroba*: develops safe playing spaces for children.

In 2012, a formal partnership between MGU and the town of Otsuchi was established and, to date, more than 1000 MGU students and 30 faculty and staff have participated in the project. Additionally, international students from Australia, England, Malaysia, New Zealand, the Philippines, Taiwan, and the USA have participated in the project since 2013.

The Study Tour

The first step for any student wishing to join the volunteer activities of the Do for Smile@East Japan Project is to participate in a three-day study tour to the affected region. I focus on the study tour in the current chapter because it is the main activity in which SA students participate due to the limited length of their stay in Japan, though some have been able to fit in additional independent volunteer trips to the region. The account that follows occurred in June 2014, but subsequent study tours in which I have participated follow a similar format. Each semester, information sessions are conducted largely by Japanese undergraduate student leaders to introduce and recruit new students to the project and its activities, outline the study tour programme and schedule, and underscore a central tenet: 'Keep in mind that you are an active volunteer, NOT a tourist.' In this regard, student leaders provide guidelines and expectations for volunteer behaviour, reminding students that their volunteer activities aim to support and help alleviate stress within the community, not contribute to it. This is a first lesson in cultivating student sensitivity towards the community and volunteer activities.

Following the information session, students interested in joining the study tour submit an application that requests general personal and contact information, details of any prior volunteering experience, and an essay prompt: 'What is your motivation for this Otsuchi Study Tour and how will you draw on the study tour experience to contribute to the tsunami-affected area or the society around you?' Students selected for the study tour must also acquire parental permission and pay 4000 yen (approximately US$35) for transportation and lodging. Additional costs are subsidised by the university. The study tour is open to 20 MGU students, with up to four of these spots reserved for SA students. The tour is conducted entirely in Japanese, though I have offered translation and language support where necessary based on the SA students' Japanese language abilities. For the most part, however, SA students do their best to keep up, consulting Japanese peers for support or clarification.

Approximately a week before the study tour, a mandatory three-hour orientation meeting is held in which participants receive background reading materials, programme details, the schedule, a packing list, and emergency and evacuation procedures in the event of another disaster. Student leaders introduce themselves and present background information on the disaster and on-going support activities. In addition, they describe the remote coastal fishing town of Otsuchi through a series of photographs from before and after the disaster. To the mostly urban Japanese MGU students, the culture of this rural region is as unfamiliar as it is to SA students.

In 2014, the study tour began with a Friday evening pre-departure meeting prior to the group boarding an overnight bus from Tokyo to Otsuchi, an 8-hour trip of about 350 miles (570 kilometres). At the meeting, travel logistics were explained, group assignments for various activities and duties during the weekend were announced, and all participants introduced themselves and discussed their reasons for joining the study tour and their learning expectations. Questions about the community were also raised and several students voiced some uncertainty about confronting a place that had suffered such devastation.

On arrival the following morning, a full schedule of activities began. After settling in at a community centre, student leaders led the group on a walk to a nearby evacuation point atop a hill and instructed everyone to escape to that location in the event of a tsunami warning. This excursion was not only about obvious safety precautions, but it is also rooted in the local Japanese concept of *tendenko* known in the region for more than a century. *Tendenko* 'primarily describes a cardinal rule for emergency tsunami evacuation, which appears to hinge on the importance of protecting one's own life' (Yamori, 2014, p. 51). In practice, everyone's chance of survival is maximised when each person evacuates individually from schools, homes, or workplaces confident in their understanding that others will do the same (Ishigaki, Higashi, Sakamoto, & Shibahara, 2013, p. 287).[1]

Later that morning, students participated on a tour of the town conducted by a local NPO, *Oraga Otsuchi*, which actively promotes the rebuilding and revitalisation of the community. As students visited local sites—including the former town office where the mayor and other town officials perished, an elementary school that completely burned in the fires following the disaster, and a hill high above the town from which some survivors witnessed their homes and loved ones being washed away—NPO members shared their own devastating personal experiences of the disaster and discussed many of the challenges that the community has faced in its aftermath. Students learned that, even years after the event, reconstruction was on-going and recovery was estimated to take over a decade.

In a measure of support for the local economy, meals during the study tour were taken at local restaurants where students also had the chance to experience the different tastes of the local maritime cuisine. During the afternoon, students visited the local junior high school located on a hilltop, and the former principal recounted how the tsunami waters swelled all the way to the entrance of the school. The school building became an evacuation centre and shelter for displaced residents, and temporary housing constructed on the school grounds was still in use at the time of our visit. The former principal also discussed the counselling needed by local students to cope with the trauma of their experiences and explained his current work focussing on curriculum planning and reform to promote disaster preparedness education.

During the second day of the study tour, students helped clean the community centre in the morning before joining programme activities in small groups headed by a student leader. I accompanied a group that was part of an on-going cultural preservation programme, and we visited the home of an elderly woman for a scheduled meeting with her and a neighbour. Sitting on floor pillows around a low table in a cramped living room, study tour participants listened and observed as the student leader began a conversation with the elderly women. They had met on numerous occasions before and the banter that ensued between them in this intimate setting was more than merely friendly, but more akin to a granddaughter returning home for a visit. This visit was part of a large archiving project to record local dialect and the history of the community, as previously recorded information and documents had been lost in the tsunami. The student leader asked about the pronunciation and meaning of some concepts that she had collected on a previous visit, and from there, stories about the women's childhoods and youth flowed as they explained the words and the contexts from which they were derived. This archiving project not only contributes to important local culture preservation, but also serves as an opportunity for social engagement for elderly community members. Following this morning visit, an afternoon discussion was led by the parent-teacher association president of the local elementary school and focussed on some of the challenges that the community continues to grapple with. He urged MGU students to consider ways in which they could draw upon what they learned during the study tour to make contributions to their own communities and beyond.

In addition to the tours around town, lectures, and participation in ongoing programme activities, the coordinator and student leaders placed great emphasis on reflection activities. At the end of each day of the study tour, students answered questions on a prepared handout. On the first day, questions included impressions of the day's activities (words, scenes, people, landscape), how students now understood the town both before and after the disaster, the significance of continuing to view the region as a site of disaster after a few years had passed, and any remaining questions that had emerged from the day's experiences. These questions were used as the basis for discussion during a 90-minute evening meeting in which small groups of students followed a post-it note pedagogy to share and record their ideas, brainstorming and then organising them on a large sheet of paper to be presented to the larger group towards the end of the session. The day two handout also asked for impressions of the day's activities, and subsequent questions prompted students to talk about what they had learned from the study tour and what they now understood about disaster and recovery. In addition, they were asked to consider how they, as students, might be able to make contributions after learning about the town and its experiences. Discussion using the same post-it note pedagogy followed that evening as well, and later that night students boarded an overnight bus for the return trip to Tokyo. At a follow-up meeting a few days after returning to campus, students discussed what stood out from the study tour for them, how they could draw on their new understanding going forward, and how the study tour could be enhanced to promote student learning.

Benefits for SA Students Joining the Do for Smile@ East Japan Study Tour

The Do for Smile@East Japan study tour is a meaningful introduction carried out with sensitivity and care for students and by students to learn about the experiences of disaster and to consider contributions that individuals can make personally to support community members in their recovery. It is sustained through the on-going partnership between MGU and the community and allows Japanese and SA students alike to gain first-hand insight from local residents who willingly share their stories of escape and resilience following the catastrophic events of the disaster. Based on my participant observation, I believe it is accurate to say that all students are prompted in some way during the study tour to reflect personally on the magnitude of the disaster and recognise the value of even small contributions in support of others.

In addition to the explicit aims of the study tour, this volunteer activity is for SA students more than merely a vehicle for learning about the disaster; it is also an opportunity to actively engage in their own SA experience. An activity like the study tour fosters the development of social networks between SA students and Japanese peers, offers authentic participation in deeply meaningful Japanese cultural experiences, and creates a forum for intercultural learning, points that are explained in more detail below. These attributes are crucial for SA students who participate in island programmes such as the one offered at MGU that are designed and administered exclusively for SA students, who take Japanese language classes and cultural content courses in English with fellow SA students. In addition, as SA students at MGU live at an externally-contracted dormitory for international exchange students located about 20 minutes from campus by train, the programme structure and housing arrangements limit SA students' opportunities to establish friendships with Japanese peers and interact in Japanese.

In contrast to the formal SA programme, participation in the study tour immediately provides SA students with entry into an authentic, organised activity with Japanese peers in a Japanese language and culture context. Through intense and even intimate shared experiences, the study tour provides a setting that fosters the development of social networks among students and feelings of connectedness to the host institution and volunteer activity. These can become important mechanisms of support for SA students upon returning to campus life and throughout their stay abroad. Motivated by the study tour experience and keen to deepen friendships with Japanese peers, one student from New Zealand independently joined two additional volunteering trips to Otsuchi. About these experiences he wrote, 'While on study exchange to MGU, I have had the opportunity to go with the Volunteer Center three times to Otsuchi township in Iwate prefecture, one of the most heavily hit areas in Japan. Each time I have travelled to Otsuchi I have learned more, and have discovered a spirit of resilience within the people of this same town.'

Research indicates that establishing social relationships can be a significant challenge for SA students (Bochner, Hutnik, & Furnham, 1985; Kudo & Simkin, 2003; Mitchell, Tracy-Ventura, & McManus, 2017). In addition to the structural barriers of island programmes mentioned above, seeking friendships may be more difficult in specific cultural settings such as Japan. In a recent US-based study on intercultural friendships, Gareis (2012, p. 320) found that East Asian students had great difficulty in establishing relationships with American peers. Likewise, in Japan, SA students note that Japanese peers tend to be shy, which makes it difficult to get to know them. Host institutions, to their credit, often try to connect SA students with domestic students through a buddy system, but frequently these arrangements are founded on domestic students' desire for language exchange rather than mutual interests. SA students at my university frequently tell me that they are matched with Japanese peers who are English majors (and who expect English conversation), but they want to have friends with whom they can speak Japanese and learn about Japan.

In contrast to language-focussed interactions, friendships fostered out of mutual interests and through authentic activity have a greater chance of enduring, and being able to develop social networks with host culture peers can greatly enhance students' SA experiences. Isabelli-García's (2006) research on SA students in Argentina demonstrates the important role that social networks can have in motivating language learning and cultural understanding as well as promoting positive social attitudes. She (2006, p. 231) writes that 'learners may not magically become fluent speakers simply by being surrounded by the target language' but, rather, motivation is driven by relationships and feelings of connectedness to the host culture. She presents Tom as a case in point. Needing to complete an SL requirement for his home institution, Tom joined volunteer work at a church, which introduced him to a new social circle of Argentines who were also volunteers. This social network subsequently allowed Tom to expand his opportunities for social interaction with native speakers and this, in turn, promoted his second language development. Isabelli-García (2006, p. 255) attributes Tom's social network of Argentine friends to helping him make notable progress in language proficiency and accuracy during his SA: 'Tom, who had success in creating a social network, changed from an instrumental motivation to an integrative and intrinsic motivation throughout the rest of his stay abroad.' Kinginger (2009, p. 149) mentions similar language development success experienced by Louis, an American student in France, who drew on social networks that emerged from volunteer activity: 'By volunteering with a local soup kitchen Louis expanded his circle of friends in Montpellier to include fellow volunteers of all ages and walks of life, thus also expanding his repertoire of formal and informal language.' The extensive study of British students' sojourns abroad by Mitchell et al. (2017) also found similar patterns of language learning efficacy among students who sought friendships with local peers and engaged in local sporting clubs or community networks. Importantly, they note that students who exercise 'agency to enter and develop local networks' make important gains in language learning (p. 163).

The study tour is also a Japanese cultural experience for SA students in several ways. At the most general level, it introduces them to the rural Japanese countryside where the dialect, diet, and daily life differ substantially from urban Tokyo and, despite the disaster, are still prominent features of the community. Volunteer activities in the community also bring SA students into close contact with Japanese people of all ages and walks of life. In Otsuchi, students meet elderly residents, town officials, local business people, and young children. All have stories from which students can learn. Perhaps because of the wounds left by the disaster, frank voices of discontent are also sometimes heard, giving SA students insight into some of the conflicts and challenges that face not only the region but also Japan as a country.[2] In terms of participating in a Japanese-organised volunteer programme, SA students gain an emic window on to how Japanese approach the various contexts of the study tour, conceptualise their work, and engage with the local community. At the most personal level, SA students experience group travel with Japanese peers. Travelling by overnight bus (which is fairly common among Japanese university students, as it is inexpensive), lodging at a community centre where groups of students sleep on futons laid out on tatami-matted floors, and sharing communal bathing facilities segregated only by gender are often new experiences for SA students. On the study tour, SA students also find themselves responsible for pitching in to clean the community centre before departure. This includes not only tidying and vacuuming rooms, cleaning the kitchen, and taking out garbage, but also cleaning sinks and toilets. While Japanese students appear to take readily—if not entirely enthusiastically—to these chores (which is a regular feature of Japanese school life beginning in the elementary years), SA students are initially somewhat baffled and unsure of how to act. After a few awkward moments of observation, however, they tend to follow the lead of their Japanese peers. As an Australian student told me, 'I didn't know what to do, but I just started doing what they were doing.' While these might be seen as insignificant and mundane activities, they are in fact spontaneous cultural learning experiences for SA students. Moreover, experiences such as these—in the margins of the official programme—are frequently where social relationships and motivation for further engagement emerge.

The study tour also offers a forum for intercultural learning, especially where SA students can make a contribution to the experience that provides benefit for all student participants. Initially, SA students are surprised by a study tour that is largely student-driven and student-led, but as Japanese peers support their participation, SA students grow in their motivation to engage in activities as fully as possible. Some SA students have suggested that they found it easier to speak Japanese in circumstances in which they focussed on activities and not specifically on language. This demonstrated to them that they could complete tasks and achieve goals in Japanese with the support of peers, which helped to promote their confidence. Subsequently, through reflective discussions in the evenings, SA students find important ways to make meaningful contributions by drawing on their own background experiences, which prove instructive for Japanese peers. One student from the Philippines, for example, described the devastating impact that Typhoon Haiyan had on her country in 2013 and the differences in response and recovery efforts from those in Otsuchi. Similarly, when a student from New Zealand mentioned the 2011 earthquake in his home country, both Japanese and SA students came to realise some common challenges faced by their countries and began to adopt a more global purpose in thinking about how to help communities move on after a disaster. Through the study tour, SA students gain benefits that exceed the explicit linguistic and culture goals of the programme, acquiring experiences, interest, and recognition in positively engaging in the host culture. One student from New Zealand even found his own way to make a contribution to the project later on by using his multimedia and computer skills to develop a photo-essay booklet, captioned throughout in English, displaying images of the town demonstrating community resilience.

Considerations for Establishing ISL for SA Educators

If the aim of SA is transformative experiences for students, educators must recognise that the demands on faculty, institutions, and collaborating partners in developing and sustaining ISL opportunities are considerable. Preparation in the form of establishing relationships, identifying placements, delineating responsibilities, scheduling, and organising travel and accommodation can be formidable obstacles to ISL. At the same time, while juggling the various organisational tasks, it is important not to overlook getting to know student participants (their backgrounds and language abilities) and shaping their expectations through orientations and other activities where possible. Wessel's (2007) discussion of setting up SL in Mexico for sociology students reveals several types of initial organisational challenges, and even after working through all of the arrangements, she found that, once on the ground in Mexico, students' limited knowledge about the community and differing levels of language ability were also constraints on the programme, highlighting the need for extensive pre-departure preparation (perhaps like the one discussed above). Lear and Abbott (2009, p. 313) also identified 'misaligned expectations' that emerged between students in a Spanish CSL course and community partners. The limitations of students' Spanish language skills, cultural misunderstandings, and a lack of professional workplace skills more generally 'create[d] an extra burden for instructors, students and community partners as they attempt[ed] to create mutually beneficial relationships that utilise and enhance the students' Spanish language skills and cultural knowledge' (Lear & Abbott, 2009, p. 313).

Although ISL models are typically either off-campus components of a home institution course or a short-term intensive travel course, student engagement with the local community may be further enhanced by working more collaboratively with overseas partner institutions, many of whom are increasingly invested in finding means to accommodate international students in their educational programmes and who have cultivated resources that can be drawn upon. In addition to perhaps easing some of the organisational and logistical challenges of setting up independent ISL opportunities that cooperating with a host partner would bring, tapping into an emic host country model of CSL (as described in the previous section) can provide a new framework for learning for SA students. Locally organised community service and volunteer work inherently operates in culturally situated ways and likely with different priorities and approaches than non-locals might expect. Joining in the activities of such a specific framework places SA students in situations that provide 'authentic contact with the host culture' (Engle & Engle, 1999, p. 41), offer direct insight into how activities are conceptualised, operationalised, and performed from an emic or native point of view, and foster social networks that can be further consolidated and enjoyed. One of the hurdles to tapping into the existing resources of the overseas partner institution is finding the appropriate contact, as the established formal contact may not be fully aware of all the opportunities on their own campus for ISL and SA students specifically. The final section (see below) provides some recommendations for undertaking this initial groundwork. In addition, from an international institutional perspective, it is often the case that SA students learn about and become involved in activities such as the Volunteer Center only late in their SA sojourn, limiting chances for participation. Through more collaborative relations with international partners, SA students could become aware of the opportunities before their departure for Japan or at least earlier in their SA experience, to their benefit.

The study tour described above serves as an illustration of the process of bringing SA students together with domestic peers in an organised setting with planned activities and spaces for reflective discussion and co-creation of ideas. It is also important to note that there was ample unstructured time in which students could pursue friendships and personal conversations. The long bus ride, group walks in the community, meals taken together, shared sleeping quarters, and cleaning duties enabled students to make the experience their own, promoting the 'connective learning' that Parker and Altman Dautoff (2007) identified as an important and enduring outcome in their study of a business school course that combined SA and SL in Nicaragua. They write:

> Connective learning, represented by feelings of personal connection and intent or action to stay connected, resulted most from informal face-to-face-interactions rather than formal presentations. We believe that free time activities and work and play with service learning villagers provided time for students to learn about others' lives, hopes, and dreams, and they provided opportunities for students also to share their own thoughts and hopes. In particular, service learning activities stimulated most personal feelings of connections. (2007, p. 48)

The connective learning afforded by an ISL experience helps to motivate engagement with the host culture beyond that experience alone and can potentially lead to personal transformation for SA students. The connective learning may also encompass experiences that are not exclusively positive. Two female SA students, for example, were surprised and uncomfortable sharing bathing facilities with Japanese peers, having never before experienced open room showers and a large soaking bath. Despite initial hesitation, they said they both engaged in the experience as part of 'Japanese culture', and perhaps also because they did not want to stand apart from Japanese peers. Being destabilised can be an important trigger for deep learning, and programmes must therefore be careful not to construct a veneer over the experience but rather to promote one in which students know they are to be engaged participants in the local community and key agents of their own learning. Facilitating cultural integration through service prods SA students into meaningful activity, prompts task-oriented language use to communicate with peers, and makes possible time together to explore social relationships beyond the framed experience. Educators need to take care in providing the overarching structure, preparing students for what they will face, ensuring they have support when needed, and helping them understand their experiences through debriefing activities after they return. The next section provides recommendations as to how overseas institutions can be engaged in this process.

Conclusion and Recommendations

In this chapter, I have described an ISL opportunity in the form of volunteer work organised through a Japanese host institution that offered SA students authentic opportunities to work alongside local peers, use their Japanese language skills, and engage in connective learning that can become a sustaining force for a transformative experience. Although the study tour presented above emerged out of the extraordinary and catastrophic circumstances of the 2011 Great East Japan Earthquake and Tsunami, five years later volunteer activities focus on supporting the community as it continues to move forward through social welfare activities, educational support for local children, and cultural preservation projects. In this sense, while the catalyst motivating community volunteer work could be considered unique, at this juncture the community partnership that has been established and the on-going activities should be seen as comparable to those volunteer activities around the world that address significant social problems, whether they stem from disaster, poverty, hunger, disadvantage, or environmental degradation. While projects are always rooted in the particulars of their context, it may be that these particulars actually help SA educators to explore new possibilities for combining SA and CSL. Citing Grünzweig and Rinehart (2002), Long et al. (2010, p. 95) write, 'International education itself is based on its innovative potential. One of its explicit purposes is to introduce alternative ways of thinking to individuals, organisations, and societies.'

In terms of developing CSL and volunteer work opportunities through a partner institution in order to optimise the opportunities for transformation, the following steps are a guideline based on my observations of the example I have described from Japan. A crucial first step is to identify partner institutions that connect with the programme director's discipline, area of research, language, or topic of interest. These may be listed on the university's website, but also consider contacting the university's international or SA office to learn of new partnerships in development. Also, check out partner institution websites (many have English pages to some extent) to learn about student support organisations and activities that may fit your aims.

Follow up by seeking a contact person at the partner institution who may be able to direct enquiries to appropriate resources in the institution. Enquire if anyone on the home campus can suggest a contact person. If language is a barrier to contacting the partner institution, search for foreign faculty on the university's website. This is also a good way to make initial informal enquiries to ascertain possible resources, contact people, and strategies for making further enquiries. Most importantly, consider both formal and informal channels to gather information. The formal contact may not be the person who is most amenable, interested, or able to develop these arrangements, so it is important to locate the appropriate person at the institution who can help.

Remember as well that students can be a rich source of information, both students who have returned from SA at the partner institution being considered as well as exchange students from the target country. Tell them about your programme aims and ask them about potential local opportunities. Also enquire about their own SA experiences and ask for their thoughts on how their programmes might have been enhanced, or could have included CSL or volunteer work. When compiling a list of potential CSL or volunteer work opportunities, focus on ones that collaborate with local peers, and emphasise learning by doing over language-intensive activities. Students, especially those with more limited foreign language skills, will find this less intimidating, and can work at their own pace to build confidence while still forging new friendships.

When designing the programme, build in supporting features for CSL or volunteer work through orientations, gatherings to get to know participating students, activities to reflect on experiences, and post-event debriefing and discussion. Remember also to include unstructured time for students to get to know local peers, use their conversational language skills, and form relationships. Unstructured time can take many forms:

such as an extended lunchtime, travelling together to a specific destination, or an independent group activity. Most importantly, keep in mind that it is likely that unstructured time will offer students some of the best opportunities to make their SA experiences their own and set them on a transformative journey.

Finally, expect that forging new connections and developing a curriculum of this nature takes time, and that you may encounter hurdles. Don't be discouraged. To observe students engaging in the host culture and becoming independent language learners with new friends while carrying out meaningful activity is worth the effort.

Summary of recommendations for setting up ISL based on an example from Japan
- Identify partner institutions and student support organisations that match the CSL or volunteer work objectives.
- Seek a contact person at the partner institution. Consider formal and informal channels.
- Talk with post-SA students and exchange students from the target country about local possibilities or desired CSL experiences.
- Focus on joining CSL or volunteer work that collaborate with local peers, and where SA students can learn through observation and participation.
- Design a programme that includes orientation, reflection, and debriefing along with unstructured time for students to form friendships with peers.
- Expect hurdles, but don't give up!

Notes

1. Unfortunately, many townspeople did not follow their own long-held local knowledge in the immediate wake of the earthquake. Many died after they had initially evacuated to safety, but then returned to the low-lying town centre in search of family members, only to succumb to the tsunami wave that breached a 30-foot protective seawall.
2. Regarding the upcoming 2020 Tokyo Olympics, for example, it is not uncommon to hear local Otsuchi voices question the government's commitment to their region as it allocates substantial funds for sports stadiums and other athletic facilities in Tokyo, which they already regard as having greater overall economic wealth.

Bibliography

Abbott, A., & Lear, D. (2010). The connections goal area in Spanish community service-learning: Possibilities and limitations. *Foreign Language Annals, 43*(2), 231–245.

Bochner, S., Hutnik, N., & Furnham, A. (1985). The friendship patterns of overseas and host students in an Oxford student residence. *Journal of Social Psychology, 125*(6), 689–694.

de Wit, H. (2013). The different faces and phases of internationalization of higher education. In A. Maldonado & R. Bassett (Eds.), *The forefront of international higher education* (pp. 95–106). New York: Springer.

Doerr, N. (2012). Study abroad as 'adventure': Construction of imaginings of social space and subjectivities. *Critical Discourse Studies, 9*(3), 257–268.

Engle, J., & Engle, L. (1999). Program intervention in the process of cultural integration: The example of French practicum. *Frontiers: The Interdisciplinary Journal of Study Abroad, 5,* 39–59.

Engle, L., & Engle, J. (2003). Study abroad levels: Toward a classification of program types. *Frontiers: The Interdisciplinary Journal of Study Abroad, 9,* 1–20.

Gareis, E. (2012). Intercultural friendship: Effects of home region and sojourn location. *Journal of International and Intercultural Communication, 5*(4), 309–328.

Grimes-MacLellan, D. (2012). Students in the field at the site of the great East Japan earthquake. *Asia Pacific Journal, 10*(4), 1–12.

Grimes-MacLellan, D. (2016). Cultural consultants in the classroom: Harnessing international student mobility for intercultural learning. *Japanese Studies Association Journal, 13*(1), 93–115.

Grünzweig, W., & Rinehart, N. (2002). International understanding and global interdependence: Towards a critique of international education. In W. Grünzweig & N. Rinehart (Eds.), *Rockin' in Red Square: Critical approaches to international education in an age of cyberculture* (pp. 5–24). Hamburg and London: LIT Verlag.

Isabelli-García, C. (2006). Study abroad social networks, motivation and attitudes: Implications for second language acquisition. In M. A. DuFon & E. Churchill (Eds.), *Language learners in study abroad contexts* (pp. 231–258). Clevedon, UK: Multilingual Matters.

Ishigaki, A., Higashi, H., Sakamoto, T., & Shibahara, S. (2013). The great East-Japan earthquake and devastating tsunami: An update and lessons from the past great earthquakes in Japan since 1923. *Tohoku Journal of Experimental Medicine, 229*, 287–299.

Itin, C. (1999). Reasserting the philosophy of experiential education as a vehicle for change in the 21st century. *The Journal of Experimental Education, 22*(2), 91–98.

Jackson, J. (2015, July 16). *Research-inspired interventions in study abroad programming.* Plenary Talk IV. The Culture of Study Abroad for Second Languages Conference, Halifax, NS, Canada.

Kiely, R. (2004). A chameleon with a complex: Searching for transformation in international service learning. *Michigan Journal of Community Service Learning, 10*(2), 5–20.

Kiely, R., & Nielsen, D. (2002). International service learning: The importance of partnerships. *Community College Journal, 73*(3), 39–41.

Kinginger, C. (2009). *Language learning and study abroad: A critical reading of research.* New York: Palgrave Macmillan.

Krathwohl, D., Bloom, B., & Masia, B. (1964). *Taxonomy of educational objectives: Handbook II, affective domain.* New York: David McKay Co.

Kudo, K., & Simkin, K. A. (2003). Intercultural friendship formation: The case of Japanese students at an Australian university. *Journal of Intercultural Studies, 24*(2), 91–114.

Langseth, M., & Troppe, M. (1997). So what? Does service-learning really foster social change? In M. Langseth & M. Troppe (Eds.), *Expanding boundaries: Building civic responsibility within higher education* (Vol. 2, pp. 37–42). Columbia, MD: Cooperative Education Association.

Lear, D., & Abbott, A. (2009). Aligning expectations for mutually beneficial service-learning: The case of Spanish language proficiency, cultural knowledge, and professional skills. *Hispania, 92*(2), 312–323.

Leeds, J. (1999). Rationales for service-learning: A critical examination. *Michigan Journal of Community Service Learning, 6*(1), 112–122.

Long, S. O., Akande, Y., Purdy, R. W., & Nakano, K. (2010). Deepening learning and inspiring rigor: Bridging academic and experiential learning using a host country approach to a study tour. *Journal of Studies in International Education, 14*(1), 89–111.

Meiji Gakuin University. (2015). *MG diary 2015.* Tokyo: Meiji Gakuin University.

Meiji Gakuin University Volunteer Center. (2015). *MGU Volunteer Center leaflet.* Tokyo: Meiji Gakuin University.

Mitchell, M., Tracy-Ventura, N., & McManus, K. (2017). *Anglophone students abroad: Identity, social relationships, and language learning.* New York: Routledge.

Parker, B., & Altman Dautoff, D. (2007). Service-learning and study abroad: Synergistic learning opportunities. *Michigan Journal of Community Service Learning, 13*(2), 40–53.

Plater, W. M., Jones, S. G., Bringle, R. G., & Clayton, P. H. (2009). Educating globally competent citizens through international service learning. In R. Lewin (Ed.), *The handbook of practice and research in study abroad: Higher education and the quest for global citizenship* (pp. 485–505). New York: Routledge.

Ramírez, G. B. (2013). Learning abroad or just going abroad? International education in opposite sides of the border. *Qualitative Report, 18*(62), 1–11.

Saito, Y., & Ichikawa, K. (2013, December 11). *The challenge of service-learning in Meiji Gakuin University (MGU)*. 14th IAVE Asia-Pacific Regional Volunteer Conference, Macau.

Vande Berg, M., Paige, R. M., & Lou, K. H. (2012). Student learning abroad: Paradigms and assumptions. In M. Vande Berg, R. M. Paige, & K. H. Lou (Eds.), *Student learning abroad: What our students are learning, what they're not and what we can do about it* (pp. 3–28). Sterling, VA: Stylus.

Wessel, N. (2007). Integrating service learning into the study abroad program: U.S. sociology students in Mexico. *Journal of Studies in International Education, 11*(1), 73–89.

Yamori, K. (2014). Revisiting the concept of tsunami tendenko: Tsunami evacuation behavior in the great East Japan earthquake. In H. Kawase (Ed.), *Studies on the 2011 off the Pacific coast of Tohoku earthquake* (pp. 49–64). Tokyo: Springer Japan.

Zlotkowski, E. (1998). A service learning approach to faculty development. In R. A. Rhodes & J. P. F. Howard (Eds.), *Academic service learning: A pedagogy of action and reflection* (pp. 21–30). San Francisco: Jossey-Bass.

Part III

Participant Experiences and Engagement

Exploring Intercultural Learning and Second Language Identities in the ERASMUS Context

Ana Beaven and Claudia Borghetti

Introduction

The increase in the number of students taking part in study abroad (SA) programmes worldwide has triggered, on the part of Higher Education institutions, the inclusion of both the linguistic and (inter)cultural preparation and guidance of students before, during, and after SA. It is in this context that the *Intercultural Education Resources for ERASMUS Students*

This work was supported by the Education, Audiovisual & Culture Executive Agency and the European Commission, Directorate General for Education and Culture, under the Lifelong Learning Programme, ERASMUS [527373-LLP-1-2012-1-IT-ERASMUS-ESMO]. We would also like to thank the students who took part in the study, and the IEREST partners who developed the activity presented here.

A. Beaven (✉)
University Language Centre, University of Bologna, Bologna, Italy
e-mail: ana.beaven@unibo.it

C. Borghetti
Department of Modern Languages, Literature, and Cultures, University of Bologna, Bologna, Italy
e-mail: claudia.borghetti@unibo.it

© The Author(s) 2018
J. L. Plews, K. Misfeldt (eds.), *Second Language Study Abroad*,
https://doi.org/10.1007/978-3-319-77134-2_7

and their Teachers (IEREST) European project was developed. The project aimed to produce a set of teaching modules to help students taking part in the European Community Action Scheme for the Mobility of University Students (ERASMUS) benefit from their sojourn in terms of personal growth and intercultural learning (Beaven & Borghetti, 2015).

This chapter explores especially the issue of how students make sense of their language experiences while studying abroad. When investigating SA outcomes, most researchers have focussed on second language (L2) gains (see, for example, Kinginger, 2009; Pérez-Vidal, 2014), while some have analysed outcomes related to interculturality such as intercultural competence (see Vande Berg, Paige, & Lou, 2012) or global citizenship (Lewin, 2009). Others still have looked at intercultural development through the L2. Jackson (2008, p. 11), for example, analyses 'the nature of language learning, identity (re)construction, and the development of intercultural communicative competence and intercultural personhood in L2 sojourners and also tests contemporary sociocultural perspectives by investigating the actual experiences of L2 sojourners'. Block (2007) has also discussed identity issues in L2 acquisition, including in SA contexts, although he did not focus specifically on the issue of intercultural development. Benson, Barkhuizen, Bodycott, and Brown (2012, 2013), on the other hand, have analysed the development of L2 identities in SA contexts in great detail and with some import for considering interculturality.

Following Benson et al.'s (2012, 2013) line of thought, in this study we argue that, in a context of L2 use such as SA, students' language experiences constitute language-mediated identity work. Moreover, in some cases, such experiences can also be conceptualised as opportunities for intercultural development according to a non-essentialist perspective of culture (Holliday, 2011, para. 2). The study intended to investigate how such opportunities arose during an IEREST course, which was taught online to 33 ERASMUS students from the University of Bologna who, at the time, were studying abroad in a variety of European countries. Students and teachers worked online for six weeks, using a set of communication tools, including a course blog. The current chapter focusses on data gathered from the blog postings.

In order to analyse the students' language-mediated identity work, we draw on Benson et al.'s (2012, 2013) framework of L2 identity development, and especially their three domains of (1) 'identity-related L2 proficiency', (2) 'linguistic self-concept', and (3) 'L2-mediated personal development'. Benson et al. adopt different terms in their two publications; we are using the terminology in the 2012 publication. The first term, 'identity-related L2 proficiency', is defined as an individual's 'ability to do things with words, to function as a person, and express desired identities' (2012, p. 183). The second, 'linguistic self-concept', relates to the individual's 'sense of who they are as language learners and users, and their ability to negotiate personal identities through a second language' (2012, p. 184). The third, 'L2-mediated personal development', refers to aspects such as personal growth and independence, as well as intercultural learning, including appreciation of culturally different others. In Benson et al.'s (2013) model, these three dimensions of L2 identity development are not mutually exclusive and are arranged along a continuum from L2 proficiency to personal development.

Although there is no single vision of what intercultural learning[1] entails, factors that have been associated with it involve cognitive, affective, and behavioural changes with regard to culturally different others (Byram, 1997; Deardorff, 2006). In addition, intercultural development can be seen as independent from knowledge of a specific culture, and therefore involving attitudes, skills, and knowledge that are applicable to any cultural group, including those one belongs to (Risager, 2005). These features assume somewhat different connotations if framed within a non-essentialist approach of culture (Holliday, 2011). Indeed, if culture is any 'discourse community that shares a common social space and history, and common imaginings' (Kramsch, 1998, p. 10), then we can also speak of the cultures of a professional community or a group of ERASMUS students, not only of nation states. What distinguishes the former 'small cultures' from the latter 'large cultures' (national or ethnic ones) are not their intrinsic features, but rather the fact that the large ones have been reified in time, mostly for political purposes (Holliday, 1999). Within this framework, an individual can belong to a varying number of different large and small cultures, identification with which is contextual (e.g., the same SA student can feel Italian when with co-nationals, but international when with other mobile students). This implies that those whom an individual considers 'others' will depend on the cultural group of reference in that specific context and can vary with it (Bucholtz & Hall, 2005, 2011). Thus, if interpreted within a non-essentialist framework, intercultural learning is the process through which individuals become aware of diversity, as well as able to act upon such awareness (Beaven & Borghetti, 2016). Moreover, intercultural development is also linked to identity development (Kramsch, 2009), as reflecting on one's experience of diversity can lead to conflicts due to the realisation of being culturally situated—but not culturally determined—individuals. Indeed, the awareness that there are as many different identity positions as cultural groups with which one identifies implies that identity is—to a certain degree—a deliberate choice. Language (L1, L2, L3) can play a main role in this process: it is also through the opportunities of language use—in terms of variety and types of contexts, interlocutors, and topics being discussed—that one can imagine possible new identities for the future (Norton, 2012), glimpsed through our encounters with cultural others.

Context: Interculturality and ERASMUS

SA is not a new phenomenon: it can be traced back to the time when medieval scholars travelled from one university to the other to expand their knowledge. Europe's flagship mobility programme, ERASMUS, is in fact named after the European scholar Erasmus of Rotterdam (1465–1536), a humanist and theologian who studied and taught in various European countries. ERASMUS was launched in 1987, substituting the previous (bilateral) Joint Study Programme Scheme, which was founded in 1976. Today, the new ERASMUS+ programme (2014–2020) enables students to go abroad for either one or two semesters, at undergraduate, Master's, or doctoral level; it is also no longer limited to European destinations and includes teachers and staff. The participants can do a work placement, or study in a different Higher Education institution, which is the most common type of experience.

Since its launch in 1987, when 3244 students from 11 countries took part, ERASMUS has enabled around 3.3 million students to study or do a placement abroad; in 2013–2014, 272,000 individuals from 28 European Union (EU) member states in addition to some non-EU countries[2] took part in the programme (European Commission, 2015). While the Joint Study Programme Scheme's main concern was to offer opportunities for the 'cultural and academic enrichment' of the students taking part (Council of Europe, 1984), since the mid-1990s the ERASMUS programme has had as its driving force the development of employability skills and active citizenship. According to the European Commission (2015):

> mobility contributes to combatting youth unemployment, an objective which features prominently in the Europe 2020 strategy for growth and jobs. It also equips the new generation with social, civic and intercultural skills, an essential element of the 2015 Paris Declaration following the terrorist attacks in Paris and Copenhagen. (European Commission, 2015, p. 4)

Thus, the aims of European student mobility go beyond those of offering participants opportunities to study in a different country and learn a new language. They include individuals' personal and professional development:

> students certainly improve their foreign language skills and develop greater intercultural awareness; but they also develop soft skills, such as being able to quickly adapt to changes and new situations, solve problems, work in teams, think critically, be tolerant of different views and communicate effectively [...] A third of former ERASMUS students now live with a partner of a different nationality. (European Commission, 2015, p. 4)

The increase in the number of students taking part in SA programmes not only in Europe but also worldwide has triggered a need to offer participants improved preparation for their SA. This preparation is not limited to language skills development. Since research has shown that intercultural skills are not automatically developed as a result of direct contact with cultural diversity (Abdallah-Pretceille, 2008; Anquetil, 2006) or that, when they are, they decrease upon return if not properly supported (Merino & Avello, 2014), much attention is now given to ways of boosting students' opportunities to develop their intercultural competence (Beaven &

Borghetti, 2015; Jackson & Oguro, 2018). Therefore, there has been an increased interest on the part of Higher Education institutions also to provide (inter)cultural preparation, guidance, and debriefing to participants before, during, and after SA. The focus on intercultural preparation and learning is clearly not limited to the European context. The USA also has a long tradition of SA, and several programmes have been preparing students from an intercultural point of view for nearly two decades. Paige and Vande Berg (2012) and related chapters in the same volume (Vande Berg et al., 2012) review some of the most significant projects. The preparation programmes described there all refer—at least in their evaluation of outcomes—to the *Intercultural Development Inventory* (Hammer, 2007; Hammer & Bennett, 1998) and to the related *Developmental Model of Intercultural Sensitivity* (Bennett, 1993). Deardorff's (2006) model of intercultural competence is also especially influential in the USA, while Jackson's (2008, 2010) work on the preparation and outcomes of SA in terms both of language and intercultural development has been instrumental in effecting change in the East Asian context over the last decade. Clearly, a review of these frameworks is beyond the scope of this chapter, but there seems to be a general agreement among scholars in Europe and globally that simply spending time abroad is not sufficient for deep intercultural learning to take place.

The IEREST Project and the Teaching Activity '24 h ERASMUS Life'

It is in this context that the IEREST project, an ERASMUS Multilateral Project (2012–2015), was developed. The three-year project was co-funded by the European Commission within the *Lifelong Learning Programme* (2007–2013). Its aim was to develop and publish—in the form of Open Educational Resources—what was termed an 'Intercultural Path', a set of three teaching modules to be provided to ERASMUS students before, during, and after their experience abroad. This includes the 'while-abroad' teaching activity '24 h ERASMUS Life' (IEREST, 2015), which provided the context for this study. The IEREST materials were not designed to teach interculturality through the L2, for intercultural development does not necessarily involve communicating in a different language. However, when the intercultural experience happens in or through a L2—as is the case of the participants in this study—this inevitably influences the experience.

IEREST is founded in an understanding of interculturality 'as a lifelong learning process which entails the recognition and appreciation of one's own and others' multiplicities' (Beaven & Borghetti, 2015, p. 8). Its theoretical underpinnings derive from the non-essentialist approach to interculturality (Holliday, 2011) mentioned above. In other words, students taking part in the project were invited to consider culture not as taken-for-granted national or ethnic characteristics, but rather as a set of meanings, values, and behaviours negotiated by (and within) any social group. Even though their SA experience foregrounded the international dimension of diversity, participants were encouraged to reflect also on the existence of 'small cultures' (e.g., the ERASMUS community or the 'locals') in Holliday's (1999) terms.

From a methodological point of view, the three teaching modules of the IEREST Intercultural Path, designed for each of the phases of mobility (before, during, and after), are divided into activities: four for Module 1 and three for Modules 2 and 3, respectively. The activities are divided again into tasks. Each activity is based on Kolb's (1984) learning cycle, which involves four phases: 'concrete experience', 'reflective observation', 'abstract conceptualisation', and 'active experimentation'. This means that, while the theoretical frame is important, it can only have a meaningful effect if, through reflection, students can interpret their lived experiences in the light of the conceptual inputs.

The 'while-abroad' module is based on two main ideas. First, it encourages students to reflect on the expectations, emotions, difficulties, and opportunities offered by their life abroad and, second, it invites them to explore the new environment and build new relationships. It comprises the three Activities: *'24 h ERASMUS Life'*, *Intercultural Geography*, and *Experiencing (Interculturality through) Volunteering* (IEREST, 2015). These three activities combine different types of field-work derived from ethnography with self-reflection carried out through the writing of personal diaries based on the students' first-hand experiences.

The activity '24 h ERASMUS Life' (for details, see IEREST, 2015, pp. 58–73) encourages students to reflect on their daily experiences using personal diaries as assignments. These are submitted at regular intervals to the teacher, who selects and anonymises relevant extracts, and offers them to the class for discussion. The topics the students are required to write about are:

1. the emotional dimension of living in a different country (possible instances of 'culture shock', homesickness, sense of autonomy, and so forth);
2. the students' social networks, including their friendships with co-nationals, other international students, or locals;
3. their views regarding the educational system of their home and host institutions, and how their opinions may be influenced by their own cultural assumption regarding what are 'normal' or 'good' learning and teaching models;
4. language experiences, including L2 identity-related aspects (how they feel when using their L1 and L2 abroad, speaking with native or non-native speakers, code-switching, and so forth).

Throughout the activity, writing the personal diary aligns with the 'reflective observation' phase in Kolb's (1984) experiential learning cycle, while elements of theory and related terminology (e.g., 'culture shock', 'large/small cultures', or 'linguistic self-concept'), provided by the teacher, correspond to the phase of 'abstract conceptualisation'.

The version of the activity contained in the IEREST (2015) manual was designed to be taught face-to-face. However, as suggested in the introduction, it can also be delivered at a distance while the students are abroad. This is the format adopted at the University of Bologna. The fact that the activity was taught online required a certain degree of adaptation of the tasks. One of the main differences regarded the substitution of the personal diaries with an online class blog.

Like other social media, blogs are increasingly used in higher education (Tess, 2013), especially in the foreign language classroom (Blake, 2013) and for intercultural learning in SA contexts (Elola & Oskoz, 2008). Like journals, blogs promote self-expression and help students reflect on their experiences (Lee, 2010; Yang, 2009). They therefore seemed a good alternative to the personal diaries in the original format of the activity. Indeed, Urlaub (2011) argues that

> this writing-intensive environment helps learners to develop the necessary level of reflectivity in order to develop nuanced ideas about their own and the foreign cultural contexts. Blogging [...] facilitate[s] epistemic writing, a stage of literacy development where writing becomes a tool to reorganize incoming information and to develop complex thoughts, reflections, and viewpoints. (p. 43)

In addition, class blogs encourage collaborative learning and interaction between the writers of each post and the rest of the class, who can respond to the posts by writing comments (Lee, 2009). In choosing to replace personal journals with a class blog, we considered this as an advantage, in that the discussions based on the reading of the journal entries in the face-to-face version of the activity could take place directly within the class blog in the online course.

The Study

The aim of this study is to explore how participants in the online version of the IEREST '24 h ERASMUS Life' activity conducted at the University of Bologna made sense of issues related to language and identity by applying the framework developed by Benson et al. (2012, 2013). In addition, with a view to observing the efficacy of IEREST, we investigated how the teaching resources facilitated intercultural learning within the non-essentialist perspective adopted.

Participants

The '24 h ERASMUS Life' activity was taught online to 33 outgoing students (26 female, 7 male) from the University of Bologna in autumn 2014, when they were doing their one-semester SA period in different European countries (Austria 1, Belgium 4, Denmark 2, Estonia 1, Finland

2, France 4, Germany 3, Hungary 2, Iceland 1, Lithuania 1, Netherlands 4, Portugal 1, Spain 5, UK 2). They were both undergraduate and postgraduate students majoring in a variety of subjects (Agricultural Science 3, Arts and Humanities 3, Communication Sciences 1, Economics 4, Education 2, Engineering 3, Law 1, Modern Languages 7, Pharmacy 2, Politics 5, Psychology 2). The course took place between 31 October and 12 December 2014, which means that the students had been abroad for about two months before the course began. In the findings below, the participants are identified by 'S' for 'student' and a number.

Data Collection

Students and teachers worked online for six weeks, using a set of communication tools, including forums, videoconferences, chat rooms, and a class blog. The present study focusses on data gathered from the blog postings. In total, 22 students wrote at least one post in the class blog. The total number of posts was 47, with some students contributing one post and some up to three. The students were also encouraged to write comments in reply to other participants' posts, and there were a total of 126 comments. The total number of words analysed was 35,975.

Although writing in the class blog was a pre-requisite for obtaining three European Credit Transfer and Accumulation System (ECTS) credits assigned to the course, 11 students did not write their posts. This was due to a number of reasons: some had technical problems with the blog and thus contributed only through the course forum; others preferred to take on a more passive role and relinquish their credits.

Data Analysis

The first analysis was carried out to identify all the extracts referring to the students' language experiences (related to any of the four different topics proposed by the tasks, that is, emotions, social networks, academic experience, and language), whether they included the terms 'language' or not. As expected, the blog posts in which the students were asked to discuss their language-related experiences had more instances, but language-related issues were also mentioned when online interactions focussed on other issues (e.g., academic achievement, international friendships). The fact that we focussed on extracts related to language means that some instances in which students discuss intercultural issues do not appear in the dataset. Nevertheless, the advantage of this choice is that instances of intercultural reflections that were included are strongly related to language use. Secondly, the extracts where language experiences (in any language, including the students' L1) were mentioned were then analysed thematically (Braun & Clarke, 2006) and codes were identified. The third phase of analysis involved associating the different codes to the three domains of L2 identities developed by Benson et al. (2012, 2013). We excluded from the analysis any codes that were not related to these three aspects (e.g., issues related to their beliefs about the most effective way to learn a language, or about whether English should be used more widely in Italy), to focus on the relationship between language, identity, and interculturality. Finally, the codes within each of the three dimensions were reviewed in order to identify themes.

Findings

The themes which emerged from the analysis are reported in this section, divided according to the three dimensions of L2 identity on Benson et al.'s (2012, 2013) framework.

Identity-Related L2 Proficiency

On L2 SA, being able to solve problems independently or succeed academically, in other words to function in everyday life and perform one's identity—and possibly expand it—as a competent individual and student is necessarily mediated through the L2. Therefore, regarding 'identity-related L2 proficiency'—that is, the ability to do things and function as a person in the L2—one of the recurring themes in the data is the difficulty of expressing oneself in the L2, even when attempting to get trivial things done. As a result, many students mentioned a sense of frustration, articulated in terms of feeling 'stupid', 'retarded', and 'inadequate' and even of 'going crazy':

Excerpt 1 S13: Even something simple like asking for a bus ticket becomes complicated. (Translation from Italian)

Excerpt 2 S12: The initial days were a massacre for my self-esteem. I found it hard to communicate well and naturally in English, above all in everyday life. (Translation from Italian)

Excerpt 2 is especially relevant as the student explicitly describes the impact of the lack of L2 fluency as a threat to her self-esteem. Most probably the utterance, expressed as a hyperbole, contains a hint of self-irony. Nevertheless, from an analytical point of view, this example is a key case: failing to project one's desired identity through the L2 can result in questioning, even momentarily, one's actual identity.

Notably, this difficulty is felt especially in the academic context, where the inability to write assignments or take part in a seminar can leave individuals with a sense of inadequacy in respect to their idea of themselves as effective students:

Excerpt 3 S1: However, while I started doing the assignment, I realised that, even though I knew the concepts/ideas, I wasn't able to express myself as I wanted. I felt constraint by my lack of fluency in French. Even if I do speak this language, I feel as I can't write as freely as I would do it, for instance, in English, or in my native language (Spanish). [...] Not only at the beginning of the exchange period, but still today, I often have a feeling of 'inadequacy' while using French language, particularly in an academic context.

Several participants remarked how this feeling of inadequacy, of disappointment about not being able to function as an individual/student, was made worse by a sense of exhaustion and of being overextended, due to the effort of having to do everything in the foreign language:

Excerpt 4 S18: After two hours I'm exhausted and my brain is burnt out. This goes on for a couple of weeks, I get back from lessons and it feels like I've been studying for 24 h non-stop.

However, in most cases this sense of frustration was compensated for by the students' motivation and determination (see Excerpt 5) or by interacting with other L1 speakers, as co-nationals can make one feel better understood and thus help re-establish self-confidence (see Excerpt 6).

Excerpt 5 S1: However, instead of getting frustrated I tell to myself: this is why you are here. It will come, don't worry … It has only been a month. You'll get better! I am sure I will. The important thing is NEVER to be discouraged.

Excerpt 6 S3: Finally, my Italian friends … I tried to force myself to avoid Italian people at the beginning. I just stayed in touch to do not be rude. And I am very lucky to have them here because sometime you need to speak about your emotions or feelings and in English it may be very hard or impossible. They made me feel self-confident and with strong roots which helps to stay balanced when everything seems wrong.

Clearly, not all difficulties related to L2 proficiency are directly linked to identity. Nevertheless, the data analysis has shown evidence that lack of language skills can threaten self-identity and, considering the SA context, especially academic identities. This can be intellectually and emotionally taxing, but our students showed that they can draw on their own personal and social resources to counterbalance these difficulties.

Linguistic Self-concept

The dimension of 'Linguistic self-concept' partially implies that of 'Identity-related L2 proficiency', as (not) being able to express one's own meanings through the L2 represents a precondition for having and developing an idea of oneself as L2 learner and user. However, our analysis helped to distinguish the cases when language proficiency, rather than being a help or a hindrance to getting things done, was linked in various ways to the feeling of being capable (or incapable) social actors in the L2-speaking community. In the vast majority of cases, this was related to being a university student abroad (see Excerpts 7 and 8).

Excerpt 7 S13: Fear of failing, fear of not being able to pass exams as well as I could have done in my natural language [...] I think I may not obtain the expected result. You think you won't be able to take exams, you won't learn a new language, you won't do anything. (Translation from Italian)

Here, S13 expresses not only the discomfort caused by not being able to use the L2 well, but also the concern that she may not be a successful language learner or user. In her words, it is possible to perceive how she links her lack of linguistic skills to a possible threat to her self-concept as a successful university student. These feelings of incompetence can also make individuals position themselves/be positioned as outsiders and abstainers in the local academic community, as the student in Excerpt 8 explains:

Excerpt 8 S1: I am pretty much an outgoing person and I don't have trouble in expressing my opinion in public. In general, I like to participate in class and communicate my questions or comments. However, due to the language barrier I am encountering during my time abroad, this started to change, and I preferred not to do it so, as I didn't feel comfortable with speaking in public in a language I am not proficient in. At the beginning this gave me the impression of being 'outside' the group discussion, 'outside' the class; indeed, I was locking me outside because of my fear to speak in a foreign language.

Feeling—or being made to feel—like an outsider because of a lack of L2 proficiency seems to affect not so much this student's *linguistic* self-concept, but rather his perception as a confident and communicative person. This identity threat triggers a kind of self-protection mechanism in which the student closes himself out or withdraws from the group. Incidentally, we notice in this extract, as in many others, a reference to the effect of time (e.g., speaking about the initial moments, or how things had changed). We will return to these changes perceived with the passing of time in the following sections.

'Linguistic self-concept' does not always manifest itself in a negative way. In a number of instances students overcome their feelings of inadequacy by developing specific learning, personal, and identity-management coping strategies (Excerpts 9, 10, and 11). Overall this leads some of them to foresee a different language-oriented future for themselves (Excerpt 12).

As for many instances identified within the 'identity-related L2 proficiency' dimension, Excerpt 9 illustrates a recurrent emotion in many students: that of feeling inadequate, even infantile, when using the L2.

Excerpt 9 S6: I feel like a child learning to speak, attentive to everything and every word, who practices on his own … for example, when I'm out or on the bus [...], I pay more attention to the words the others say and I try to understand what they're talking about, and I check if I've understood all the words or not, in short it's like mental notebook. (Translation from Italian)

What distinguishes this particular case from others is that the student also feels like she has a 'mental notebook', on which all new learning can be recorded. In other words, there is a sense that being like a child also means being able to start learning again, paying attention to how the language is used in the environment, being a conscious (and conscientious) learner. This is a clear example of how Benson et al.'s (2012) dimensions describe a continuum in L2 identity development. In the previous section, we saw how a lack of proficiency in the L2 can impinge on an individual's pragmatic abilities to perform even basic transactions (Excerpts 1 and 2), and make the learner feel physically and intellectually overextended (Excerpt 4), which prevent the individual's ability to express their own desired identity. On the other hand, here (Excerpt 9) we also see how individuals can change these difficulties into opportunities to develop their 'linguistic self-concept' through the autonomous acquisition of effective learning strategies.

Two personal coping strategies are manifested in Excerpt 10, which is a comment to another student's blog post.

Excerpt 10 S1: You're great! Because of your desire to improve what seems to me your already excellent level of German … great also because you're able to laugh at yourself! When I mixed my languages, I felt stupid and desperate … I believed I would end up not speaking anything!! But now I even enjoy doing it ☺ (Translation from Italian)

Here S1 values her peer's ability to laugh at herself instead of feeling discouraged; in fact, not taking oneself too seriously may have a positive effect on diffusing stress and thereby encourage language learning. In addition, she also admits having changed her appreciation of the practice of code-switching, no longer a sign of failing to learn and use the new language but, rather, a resource that can also be fun.

A further coping strategy is shown in Excerpt 11. As Benson et al. (2012) point out, the development of linguistic self-concept is strongly linked to recognised identities, in other words how others see you. In this sense, we can see how S2, who does not feel particularly successful in the L2, views himself as a competent user of the target language through the eyes of his Italian friends:

Excerpt 11 S2: Put in that way it would seem a disaster, but it really went quite well in not too long time (though I still remain among one of the worst to speak English), I noticed it especially when some Italian friends came to visit me and I had to present them to my ERASMUS friends: I felt proud of me when they noticed my improvements.

As mentioned before, positive effects of the SA experience on the individuals' self-concept can emerge, particularly at the end of their period abroad, in the way they imagine their future selves as language learners and users:

Excerpt 12 S18: This experience [...] has made me realise how wonderful it can be to speak other languages and interact with others and that's why I think that, when I go back, I'll dedicate myself to other languages because it's really satisfying to be able to understand and speak another language. (Translation from Italian)

As we can see in S18's statement, expanding self-concept concerning one specific L2 experience can also have an effect on willingness to invest in language learning in general, and to increase linguistic repertoires in the future. For this reason, Excerpt 12 also provides a good link between the dimension of 'linguistic self-concept' and that of 'L2-mediated personal development', in that it can be interpreted in terms of individual change as an effect of the SA period.

L2-Mediated Personal Development

Jackson (2008, p. 214) claims that SA has the potential to stimulate personal development in terms of 'enhanced personal growth, self-confidence, and maturity; a higher degree of independence; a broader world view'. In our study, there are fewer instances of this dimension than of the previous two. This in itself is not surprising, as it is important to remember that the students had been abroad for only two to three months at the time of the IEREST course, and that they still had a similar period ahead of them. Excerpt 13 is illustrative of comments concerning aspects of personal development, but it is not clear if they are related to L2 identity:

Excerpt 13 S14: What you wrote led me to reflect on one of the many positive aspects of the ERASMUS experience, that of becoming more mature and independent people. Dealing with negative experiences, having to get out of trouble alone and succeed in this intent is one of the aspects that I think characterise this period abroad for many of us, and it's amazing how one can change as a result of these events. It is precisely for this reason that in difficult times we must remind ourselves that every bad experience can serve as a starting point in the process of becoming more mature and learning new things about ourselves. (Translation from Italian)

While it is clear that S14's words refer to forms of personal development, her focus is on 'experiences', 'this period abroad', and 'events', rather than any specific mention of the L2. Thus, recalling Jackson's (2009) words about L2 SA not necessarily leading to intercultural awareness, this excerpt does not allow us to know for certain whether the 'negative experiences' that triggered changes in S14's personality were linked in any way to the fact of using a L2, or even being immersed in a L2 context. We thus eliminated such comments from our focussed data set in order to bring to the fore precisely those aspects of intercultural development that were closely linked to language use.

Given the relatively brief time that the participants were abroad when these data were recorded, the participants' comments refer mostly to the difficulties they have encountered and how they see themselves in the future (see Excerpt 14), while only a few of them are yet inclined to appraise their experience, especially in terms of personal development (see Excerpt 15).

Excerpt 14 S13: But the advice I can give you is to really start thinking positively about all these obstacles. We're all capable with our own language and with things we've been used to forever, but it's new things that make us grow, even though they are difficult because they're unknown. I think all these difficulties will make us stronger.

Excerpt 15 S8: When you start getting confident and familiar with the language, it becomes a source of satisfaction and courage. And when you start mastering English, you feel stronger, readier and less frightened.

According to a non-essentialist approach to culture, the data also enables us to identify some phenomena in the students' intercultural reasoning. Excerpt 16 illustrates the way in which the students explore processes of categorisation into 'us' and 'others' that is different from the conventional one linked to 'large cultures' (national and ethnic) (Holliday, 2011).

Excerpt 16 S1: As soon as you hear the 'funny accent' (meaning when you spot somebody who is not native French) you just feel the need to say 'Ey! where are you from? we are on the same boat!!'

Here, the S1 uses categories that distinguish natives from non-natives, where it is language—or, rather, lack of language proficiency—that bonds ERASMUS students together. On the one hand, these traces of reasoning in the data do not tell us much about the actual intercultural development of the students. On the other hand, they were significant for IEREST from a pedagogical point of view, as the students' initial discursive hints of moving from, or re-fashioning, commonly essentialist, large-culture terms ('native' speakers v. non-native speakers) to non-essentialism by perceiving different non-native speakers (with a 'funny accent') as its own self-defining small-culture group ('on the same boat') were used to stimulate class discussions on categorisation processes and interculturality during the videoconferences and in the forum.

The same phenomenon is even more evident in Excerpt 17. Here, S2 shows an awareness of the concept of culture as negotiated by its members, and as belonging to a small social group—in this case, an ERASMUS community—constructed among other things on the inability to speak the target language well.

Excerpt 17 S2: Yes, I miss speak Italian (though Skype is a great way to stay in touch) [...] but after more than 3 months here I'd say that I'm definitely settled. Living with the ERASMUS group during the day (in the university and in the city) and night (in the student house) helped me to realise that I couldn't feel shock to live in a new country, simply because me and the other guys were building a 'small community' with its new rules which ourselves decided and a culture to which each of us could add its contribution; and that's not shocking.

We believe then that, while the data did not yield a large number of instances of personal development linked to L2 identity, it does show that the IEREST '24 h ERASMUS Life' activity created opportunities for the students to reflect on their experiences through a non-essentialist view of culture and identity.

Discussion

The framework proposed by Benson et al. (2012, 2013) has proven useful for investigating the possible development of L2 identities and exploring what aspects of intercultural learning emerged that were linked to language learning and use abroad. Considering that our study was not designed as a longitudinal investigation of how the students' identities changed over time, what emerges from the data analysis is mainly a multifaceted picture of the ways in which language use abroad and identity interact with each other.

The first aspect that arose clearly from the data is the fact that the participants in the IEREST course focussed their attention on one particular facet of their sense of self, namely their role as students and social actors in the new academic community. This theme spans across the first and the second dimensions of the framework ('identity-related L2 proficiency' and 'linguistic self-concept'). Although life abroad also involves daily routines such as shopping or using public transport, a crucial concern for the participants is both being able to study effectively in a L2 (dimension 1, Excerpts 3 and 4) and negotiating their identity as active and competent students through the L2 (dimension 2, Excerpts 7 and 8). Overall, both of these perspectives on L2 identity are strongly linked to the anxiety, fatigue, and feelings of inadequacy caused by a perceived lack of L2 proficiency (e.g., Excerpts 1, 2, 4, 7, and 8). The fact that participants focus on their role as students is not surprising, since the main purpose of the ERASMUS programme is to provide an academic experience in a different country and the goals of the '24 h ERASMUS Life' activity included encouraging students to reflect on their lives in the host university. However, it is also noteworthy that the IEREST activity succeeded in stimulating not only the students' personal manifestations of discomfort, but also their willingness to share with the rest of the group their strategies for overcoming negative feelings; these ranged from investing in a number of resources, including drawing on personal strength (Excerpt 5), keeping L1-mediated social contacts (Excerpt 6), adopting new ways of language learning (Excerpts 9 and 10), code-switching and having fun with languages (Excerpt 10), and acknowledging compatriots' praise (Excerpt 11). Though the L2 identity work cannot be traced chronologically due to the research design adopted, there is nonetheless much evidence of it in the corpus analysed, with the students evaluating themselves as L2 users and actively creating the social and personal conditions necessary to reach their 'Ideal L2 Self' (Dörnyei, 2009) by investing in language learning and use (Norton, 2012).

Regarding the third dimension of identity in Benson et al.'s (2012, 2013) framework, things are a little different. As mentioned above, due to our methodological decision to focus on the students' accounts linked to L2 identity, our study says little about aspects of personal growth accomplished regardless of language mediation. In addition, participants in the IEREST course were in the middle of their SA experience and thus were—unsurprisingly—little inclined yet to reflect on how living through the L2 in the host country was changing them overall. Nevertheless, in addition to the cases where the students make explicit reference to 'L2-mediated personal development' (Excerpts 14 and 15), there are many blog posts and comments discussing comparisons between past and present situations. Although still immersed in the new experience, students' stories often suggest a temporal shift between the initial phase of their stay abroad and the moment of data collection: at times, personal challenges are reported as having been solved (e.g., Excerpts 5 and 8), while others not entirely (Excerpt 3). In any case, participants' early reflections can be interpreted as indications, to themselves and to others, of the developmental path they have been following. Crucially for our analysis, the students conceptualise their own L2 experiences both as the cause (in the initial phase) and as the solution to a given problem. The centrality attributed to language in the present study makes it difficult to discuss results in the light of the existing literature on the effects of SA on students' personal development. In the research that has been conducted, there is no specific focus on the role of L2 learning and use on the students' self-reported (e.g., Jackson, 2008; Meier & Daniels, 2013) or confirmed emotional stability, self-efficacy, or independence (e.g., Brown, 2009; Mitchell, Tracy-Ventura, & McManus, 2017).

Overall, Benson et al.'s (2012, 2013) framework proved useful to analyse the processes linked to L2 identity in the students' accounts of their experiences abroad. Nevertheless, its application to the IEREST data has highlighted that it tends to categorise the different aspects of L2 identity development too distinctly; our findings show that some aspects can span the three dimensions of language-related identity work. As discussed above in respect to dimensions 1 and 2, this is the case of the academic domain, which relates to L2 proficiency and at the same time affects the students' 'linguistic self-concept' as active social actors, capable of negotiating their identities at the host university. The affective domain was also found to cut across dimensions in its impact on L2 identity. While these conceptual overlaps are implied in Benson et al.'s framework, which conceives identity dimensions as a continuum, our experience with operationalising the model and coding the data suggests that the distinction between the ability of expressing desired identities by achieving pragmatic objectives (dimension 1) and the 'ability to negotiate personal identities through a second language' (2012, p. 184; dimension 2) is especially challenging, probably partly because the difference between 'projecting' and 'negotiating' is blurred. After all, as highlighted by Bucholtz and Hall (2005):

> Any given construction of identity may be in part deliberate and intentional, in part habitual and hence often less than fully conscious, in part an outcome of interactional negotiation and contestation, in part an outcome of others' perceptions and representations, and in part an effect of larger ideological processes and material structures that may become relevant to interaction. (p. 606)

Since identity is a complex construct where the individual's intention to project a self-image is intrinsically linked to the negotiation of that image, it is not surprising that analytically distinguishing between the two facets—individual and social—can be difficult.

As far the opportunities of intercultural learning are concerned, again following Benson et al. (2012, 2013), we have assumed that personal development includes forms of intercultural learning and that the latter—in L2 SA programmes—is necessarily woven into L2 experiences. However, diverging from the Benson et al. framework, in our analysis we adopted a non-essentialist view of culture (Holliday, 2011), which also characterises the IEREST pedagogy. Consequently, as expected, the students' accounts of their experiences are full of references to forms of categorisations based on small cultures (see Excerpts 16 and 17). This does not imply intercultural learning in itself. But the fact that the students expressed themselves in such terms gave the teachers the opportunity to raise their awareness that, as individuals, we belong not only to large cultures, but also to smaller cultures, even if sometimes only temporarily. In addition, the awareness that terms and cultures are negotiated by their members—a concept more easily understood when thinking about small cultures—opens up opportunities to understand how the larger cultures are also negotiated by their members, and not something solid and unchangeable. An interesting aspect is that in many blog posts these small cultures are linked to language use (e.g., native v. non-native speakers and L1 v. L2 use). This too provided an opportunity for the class to reflect on how language is an important aspect of culture.

Conclusion and Recommendations

The current chapter has focused on the data collected during the teaching and fulfilment of an activity within the context of an intercultural preparation programme for ERASMUS students while they were already abroad. The data—the blog posts and related online comments written by the students—were reviewed and analysed through the lens of Benson et al.'s (2012, 2013) framework of L2-identity development. In addition, the study was useful for investigating the ways in which the resources encouraged discussions related to intercultural issues among the students.

Related to the latter objective, from our experience implementing and studying the impact of the '24 h ERASMUS Life' activity, we believe its efficacy can be boosted by paying attention to four measures. First of all, peer-to-peer interaction is at the core of the learning process. In our implementation, the students were highly involved in the discussions, as seen by the numerous comments each blog post received. This made it possible for them to dig deep into their own reasoning on cultural and identity issues. In fact, some scholars have claimed that interaction plays a key role in intercultural learning (Kearney, 2016; Liddicoat & Scarino, 2013). A second recommendation is that, while learning based on the students' lived experiences is natural in a SA context, this needs to be supported by theoretical input, which enables them to make better and deeper sense of what they go through while abroad (e.g., Holliday, 1999, 2011; IEREST, 2015). The third point is linked to the second: it is important to pace the activity in such a way as to allow the students the necessary time to process the new input and link it to their lived experiences. This can be done by allowing enough time to reflect in class but also providing regular reflection tasks for homework. We cannot provide an indication of how often questions need to be asked; in fact, they probably need to be asked in every lesson, but the task and the students' discussions would guide these. Similarly, there are many ways in which students can be asked to reflect, but in terms of requiring blog posts (or diary entries) to be written, this would depend on the frequency of the lessons and the duration of the entire course. In our case, they had a reflective task once a week. Finally, it is important for the teachers to be aware that a non-essentialist view of culture can be conceptually challenging for many students, who may expect to receive culture-specific information regarding the country in which they are studying. This risk can be limited by providing information on the contents of the course before it begins, so that the students understand what the course will include and what it will not.

Summary of recommendations for encouraging intercultural learning and L2 identity development in SA
• Class discussions (including online discussions), which are guided—but not dominated—by the teacher and focus on peer engagement are essential, as it is through interactions and negotiation of meaning that intercultural learning can take place. • Preparation and guided reflection need to be based on the student's lived experiences, but theoretical input is also necessary if the students are to make deeper sense of these experiences and learn through them. • It is necessary to allow time for the students to process the new theoretical input and alternating this with discussions and reflections on their experiences abroad. • Teachers need to be aware that a non-essentialist view of culture can be conceptually challenging for their students and therefore must clarify this approach explicitly at the beginning of the course in order to manage the students' expectations.

Notes

1. Although various authors use the following terms slightly differently, for the purposes of the current chapter, the phrases 'intercultural learning', 'intercultural development', 'interculturality', and 'development of intercultural competence' are used interchangeably.
2. The Former Yugoslav Republic of Macedonia, Iceland, Liechtenstein, Norway, Switzerland, and Turkey.

Bibliography

Abdallah-Pretceille, M. (2008). Mobilité … sans conscience! In F. Dervin & M. Byram (Eds.), *Echanges et mobilités académiques—Quel bilan?* (pp. 215–231). Paris: L'Harmattan.

Anquetil, M. (2006). *Mobilité ERASMUS et communication interculturelle, une recherche-action pour un parcours de formation*. Bern: Peter Lang.

Beaven, A., & Borghetti, C. (2015). Editorial. *Intercultural Education, 26*(1), 1–5.

Beaven, A., & Borghetti, C. (2016). Editorial: Interculturality in study abroad. Special issue: Perspectives and discourses on student mobility and interculturality. *Language and Intercultural Communication, 16*(3), 313–317.

Bennett, M. J. (1993). Beyond ethnorelativism: The developmental model of inter-cultural sensitivity. In R. M. Paige (Ed.), *Education for the intercultural experience* (pp. 21–71). Yarmouth, ME: Intercultural Press.

Benson, P., Barkhuizen, G., Bodycott, P., & Brown, J. (2012). Study abroad and the development of second language identities. *Applied Linguistics Review, 3*(1), 173–193.

Benson, P., Barkhuizen, G., Bodycott, P., & Brown, J. (2013). *Second language identity in narratives of study abroad*. New York: Palgrave Macmillan.

Blake, R. J. (2013). *Brave new digital classroom: Technology and foreign language learning*. Washington, DC: Georgetown University Press.

Block, D. (2007). *Second language identities*. London: Continuum.

Braun, V., & Clarke, V. (2006). Using thematic analysis in psychology. *Qualitative Research in Psychology, 3*(2), 77–101.

Brown, L. (2009). The transformative power of the international sojourn: An ethnographic study of the international student experience. *Annals of Tourism Research, 36*(3), 502–521.

Bucholtz, M., & Hall, K. (2005). Identity and interaction: A sociocultural linguistic approach. *Discourse Studies, 7*(4–5), 584–614.

Bucholtz, M., & Hall, K. (2011). Locating identity in language. In C. Llamas & D. Watt (Eds.), *Language and identities* (pp. 18–28). Edinburgh: Edinburgh University Press.

Byram, M. (1997). *Teaching and assessing intercultural communicative competence*. Clevedon: Multilingual Matters.

Council of Europe. (1984). *Recommendation no. R (84) 13 of the Committee of Ministers to member states concerning the situation of foreign students*. Strasbourg: Council of Europe.

Deardorff, D. K. (2006). Identification and assessment of intercultural competence as a student outcome of internationalization. *Journal of Studies in Intercultural Education, 10*, 241–266.

Dörnyei, Z. (2009). The L2 motivational self system. In Z. Dörnyei & E. Ushioda (Eds.), *Motivation, language identity and the L2 self* (pp. 9–42). Bristol: Multilingual Matters.

Elola, I., & Oskoz, A. (2008). Blogging: Fostering intercultural competence development in foreign language and study abroad contexts. *Foreign Language Annals, 41*(3), 454–477.

European Commission. (2015). ERASMUS—Facts, figures & trends. In *The European Union support for student and staff exchanges and university cooperation in 2013–14*. Luxembourg: Publications Office of the European Union.

Hammer, M. R. (2007). *The intercultural development inventory (IDI) manual* (Vol. 3). Ocean Pines, MD: IDI, LLC.

Hammer, M. R., & Bennett, M. J. (1998). *The intercultural development inventory*. Portland, OR: Intercultural Communication Institute.

Holliday, A. (1999). Small cultures. *Applied Linguistics, 20*(2), 237–264.

Holliday, A. (2011). *Intercultural communication and ideology*. London: Sage.

IEREST. (2015). *Intercultural education resources for ERASMUS students and their teachers*. Koper: Annales University Press.

Jackson, J. (2008). *Language, identity, and study abroad: Sociocultural perspectives*. London: Equinox.

Jackson, J. (2009). Intercultural learning on short-term sojourns. *Intercultural Education, 20*, 59–71.

Jackson, J. (2010). *Intercultural journeys: From study to residence abroad*. Basingstoke, UK: Palgrave Macmillan.

Jackson, J., & Oguro, S. (Eds.). (2018). *Intercultural interventions in study abroad*. New York: Routledge.

Kearney, E. (2016). *Intercultural learning in modern language education: Expanding meaning-making potentials*. Bristol: Multilingual Matters.

Kinginger, C. (2009). *Language learning and study abroad: A critical reading of research*. Basingstoke, UK: Palgrave Macmillan.

Kolb, D. A. (1984). *Experiential learning: Experience as the source of learning and development*. Englewood Cliffs, NJ: Prentice Hall.

Kramsch, C. (1998). *Language and culture*. Oxford: Oxford University Press.

Kramsch, C. (2009). *The multilingual subject: What foreign language learners say about their experience and why it matters*. Oxford: Oxford University Press.

Lee, L. (2009). Promoting intercultural exchanges with blogs and podcasting: A study of Spanish-American telecollaboration. *Computer Assisted Language Learning, 22*(5), 425–443.

Lee, L. (2010). Fostering reflective writing and interactive exchange through blogging in an advanced language course. *ReCALL, 22*(2), 212–222.

Lewin, R. (Ed.). (2009). *The handbook of practice and research in study abroad: Higher education and the quest for global citizenship*. New York: Routledge.

Liddicoat, A. J., & Scarino, A. (2013). *Intercultural language teaching and learning*. New York: Wiley.

Meier, G., & Daniels, H. (2013). 'Just not being able to make friends': Social interaction during the year abroad in modern foreign language degrees. *Research Papers in Education, 28*(2), 212–238.

Merino, E., & Avello, P. (2014). Contrasting intercultural awareness at home and abroad. In C. Pérez-Vidal (Ed.), *Language acquisition in study abroad and formal instruction contexts* (pp. 283–309). Amsterdam: Benjamins.

Mitchell, R., Tracy-Ventura, N., & McManus, K. (2017). *Anglophone students abroad: Identity, social relationships and language learning*. London: Routledge.

Norton, B. (2012). *Identity and language learning: Extending the conversation*. Bristol: Multilingual Matters.

Paige, R. M., & Vande Berg, M. (2012). Why students are and are not learning abroad: A review of recent research. In M. Vande Berg, R. M. Paige, & K. H. Lou (Eds.), *Student learning abroad: What our students are learning, what they're not, and what we can do about it* (pp. 29–60). Sterling, VA: Stylus.

Pérez-Vidal, C. (Ed.). (2014). *Language acquisition in study abroad and formal instruction contexts*. Amsterdam: Benjamins.

Risager, K. (2005). Foreword. In L. Sercu, E. Bandura, P. Castro, L. Davcheva, C. Laskaridou, U. Lundgren, M. C. Méndez García, & P. Ryan (Eds.), *Foreign language teachers and intercultural competence: An international investigation* (pp. VII–VIX). Clevedon: Multilingual Matters.

Tess, P. A. (2013). The role of social media in higher education classes (real and virtual)—A literature review. *Computers in Human Behavior, 29*(5), A60–A68.

Urlaub, P. (2011). Intercultural blogs in study-abroad contexts. *Academic Exchange Quarterly, 15*(3), 42–50.

Vande Berg, M., Paige, R. M., & Lou, K. H. (2012). Student learning abroad: Paradigms and assumptions. In M. Vande Berg, R. M. Paige, & K. H. Lou (Eds.), *Student learning abroad: What our students are learning, what they're not, and what we can do about it* (pp. 3–28). Stirling, VA: Stylus.

Yang, S.-H. (2009). Using blogs to enhance critical reflection and community of practice. *Journal of Educational Technology & Society, 12*(2), 11–21.

'I Thought I Was Prepared.' ERASMUS Students' Voices on Their Transition from L2 Learners to L2 Users

Sònia Mas-Alcolea

Introduction

Study abroad (SA) is socially constructed as an undoubtedly positive phenomenon with different overlapping objectives: 'linguistic ones certainly, but equally cultural, academic, personal and professional ones' (Coleman, 1998, p. 197). This common, social discourse has been well noted in and complemented by scholarship and academic discourse. Mitchell, Tracy-Ventura, and McManus (2017, p. 19) assert that 'the [enduring] metaphor of linguistic and cultural "immersion" [is still] a powerful driver in historical thinking about the sojourn abroad'. For sure, SA is a positive phenomenon for which 'schools, parents and students believe that a period spent studying or working abroad will bring substantive benefits' (Benson, Barkhuizen, Bodycott, & Brown, 2013, p. 147). Among these benefits—which may include increased intercultural knowledge and understanding, greater confidence and independence, future employability, and so forth—second

S. Mas-Alcolea (✉)
University of Lleida, Catalonia, Spain
e-mail: sonia.mas@dal.udl.cat

language (L2) learning appears to be the most popular, with many assuming that 'students who go abroad are those who will ultimately become the most proficient in the use of their [second] language' (Freed, 1995, p. 5). Many seem to have almost blind faith in the SA setting as the ideal environment which provides the desired amount of input and contact with native speakers (DeKeyser, 2007; Magnan & Lafford, 2012), and thus, adhere to the 'study-abroad social imaginary'[1] (Kubota, 2016) or the social construction of SA as a 'magical formula for the development of language ability' (Kinginger, 2011, p. 58), as 'a short cut to linguistic fluency' (Wilkinson, 1998, p. 23), or as the 'ideal means of learning a foreign language' (Allen, 2010, p. 27). Indeed, research has demonstrated that SA does make a difference (Llanes & Muñoz, 2009) and that it may favour (1) the improvement of the students' oral production skills (e.g., Freed, Segalowitz, & Dewey, 2004; Juan-Garau & Pérez-Vidal, 2007; Llanes & Muñoz, 2009); (2) the students' lexical growth (e.g., Foster, 2009; Ife, Vives Boix, & Meara, 2000; Llanes & Muñoz, 2009), and (3) the development of pragmatic and sociolinguistic skills (e.g., Kinginger & Farrell, 2004; Shively, 2011; Taguchi, 2008). These studies, which reflect the 'desire to prove the effectiveness of SA, with learners developing language abilities analogous to "concrete" products' (Kinginger, 2009, p. 29), certainly advance the idea of SA as having 'the potential to enhance students' language ability in every domain' (Kinginger, 2013, p. 4). However, while it is true that 'exposure to an immersion setting [does lead] to some kinds of learning' (Plews, Breckenridge, Cambre, & Fernandes, 2014, p. 69), both the educational institutions and the learners themselves have a role to play in the actual L2 learning process and, thus, cannot leave it all up to the immersion setting. Research has primarily focussed on the linguistic gains of SA (immediate post-sojourn stage), and not so much on the different variables that ultimately condition such gains. In this regard, more research is needed investigating how well-prepared students are linguistically before leaving, what role (if any) their home institution and the students themselves adopt in order to be prepared linguistically (and in which languages), and how this preparation (or the lack of it) affects the overall evolution of their identities as L2 learners/users.

Clearly, L2 learning—and most often the learning of English as an L2—is one of the main reasons why the number of higher-education students contemplating SA is on the increase (Feyen & Krzaklewska, 2013).

Crucially, for many of those students who live in a context where English is a school subject for learning and studying, and not a communicative tool that they need as part of everyday life, the SA experience constitutes the first time abroad with the explicit intention of *using* the foreign language *to live*. Such students, as is the case of the participants in this study, may suddenly be facing the transition from memorising long lists of vocabulary and grammar rules to actually *applying* and *using* these words and forms in their lives abroad. This is important because a change in the role and prominence of an L2 and one's lived experiences of that change can precipitate a shift in (linguistic) identity and personal outlook; as Benson et al. (2013, p. 3) show, SA is 'a potentially "critical" experience that opens up second language identities to change'. But are the SA students prepared by domestic curricula for this?

The objective of the present chapter is not to demolish the robust social construction of SA and refute the idea or scholarly evidence that the SA context is a critical variable that might positively affect students' learning and use of a given L2. Indeed, the study at the heart of this chapter set out to explore and possibly support Kubota's (2016, p. 355) claim that, despite the common insistence on the linguistic, cultural, personal, and career benefits of SA, 'the student sojourn experience and these alleged benefits do not have a simple causal relationship' and that policymakers should be aware of this in order to 'facilitate the narrowing of the gaps'. The chapter thus seeks to examine the critical moment of specifically ERASMUS[2] students' transition from being L2 learners to L2 users, for this is surely most pertinent for those using the L2 to live for the first time. In doing so, I explore especially the social consequences of successfully managing, feeling comfortable with, and taking advantage of this transition, or not. To do this, I first describe the context for the study and chapter, namely the move from a domestic educational arena to the immersion education setting of ERASMUS. Second, I present the design and methodology of data collection and analysis that allowed me to document and make sense of the way(s) in which the students accounted for the development of their L2 identities. Third, I provide an analysis of the students' perception of their evolution as L2 learners and/or users. Then, I present the overall findings and discussion. Finally, I present the conclusion together with some recommendations that are meant to contribute to a successful design and implementation of an SA programme.

In tackling this issue of students' successful or less than successful transition from L2 learner to L2 user, the present chapter contributes to research on SA in the following ways. First, bringing to the fore students' discursive construction of their *individual* trajectories may undermine what is often assumed to be common knowledge about the ERASMUS experience—such as the learning and use of a foreign language—and allows scholars and practitioners to better understand (1) the process the students undergo; (2) the complexity of the sojourn abroad and the multiple factors (internal and external) that ultimately affect the different learning outcomes; and, therefore, (3) why many results and conclusions report 'inconsistency' and 'individual differences' (Kinginger, 2015, p. 7). Indeed, the multiplicity of discourses presented in this study showcases the fragmented nature of the 'ERASMUS culture', or the complexity and heterogeneity of both the experiences and outcomes of the stay which are, in turn, conditioned by internal and external factors. Second, this chapter addresses a very important yet under-researched aspect of SA experience, namely, the students' linguistic pre-sojourn preparation.

Context: Domestic L2 Curricula and ERASMUS Immersion

'Why study abroad?' is one of the questions the participants of this study were asked prior to departure. The majority of them mentioned the learning and/or improvement of a foreign language—mostly of English—as the main reason why they decided to leave their home educational setting in Catalonia to undertake a sojourn abroad where, unlike in their home country, they expected to be able to achieve their language acquisition goal. Before leaving, all the students clearly displayed two different stances towards their educational home context and towards the SA context. On the one hand, the students saw their at-home (AH) context as a site where they had been *studying—not using*—English compulsorily in both primary and secondary school. In this context, the ideal objectives of the official curricula in secondary education in Catalonia—for example, 'understanding and communicating in the new language' (DGESOB, 2015, p. 7) and becoming 'an effective user of the target language in real communication activities' (DGESOB, 2008, p. 3)—remain ideal and detached from a specific implementation context: students attend only two to four hours of English per week in both primary and secondary school, with one teacher for 25 students on average (Generalitat de Catalunya, 2016). The negative stance towards the AH context as regards L2 learning and use is supported by (1) the poor presence of English at Catalan universities—only 10 per cent according to the Generalitat de Catalunya (2016)—despite the objective of the European Commission (2003, p. 3) to 'make sure that everyone can speak two languages as well as their mother tongue'; and (2) the low percentage of Catalan citizens who declare having a good command of English—according to the Catalonia Statistics Institute (IDESCAT, 2015) only 28.31 per cent of the population claims to have a good command of English.

On the other hand, the participants in this study saw the SA context as a somewhat unique opportunity that would allow them to be exposed to a foreign language (mainly English) and, thus, to achieve what in the AH context seems utopian: the *use* of this L2 as part of their everyday lives. They imagined and described studying abroad as involving switching from (L2) learner to user identities (Benson et al., 2013)—and for some of them to 'user-for-the-first-time' identities; or the 'crossing [of] the language threshold' (Murphy-Lejeune, 2002, p. 117). However, most participants in this study had to, and actually did, meet the linguistic requirements established by their home university as stated on its website: all of them had to show proof of their language proficiency; following the *Common European Framework of Reference for Languages* (CEFR), they needed at least a B1 level and preferably a B2 level of the language of instruction in the host university. This applied to all ERASMUS students except for those going to Italy and Portugal, who were just asked to express their commitment to enrol in a language course, before departure.

Indeed, the students considered this language requirement as guaranteeing their well-being as L2 users while abroad. However, as Murphy-Lejeune (2002, p. 120) points out, 'alienation, which sometimes marks the early stages of the experience, feeds on communication difficulties and the frustration felt by individuals whose personality is [often] perceived as diminished for want of being fully expressed' (Murphy-Lejeune, 2002, p. 120). Taking this into account, I believe that more research is needed on the students' linguistic preparation, on the linguistic requirements they are often asked to meet, and how these include (or not) the communicative needs that the students actually find once abroad as well as the impact that this has on the students' well-being mainly during the early stages of their experience or during this 'initial trying period of linguistic fatigue' (Murphy-Lejeune, 2002, p. 120).

To this aim, the research questions this study attempts to answer are the following: (1) pre-sojourn. How do the ERASMUS students express their expectation and motivation to learn and *use* an L2? Do the students construct themselves as being linguistically prepared for the stay abroad? In what ways do the students' discourses on mobility align with that of their home university? (2) In-sojourn. How do the ERASMUS students experience the transition from being an L2 learner to being an L2 user once they set foot in their host countries? Do the students present the language requirement set by their home university as guaranteeing their well-being as L2 users while abroad, or do they discover specific aspects of their linguistic preparation and needs lacking? What are the consequences of succeeding or not succeeding in going through this transition?

The answers to these questions may lead us to unravelling the complexities of this transitional process of the SA experience, which, as will be shown in this chapter, generated the greatest affective reactions on the part of the participants in this study. They may also allow us to draw further pedagogical implications that might help improve the ERASMUS experience.

Research Design: A Multiple Case Study

This chapter is based on a larger research project that investigated the impact that the ERASMUS SA experience had on the identities of nine undergraduate students from a university in Catalonia. The project used a longitudinal, qualitative approach, combining both textual and observational data to explore the students' experiences of (inter)cultural learning and language learning/use—the latter being the focus of the current chapter. The longitudinality and the multiple methods used for data collection allowed me to track and focus on the *process* that students undergo or on the 'developmental factor' since it is expected that 'a case typically evolves in time, often as a string of concrete and interrelated events that occur' (Flyvbjerg, 2011, p. 301) at a particular time and within a particular context, and influenced by various internal and external factors. As is common in a multiple case study, the 'cases' were conceived as 'actors' (Stake, 1995) and the overall objective of this project was to 'enter the scene with a sincere interest in learning how they function in their ordinary pursuits and milieus' (Stake, 1995, p. 1). To this effect, the current study is based on a 'detailed, in-depth data collection involving multiple sources of information rich in context' (Creswell, 1998, p. 61), which included verbal data gathered from focus group interviews, a short written questionnaire, written experiential accounts while abroad, and a final individual narrative interview. The verbal data were complemented with observational data gathered from another method known as 'shadowing', which entails 'a researcher closely following a subject over a period of time to investigate what people actually do in the course of their everyday lives, not what their roles dictate of them' (Quinlan, 2008, p. 1480). This method was useful given that it allowed me not only to draw on the students' reports of what was occurring abroad and of their experiences as L2 learners/users, but also to observe them directly. The different methods are summarised by phase in Table 1.

The project, from which the current study draws, followed nine students, ranging in age from 22 to 26, as they participated in the ERASMUS SA programme in 2013–2014. All the students were born in Catalonia and constructed themselves as being Catalan—rather than Spanish. Additionally, they all saw themselves as being bilingual speakers of Catalan and Spanish

Table 1 A longitudinal data collection

PRE-SOJOURN	Focus group interview
	Short, written questionnaire
IN-SOJOURN	Written experiential accounts
	Individual semi-structured interview (on site)
	Shadowing (visiting the students' in their host country)
POST-SOJOURN	Focus group interview
	Individual narrative interview

Table 2 Participant profiles

Host country	Students' names	Gender	Age	Degree
Denmark	Ariadna	Female	26	Social Education
	Joan	Male	24	Industrial Engineering
	Mònica	Female	22	Education
Italy	Josep Miquel	Male	23	Law
	Patrícia	Female	23	Law
	Verònica	Female	22	Business Administration
Wales (UK)	Amanda	Female	22	Law
	Marina	Female	22	English Studies
	Roger	Male	22	Law

and as prospective multilingual speakers after the SA experience. As Table 2 illustrates, out of the nine students, only one (Marina) was majoring in languages (English), four (Amanda, Josep Miquel, Patrícia, and Roger) were majoring in law, one (Ariadna) in social education, one (Joan) in industrial engineering, one (Mònica) in education, and one (Verònica) in business administration. All names are pseudonyms. Their destinations included three different (sociolinguistic) contexts in which the presence of English varied: Wales (UK), where English was both the language of instruction and the one used outside the university, though Welsh was also present; Denmark, where English was the medium of instruction while Danish was the everyday language; and Italy, where Italian was both the language of instruction and the everyday language, but where global English was to be expected.

The data presented here are analysed using the notion of *stance* (Du Bois, 2007; Jaffe, 2009), for which the focus is placed on the mechanisms the students use in order to discursively construct the impact that the SA experience has on their identities as L2 learners/users. By way of illustration, Du Bois (2007, p. 166) provides the following example that shows the different elements that are part of two stance utterances produced by two speakers in a conversation (Table 3).

As I will show, the students did not offer an objective description of facts, but a representation of their social reality from their particular perspective or *stance*, which they made more or less explicit by means of the linguistic resources that they chose. Thus, it is through the analysis of the participants' 'language of evaluation' (Johnstone, 2009, p. 31) that I attempted to discover the feelings, attitudes, or perspectives with which

Table 3 Examples (*adapted from* Du Bois, 2007)

Speaker	Stance subject	Positioning	Stance Object	Alignment
SAM:	I	Don't like	Those	
ANGELA:	I	Don't like	Those	Either

they constructed the impact that their SA experience had on their L2 identities, while taking into account their initial L2 self-perceived competence as well as the university language requirement. Working on case-specific positionings and/or understandings of what the ERASMUS experience had meant for the participants might help student exchange programmes be more insightful when designing and planning the desired personal and professional outcomes.

Findings and Discussion

Pre-sojourn. The Students' Imagined Identities as Future L2 *Users*

The learning of English—and not of any other language—was indeed the most mentioned expectation and motivation of those students who went to Wales and Denmark (despite English not being an official language of Denmark). All these students expected their sojourn abroad to provide them with 'a round-the-clock exposure to the language' (Engle & Engle, 2004, p. 234), which would help them benefit from the experience linguistically. Indeed, the analysis of these students' discourse at the pre-sojourn stage does not show heterogeneity regarding their expectations and motivations for going abroad but, rather, reveals a clear homogeneity of their *imagined identities* (Barkhuizen & De Klerk, 2006; Norton, 2001) as future ERASMUS students who would become better users—rather than learners—of English as a result of their SA experience. This is illustrated in the following excerpts, in which I quote the students' expression of their hope to 'speak foreignness' (Murphy-Lejeune, 2002). The excerpts come from those data sources in which the students made this *initial* motive explicit.

Excerpt 1:	'to know the language [English] perfectly' (*From the short written questionnaire—pre-sojourn; Marina—Wales*)
MARINA:	What has motivated me to participate in this stay has been my wish to know the language perfectly, which since I was a kid I always wanted to study. [...] What is more, thanks to the experiences of other people I know, I have realised that this programme is of great help to reach my goals. In a way, these experiences have also influenced this decision.
Excerpt 2:	'to practice English' (*From the short written questionnaire—pre-sojourn; Amanda—Wales*)
AMANDA:	I want to practice English because I haven't been away from home more than two weeks.
Excerpt 3:	'perfect my level of English' (*From the short written questionnaire—pre-sojourn; Roger—Wales*)
ROGER:	I hope and will work so that my stay in the UK helps me perfect my level of English.
Excerpt 4:	'practice [English]' (*From the pre-focus group; Mònica—Denmark*)
MÒNICA:	The objective for doing an ERASMUS is in the first place_ for the language\ right/because··_ * well_ my idea is_ [...] I go abroad_ I practice· quite a while and upon my return I will feel better [with my English]\.[3]
Excerpt 5:	'to improve my English' (*From the short written questionnaire—pre-sojourn; Ariadna—Denmark*)
ARIADNA:	I'm going to Denmark because I would like to improve my English.
Excerpt 6:	'to improve my English' (*From the pre-focus group; Joan—Denmark*)
JOAN:	I finally decided to go to Denmark because I thought it was a very good opportunity to··_ * well_ to improve my English\

As these excerpts illustrate, these students chose Wales and Denmark as their host destinations because they hoped and expected to achieve one of their main goals: practising, improving, and perfecting English.

The wish of some of the students to go to Wales was born out of the fact that they expected it to be the best site to learn English and, for Amanda in particular, the best site to learn what she described as 'the correct English'. This idealisation of and an expectation to find native speakers of English who have a 'complete and possibly innate competence in the language' (Pennycook, 1994, p. 175) is illustrated in the following excerpt, in which we observe another student (David), who was not part of the in-depth study but was also about to participate in the ERASMUS programme, and Amanda talking about the United Kingdom (UK) as the best destination to learn English.

Excerpt 7: 'what better than going to the UK/' (*From the pre-focus group; Amanda—Wales*)
DAVID: I looked at the list_ and there was Germany_ Finland_ and you say_ what better than going to the UK/
AMANDA: of course\
DAVID: because you will find all the signs in English_ you will meet people who speak English_
AMANDA: and the correct English\
DAVID: exactly\

In Excerpt 7, using linguistic mechanisms such as 'of course' and 'exactly', David and Amanda verbally indicate their *alignment* with each other about the UK as the best destination to learn English. Furthermore, Amanda uses the coordinating conjunction 'and', in order to contribute to the construction of a common *stance* regarding the reasons why the UK is the perfect site, while adding the reason that it is a country where you find 'the correct English'.

This expectation and motivation for learning English—and not any other language—may be influenced by the language certificate the students are required to have in order to participate in the mobility programme. As stated on the website of the students' home university, all potential ERASMUS students are asked to certify an intermediate level of the language of instruction in the host university, which in these instances is English (not Danish or Welsh). The language motive also appeared in the discourse of the participants of this study who went to

Italy, although they did not mention it as being a priority for them and the same language requirement did not apply. The three of them expressed their expectation to learn Italian, which Patrícia describes as 'new' because it is not a language they had to study at school. Likewise, Verònica presents English as a language she does not expect to be able to practise as much as she would like to in that particular context.

Excerpt 8:	'I want to learn Italian' (*From the short written questionnaire—pre-stay; Verònica—Italy*)
VERÒNICA:	[I want to] learn Italian because, since I will not be able to practice English as much as I wanted, I will learn Italian as much as I can and this will be a positive aspect personally speaking and for my CV.
Excerpt 9:	'I want to learn Italian' (*From the short written questionnaire—pre-stay; Josep M.—Italy*)
JOSEP M.:	I want to learn Italian because it is a very basic language which I have always liked.
Excerpt 10:	'to learn a new language [Italian]' (*From the short written questionnaire—pre-stay; Patrícia—Italy*)
PATRÍCIA:	It is a new experience to learn a new language [Italian]. […] Also I want to attend an intensive course in Italian before leaving, at the Official Language School or at university, and also any course offered by the host university.

The three students seem to display a positive stance towards the learning of this foreign language (Italian), not only because, as Josep M. suggests, it is easy or 'basic' to learn for speakers of Romance languages, but also for a future job or career, as suggested by Verònica. This expectation and motivation to learn and/or to improve a foreign language as a result of studying abroad that all the participants in this study shared could be claimed to be affected by the 'language pledge' (Mitchell et al., 2017) still present in many circulating discourses on mobility.

The institutional discourse of the students' home university illustrates this pledge well. As the following excerpt shows, the university displays a positive stance towards mobility by highlighting the linguistic benefits, among others, that an SA experience somewhat unquestionably entails.

Excerpt 11: The linguistic benefits of studying abroad (From a leaflet about mobility of the students' home university; my translation[4])
There are various good reasons to take the opportunity of participating in one or more mobility programmes and pursuing part of your studies at a foreign university. Academically, you will be able to [...] *improve* your foreign language skills and to *learn* new ones. [...] [Y]ou will *strengthen* your aptitudes like [...] your fluency in foreign languages. (Emphasis added)

Excerpt 11 is a clear instance of the inscribed positive judgement of mobility programmes that this university evokes in, and through, its institutional discourse, for which the learning and/or the improvement of a foreign language is presented as being one of the promises of studying abroad. Through the use of the second person singular, the discourse of the university is directly addressed to individuals thinking about the possibility of participating in a mobility programme; their future development is implicated. It is a discourse that presents mobility as an experience with different academic stimuli, making the individual an active participant, instead of a passive consumer; someone who will 'learn' (*aprendrà*), 'improve' (*millorarà*), and 'strengthen' (*reforçarà*) their language skills in a different and new environment.

In sum, the analysis of the students' discourse pre-departure shows that there is a clear alignment with the institutional discourse of their home university on the linguistic benefits that an SA experience presumably entails. At this stage, however, none of the participants mentioned that they needed to prepare themselves linguistically for going abroad, probably because of the language requirement they had to meet (in the case of those who went to Denmark or Wales), or the lack of it (in the case of those who went to Italy).

The apparent casual assuredness with which the participants faced their language learning on the ERASMUS programme positions them on the verge of potentially effortless success. However, how do the students experience the transition from being an L2 learner to being an L2 user once they set foot in their host countries? For those students who went to Denmark or Wales, the language certificate they are required to have prior to departure assures them that they can leave. Yet, does it guarantee the students a sense of well-being as English users and, for some of them, as English users for the first time? Does it create a false sense of security for those students who went to Italy who were not required to certify any foreign language level? Can these students survive, linguistically speaking, simply because they already speak another Romance language?

The next section attempts to explore such questions by focusing on the students' discourses upon arrival in their chosen host country and on their perception of their transition from being L2 learners at home to becoming L2 users abroad.

In-sojourn. The Students' Transition from Learning to Using an L2: Coping with the Unexpected

Most participants recalled their arrival in the host country as a tough period mainly due to their language difficulties or what resembles 'the intense suffering of being deprived of the ability to express oneself fully and as a consequence of being reduced to a talkative mask, a masquerade' (Murphy-Lejeune, 2002, p. 82). Even though the university required students to show proof of language proficiency prior to their departure, when reflecting upon their own 'linguistic self-concept'[5] (Benson et al., 2013, p. 80), most students—whether in Denmark, Italy, or Wales—felt that they should have prepared themselves better linguistically. In fact, the realisation of the need to have prepared oneself better applied exclusively to the L2 and to no other aspect of the sojourn. Let us consider the elicited reflections of one participant per host country on their self-perceptions not only as language learners, but also as poor L2 users at the beginning of their SA experience.

Excerpt 12:	'it is a huge feeling of impotence' (*From the semi-structured interview while shadowing Patrícia—Italy*)
SÒNIA:	and how prepared would you say you were in relation to […] language for instance/
GEORGINA:	I wasn't prepared linguistically speaking\
PATRÍCIA:	no\ me neither really\ I took that two week course bu…t_ […] since I came here in the second semester

	* I did it in the summer and I had totally forgotten it\ [...] when I got here I didn't know anything\
SÒNIA:	[...] you would recommend this\ right/you would say_ hey_ prepare yourself well because Italian is similar bu...t_
PATRÍCIA:	yes\ exactly\ they don't ask you for this in order to come here but it is necessary\ (...) yes\ it is a huge feeling of impotence when you say I can't handle a conversation because * I understand it but I can't_ I can't say what I want\
Excerpt 13:	'I was blocked\' (*From the semi-structured interview while shadowing Ariadna—Denmark*)
SÒNIA:	and now that you have bee··n here for a while_ how prepared would you say you were [linguistically speaking] at the beginning of this stay/
ARIADNA:	no\ I should have gone ... do a little bit of speaking before coming here because ... I remember that when the buddies picked me up (...) at the train station_ I was inside the car and wanted to say that it was very windy in my home town and I just couldn't\ you know/I was blocked\
Excerpt 14:	'I thought I was prepared' (*From the semi-structured interview while shadowing Amanda—Wales*)
RESEARCHER:	did you feel you were well-prepared with English/
AMANDA:	I wasn't\ I wasn't\ I thought I was prepared\ if I have a C1 level_ I thought I had the level to participate in an ERASMUS\ right/a··nd and I have had to overcome this\

These three students' utterances (such as 'a huge feeling of impotence', 'I was blocked', 'I should have done a little bit of speaking', 'I thought I was prepared', and 'I have had to overcome this') clearly index their sense of angst, powerlessness, self-reproach, and frustration at not being able to communicate with others in an L2. They all display a negative affective stance towards the fact of realising that they were not as prepared for the sojourn as they had thought, despite the initial language requirement they had to meet prior to departure. For Amanda, the stay was even like a trial, a challenge she had to survive, or 'overcome'.

Although English was not the language of instruction in Italy, the students remarked that it was the language used within the ERASMUS community. The following excerpt taken from the semi-structured interview with Verònica shows her expressing her discontent towards not being able to communicate in English once abroad, even though she had 'studied' the language for many years at school:

Excerpt 15:	'the language (…) is what worries me the most\' (*From the semi-structured interview while shadowing Verònica—Italy*)
VERÒNICA:	the language (…) is what worries me the most\ I knew this would happen to me because every time I have travelled_ (…) the same has happened to me\ we [Spaniards] are the ones who speak the worst English_ we are the worst\ (…) but the thing is that I have got here and they have confirmed this to me\ I feel bad\ I don't understand why this happens\ (…) I don't even think this is normal\ I don't understand why we can't reach this level and they can\ and I think * I have been studying English for a lot of years\ 12 years studying and I have a B1 level\ is this a joke/

Verònica's use of the affective verb 'worries' clearly indexes her concern and her shame of her poor competence in English, a stance object that she treated as a defining feature not only of herself, but also of Spanish students in general. Speaking the 'worst' English clearly constitutes a stance object to which she oriented affectively ('I feel bad') and which she negatively evaluated as not 'normal' and even as 'a joke'. This was, for Verònica, something for which she could not seem to find an explanation, given the number of years she had been studying—though not necessarily using—English as a compulsory subject at school. Verònica's affective stance evidences Prior's (2016, p. 3) concept of emotion as 'an integral part in the lives and practices of L2 users'. In fact, the students' accounts of their experiences abroad tend to highlight the negative affective dimension of many aspects of the stay and especially their language learning and use.

The next excerpt shows a similar stance from another student, Marina, who displays a rather negative stance towards her first weeks in Wales due to her lacking sufficient competence in English.

Excerpt 16: 'you would like to say many things but you don't know how\' (*From the narrative interview with Marina—Wales*)

SÒNIA: one of the most negative aspects that I have heard in·_ in your discourse has been_ that * you have said that you get blocked_ that you don't know how to say things\ therefore one of the problems that you probably encountered at some point was with the language/with English/

MARINA: yes\ yes_ yes\ because obviously_ when_ when you arrive_ you don't have enough level to_ to [talk about] everyday aspects\ for instance_ I had to manage to call the gas companies_ the water companies_ all this\ to have Internet at home_ * everything\ I mean_ things that I didn't even know how to do_ I had to take the phone and say_

SÒNIA: +*mhm*\+

MARINA: look_ I want this_ I want this_ * I mean * and_ and obviously_ * I mean_ it's hard because_ it is a * they are aspects that_ that you have never studied\ bu·t_ but * well_ you end up managing and you end up knowing it\ and also_ * I don't know_ here··_ wi··th_ * well_ since we start to· to learn English_ what we need to work on the most should be speaking and we don't do this\ and I think it is essential a·nd and * when you arrive there you would obviously like to say a lot of things but you don't know how\

As illustrated in this excerpt, Marina explicitly displays alignment with the researcher by repeating three times the stance marker 'yes', in evaluating the linguistic aspect of the stay as one of the 'problems encountered' at the beginning. As she also seemed to suggest in the interview, once abroad she realised the importance of working on 'speaking', which she deemed 'essential' and yet, at the same time, an aspect which should be given more emphasis in the instructional approach to English at school in Catalonia.

Additionally, it is important to note how Marina uses generalising 'you' utterances when talking about the inability of communicating with others in a foreign language ('you don't have enough level', 'you want to say a lot of things but you don't know how'). By generalising her stance, she seems to indicate a desire for group responsibility and/or refers to knowledge that other ERASMUS students would undoubtedly share. However, she also uses the 'I' in order to clearly signal her personal achievement in 'managing to call the gas companies', for instance—this indicates a necessity to be individually responsible for one's evolution as an L2 learner/user and a growing sense of confidence, triumph, or pride.

Similarly, Joan contended that '[he] wasn't as well prepared as [he] thought' and that he lacked basic vocabulary, and Mònica expressed her surprise about not feeling prepared for her stay abroad. These experiences were in spite of the B1 English language requirement of their home university prior to departure.

Excerpt 17: 'you need more' (*From the semi-structured interview while shadowing Mònica—Denmark*)
MÒNICA: the girl from the Philippines had to take the TOEFL exam_ to be here_ for the international relations office\ we needed almost nothing\ [...] well_ it's not that we can't follow the classes\ but obviously if we had a better level_ * I mean_ I believe that you can be here with a B1 level\ right/ [...] but of course it is like if you need mo··re_ * I don't know\
SÒNIA: it's hard for you\ right/
MÒNICA: yes\ [...] if the programme you are participating in is in E& * is in English_ they should make you take a test in [our home town]_ of speaki·ng_ of * I don't know what\

In this excerpt, Mònica refers to a student from the Philippines she has met in Denmark who was required to certify a higher level of English prior to departure. Mònica evaluates her B1 language requirement negatively, as 'almost nothing', as not helpful for going to a university in which English is the language of instruction, and as making the beginning of her ERASMUS experience 'hard'. Her stance utterance 'they should make you take a test' also illustrates Mònica's sense of responsibility in her linguistic preparation, by shifting it away from herself and onto the home university.

Indeed, frustration seems to mark the first stages of the ERASMUS experiences for most participants, 'whose personality is [somehow] perceived as diminished for want of being fully expressed' (Murphy-Lejeune, 2002, p. 120). According to the students, and as this section shows, their self-perceived poor L2 competence had two main consequences, namely, not being able to follow classes in an L2 and not being able to forge relationships with speakers of other L1s. Likewise, according to the students, the reasons for the poor L2 competence lie squarely with the home school and university and not so much with themselves.

Regarding the students' inability to follow classes in an L2, the following excerpt shows how Patrícia recalls her first classes at an Italian university.

Excerpt 18: 'difficult to follow the classes\' (*From the narrative interview with Patrícia—Italy*)
PATRÍCIA: at the beginning we found it a little bit difficult to follow the classes\ but (…) there were also a lot of people * when we said hey_ we are ERASMUS students_ they already told you oh_ don't worry_ we'll lend you our class notes_ don't worry\ that was great\

Patrícia uses the evaluative adjective 'difficult' to describe her only basic ability to follow classes in Italian, despite this being a Romance language. Besides this, she also constructs herself overtly as a member of the identity category 'ERASMUS student' and explains how this self-categorisation immediately produced an empathetic response from her Italian interlocutors, for whom sharing notes with ERASMUS students seemed to be a common practice. Patrícia evaluates positively their willingness to share notes with her through the use of the evaluative adjective 'great'.

Verònica also contended that 'we didn't understand anything' in class. By using the first-person-plural pronoun 'we', Verònica explicitly voices other Spanish/Catalan ERASMUS students who, like her, would position themselves as not able to follow classes in Italian. The following excerpt shows Verònica's negative affective stance towards the way in which, according to her, Spanish ERASMUS students were treated in a partial manner at her Italian university because of their inadequate competence in the language of instruction (Italian).

Excerpt 19:	'you will do something different\' (*From the semi-structured interview while abroad with Verònica—Italy*)
SÒNIA:	you don't go to class_ why not/
VERÒNICA:	(…) what enraged me was tha··t_ in many subjects they told you don't_ don't come because you will do something different\
SÒNIA:	+*mhm*\+
VERÒNICA:	there was one subject which was political economy (…) in which the teacher had been on an ERASMUS i··n_ in the Canary Islands_ and * he took all the Spanish students and told us that no_ that he would_ he would give us a book and that we should study it in Spanish_ and that we would take the exam in Spanish because he understood Spanish\

As evidenced in excerpt 19, using Spanish was the easy way out, not only for the students, but also for the teacher. Verònica's attempt to improve her Italian was cut short by the teacher's gesture to help them— but also himself—by sticking to Spanish. In this instance, L2 learning was hampered by the host university teacher and students who dissuaded the Spanish/Catalonian students from making an effort to understand and use the Italian language within the university context. The affective stance predicate 'enraged', along with the shift in pronouns from 'me' to 'you' (a Spanish student) to 'us' and 'we' (all Spanish students), clearly indexes Verònica's feelings and/or positioning towards the way classes in Italy worked as well as the Spanish ERASMUS students' feelings of alienation from local and other international students. This is not necessarily an unusual pattern in the SA context, for Churchill (2006, p. 207) points out that certain individual teaching decisions and approaches may become a 'negative factor affecting student participation' in the SA classroom. Churchill suggests this can be addressed by pre-programme planning that considers the SA classroom experience not as 'a loss of precious time' (p. 221).

Amanda also reported not being able to follow classes at the beginning of her stay in Wales. Although she also stated feeling at ease with foreign language use after a few months:

Excerpt 20:   'I don't understand anything\' (*From the narrative interview with Amanda—Wales*)
AMANDA: and the classes (…) at the beginning I also +uh···+ thought * I don't understand anything_ +uh+ they speak very fast_ maybe I don't pass [the subject]_ (…) but at the end as days go by you start adapting_ you see·_ that you can perfectly go through this\

Amanda's affective stance is displayed in expressing her initial worry about failing the subject due to her lack of language competence. Her use of generic 'you' subjects enables her also to generalise her epistemic stance to other possible members of the category 'ERASMUS student' who, despite experiencing language difficulties at the beginning of their sojourn, would finally 'go through this'. Thus, although Amanda described how hard that beginning was, she now seems to highlight the transformative process she has undergone by finally displaying a positive stance of being able to cope and experiencing success ('you start adapting', 'you can perfectly go through this').

Considering that the ERASMUS programme is 'perceived as a social experience rather than exclusively an academic one' (Krupnik & Krzaklewska, 2013, p. 212), being able to cross this language threshold from language learner to user was important not only to follow classes, but also to forge social ties with other exchange students who spoke other L1s. As Murphy-Lejeune (2002, p. 117) claims, 'language limitations isolate socially'. The students in the current study also perceived this as another consequence of poor L2 competence. For example, the following excerpt shows how Joan views interacting with co-nationals and lacking confidence in English as defining features of all Spanish ERASMUS students. He evaluates this as 'a total tendency'.

Excerpt 21: 'they got together because of the language\' (*From the narrative interview with Joan—Denmark*)

SÒNIA: did you see that the Spanish students tended to stay_ to stay with Spanish students/why do you think this is so/

JOAN: ye··s\ a total trend\ total\ I don't know_ I think it is because_ they feel more confident\ I think it is also due to the fact that they leave with a level of English_ * many of them left without a certificate of English\ I mean_ they had a B1 a·nd * you know/well_ they spoke poor English\ you know/ (…)

SÒNIA: poor English\

JOAN: yes\ many thought_ it is better if I can be with people of my country\ (…) I think they got together because of_ because of the language\ you know/because many people were embarrassed to speak ca& * in English\ I remember I was_ in an office of a * of my supervisor and there were groups outside that were speaking Spanish\ right/they were Spanish groups\ and one said to the other_ {(Spa) you ask because your English is better\} (…) {(Spa) it's always me asking\} you know/I mean_ there was…_

SÒNIA: no confidence with the language/

JOAN: yes\ mainly the people fro··m outside Catalonia\

As shown in this case, Joan presents the inevitable connection among Spanish ERASMUS students as related to their embarrassment for their poor competence in English and the comfort that comes from acting as a familiar group. Furthermore, Joan highlights the distinction between the Spanish group ('the people from outside Catalonia'—'they') and the Catalan group ('we'), the former having 'no confidence with the language'.

In another similar example in excerpt 22, Verònica evaluates her poor competence in English as 'the problem' preventing her from socialising with non-Spanish ERASMUS students and, therefore, hindering her improvement of this L2.

Excerpt 22: 'my English is not enough\' (*From the narrative; Verònica—Italy*)

VERÒNICA: the problem is that if I could speak English the same way I speak Catalan (...) well of course I would be able to speak with them_ with_ with those people and I could have contact with them but the truth is that my English is not enough\

SÒNIA: (...) the majority of your ERASMUS colleagues * well_ the ERASMUS students in general speak English\ right/ would you say that the majority speak English/

VERÒNICA: they speak or try to speak [English]\

SÒNIA: are you talking about Spanish [ERASMUS] students/

VERÒNICA: yes\ look_ there's a huge difference and that is that the Spanish do not know how to speak in English_ and the others know English very well\

SÒNIA: (...) and Italian* do the Spanish speak Italian and the others don't o··r_

VERÒNICA: the Spanish can understand Italian and it is much easier and the others find it more difficult\ there are people who have come here without taking any course [in Italian] and without doing anything\ but what I don't understand is how it can be that everybody who is not Spanish know how to speak English_ and we don't\

In her interview, Verònica constantly emphasises the distinction between 'non-Spanish [ERASMUS] students' who 'know how to speak English' and 'Spanish [ERASMUS] students' who 'do not know how to speak in English' in the context of the social consequences that this entailed. Put simply, from her perspective, all ERASMUS students could interact with each other in proficient English except for Verònica and her cohort. This is the reason why Verònica later recognises she interacted mostly with other co-nationals, who finally became a resource that 'provided a basis for emotional closeness and support' (Papatsiba, 2006, p. 123). To a certain extent, these co-nationals acted as their families, even though this contact somehow defeats the main transnational or pan-European aim of the ERASMUS programme, which is 'to strengthen the interaction between citizens in different Member States with a view to consolidating the concept of a People's Europe' (Council of Ministers, 1987, p. 21).

In sum, the analysis of the participants' discourses shows that they all expected to improve or perfect their L2 and that the SA experience raised their awareness of their actual L2 proficiency and their lack of linguistic preparation in their initial communicative situations in a given foreign language (i.e., English or Italian). Their use of evaluative adjectives (e.g., 'difficult', 'horrible', 'hard'), affective verbs (e.g., 'enrages', 'feel'), and negated modal verbs like 'can't' all index their affective negative stance towards their initial language-based experiences as ill-prepared users of a given foreign language. Initially, they could not fully express themselves through the L2 and therefore realised once in-sojourn that a pre-sojourn linguistic preparation is 'essential' and 'necessary'. In fact, most categorised themselves as 'not prepared' sufficiently linguistically so as to follow classes at the beginning of their stay. What is more, according to some, this poor competence in the L2 also crystallised into social isolation, the impossibility of building a rich social network formed by people from different countries and, ultimately, a somehow inevitable joining with other co-nationals who spoke the same L1. Even though most students did finally report having made progress in their learning and use of foreign languages over the stay (Mas-Alcolea, 2017), the almost unanimous experience and realisation of insufficient L2 proficiency and preparation delayed and limited the extent of that progress.

Conclusion and Recommendations

The main aim of this chapter has been to examine how Catalan ERASMUS students discursively constructed their transition from being L2 learners at home to being L2 users during and as a consequence of their SA experience. This is especially useful to SA research since the ERASMUS exchange represented the first time that these participants were living in the L2. The focus was placed on the students' development of their 'second language identity' (Benson et al., 2013) and on 'the differences languages make to individuals, and of the ways in which individuals construct their identities and relationships' (Burck, 2005, p. 3) through different languages. Regarding the pre-sojourn stage, the analysis of the students' discourses revealed, on the one hand, how they projected their *imagined identities* (Barkhuizen & De Klerk, 2006; Norton, 2001) as future competent L2 users in the SA context, which, unlike the AH context, they believed would offer multiple opportunities for using—and not just learning—a foreign language. The students' imagined identities appear to have been influenced by circulating discourses on mobility—including that of their home university—which present 'an encouraging picture' of the SA experience as having 'the potential to enhance students' language ability in every domain' (Kinginger, 2013, p. 4). The students also took for granted that the home university language requirement would guarantee their linguistic needs once abroad.

Regarding the in-sojourn stage, and to the students' surprise, it has been shown that this longed-for transition to L2 user was not a smooth process and that it depended on whether they succeeded in bridging the gap between their previously imagined identities and their actual lived identities abroad. Certainly, the language requirement set by their home university did not seem to guarantee this transition. Despite the final generally positive evaluation of the ERASMUS experience by the students (Mas-Alcolea, 2017), their interviews and essays quickly exposed the difficulties most of them faced at the initial stage of the sojourn. These were mainly related to the students' self-perceived poor L2 competence, especially in English, which was both the language of instruction in Denmark and Wales and the language used within the ERASMUS community in all three destination countries for socialising. Although they had met their home university's linguistic requirement, this proved to be no safeguard for their actual linguistic needs once abroad. Daily communicative practices, such as getting home Internet service, politely making small talk about the weather, and following university lessons, turned out to be extremely difficult in the L2 at first. This generated a sense of surprise and even frustration, shame, and embarrassment on the part of the students, for not being able to meet the linguistic requirements of certain communicative situations abroad meant—at least initially—neither attaining their personal intentions and imagined identities nor fulfilling the accepted goals of ERASMUS. The students' display of a negative affective stance towards their initial inability to communicate and live through an L2 is in line with Murphy-Lejeune's (2002, p. 117) study in which she discerns the students' 'communication strain' and the ways in which they regard language as 'an indelible stigma'.

Besides affecting the students' emotional well-being, this initial linguistic limitation had consequences on their socialisation abroad, which in most cases also marked the whole SA period. Students who had difficulties interacting in English, the chief lingua franca or a 'shared practice' within the international student community (Kalocsai, 2014), tended to limit their interactions to other co-nationals which, in turn, reduced their opportunities for using and improving their L2. This often constituted further frustration, since developing international networks through various interactions with local and other international students was an expectation of most of the participants. Soon, this circumstance challenged the students' perception of their home university's intercultural and linguistic exchange ideal of the ERASMUS mobility programme.

The pre-sojourn requirements set by the home university, which were interpreted by the students as guaranteeing their 'linguistic safety' abroad, were based on the CEFR and issued by external entities, not necessarily related with the ERASMUS programme or with the university's international office. These external and generalist mechanisms seemed to generate expectations on the part of the participants as to what languages they would encounter abroad (such as the medium of instruction and the language of socialisation) and what L2 proficiency they would need in order to have a successful experience. In Denmark and Wales, a B1 English proficiency level was deemed necessary and sufficient, while no compulsory L2 proficiency—whether Italian or English—was required for the Spanish/Catalonian students to travel to Italy. Consequently, English was the only language expected to be used and needed by students going to Denmark and Wales, and students going to Italy were expected to be able to 'survive' through their L1s (Spanish and Catalan) in an Italian-medium environment.

The testimonies analysed in this chapter have evidenced the shortcomings of the pre-departure requirements by the students' home university and also the students' lack of self-responsibility for their preparedness and future learning. On the one hand, the pre-departure requirements do not seem to be based on the students' real potential needs abroad; on the other hand, they should not only validate the students' knowledge about the language but also their knowledge about how to use the language in those social domains in which they will presumably engage abroad.

Hence, some questions in this respect need further answers: Whom do these linguistic pre-sojourn requirements benefit? What do they really guarantee? How can they be adjusted to the *real* linguistic requirements of an SA experience? More research in this respect across various ERASMUS-sending countries is needed in order to inform the decisions of university policymakers and to improve exchange students' linguistic well-being abroad. Based on the experiences of the students in the current study, I offer some recommendations in the following paragraphs.

First, universities should be more engaged in guaranteeing the students' linguistic well-being abroad. This should involve not only a set of pre-sojourn requirements, but also adequate pre-sojourn preparation as well as support during the stay. Before departing, students could access online orientations designed specifically for linguistic needs upon arrival. In-sojourn support could take the form of reception language courses, linguistic consulting services, and support in offering international students opportunities to participate in local activities, such as being part of a local—and not exclusively international—sports team, among others.

Second, universities should prioritise pedagogical strategies over SA marketing strategies. They should not only advertise the benefits and virtues of SA, but also publicise the potential ways of achieving these outcomes or possibly avoiding any complications so that future participants might learn from others' positive and negative past experiences. This surely would include the compilation and sharing of different testimonies that show and tackle the negative consequences of leaving without being prepared linguistically especially for everyday language, for instance.

Third, recommendations about their linguistic pre-sojourn preparation should be made by home universities and not external entities. These recommendations can be developed through consultation with past participants and the students' current professors or language faculty. On the basis of those past experiences, universities should provide general guidelines for the students' adequate (to their environment and potential language use) language preparation before departure that can be expanded upon individually.

Fourth, educational activities should be adopted, in the form of pre-sojourn language preparation courses, based on the students' actual potential needs abroad. These should be inspired by examples from studies like the current one, which has accessed the students' own reported needs and difficulties. Other examples include Jackson's (2009, p. 60) ethnographic work on L2 students from Hong Kong, which concludes that 'inadequate preparation [...] can have detrimental effects on sojourner perceptions, adjustment, and willingness to engage with host nationals' and Murphy-Lejeune's (2002, p. 84) study on European mobility, in which she asserts that 'language preparation for non-specialist students suffers from the same uncertainties as orientation courses for the actual period abroad and [that] it could be suggested that many students leave ill-prepared for what lies ahead of them'.

Fifth, pre-sojourn linguistic requirements should not be based on generalist degrees but on specialised tests. Research on SA could potentially inform pre-SA language tests so that these could act as a more trustworthy guarantee of linguistic safety. Finally, prior to departure, universities should foster the students' awareness of their own potential active role in their L2 learning processes, by providing information on the different strategies they could use that would facilitate their L2 learning. This would foster not only their awareness and knowledge of such strategies, but also their sense of agency and responsibility in this process. Indeed, this chapter reveals that both sending universities and individual students need to take more responsibility for L2 learning in SA.

Summary of recommendations for L2 preparedness for ERASMUS exchanges based on participants' lived experiences:

- Universities should be more engaged in guaranteeing the students' linguistic well-being abroad through a set of pre-sojourn requirements, but also adequate pre-sojourn preparation and in-sojourn support.
- Universities should prioritise pedagogical strategies over SA marketing strategies and, thus, also publicise the potential ways of achieving these outcomes or possibly avoiding complications.
- Recommendations about the students' linguistic pre-sojourn preparation should be made by home universities and not external entities.
- Educational activities should be adopted, in the form of pre-sojourn language preparation courses, based on the students' most likely potential needs abroad.
- Research on SA could potentially inform pre-SA linguistic requirement language tests so that these could act as a more trustworthy guarantee of linguistic safety.
- Prior to departure, universities should foster the students' awareness of their own agency and responsibility in their L2 learning process in SA.

Notes

1. Kubota (2016, p. 349) writes about 'the study-abroad social imaginary' in order to make reference to 'the alleged benefits of study abroad found in common discourse'. These *social imaginaries*, following Rizvi and Lingard (2010, p. 34), are spread through 'images, myths, parables, stories, legends and other narratives and most significantly, in the contemporary era, the mass media, as well as popular culture'.
2. ERASMUS is an acronym for '**EuR**opean Community **A**ction **S**cheme for the **M**obility of **U**niversity **S**tudents'. As the name indicates, it is an independently run student exchange programme that allows students to spend 3 to 12 months abroad in a European country. The general rationale of the programme is to promote student mobility within the European Union on the assumption that those mobile students will become more pro-European.
3. The transcription conventions are based on Payrató and Alturó (2002): (1) Laughter: Laughter particles are indicated with the @ symbol between the '+' symbol, approximating syllable number; utterances spoken laughingly appear between square brackets. (2) Lengthening: Dots (.) indicate prolongation of the immediately prior sound. (3) Repetition: All voluntary and involuntary repetitions of words and phrases are transcribed. (4) Terminal pitch movement: Rising pitch movement is marked with a slash (/); falling pitch movement is marked with a backslash (\); continuing or level pitch movement is marked with an underscore (_). (5) Reformulation of an idea: An asterisk (*) indicates that the speaker has reformulated an idea. (6) Omissions: words omitted are indicated with three dots between square brackets [...]; a word that was started but left unfinished is indicated by the ampersand symbol &. (7) Non-Catalan speech: utterances in languages, which are not the speaker's first language (Catalan), appear between square brackets with the language indicated.
4. Hi ha unes quantes bones raons per aprofitar l'oportunitat de participar en un o diversos programes de mobilitat i cursar una part dels teus estudis en una universitat estrangera. Acadèmicament, podràs [...] millorar els teus coneixements de llengües estrangeres i aprendre'n de noves. [...] reforçaràs aptituds com ara [...] la teva fluïdesa en idiomes estrangers. I have withheld the citation to preserve the participants' anonymity.

5. The notion of 'linguistic self-concept' put forward by Benson et al. (2013, p. 80) has to do with the ways in which 'learners perceived their ability as users and as learners of a second language, and also to their beliefs and emotions' or with their answer to the question 'Who am I and who do I become as I learn and use English in my study abroad context?'.

Bibliography

Allen, H. W. (2010). Language learning motivation during short term study abroad: An activity theory perspective. *Foreign Language Annals, 43*(1), 27–49.

Barkhuizen, G., & de Klerk, V. (2006). Imagined identities: Pre-immigrants' narratives on language and identity. *International Journal of Bilingualism, 10*(3), 277–299.

Benson, P., Barkhuizen, G., Bodycott, P., & Brown, J. (2013). *Second language identity in narratives of study abroad*. Basingstoke, UK: Palgrave Macmillan.

Burck, C. (2005). *Multilingual living: Explorations of language and subjectivity*. Basingstoke, UK: Palgrave Macmillan.

Churchill, E. (2006). Variability in the study abroad classroom and learner competence. In M. A. DuFon & E. Churchill (Eds.), *Language learners in study abroad contexts* (pp. 203–227). Clevedon, UK: Multilingual Matters.

Coleman, J. A. (1998). Language learning and study abroad: The European perspective. *Frontiers. The Interdisciplinary Journal of Study Abroad, 4*(2), 167–203.

Council of Ministers. (1987). Council decision of 15 June 1987 adopting the European Community action scheme for the mobility of university students (ERASMUS) (doc. 87/327/EEC). In *Official Journal of the European Communities*, L 166, pp. 20–24.

Creswell, J. W. (1998). *Qualitative inquiry and research design: Choosing among five approaches*. London: Sage.

DeKeyser, R. (Ed.). (2007). *Practice in a second language: Perspectives from applied linguistics and cognitive psychology*. New York: Cambridge University Press.

DGESOB (Direcció General d'Educació Secundària Obligatòria i Batxillerat). (2008). *Currículum batxillerat: àmbit de llengües, Decret 142/2008 – DOGC núm. 5183*. Barcelona: Generalitat de Catalunya.

DGESOB (Direcció General d'Educació Secundària Obligatòria i Batxillerat). (2015). *Competències bàsiques de l'àmbit lingüístic: Llengües estrangeres, Servei de Comunicació i Publicacions*. Barcelona: Generalitat de Catalunya.

Du Bois, J. W. (2007). The stance triangle. In R. Englebretson (Ed.), *Stancetaking in discourse: Subjectivity, evaluation, interaction* (pp. 139–182). Amsterdam: Benjamins.

Engle, L., & Engle, J. (2004). Assessing language acquisition and intercultural sensitivity development in relation to study abroad program design. *Frontiers: The Interdisciplinary Journal of Study Abroad, 10,* 219–236.

European Commission. (2003). *Promoting language learning and linguistic diversity: An action plan 2004–2006 (COM (2003) 449 final).* Luxembourg: Office for Official Publications of the European Communities.

Feyen, B., & Krzaklewska, E. (Eds.). (2013). *The ERASMUS Phenomenon: Symbol of a New European Generation?* Frankfurt & Bern: Peter Lang.

Flyvbjerg, B. (2011). Case study. In N. K. Denzin & Y. S. Lincoln (Eds.), *The Sage handbook of qualitative research* (4th ed., pp. 301–316). Thousand Oaks, CA: Sage.

Foster, P. (2009). Lexical diversity and native-like selection: The bonus of studying abroad. In B. Richards, M. Daller, D. Malvern, P. Meara, J. Milton, & J. Treffers-Daller (Eds.), *Vocabulary studies in first and second language acquisition* (pp. 91–106). New York: Palgrave Macmillan.

Freed, B. F. (Ed.). (1995). *Second language acquisition in a study abroad context.* Philadelphia: Benjamins.

Freed, B. F., Segalowitz, N., & Dewey, D. P. (2004). Context of learning and second language fluency in French: Comparing regular classroom, study abroad, and intensive domestic immersion programs. *Studies in Second Language Acquisition, 26*(2), 275–301.

Generalitat de Catalunya. (2016, September 1). *S'incrementa la taxa de graduació a l'ESO fins al 88%.* Retrieved from http://web.gencat.cat/es/actualitat/detall/Curs-escolar-2016-2017

Idescat. (2015). *Enquesta d'usos lingüístics de la població 2013.* Generalitat de Catalunya. Retrieved from https://www.idescat.cat/cat/idescat/publicacions/cataleg/pdfdocs/eulp2013.pdf

Ife, A., Vives Boix, G., & Meara, P. (2000). The impact of study abroad on the vocabulary development of different proficiency groups. *Spanish Applied Linguistics, 4*(1), 55–84.

Jackson, J. (2009). Intercultural learning on short term sojourns. *Intercultural Education, 20*(1), S59–S71.

Jaffe, A. (Ed.). (2009). *Stance: Sociolinguistic perspectives.* New York: Oxford University Press.

Johnstone, B. (2009). Stance, style, and the linguistic individual. In A. Jaffe (Ed.), *Stance: Sociolinguistic perspectives* (pp. 29–52). New York: Oxford University Press.

Juan-Garau, M., & Pérez-Vidal, C. (2007). The effect of context and contact on oral performance in students who go on a stay abroad. *Vigo International Journal of Applied Linguistics, 4*, 117–134.

Kalocsai, K. (2014). *Communities of practice and English as a lingua franca. A study of ERASMUS students in a central European context.* Berlin: Walter de Gruyter.

Kinginger, C. (2009). *Language learning and study abroad: A critical reading of research.* New York: Palgrave Macmillan.

Kinginger, C. (2011). Enhancing language learning in study abroad. *Annual Review of Applied Linguistics, 31*, 58–73.

Kinginger, C. (2013). Identity and language learning in study abroad. *Foreign Language Annals, 46*(3), 339–358.

Kinginger, C. (2015). Student mobility and identity-related language learning. *Intercultural Education, 26*(1), 6–15.

Kinginger, C., & Farrell, K. (2004). Assessing development of meta-pragmatic awareness in study abroad. *Frontiers: The Interdisciplinary Journal of Study Abroad, 10*, 19–42.

Krupnik, S., & Krzaklewska, E. (2013). Researching the impact of ERASMUS on European identification—proposal for a conceptual framework. In B. Feyen & E. Krzaklewska (Eds.), *The ERASMUS phenomenon-symbol of a new European generation?* (pp. 207–225). New York: Peter Lang.

Kubota, R. (2016). The social imaginary of study abroad: Complexities and contradictions. *Language Learning Journal, 44*(3), 347–357.

Llanes, À., & Muñoz, C. (2009). A short stay abroad: Does it make a difference? *System, 37*(3), 353–365.

Magnan, S., & Lafford, B. (2012). Learning through immersion during study abroad. In S. Gass & A. Mackey (Eds.), *The Routledge handbook of second language acquisition* (pp. 525–540). New York: Routledge.

Mas-Alcolea, S. (2017). *Discourses on Study Abroad: The Experience of ERASMUS Students from a University in Catalonia.* Tesis Doctorales en Red, University of Lleida. Retrieved from http://hdl.handle.net/10803/456557

Mitchell, R., Tracy-Ventura, N., & McManus, K. (2017). *Anglophone students abroad: Identity, social relationships, and language learning.* New York: Routledge.

Murphy-Lejeune, E. (2002). *Student mobility and narrative in Europe: The new strangers.* London: Routledge.

Norton, B. (2001). Non-participation, imagined communities and the language classroom. *Learner Contributions to Language Learning: New Directions in Research, 6*(2), 159–171.

Papatsiba, V. (2006). Study abroad and experiences of cultural distance and proximity: French ERASMUS students. In M. Byram & A. Feng (Eds.),

Living and studying abroad: Research and practice (pp. 108–133). Clevedon, UK: Multilingual Matters.

Payrató, L. L., & Alturó, N. (Eds.). (2002). *Corpus oral de conversa col·loquial*. Barcelona: Universitat de Barcelona.

Pennycook, A. (1994). *The cultural politics of English as an international language*. London: Longman.

Plews, J. L., Breckenridge, Y., Cambre, M. C., & Fernandes, G. M. d. F. (2014). Mexican English teachers' experiences of international professional development in Canada: A narrative sequel. *Electronic Journal of Foreign Language Teaching, 11*(1), 52–75. Retrieved from http://e-flt.nus.edu.sg/v11n12014/plews.pdf

Prior, M. T. (2016). *Emotion and discourse in L2 narrative research*. Tonawanda, NY: Multilingual Matters.

Quinlan, E. (2008). Conspicuous invisibility: Shadowing as a data collection strategy. *Qualitative Inquiry, 14*(8), 1480–1499.

Rizvi, F., & Lingard, R. (2010). *Globalizing education policy*. London: Routledge.

Shively, R. L. (2011). L2 pragmatic development in study abroad: A longitudinal study of Spanish service encounters. *Journal of Pragmatics, 43*(6), 1818–1835.

Stake, R. E. (1995). *The art of case study research*. Thousand Oaks: Sage.

Taguchi, N. (2008). Cognition, language contact, and the development of pragmatic comprehension in a study abroad context. *Language Learning, 58*(1), 33–71.

Wilkinson, S. (1998). Study abroad from the participants' perspective: A challenge to common beliefs. *Foreign Language Annals, 31*(1), 23–39.

Language Teachers on Study Abroad Programmes: The Characteristics and Strategies of Those Most Likely to Increase Their Intercultural Communicative Competence

Deborah Corder, Annelies Roskvist, Sharon Harvey, and Karen Stacey

Introduction

The shift in educational goals to incorporate intercultural communicative competence (ICC) and the increasing discourse around intercultural citizenship and intercultural dialogue mean that the expectations of the role of the language teacher are changing. Language teachers now need to be interculturally competent, understand the processes of intercultural development, the language and culture nexus (Byram, 2008, 2012b; Risager, 2012), and be able to include the intercultural dimension in their classrooms to meet the expectations of intercultural communicative language teaching (iCLT) (Bastos & Araújo e Sá, 2014; Byram, 2008, 2014; Jackson, 2012b; Kelly, 2012; Ryan, 2012). This has implications for the teacher training and professional development (PD) of in-service teachers, and the analysis of data in this chapter illustrates such implications.

Since 2005, the New Zealand (NZ) government has funded PD language and culture immersion experiences (LCIEs) or sojourns for in-service language teachers as part of its aim to develop capacity and capability in language teaching. The effectiveness of the LCIEs was evaluated by Harvey, Roskvist, Corder, and Stacey (2011) in a report commissioned by the NZ Ministry of Education (MoE). The findings of the report indicated gains in language ability, confidence, and cultural knowledge. The evidence was less convincing for understanding the relationship between language and culture and the concept of ICC. However, the concept of ICC was officially introduced to NZ schoolteachers with a new curriculum in 2007 (MoE, 2007), and for many of the teacher-participants in the 2011 study, it was still a new concept about which they may not have had a great deal of PD.

As part of the brief for the Harvey et al. (2011) study, the NZ MoE wanted to know if it was possible to determine the characteristics of teachers who were likely to increase their ICC as a result of a LCIE. This chapter explores the experiences of three in-service language teachers who participated in the LCIE programme. It examines data from the 2011 study for evidence of the characteristics of ICC and strategies used by teachers, interpreting how these strategies led to transformative intercultural learning. It also explores what could have been different and what needs to happen in order to maximise the experience and translate it into improved experiences and outcomes for students in these teachers' domestic classrooms. The data are examined using the objectives related to Byram's model of intercultural competence (2008), which was used by Harvey et al. (2011), as well as a number of other constructs and models used in the emerging body of intercultural development and study abroad (SA) research. Byram (2009, 2012b) acknowledges that his model is not exhaustive and does not include personality or every detail of the intercultural speaker. While case studies are individual and cannot be generalised, the aim of the chapter is nonetheless to provide insight into the processes in the development of intercultural competence in the case of teachers as participants in LCIEs, and what characteristics and strategies demonstrated by individuals might facilitate their intercultural development.

After briefly explaining the NZ LCIEs programmes, we review the literature on ICC and SA. The literature refers to both 'intercultural competence' and ICC. ICC embodies the intercultural competences of knowledge, skills, attitude, and critical cultural awareness, which characterises many models, but incorporates the linguistic as well as the cultural dimension (Byram, 2012a, 2012b), and is used in the context of language teaching.

Context

The NZ teachers, LCIE programmes are available for in-service teachers of second languages (L2s) in the NZ curriculum. The programmes are either short term, ranging from one to three months, one semester, or one year, and participants usually go abroad individually and not as a group. The programmes are contracted by the MoE to two organisations: International Languages Exchanges and Pathways (ILEP, n.d.) and AFS New Zealand (formerly the American Field Service) (n.d.-a). Each organisation differs in the programmes it offers, meaning that LCIE experiences can vary.

ILEP is funded by the MoE and a number of international organisations. ILEP programmes tend to offer language and culture immersion through enrolment in SA courses, which can include ICC development and language teaching pedagogy, as well as observations in schools. Teachers can go in groups accompanied by an MoE language advisor, who may or may not be seconded by an international organisation. The role of the language advisors in NZ is to support language teaching and learning in NZ schools.

AFS New Zealand is a non-governmental, non-profit organisation that provides teachers opportunities to improve their language proficiency and cultural knowledge. Teachers are placed in a country in which the teaching language is an official language. They usually teach in schools as first-language teaching assistants, observe classes in their teaching language, and sometimes enrol in language, culture, or teaching methodology courses. Most reside with host families. One of the main outcomes is for teachers to develop their own ICC to support the improvement of the teaching and learning of languages in NZ classrooms (AFS, n.d.-b).

Teachers set their own language-learning goals for PD and as eventual learning outcomes for their students with an advisor before departure and subsequently submit scheduled reports (AFS, n.d.-a, n.d.-b). The emphasis on setting learning goals has increased since Harvey et al.'s (2011) findings. However, there is no clear mention of pre-departure preparation linking goals to theory and research, which was one of the recommendations of the 2011 report.

According to Harvey et al. (2011), more than 140 teachers from primary (aged 5–12) through to secondary (aged 12–17) level had participated in the LCIE programmes in the period 2005–2011. Immersion countries were Argentina, Belgium, France, Canada (Québec), Chile, China, Germany, Japan, New Caledonia, Samoa, and Spain. Their perceived language proficiency ranged from beginners through to advanced and expert user level. In NZ, primary teachers are generalist teachers and not trained as language teachers. Many have not studied a language beyond school level, if at all. Since 2005, the Government aim has been to build language provision for all students and the LCIEs were initiated as part of teacher PD. Two of the teachers who are the focus of this chapter participated in AFS NZ programmes, and one in the ILEP programme.

Literature Review

SA/cultural immersion experiences have long been considered as providing the potential for language and culture learning as well as increased intercultural understanding, and increasing numbers of students and teachers are participating (Jackson & Oguro, 2017; Smolcic & Katunich, 2017). However, studies are increasingly indicating that individual participant experiences and language development are varied and that SA does not necessarily result in ICC development (Ehrenreich, 2006; Vogt, 2016). SA involves a complex interplay of individual worldviews and expectations (Jackson, 2012a; Kinginger, 2015), with the added professional dimension in the case of teachers (Bastos & Araújo e Sá, 2014;

Plews, Breckenridge, & Cambre, 2010; Wernicke, 2010). Research on the SA experiences of teachers in particular is slowly increasing, although it is mostly on pre-service rather than on in-service teachers. Like Harvey et al. (2011), these studies suggest gains especially in linguistic competence and cultural knowledge. However, when the aims of the programme also include the development of ICC—again, like Harvey et al. (2011)—the studies indicate that maximal gains cannot be taken for granted and changes in the traditional approaches to SA programmes are required (East, 2013; Ehrenreich, 2006; Harvey et al., 2011; Kırkgöz, 2016; Marx & Moss, 2011; Plews, Breckenridge, Cambre, & Fernandes, 2014; Vogt, 2016). These findings echo the themes in related studies on SA for L2 students. Some studies indicate the potential for learning but question its nature and extent as well as the effectiveness of how gains are measured (Jackson, 2012a; Kinginger, 2015; Vande Berg, Paige, & Lou, 2012). SA research has identified the need for the intentional development of ICC knowledge and skills (Jackson, 2009; Jackson & Oguro, 2017; Vande Berg et al., 2012).

Intercultural Competence

The increasing body of work on intercultural competence/communication, which problematises its own concepts and frequently introduces new ones, can be overwhelming for a language teacher to translate to classroom practice. While there is a plethora of models, terminologies, and definitions (Byram, 2009; Holmes & O'Neill, 2012; Jackson, 2012b), there seems to be consensus that the common goal of intercultural competence is 'the appropriate and effective management of interaction between people who, to some degree or another, represent different or divergent affective, cognitive, and behavioural orientations to the world' (Spitzberg & Changnon, 2009, p. 7). Spitzberg and Changnon (2009) have identified commonalities across the models that include motivation (attitude, values, beliefs), knowledge (cultural, theoretical), skills (flexibility, openness), context (relational/conflict management, environment), and outcomes (critical self-assessment, awareness of identity, maintaining relationships).

Intercultural Communicative Competence (ICC)

Applied linguists concerned with ICC have discussed the holistic development of the individual and focussed on the fundamental competence of the critical cultural self-awareness of one's own culture and how culture, underpinned by values, beliefs, and norms, influences one's identity, worldviews, behaviour, and also awareness of the use of language (Byram, 1997, 2008, 2009; Deardorff, 2006, 2009; Holmes & O'Neill, 2012; Jackson, 2012a; Witte, 2011). Without this ability to question and analyse one's own cultural framework, it is not possible fully to understand and respect personal and cultural differences and contexts, be open to multiple perspectives, and develop the necessary behavioural characteristics or outcomes of intercultural competence. Having language awareness as well as cultural awareness is what Byram (2012b) calls the language–culture nexus. It requires the ability to analyse the relationship between language and culture as it relates to oneself and society and how it links to personal and social identities. Critical language and cultural awareness and the concept of interculturality and intercultural dialogue are now seen as complementing citizenship education (Byram, 2014). Linguistic competence and critical cultural awareness of one's own worldviews and ideologies enable an individual to interact both with people who speak the same language but have different worldviews and with people from other countries, through other languages, as cultural mediators (Byram, 2008, 2012a; Lázár, 2011).

ICC behaviours and outcomes such as adaptability, being able to move out of one's comfort zone when faced with uncertainty and difference, and making sense of the experiences and emotional responses in intercultural encounters are especially significant for cultural immersion experiences such as SA. It is clear from ICC literature (Bastos & Araújo e Sá, 2014; Byram, 2012b, 2014; Jackson, 2012b; Kelly, 2012; Ryan, 2012; Sercu, 2004a, 2004b) and from the NZ MoE support materials, such as the Newton, Yates, Shearn, and Nowitzki (2010) report, that language teachers are expected to be familiar with ICC theory and iCLT. The expectations on language teachers now are different from when most current teachers completed their teacher education or were at school, when language teaching focussed on lexical and grammatical competence. This has clear and urgent implications for PD, requiring the aims of the LCIE immersion programmes for teachers to be clarified and processes put in place to enable participants to meet these new aims.

The Development of ICC and Cultural Immersion

Researchers such as Deardorff (2011), Driscoll, Rowe, and Thomae (2014), Mezirow (1997), Shaules (2015), Vatalaro, Szente, and Levin (2015), and Witte (2011) maintain that, for ICC to develop, assumptions underlying one's values and beliefs need to be challenged to bring about the shift in taken-for-granted frames of reference. Immersion in another culture such as through SA can provide the required dissonance and disorientation when encountering difference. It provides opportunities to question assumptions and evaluate the dynamic between self and other through exposure to new discourses and practices that can trigger the epistemological changes required for transformative intercultural learning to take place (Corder & U-Mackey, 2015; Driscoll et al., 2014; Marx & Moss, 2011).

However, literature on ICC consistently shows that development does not occur automatically, is individual and complex, and can be very emotional. The process involves changes in attitudes, values, and beliefs that underpin one's identity and worldview that have developed through socialisation and life experiences (Holmes & O'Neill, 2012; Kinginger, 2015; Sercu, 2004b). A variety of factors such as age, gender, ethnicity, social background, prior intercultural experiences, and language-learning aptitude (which might include memory efficiency, willingness to take risks, motivation, strategies, and self-efficacy) can affect transformative learning in SA. In the case of teachers, there is also the interplay between their individual and professional identities, worldviews, and experiences (Bastos & Araújo e Sá, 2014; Lázár, 2011; Peiser & Jones, 2014). This interplay affects their educational beliefs: their views on language teaching, the teaching of culture, and the role of ICC in language teaching. Peiser and Jones (2014) maintain that teachers need to understand 'self' to understand how their values and beliefs influence their roles as professionals.

In addition, actively engaging in the intercultural experiences, especially when pushed beyond one's comfort zone, involves emotional and psychological factors like motivation and the resilience to manage culture shock, embarrassment, and other emotional responses such as fear and anger (Corder & U-Mackey, 2015; Driscoll et al., 2014; Engberg, Jourian, & Davidson, 2015; Harrison & Brower, 2011; Shaules, 2015). Paige (1993) identifies ten situational and personal factors that can cause intense emotions and psychological stress when faced with cultural differences, and hence cause culture shock. These include the extent of the cultural differences, ethnocentrism, cultural immersion, cultural isolation, language, prior intercultural experience, expectations, status, loss of power and control, as well as challenges to sense of identity. Jackson (2009) found that even with high levels of language ability, participants can still have ethnocentric tendencies. Neuroscience research (Doidge, 2010; Shaules, 2015) explains culture shock as brain shock from cognitive overload, which prevents shifting between differing cultural perspectives and worldviews. Greater cognitive flexibility brings more capabilities to manage emotional responses to difference. According to Bennett (1993), cognitive flexibility is necessary for increased cultural sensitivity. In their study of SA students, Harrison and Brower (2011) found that most SA measures only captured student satisfaction, unlike measures used for international job placements that assess cultural intelligence (CQ), the ability to adapt across cultures not just at the sociocultural level but also at the psychological level. CQ involves three dimensions: cognitive, emotional/motivational, and physical factors, that is, 'head, heart and body' (Harrison & Brower, 2011, p. 42). CQ gives individuals the confidence and understanding of the context to capitalise on their personalities and tendency towards commitment, control, and challenge (psychological hardiness) and to adapt successfully to different cultures. Psychological hardiness relates to the ability to adopt active and problem-focussed coping strategies rather than withdrawing and emotion-focussed strategies. It influences whether individuals perceive experiences as learning opportunities or as threats, and whether they are motivated to engage actively. Harrison and Brower's (2011) study found a correlation between CQ, psychological hardiness (stress resiliency), and homesickness. Culture shock can trigger homesickness. These individual factors can influence the nature of the SA experience, including expectations and goal setting, the ability to adapt attitudes and behaviour to be more effective in the different cultural environment, feelings of well-being and mood levels, performance, perceptions of the experience, and ultimately gains in linguistic, cultural, and intercultural competencies. Harrison and Brower (2011) conclude that, while preparation for SA should include cognitive and physical dimensions, careful consideration should also be given to the emotional dimension involving CQ and psychological hardiness, especially as they are the strongest predictor of homesickness and psychological adjustment to a different culture and, ultimately, successful outcomes.

Research indicates that SA experiences are inconsistent across participants and that ICC development is haphazard and subject to chance (Driscoll et al., 2014; Harvey et al., 2011; Holmes, Bavieri, & Ganassin, 2015; Jackson, 2012a; Jackson & Oguro, 2017; Marx & Moss, 2011; Plews et al., 2010; Vande Berg et al., 2012). Studies have highlighted the need to clarify the aims of programmes as well as the commonly used approaches and tools used to measure gains. If ICC development is an aim, programmes need to be structured accordingly for transformative intercultural learning to take place. Analysed using Byram's (2008) ICC model, the teachers in Harvey et al. (2011) showed evidence of subcompetences and objectives such as attitude (willingness to engage with otherness), cultural knowledge, and skills of discovery and interaction. However, evidence of understanding ICC and the language and culture nexus was less convincing. While some appeared to understand the aims of ICC, such as preventing overemphasis on foreignness and stereotyping, their understanding was varied and largely descriptive. There was no explicit mention of ICC theory, pertinent research on iCLT, or of their own experiences in this regard. Like the students in Müller and Schmenk (2016, p. 145), the teachers lacked a 'framework of reference'. This may explain why, significantly, the teachers lacked the ability to reflect critically on their experiences as leverage for personal transformation. To maximise the LCIE, Harvey et al. (2011) recommended that programmes should have a more holistic structure, starting with pre-departure preparation that includes language classes, goal setting that draws on theory and research, and clear understanding of professional aims with hosts. Other useful considerations were reflective journals or blogs, ethnographic projects, establishment of a learning community of sojourners and/or colleagues and students in NZ, post-sojourn debriefings, and ongoing opportunities to reflect on and discuss experiences.

Other studies on students (Holmes et al., 2015; Jackson & Oguro, 2017; Root & Ngampornchai, 2012; Vande Berg et al., 2012; Wernicke, 2010), pre-service teachers (Cushner & Chang, 2015; Vatalaro et al., 2015), and in-service teachers (Driscoll et al., 2014; Plews et al., 2010, 2014) also indicate the importance of pre-immersion preparation that has included intercultural learning, reflection skills, and in-country mentoring for individual development. Studies on post-immersion experience (Kartoshkina, 2015; Root & Ngampornchai, 2012) indicate that this stage of the immersion experience is equally important but neglected. In their study investigating in-service primary teachers after their pre-service four-week immersion course, Driscoll et al. (2014) found that the teachers' experiences had been transformative largely thanks to the structured holistic support they had received. This support had been 'designed to raise the level of analysis and critical discourse and enhanced students' critical cultural awareness' (Driscoll et al., 2014, p. 317). In their study of pre-service teachers, Marx and Moss (2011) found that the SA programme design must be informed by intercultural development theory and provide supportive environments that foster critically reflective thinking about culture. East's (2013) study of a short-term immersion PD experience for in-service teachers indicates that gains in understanding the concept of ICC could be attributed to an input session dedicated to iCLT during the immersion. Similarly, Vogt's (2016, p. 567) study of 35 pre-service teachers who did a work placement as part of their SA indicates a need for intercultural learning to be 'guided'.

As can be seen, SA research shows that both experiences and the evaluation of gains are complex. Individual values and beliefs influence aims and expectations and ultimately the experience and perceptions of gains (Jackson, 2012a; Kinginger, 2015). If the development of ICC is the goal of SA, then this influence can be even more complex. Furthermore, as Wernicke (2010, p. 11) points out, students tend to focus on gaining knowledge, plain and simple, but, when teachers are SA participants, they engage in acquiring new knowledge also 'with the view of later transforming this into learning opportunities for their students'. Because of the complexity of ICC learning and the individual nature of influences, researchers maintain that there is a need for more in-depth study of individual learning experiences to provide deeper understandings of the processes involved (Holmes & O'Neill, 2012; Marx & Moss, 2011; Wernicke, 2010). This chapter contributes to understanding ICC development by looking at the different immersion experiences of three in-service teachers from the NZ school sector.

Methodology

The question pursued in this chapter is whether it is possible to determine the characteristics and strategies of teachers most likely to increase their ICC during their LCIEs. This was part of the MoE brief for the evaluative study by Harvey et al. (2011, p. 9) and relates to one of their research questions: 'What is the effect of the immersion programmes on the development of teachers' intercultural awareness and competence?' As discussed in the literature review, ICC learning is individualised, complex, has several contributing factors and requires more in-depth study. The data in this chapter draw on the individual experiences of three teachers who took part in the Harvey et al. (2011) study. We use an exploratory interpretative approach to gain an understanding of the varied nature of their intercultural experiences and learning. As Duff (2008) maintains, such approaches provide rich descriptions of the processes involved that quantitative methods alone do not capture. Interaction and engagement with different social and cultural practices can be analysed and interpreted for triggers that cause participants to try to make sense of what is happening, along with subsequent shifts in perspectives and behaviours from learning processes.

The 3 teachers in this chapter were among 55 in-service teachers who completed a qualitative and quantitative questionnaire administered at the end of 2008 to 114 participants. Of the 55 teachers who responded to the questionnaire, 45 were female; 48 teachers had taken part in short-term sojourns (three weeks to three months) and 7 had participated in long-term sojourns (up to one year). French was the main teaching language ($n = 18$), followed by German ($n = 11$), and Japanese ($n = 10$), with a few teaching Chinese, Samoan, and Spanish. Thirty-two of the teachers taught secondary school students aged 13–17 and were specialist language teachers. The remaining teachers were generalist teachers, with 15 teaching students aged 10–12, and 1 teaching younger students. In terms of language proficiency, approximately 30 per cent considered themselves at the expert level or advanced level, 9 per cent at the beginner level, and the remainder at intermediate or elementary level before the LCIE.

Two of the participants in this chapter, Amie and Kate, are generalist (primary) teachers and new to language teaching (one–three years in service). Both were on short-term sojourns: Amie's was three weeks in China, and Kate's was one month in Germany. Amie had not reported any prior overseas experience. Kate had visited Korea and Australia for ten days and two weeks, respectively. The third teacher, Paula, is an experienced specialist secondary schoolteacher, and her sojourn was one year in France. She had previously lived in France for one year and England for two years. All three teachers are European New Zealanders. Amie and Kate took part in a qualitative study of 10 short-term LCIE teachers, which was conducted from the end of 2008 to early 2009. Paula was one of four case studies of long-term (10 months to one year) LCIE teachers in the second half of 2008. According to Stake (1995, p. 4), when selecting case studies 'the first criterion should be to maximise what we can learn'. The 3 teachers selected for this study were chosen because their LCIEs were different durations and each teacher had very different perceptions of gains from their experience. While all three SA programmes had the potential for being effective learning experiences, they were also examples of how opportunities to maximise the experiences could have been greater. The teachers' reflections on the experiences provided insight into various characteristics and strategies that could be analysed for effectiveness in facilitating the development of intercultural competence.

The study of short-term participants (e.g., Amie and Kate) included pre- and post-sojourn interviews, and pre- and post-sojourn classroom observations. They were interviewed and observed in NZ one month before their sojourn and one month after their return; no data were collected during their sojourn. The study of long-term participants (e.g., Paula) involved only post-sojourn data collection. At the time of the study, some of these participants had been back in the classroom for over a year and were interviewed three times, thus making it possible to explore the impact of the immersion in depth. Paula was first interviewed seven months after her return and the final interview was 11 months after her return. The interview questions were semi-structured and designed to probe understandings, attitudes, and beliefs in relation to language teaching, iCLT, learning from the immersion experience, and the impact on teaching. The observation guides were developed from a range of literature (e.g., Crozet & Liddicoat, 1997; Erlam, 2005) and milestone reports from the contracted agencies.

The Harvey et al. (2011) study used Byram's (2008) model of intercultural competence to analyse the data because it had been developed specifically for foreign language teaching (Byram, 1997, 2008) and identifies the essential components of an intercultural model (Spitzberg & Changnon, 2009). We use it also in the current in-depth study to explore and interpret Amie, Kate, and Paula's experiences because it is an effective model to 'determine the presence or absence of subcompetences, and then to predict the success or failure of individuals in intercultural interaction' (Byram, 2009, p. 326). Byram's model consists of five subcompetences or 'savoirs' (2008, p. 230): knowledge (*savoir*), skills of interpreting and relating (*savoir comprendre*), skills of discovery and interaction (*savoir apprendre/faire*), attitudes (*savoir être*), and critical cultural awareness (*savoir s'engager*). We also include Houghton's (2010, 2013) additional subcompetence, knowing how to become (*savoir se transformer*). Houghton maintains this savoir emphasises Byram's critical cultural awareness as it focusses on the importance of being able to evaluate 'SELF' and 'OTHER' (Houghton, 2010, p. 225) and to consciously recognise shifts in, or deciding on, adjustment to one's worldview (values and beliefs) as a result of reflecting on challenges from exposure to different worldviews (Houghton, 2010, 2013). However, as Byram (2009, p. 325) has noted, his model is not exhaustive because 'it is a simplification of the complexity of acting as an intercultural person', does not include personality and psychological factors, and does not account for links between the subcompetences. Because predictions could be limited, Byram has suggested his model be complemented by others. Therefore, we also used a number of other constructs and models discussed in the literature review, such as transformative learning, culture shock, recent findings in cognitive neuroscience, and CQ. Jackson (2012b) maintains that this triangulation of interdisciplinary perspectives enriches research and has the potential to lead to deeper understandings of the processes needed to improve participants' experiences and programmes generally. The participants in the Harvey et al. (2011) study were predominantly female, which may have reflected the fact that there are more female language teachers than male teachers in NZ. In addition, because the teaching community is very small and close-knit, all the participants in the study were referred to as females to ensure anonymity. It is acknowledged that gender in SA research (see Galindo in the current book) is a factor; however, it is not a focus of this chapter because of the small number of male participants.

In-depth Studies

Amie

Amie went to China in January (during the summer break in NZ) for a three-week study LCIE programme organised through ILEP with seven other teachers, two of whom were from her school, and the language advisors. She had started language teaching only that school year and rated her language ability as being only 'just ahead of the students'. As a generalist, she felt qualified to teach English, maths, and science, but not Mandarin as a foreign language. She found teaching Mandarin difficult and sometimes got bored with it—'it's so hard to teach what you don't know'—and felt that she had not taught very well so far.

Before

Prior to the sojourn, Amie had had only one PD day with the language advisor and had been so busy that she had not had much time to think about the trip or read the information pack. She was concerned about the practicalities of the upcoming sojourn and the course she would be attending and thought she would be staying in a hostel. She had not set any specific goals, but expected she would find out why the Chinese she had met interacted with her in the way they had, why they bowed and showed her respect. She thought the sojourn would give her the need to learn and she would find out about taboos, such as those around the emperor. She saw herself being more motivated with greater knowledge after the sojourn and able to measure improvements in her teaching from changes in students' attitudes. Her students did not have to learn Mandarin and she could not tell them why they should when they asked her, saying 'some enjoy it but some don't'. She had not thought about how language affects culture, but expected she would see how it was used by a variety of people in everyday life, compared to the more formal language she had been learning. She had never heard of ICC, but guessed it might be the ability to speak two languages and recognise similarities.

After

The course she attended had been full immersion and very good in her opinion. It focussed on language with very little culture (limited to for example paper cutting and music) or history; anything 'bad' in history, like the Tiananmen Square incident, was avoided. Although she was with a group of English speakers in university accommodation, she felt her language ability had improved and was more confident using Mandarin in the classroom. However, she still found it hard to explain to students why they were learning Mandarin but tried to make the class fun and enjoyable. She did not have enough knowledge to teach much Chinese culture, or the time and sufficient language to encourage the students to question, compare, and contrast with their own worldviews and cultural backgrounds.

When asked about her new knowledge of Chinese culture, Amie mentioned that she had learned about taboos and that there seemed to be a different attitude towards women, but she could not remember everything. She noticed differences especially in diet and food, saying 'nothing back in New Zealand could have prepared me for that'. In her advice on strategies for future participants, she stressed how important it was to be able to order food in Chinese; gestures were not sufficient especially for dietary needs. Initially she liked the differences, but then felt resistance and found being away from home for three weeks stressful. Not being able to communicate was challenging for Amie. Classes were four hours a day, Monday to Friday, with a lot of homework, so any travel was limited to weekends. She felt the homework was an imposition—she did not enforce it with her own students—and was frustrated that she did not have the freedom to explore and experience China more. The newness she had experienced became familiar because of imposed daily routines. She also found the city and the area around the terracotta warriors in Xian dirty. In response to prompts about more ICC understanding, Amie said she had not noticed body language because she did not have the language to notice and match up. However, she did notice there were different levels of language for different strata of society in the Forbidden City.

Amie kept up the momentum from the LCIE once back in NZ by attending some language classes but she found no opportunities to network, being the only one in her grade-year teaching Mandarin. She found it hard to keep motivated to improve her language ability when there were so many other demands in the curriculum. She was teaching Mandarin because she had been on the LCIE, and was not sure whether she really wanted to continue doing so.

Kate

Kate had over 30 years teaching experience, with management responsibilities including being in charge of languages in the school. She had learned French at school and studied and taught an Asian language for two years, but this had ceased as there was not much support for the language. She took up German instead, which she had been teaching for two years. Her immersion was in Germany for one month through the AFS.

Before

Kate considered her LCIE was going to be very important for her PD. She judged her language skills to be beginner level and her first two goals were improving her listening skills and developing speaking ability. Learning about German culture was her third goal. She had also set herself personal goals to explore her prejudices and manage her responses to them, as well as coping with the experience of being away from family. She said she had very little knowledge of Germany and the Germans apart from some stereotypical views, such as aspects of the two world wars and how Germans are said to conform to rules. Because her father had been a prisoner of war, she wanted to know what had led to World War II. Her understanding of the relationship between language and culture was that they are inseparable, and she was surprised by the similarity between German and English, and considered Germans to be different types of English people with different backgrounds. She understood ICC to occur at different levels, the first being able to carry out basic functions like shopping and buying tickets and the next level involving deeper thinking and emotions and functioning at a more profound level. She believed that thinking had to be deeper for real understanding to take place, but doubted she would have enough time in a single month to reach this level of thinking. She believed that improved language skills after the immersion would enable her to teach beyond a superficial level. She expected she would be able to use German more and be more effective developing her students' ICC. She realised she would be making changes when she returned and that it was necessary to have someone with whom she could bounce around ideas.

After

Kate had not travelled very much before and found her initial experiences difficult. She went earlier than needed and found she lacked information on travel and who would meet her on arrival. She arrived thoroughly exhausted and was sick in the first week. Because of her lack of travel experience, she was challenged by needing to find her own way around, being without her cell phone, adjusting to the time zone, dealing with some financial constraints, and coping with unexpected aspects of teaching in a German secondary school. Nevertheless, she considered her experience life-changing and wished it had been six weeks instead of just a month.

Kate said her attitude to her language ability had changed rather than her proficiency. Her German vocabulary had increased greatly. She could understand more if it was not spoken too fast and she was prepared to 'have a go more now', even though she made mistakes. She had deliberately gone out in order to talk to people who spoke no English, such as bus drivers and people waiting at bus stops. She also prepared the evening before the vocabulary she thought she would need for the events planned the next day.

Kate had many experiences and described how on her first day at school in Germany she found herself explaining to a secondary school English class why NZ had sent soldiers to Gallipoli, and how on her second day she had to speak about attitudes towards the war as expressed in an Australian's World War I war poems. She thought these experiences were bizarre because her personal goals were to dispel her stereotypes of Germany's role in World War II. When asked whether she had achieved her goals, she said it had removed her 'block' of stereotyping German culture, history, and World War II. Although she found German society to be conforming and more monocultural than NZ, she also thought Germans were very caring and had a very positive experience. She noticed how strangers would point out transgressions, like parking in the wrong direction, and that her host had explained that it would be rude to ignore them. She noticed that teachers 'don't seem to "do" discipline', and rather 'growl' at students.

After overcoming her initial exhaustion Kate was determined to make the most of being able to absorb the culture. She had learned many new aspects of the culture and gained deeper knowledge of things she had known about only fleetingly. She experienced how it felt to be a minority and uncertain about expectations in behaviour and cultural practices. She enjoyed going to movies and talking about them afterwards, especially with her host family who knew some English. These discussions deepened her understanding of German attitudes towards films and helped her to make sense of what she watched, and she felt lucky because her family enjoyed discussions and questioned everything that was traditional. She said that her whole attitude had changed, and she would share this with her students, and talk her parents through some issues. She did not have language classes but maintained that, if she did, this would have taken away cultural opportunities.

Kate said her understanding of the language and culture nexus had deepened and spoke about noticing how direct the language was and that her hostess would get irritated if she was indecisive or when people were vague while making arrangements. She had gained much more understanding of the language-learning process, appreciated how much time and effort are needed, and how to support her students. She would provide opportunities for her students to develop ICC by teaching 'more with a German attitude', and try to adopt a German approach and talk about students' responsibilities, as well as show differences in cultural practices, even something as commonplace as eating boiled eggs at breakfast. With her increased confidence, she could go deeper than superficial statements about culture and provide more authentic learning opportunities for her students, as facilitated by technology and other resources. She found her students were more engaged and communicating more in German in class. She also noticed that the NZ students were more sensitive to the needs of the Asian students, and those with any German heritage were proud of it.

Kate had come back to NZ more motivated and felt an obligation to develop language teaching in the school, understanding more the importance of bilingualism and multilingualism. Unfortunately, she had difficulty maintaining her language as there were no other German teachers locally and it was difficult to travel to evening classes. She thought a link to a German teacher would be good and was therefore communicating with the language advisor. Her strategies for future participants included the need to be brave and not to mull over things when they go wrong—such as wearing outside shoes inside—and to acknowledge 'I've been insensitive and move on'. She also recommended going out on one's own, persevering with the language, and understanding the cultural value of conformity.

Paula

Paula's LCIE was one year in France through the AFS, where she lived in an apartment. She had been back in NZ for six months when first interviewed. As mentioned, she had spent a year in France a number of years previously, felt comfortable with both the language and the culture, and did not experience dissonance. Her biggest challenge was having no mentor before she departed with whom she could check her goals, which were to improve her speaking ability, cultural knowledge, and French grammar. She believed she gained a great deal from the immersion in terms of linguistic skills, cultural knowledge, and effectiveness as a teacher, even though she had overestimated just how much she could do as she spent a lot of time teaching in a school and studying at the university, which reduced her free time. In her interviews, she focussed on the importance of improving her grammatical understanding with students' proficiency in mind and said factors that helped her increase her cultural knowledge included attending festivals, experiencing family life, collecting realia, and buying resources such as DVDs. She thoroughly enjoyed the LCIE and believed an important factor was making friends with locals—which increased opportunities for interaction because she did not have a homestay—and that it was opportune she had a school that was used to foreign visitors. She believed that people and relationships were the key to the success of the whole programme: 'To improve proficiency, you have to mix with French speakers, and that is one of the reasons why I loved working practically full time at the school.' She maintained she was teaching more enthusiastically with good, varied resources.

In her first interview, Paula was unsure of the meaning of ICC as she had been on the immersion when the new curriculum had been introduced. She thought it might be cultural mores that guided behaviour and language use, such as greetings. When asked how her ICC might have improved on the immersion, she mentioned how she now understood register and cultural practices, such as different seasonal foods and gift giving. However, she was concerned that she did not understand ICC and asked for readings so she could learn about it. By her second interview, she had received information about ICC from the language advisor and quoted Crozet and Liddicoat (1997) and Kramsch (1998). She liked the concept that intercultural competence involves the whole person, self-reflection, and making meaning, and not just learning skills. She was teaching culture, but her teaching was assessment-driven and that restricted the time in class to spend on cultural aspects. However, by the third interview she was talking more about integrating culture into her teaching, explaining how practices differ across the regions of France, and asking students about regional differences in NZ. She understood the concept of different worldviews, showed how expressions for the same concept differ between English and French, encouraged students to compare, and tried to choose topics to engage them. She noticed that the students were more enthusiastic, which she attributed to her own enthusiasm. She maintained that they showed more curiosity, sought information and comparisons, and asked her questions about her experiences.

Post-immersion, Paula was much more confident in her teaching, more empathetic with learners, and an active member of language teacher networks and organisations despite the pressures of work that made it difficult to keep up the momentum of learning. She had not yet had any debriefings and felt strongly about the need to talk about her ongoing goals. She was experiencing reverse culture shock and readjusting to routines was the most challenging aspect of the post-immersion for her.

As for strategies for future participants, Paula stressed the importance of being very clear about what one wants to get out of the SA experience, which for her was improving language and getting good resources. She emphasised the need for a mentor to work on goals to maximise the experience and stressed the importance of making the most of every opportunity and accepting all invitations, whether they be for dinner or for outings. She also recited a long list of strategies that related to practical matters such as accommodation, documentation, health, insurance, and language courses.

Analysis of the Three Case Studies

Each teacher perceived gains in language and cultural knowledge and each demonstrated the characteristics of ICC by adapting and learning to get along with people in the immersion culture. SA research has suggested that quickly adapting one's behaviour is usual, but that it often remains at the level of socialising, or what Harrison and Brower (2011) describe as the sociocultural level without achieving the psychological level, and so is not necessarily accompanied by transformative intercultural learning (Vande Berg et al., 2012). Transformative learning results from identifying responses to triggers that lead to shifts in worldviews and being able to process these responses as a result of psychological adjustment. While each teacher had different experiences on LCIE and the potential to develop

ICC, each also responded differently to her experiences, and the data suggest that there were differences in their respective ICC development and degree of transformative intercultural learning. A number of personal and unique factors may have caused these differences, characteristics, and strategies, including motivation, identities as language teachers, their personal theories and beliefs about language teaching, their attitudes to the immersion language and culture, their understanding and level of ICC before the immersion, and their language ability.

Despite recognising the potential PD benefits of the trip, Amie seemed the least motivated of the three and unprepared in terms of goals and expectations. She seemed to rely on extrinsic factors to motivate her to learn, such as the briefing at the airport and being in China. She did not have a strong identity as a language teacher before or after the immersion and was not convinced of the value of teaching Mandarin, as it was only an elective topic of interest for her students and not part of the curriculum or assessed as strictly as mandatory curriculum topics. Nevertheless, she had a positive attitude initially, curious to explore China and engage with a different culture. She demonstrated the subcompetence of skills of discovery and noticed differences in cultural practices and the use of language despite feeling that her low level of language had inhibited gains.

However, Amie became increasingly negative as she found the environment emotionally and physically challenging. Lack of agency to control her own schedule and to nurture her curiosity led to frustration and loss of motivation, and her professional beliefs were challenged by the excessive homework. She demonstrated the characteristics of culture shock and was homesick, which can be a strong indicator of being unable to adapt to a different culture (Harrison & Brower, 2011). Paige (1993) has found that the more negative the reaction to a situation is, the more stressful that situation becomes. Amie's various experiences seem to have caused what Doidge (2010) and Shaules (2015) term cognitive overload, which prevented her from managing her emotional responses to different cultural perspectives; for sure, she lacked the cognitive flexibility to process the amount of new information to which she was being exposed. She also seemed to lack the theoretical knowledge (e.g., CQ, culture shock) to understand what was happening to her as well as the resilience to manage the challenges to her 'head, heart and body' (Harrison & Brower, 2011, p. 42). As she said, her experiences were counter to her expectations and nothing could have prepared her for her emotional responses.

According to Shaules (2015), experiences like Amie's have the potential for deep intercultural learning, but that learning relies on understanding the process and recognising the unconscious expectations that shape one's thinking and behaviour. The better one understands the intuitive hidden processes influenced by one's pre-existing cultural framework, and how these interact with the attentive or conscious mind, the better one can manage the experience and identify the shifts in one's perspectives. Shaules' emphasis on the importance of introspection and self-awareness echoes SA studies such as those by Harvey et al. (2011), Holmes et al. (2015), Jackson (2012a), Marx and Moss (2011), and Vatalaro et al. (2015). These scholars maintain that intellectual knowledge alone is not sufficient to prepare for cultural difference, for adapting, or for transformative learning, and that introspection or the ability to reflect critically is fundamental. This requires much more than simply noticing difference and responding to it. It involves having an interpretative framework to make sense of one's experiences at both the objective level (different food, dirty streets) and the subjective level (values, beliefs, communication styles). Research indicates that one negative experience can dominate one's perspective on a culture, prevent language acquisition and culture learning, or reinforce negative generalisations (Sercu, 2004b). Amie's experience may have contributed to her sense of despondency around her ability as a language teacher and her uncertainty about continuing to teach Mandarin. Pre-immersion preparation that included the psychological/affective dimensions and a mentor during and after the experience might have leveraged transformative learning for Amie by helping her to understand her emotional responses to experiences in China, to perceive them to be valuable learning opportunities, and to identify intercultural gains. Because of her apparent despondency in her language-teaching ability, it is unfortunate that she did not appear to realise that in the post-immersion observation, she was integrating culture much more through practical use of language–cultural activities, and the students were very engaged—both positive outcomes of her sojourn.

Kate and Paula were both intrinsically motivated, positive, and determined to engage as much as they could, demonstrating the subcompetences of attitude/intercultural wonderment and skills of discovery and interaction. They both also had clear goals. Their knowledge of the respective cultures was different, as were their levels of language proficiency and experience as language teachers, but they appeared to have well-developed identities as language teachers. Both experienced challenges with the organisation of their LCIE initially: Kate expected and experienced challenges to her worldview and ability to communicate during immersion; Paula did not expect her experience of reverse culture shock upon her return home. Both had beneficial experiences, but Kate's experience appeared to encompass both professional and personal goals that included the affective dimension and intercultural understanding, while Paula's focussed very much on professional goals around language acquisition and resource accumulation.

Kate's experience seems to have resulted in more ICC development in that she processed her experience of being an 'outsider', indicating characteristics of CQ as defined by Harrison and Brower (2011, p. 41): 'People with high cultural intelligence make sense of new and different situations related to cultural differences and they are motivated to act on the new understanding of cues that they see and experience.' Despite having language difficulties, adjusting to different cultural practices, overcoming initial exhaustion and sickness, and experiencing challenges to her worldview, Kate demonstrated psychological hardiness in her motivation to adopt what Harrison and Brower (2011, p. 44) describe as 'active and problem-focussed strategies'. Although she might not have been familiar with ICC theory, Kate's answers in interviews were rich in intercultural concepts and competences such as assumptions, noticing, questioning, the importance of dialogue to gain deeper understanding, changes in attitude, and that ICC was about deep learning from thinking at a more profound level and experiencing emotions. She showed evidence of critical cultural awareness in that she recognised she had stereotypes of Germans and wanted to dispel her prejudiced views. She was aware that it would be challenging to manage her responses to being in Germany and away from her family. Her transformative learning after she returned was evident in the shift in her perspective towards Germans, having discovered more about their history and interacted with them on a personal level. The different patterns of behaviour that she had noticed, such as the appropriateness of strangers pointing out transgressions, puzzled her, possibly because it challenged her assumptions about German society. She explained it to herself as Germans being caring. According to Triandis (1995), they would be displaying collectivist values in a society that has largely individualistic values. Knowledge of theoretical frameworks and a mentor's guidance in reflection would have enabled Kate to interpret both the behaviour and her response to it, form abstract conceptualisations, and ultimately understand the implications for interaction.

Kate's comment about the directness of the German language serves as evidence of awareness of the language and culture nexus, although she did not articulate the connection or know theoretical concepts such as low context language. Like Amie, she believed she would have 'noticed' more had her language ability been higher, which would seem to indicate some awareness of the language and culture nexus, but she was not able to explore this to a deeper level. With theoretical knowledge, she might have known that Kramsch (1998) and Sercu (2004a, 2004b) maintain that language is the most sensitive indicator of the relationship between an individual and a given social group. She might have been able to explore how registers, speech acts, politeness strategies, and non-verbal communication are indicators of cultural differences, and how she could develop strategies to deal with the cultural and social expectations of behaviour in her intercultural interactions.

In sharp contrast to Amie's uncertainty about the value of teaching Mandarin, Kate returned more motivated to continue teaching German and recognised the value of language learning as being much more than mere linguistic competence. Her increased understanding of German history, society, and culture, along with her own personal changes in attitude and initiation into an insider perspective, strengthened her belief in the value of being a language teacher. She integrated both general and specific culture into her language teaching in ways that Sercu (2004a) believes would enhance the performativity of students in intercultural interactions. It is significant that she talked about attitude changes. She identified her changed attitude towards communicating as being more important than increased language proficiency and was therefore more willing to interact even if she made mistakes. She also realised that it had been her 'attitude of finding out' and being willing to put herself at 'risk' or experience 'humiliation' that enabled her to benefit as much as she had from her LCIE experience. Her ability to perceive the challenges from dissonance as learning opportunities rather than threats would be described by Harrison and Brower (2011) as a characteristic of CQ. Despite not yet having any PD in iCLT after her immersion, her approach to teaching had changed; it appeared to be influencing her students' ICC development, and she could see shifts in perspectives. This was evidence of meeting the aims of the LCIE programme in terms of student intercultural gains and was remarkable considering the level of the students, that is, in classes of 30 minutes twice a week early in term one of language learning.

Paula's accounts and goals revealed strong beliefs that her role as a language teacher was to develop students' language acquisition. Unlike Amie and Kate, she did not appear to have experienced challenges from dissonance considered necessary to trigger intercultural development and transformative learning. She loved the whole experience, was comfortable in French culture as it was familiar to her, and she had the intercultural competence and language ability to adapt to the environment, get along with the French, and meet sociocultural expectations. Her identity and worldviews were not challenged and she did not mention experiencing any psychological factors of culture shock until her difficulty to adapt on return to NZ. However, she identified two factors that studies like those by Driscoll et al. (2014), Lou, Vande Berg, and Paige (2012), and Marx and Moss (2011) have identified as important for ICC development: (1) having friends and opportunities to interact with the local community; and (2) needing a mentor to check goals. Lou et al. (2012) have stressed that while other strategies like homestay and theoretical knowledge are important, their effectiveness is dependent on the provision of skilled mentors to help participants process and make sense of their experiences before, during, and after immersion, and that provision of skilled mentors must take priority.

Paula's discussion focussed on gains in language acquisition and the collection of resources, and her increased understanding of cultural knowledge remained descriptive about 'objective culture' (Sercu, 2004a, 2004b) probably because she lacked knowledge of ICC and iCLT. Having contacted the language advisor for more information following the first research interview, during the second and third interviews she had more knowledge of intercultural concepts, could quote from the literature about the language and culture nexus, and liked the shift in focus from just linguistic skills to include the whole person and the need for self-reflection. The interviews therefore became interventions and provided potential opportunities for Paula to continue to develop her learning abroad. However, even with the ICC knowledge and understanding, and despite recognising the intercultural importance of register, friendships, and relationships, Paula's discussion remained at a superficial level and there was little evidence that she had 'transcended her own way of thinking' (Driscoll et al., 2014, p. 312). In terms of student gains, Paula was integrating more culture into her classes and getting students to compare French and NZ cultural practices. Yet, while her students were more enthusiastic language learners and interested in French culture, unlike Kate's students, there did not seem to be the same shift in worldviews.

Discussion

Complexity of ICC Development

Predicting ICC development just by identifying ICC characteristics and strategies is far too simplistic to yield meaningful results and insight. This in-depth exploration confirms research by Holmes and O'Neill (2012), Jackson (2012a), and Kinginger (2015) that ICC learning is individual, complex, and involves several interplaying factors unique to the individual. Amie, Kate, and Paula each responded differently to their experiences and thus the opportunities for ICC development. The accounts of their experiences and choice of goals, or lack of goals, revealed a complex interplay between personal and professional identities, personality (CQ), life experiences, teaching ideology, individual language ability, and the extent to which they were interculturally competent or had an understanding of critical cultural awareness before their experience. Amie did not have clear goals, was not confident, and was not convinced of the value of language teaching as part of her professional identity; she identified some linguistic and cultural knowledge gains. Kate set both personal and professional goals, was more aware of 'self' and 'other' before the immersion, and was able to identify intercultural gains even though she did not have the theoretical framework to reflect critically on them at depth. Paula was clear about her identity and role as a language teacher and her goals were all professional; the gains she identified mainly reflected the value she placed on linguistic competence, gaining specific culture knowledge, and accumulating authentic resources. Significantly for the individual teacher and her domestic students, Kate's ICC development was more evident than Amie's or Paula's, and her students have, in turn, had the most ICC gains. Amie equated ICC with body language and Paula referred to cultural mores, both limited visions of the scope of ICC; even Kate's understanding of ICC was primarily concerned with a view of language fulfilling hierarchised functional–notional needs before ultimately serving self-reflective intercultural enquiry. The variance in the ICC development of the three teachers and the characteristics and strategies demonstrated especially by Kate support the argument for intentional development in ICC literature (Deardorff, 2011; Harvey et al., 2011; Holmes et al., 2015; Marx & Moss, 2011; Vande Berg et al., 2012). It is important not just to know about ICC theory or research but also to develop and possess critical cultural self-awareness. Peiser and Jones (2014) maintain that teachers need to understand the complexity of 'self' and how personal and cultural values and beliefs influence the professional self and professional role. This is especially important for teachers on LCIE programmes, who are expected not only to develop their own personal ICC but also to transfer this to their professional practice and facilitate their students' intercultural development.

The Dissonance Factor

Deardorff (2011), Marx and Moss (2011), and Witte (2011) have stated that for ICC to develop it is necessary to have one's values and beliefs challenged by cultural dissonance. Dissonance helps increase awareness of assumptions and expectations. Driscoll et al. (2014) liken this to an epistemological change, which in essence is transformative intercultural learning and not just change in behaviour. Marx and Moss (2011, p. 43) advocate that SA 'should not try to alleviate students' experience of culture shock; rather, they need to leverage the intercultural challenges inherent in these experiences and provide support for students as they struggle to make sense of what they are experiencing'. The existence or non-existence and nature of dissonance seemed to have been an important factor in the ICC development for Amie, Kate, and Paula.

Amie and Kate experienced much more dissonance during their LCIE than Paula, but their responses and learning were different. Both Amie and Kate had been willing to engage in the experience, but Amie demonstrated what Harrison and Brower (2011, p. 45) would describe as 'accommodation', while Kate showed 'adjustment'. Amie's experience was demotivating, reinforced her belief in the lack of value of teaching Mandarin, and inhibited her from evaluating how effectively she integrated culture into her teaching. Kate perceived challenges to be learning opportunities, revealed transformative learning, and returned motivated, more confident in her ability to teach German, and valuing her changed attitude to intercultural communication and understanding. She eagerly shared her learning with her students, and her classroom practice reflected her changed worldview, greater cultural knowledge, and increased understanding of being a language learner.

Paula's prior experiences of and familiarity with French culture and her language proficiency appear to have helped her not to feel being 'other'. This could have hindered her ability to notice cultural difference and to question her assumptions as she 'loved it all'. While she shared her immersion experiences with her students, this did not appear to effect shifts in their attitudes.

Mentoring

Increasingly studies have identified the need for reflection to facilitate transformative learning (Harvey et al., 2011; Holmes et al., 2015; Holmes & O'Neill, 2012; Jackson & Oguro, 2017; Lázár, 2011; Peiser & Jones, 2014; Vogt, 2016). Similarly, the three teachers' experiences highlight the need for effective and skilled mentoring throughout the LCIE programme and confirm findings of previous studies by Harvey et al. (2011), Marx and Moss (2011), and Plews et al. (2010, 2014). Lou et al. (2012) have pointed to studies that show expert individualised cultural mentoring at all three stages of the LCIE and how this should take priority over other factors such as homestays and enrolment in host university courses, for deep learning and ICC development to occur.

None of the three teachers possessed the intercultural theoretical framework or critical reflection skills required fully to understand or articulate the cognitive, affective, and behavioural processes they experienced. Amie and Kate experienced personal and professional challenges and the affective dimension of their sojourns was evident in their interviews. Amie's account of her difficulties and negative responses was emotional but remained descriptive. Kate noticed shifts in attitude and tried to identify their causes, but did not explore them further. Without challenges to her values and beliefs, Paula had no triggers to make her consciously engage with experiences and reposition self (Hutchison & Rea, 2011). According to Shaules (2015), this is probably the hardest scenario in which to develop ICC. A mentor would have helped Amie to reflect on her 'head, heart and body' (Harrison & Brower, 2011) challenges. Kate would have benefitted from a mentor's help in reflecting on her shifts in attitude. Paula needed a mentor to help her make the familiar strange, question her assumptions, go below surface culture, identify triggers, and explore the language and culture nexus. She would also have been able to explore the potentially rich learning from the reverse culture shock she experienced on her return to NZ. Individual mentors would have facilitated each teacher to maximise the transformative intercultural learning opportunities from their immersion experiences.

Conclusion and Recommendations

This chapter has explored the immersion experiences of three NZ language teachers to identify characteristics and strategies that could be predictors of ICC development. Byram's (2008, 2009) model of ICC was used as a framework to interpret their experiences, supplemented by other constructs to explore the psychological dimension. Among the participants, Amie and Kate were both generalist teachers, while Paula was a specialist language teacher. They all demonstrated ICC characteristics such as willingness to engage with 'otherness' (attitudes), culture-specific knowledge, skills of discovery, and to some extent skills of interpreting. However, there was much less evidence of theoretical knowledge and critical cultural awareness of 'self' and 'other'. The teachers were therefore limited in their ability to critically interpret and evaluate the processes they experienced or shifts in perspective. These findings reflect those in the larger Harvey et al. (2011) study, but this in-depth exploration of the three teachers' experiences has highlighted a number of other interrelated factors that add to the understanding of the process of intercultural development. The experiences reveal the complexity of attaining ICC development because of the uniqueness of individuals in terms of their personal beliefs and their professional circumstances as well as their level of ICC and CQ before the immersion, especially concerning awareness of the personal and professional 'self', motivation, and resilience. These factors appear to have determined the individual's extent and nature of engagement in the learning process, no matter the situations in which they found themselves or whether they had the competences for the epistemological changes needed for transformative learning to take place.

The existence or non-existence, timing, and nature of the dissonance considered to be necessary to trigger intercultural development and transformative learning seemed to have been an important factor. There was a correlation between the extent of dissonance perceived/experienced by the three participants, whether challenges were perceived as learning opportunities rather than threats, and how the participants managed their emotional responses to them.

The concomitant need to provide skilled mentors at all stages of the LCIE to help teachers maximise the transformative intercultural learning opportunities was also clearly revealed, reinforcing the findings of the Harvey et al. (2011) report and other studies (Giovanangeli, Oguro, & Harbon, 2017; Lou et al., 2012). The experiences of all three participants had the potential for intercultural development and transformative learning, and in each case there were lost opportunities to maximise the experiences. During their LCIEs, skilled mentoring could have been provided online (Jackson, 2017) or, as suggested by Plews et al. (2014), by local mentors who could also have introduced participants to local social and professional networks and therefore increased opportunities for engagement. Post-LCIEs experiences can be challenging, as one participant found, but tend to receive less attention from programme organisers and are also under-researched (Kartoshkina, 2015; Root & Ngampornchai, 2012). Mentors could have provided the opportunities for debriefing, interpretation, and evaluation of learning that our research provided. They could also have provided links to local professional networks to maintain the momentum of learning and development, which could lead to sharing of new knowledge and collaboration on different classroom intercultural language-learning and language-teaching activities.

The length of time was not a factor as the one-year LCIE did not lead to greater ICC development than the one-month experience, and in fact there was more development in the latter. However, prior experience of, and familiarity with, a country, while proving effective for language and specific culture knowledge gains, can prove more challenging for transformational learning to take place, especially without a mentor. In addition, the amount of free time available to immerse in the local community, interact, and explore, rather than be overly constrained by course or teaching commitments, seemed an important factor.

There was no guarantee how each participant's ICC would develop on the LCIE. However, a number of controllable interventions would have increased the potential for transformative learning to take place. Such interventions together with individual mentoring at each stage of the LCIE programme ensure that participants have the intercultural knowledge and skills necessary to develop an awareness of the influence of personal and professional identities, worldviews (embodying values, beliefs, and behaviour), and CQ. These would have facilitated critical reflection on different experiences, the learning opportunities they represent, and the ways in which the teachers could translate them into classroom practice.

Personal and professional identities emerged in the findings as important factors in ICC development. Identity was not a research topic in the original study (Harvey et al., 2011) and researcher interpretations of the teachers' identities in this chapter were based on data from the interviews.

Because of the complexity of ICC development, identity would need to be a key concern in further research evaluating LCIE programmes. Also, the findings of this in-depth study are based on the personal accounts of LCIEs of three individuals and are therefore not generalisable. However, the aim of the current study was to respond to the need identified in the literature for more in-depth exploration of individual learning experiences to increase understandings of the complex processes involved in ICC development and to further inform the design of LCIE programmes in order to maximise ICC gains. The current study has identified interrelated, pivotal factors for LCIE programmes to meet intercultural aims and these form the basis of the following recommendations.

We recommend that the aims and desired outcomes of the programme should be clear, especially if they include ICC and iCLT. The aims and outcomes should be reflected in the goals set by participants, which would then provide a working framework for mentors and participants pre-, during, and post-immersion. Also, pre-departure PD should be provided to enable participants to become familiar with ICC theory and research and so begin to develop the determining intercultural subcompetences prior to departure. It would be beneficial to include the psychological dimension (CQ), guidance in skills in critical reflection on self and other, and opportunities to explore personal and professional identities and worldviews, iCLT pedagogy, and the shift from learning *about* to learning *involving* other values, beliefs, and behaviour (Byram, 2012a). This would provide individuals with the strategies for intercultural development and transformational learning.

The language level and prior experience of participants must be considered in order to optimise the dissonance factor. If the aim is ICC development, too low a language level might reduce opportunities for engagement and noticing the language and culture nexus; too high a level coupled with prior experience might obscure the dissonance factor.

The aims of the programme would surely benefit from a judicious selection of host culture for the LCIE. If the aims include ICC development, immersion in an unfamiliar culture in which the participant would more likely face language and culture challenges might be more effective in producing the requisite triggers for intercultural development and transformational learning. Thus, greater consideration could be given to immersion in cultures other than the ones traditionally selected for a particular language, as suggested by Wernicke (2016). For NZ teachers especially of European languages who are already familiar with European countries, such non-traditional destinations could be, for example, Brazil for Portuguese, Québec for French, and South and Central America for Spanish. Here, they could explore Eurocentric assumptions about the authenticity of language varieties as well as the concept of the pluricentric nature of languages and cultures. Whenever possible, such aspects of immersion could be anticipated at home before going overseas, for example, with immersion in an online virtual world such as Second Life (Corder & U-Mackey, 2015) or in a local ethnic or heritage language community (Harvey et al., 2011; Wicke, 2007).

Priority should be given to ensuring that each participant has a skilled mentor for each stage of the LCIE. Availability of a mentor before, during, and after the sojourn is required to leverage maximum learning from the experience. The mentor should be someone in whom the participant has confidence so that they can be comfortable about sharing experiences. The mentor would help scaffold individual needs, including pre-immersion goal setting, advising on ethnographic studies to provide a focus during the immersion, and guide the participant to interpret intercultural experiences. The mentor would facilitate a participant's transformative intercultural learning and help to transfer that learning into classroom practice for student intercultural gains. Reflective journals, blogs, or portfolios are useful for fostering critical reflection, working through feedback from mentors, and undertaking collaborative learning with other participants. These would not only provide leverage for personal transformation, but could be used to evaluate gains in and after the LCIE. Returnees must also have access to a network of language teachers to share new learnings and collaborate on new resources for iCLT. This will foster ongoing transformational learning from the LCIE.

Finally, follow-up studies should be implemented at a number of predetermined intervals following the LCIEs to evaluate ongoing gains. Such evaluation (e.g., see Bird & Belnap, this volume) would inform continued planning and future implementation of programme components that could more effectively meet the complexities of both individual teacher-participants and their intercultural learning, including personal and professional identities, their level of CQ, motivation, goals, and prior knowledge and experience.

Summary of recommendations for increasing the ICC of language teachers on SA programmes
• Programme aims and outcomes must be clear, especially if they include ICC and iCLT, and these ought to be reflected in participants' goals to provide a framework for LCIE. • Flexible programme designs would support and meet the complexities of participants for ICC development. • Pre-sojourn PD in ICC and CQ could help to ensure participants have the strategies to optimise outcomes from their experiences and stated goals. • A considered selection of participants would help to ensure sufficient level of L2 competence to engage in the experience for professional purposes. • Host culture placement should consider the potential of the particular location for ensuring sufficient dissonance. • Provision of skilled mentors pre-, during, and post-LCIE is necessary for preparation, ongoing support, debriefing, and sustained gains. • An ethnographic study and/or online reflective journals or portfolios would help leverage transformational learning, foster collaboration, and evaluate LCIE gains. • Pre-, during, and post-sojourn provision of professional networks would help optimise the experience for the benefit of individual teacher-participants and their students. • In-depth debriefing on return and follow-up studies would evaluate ongoing gains and inform programme planning.

Bibliography

AFS. (n.d.-a). *Professional development for educators*. Retrieved from http://www.afs.org.nz/educators/professional-development-for-educators/

AFS New Zealand. (n.d.-b). *Language immersion awards (LIA) for teachers*. Retrieved from http://www.afs.org.nz/language-immersion-awards-lia-teachers/

Bastos, M., & Araújo e Sá, H. (2014). Pathways to teacher education for intercultural communicative competence: Teachers' perceptions. *Language Learning Journal, 43*(2), 131–147. https://doi.org/10.1080/09571736.2013.869940

Bennett, M. (1993). Towards ethnorelativism: A developmental model of intercultural sensitivity (revised). In R. M. Paige (Ed.), *Education for the intercultural experience* (2nd ed., pp. 21–71). Yarmouth, ME: Intercultural Press.

Byram, M. (1997). *Teaching and assessing intercultural communicative competence*. Clevedon, UK: Multilingual Matters.

Byram, M. (2008). *From foreign language education to education for intercultural citizenship*. Clevedon, UK: Multilingual Matters.

Byram, M. (2009). Intercultural competence in foreign languages: The intercultural speaker and the pedagogy of foreign language education. In D. K. Deardorff (Ed.), *The SAGE handbook of intercultural competence* (pp. 321–332). Thousand Oaks, CA: Sage.

Byram, M. (2012a). Conceptualizing intercultural (communicative) competence and intercultural citizenship. In J. Jackson (Ed.), *The Routledge handbook of language and intercultural communication* (pp. 85–97). Abingdon, UK: Routledge.

Byram, M. (2012b). Language awareness and (critical) cultural awareness—Relationships, comparisons and contrasts. *Language Awareness, 21*(1–2), 5–13. https://doi.org/10.1080/09658416.2011.639887

Byram, M. (2014). Twenty-five years on—From cultural studies to intercultural citizenship. *Language, Culture and Curriculum, 27*(3), 209–255. https://doi.org/10.1080/07908318.2014.974329

Corder, D. M., & U-Mackey, A. (2015). Encountering and dealing with difference: Second life and intercultural competence. *Intercultural Education, 16*(5), 409–424. https://doi.org/10.1080/14675986.2015.1091213

Crozet, C., & Liddicoat, A. (1997). The challenge of intercultural language teaching: Engaging with culture in the classroom. In J. Lo Bianco, A. Liddicoat, & C. Crozet (Eds.), *Striving for the third place: ICC through language education* (pp. 113–115). Melbourne, VIC: Language Australia.

Cushner, K., & Chang, S. (2015). Developing intercultural competence through overseas student teaching: Checking our assumptions. *Intercultural Education, 26*(3), 165–178. https://doi.org/10.1080/14675986.2015.104326

Deardorff, D. (2011). Intercultural competence in foreign language classrooms: A framework and implications for educators. In A. Witte & T. Harden (Eds.), *Intercultural competence: Concepts, challenges, evaluations* (Vol. 10, pp. 37–54). Bern: Peter Lang.

Deardorff, D. K. (2006). Identification and assessment of intercultural competence as a student outcome of internationalization. *Journal of Studies in International Education, 10*(3), 241–266. https://doi.org/10.1177/1028315306287002

Deardorff, D. K. (2009). Preface. In D. K. Deardorff (Ed.), *The SAGE handbook of ICC* (pp. xi–xiv). Thousand Oaks, CA: Sage.

Doidge, N. (2010). *The brain that changes itself: Stories of personal triumph from the frontiers of brain science*. Carlton North, VIC: Scribe Publications.

Driscoll, P., Rowe, J. E., & Thomae, M. (2014). The sustainable impact of a short comparative teaching placement abroad on primary school language teachers' professional, linguistic and cultural skills. *Language Learning Journal, 42*(3), 307–320. https://doi.org/10.1080/09571736.2014.917332

Duff, P. (2008). *Case study research in applied linguistics.* Oxford, UK: Routledge.

East, M. (2013). The impact of short term in-country experience on the professional development of teachers of French. *New Zealand Language Teacher, 39,* 32–43. Retrieved from http://search.informit.com.au.ezproxy.aut.ac.nz/documentSummary;dn=806698413201725;res=IELHSS

Ehrenreich, S. (2006). The assistant experience in retrospect and its educational and professional significance in teachers' biographies. In M. Byram & A. Feng (Eds.), *Living and studying abroad: Research and practice* (pp. 186–209). Clevedon, UK: Multilingual Matters.

Engberg, M. E., Jourian, T. J., & Davidson, L. M. (2015, April). The mediating role of intercultural wonderment: Connecting programmatic components to global outcomes in study abroad. *Higher Education.* https://doi.org/10.1007/s10734-015-9886-6

Erlam, R. (2005). Maximising instructional effectiveness in the language classroom. *New Zealand Language Teacher, 31,* 38–40.

Giovanangeli, A., Oguro, S., & Harbon, L. (2017). Mentoring students' intercultural learning during study abroad. In J. Jackson & S. Oguro (Eds.), *Intercultural interventions in study abroad* (pp. 88–102). London: Routledge. Retrieved from https://ebookcentral-proquest-com.ezproxy.aut.ac.nz/lib/AUT/reader.action?docID=5050760&ppg=207

Harrison, J. K., & Brower, H. H. (2011). The impact of cultural intelligence and psychological hardiness on homesickness among study abroad students. *Frontiers: The Interdisciplinary Journal of Study Abroad, 11,* 41–62.

Harvey, S., Roskvist, A., Corder, D., & Stacey, K. (2011). *An evaluation of the language and culture immersion experiences (LCIE) for teachers programmes: Their impact on teachers and their contribution to effective second language learning.* Wellington, NZ: Ministry of Education. Retrieved from http://www.educationcounts.govt.nz/publications/schooling/103409

Holmes, P., Bavieri, L., & Ganassin, S. (2015). Developing intercultural understanding for study abroad: Students' and teachers' perspectives on pre-departure intercultural learning. *Intercultural Education, 26*(1), 16–30.

Holmes, P., & O'Neill, G. (2012). Developing and evaluating intercultural competence: Ethnographies of intercultural encounters. *International Journal of Intercultural Relations, 36*(5), 707–718.

Houghton, S. (2010). Savoir se transformer: Knowing how to become. In Y. Tsai & S. Houghton (Eds.), *Becoming intercultural: Inside and outside the classroom* (pp. 194–233). Newcastle: Cambridge Scholars.

Houghton, S. A. (2013). Making intercultural communicative competence and identity development visible for assessment purposes in foreign language education. *Language Learning Journal, 41*(3), 311–325. https://doi.org/10.1080/09571736.2013.836348

Hutchison, A., & Rea, T. (2011). Transformative learning and identity formation on the 'Smiling Coast' of West Africa. *Teaching and Teacher Education, 27*(3), 552–559. https://doi.org/10.1016/j.tate.2010.10.009

International Languages Exchanges and Pathways (ILEP). (n.d.). Immersion scholarship programmes. Retrieved from http://www.ilep.ac.nz/scholarship-programmes

Jackson, J. (2009). Intercultural learning on short-term sojourns. *Intercultural Education, 20*(1), 59–71. https://doi.org/10.1080/14675980903370870

Jackson, J. (2012a). Education abroad. In J. Jackson (Ed.), *The Routledge handbook of language and intercultural communication* (pp. 449–463). Abingdon, UK: Routledge.

Jackson, J. (2012b). Introduction and overview. In J. Jackson (Ed.), *The Routledge handbook of language and intercultural communication* (pp. 1–3). Abingdon, UK: Routledge.

Jackson, J. (2017). Optimizing intercultural learning and engagement in study abroad through online mentoring. In J. Jackson & S. Oguro (Eds.), *Intercultural interventions in study abroad* (pp. 1–17). London: Routledge. Retrieved from https://ebookcentral-proquest-com.ezproxy.aut.ac.nz/lib/AUT/reader.action?docID=5050760&ppg=207

Jackson, J., & Oguro, S. (2017). Enhancing and extending study abroad learning through intercultural interventions. In J. Jackson & S. Oguro (Eds.), *Intercultural interventions in study abroad* (pp. 190–205). London: Routledge. Retrieved from https://ebookcentral-proquest-com.ezproxy.aut.ac.nz/lib/AUT/reader.action?docID=5050760&ppg=207

Kartoshkina, Y. (2015). Bitter-sweet reentry after studying abroad. *International Journal of Intercultural Relations, 44*, 35–45. https://doi.org/10.1016/j.ijintrel.2014.11.001

Kelly, M. (2012). Second language teacher education. In J. Jackson (Ed.), *The Routledge handbook of language and intercultural communication* (pp. 409–421). Abingdon, UK: Routledge.

Kinginger, C. (2015). Student mobility and identity-related language learning. *Intercultural Education, 26*(1), 6–15. https://doi.org/10.1080/14675986.2015.992199

Kırkgöz, Y. (2016). Integrating study abroad in teacher education: Enhancing the curriculum. In D. M. Velliaris & D. Coleman-George (Eds.), *Handbook of research on study abroad programs and outward mobility* (pp. 601–620). Hershey, PA: Information Science Reference.

Kramsch, C. (1998). *Language and culture.* Oxford: Oxford University Press.

Lázár, I. (2011). Teachers' beliefs about integrating the development of intercultural communicative competence in language teaching. *Forum Sprache, 5*(5), 113–127.

Lou, K. H., Vande Berg, M., & Paige, R. M. (2012). Intervening in student learning abroad. In M. Vande Berg, R. M. Paige, & K. H. Lou (Eds.), *Student learning abroad: What our students are learning, what they're not, and what we can do about it* (pp. 3–28). Sterling, VA: Stylus.

Marx, H., & Moss, D. M. (2011). Please mind the culture gap: Intercultural development during a teacher education study abroad program. *Journal of Teacher Education, 62*(1), 35–47. https://doi.org/10.1177/0022487110381988

Mezirow, J. (1997). Transformative learning: Theory to practice. *New Directions for Adult and Continuing Education,* (74), 5–12. https://doi.org/10.1002/ace.7401

Ministry of Education (MoE). (2007). *The New Zealand curriculum.* The Ministry of Education, The New Zealand Curriculum. Online. Retrieved from http://nzcurriculum.tki.org.nz/

Müller, M., & Schmenk, B. (2016). Conceptualizations, images, and evaluations of culture in study abroad students. *Canadian Journal of Applied Linguistics, 19*(2), 128–150. Retrieved from https://journals.lib.unb.ca/index.php/CJAL/article/view/24235/29565

Newton, J., Yates, E., Shearn, S., & Nowitzki, W. (2010). *Intercultural communicative language teaching (iCLT): Implications for effective teaching and learning. A literature review and evidence-based framework for effective teaching.* Wellington, NZ: Ministry of Education. Retrieved from http://www.educationcounts.govt.nz/publications/curriculum/76637/introduction

Paige, R. M. (1993). On the nature of intercultural experiences and intercultural education. In R. M. Paige (Ed.), *Education for the intercultural experience* (pp. 1–19). Yarmouth, ME: Intercultural Press.

Peiser, G., & Jones, M. (2014). The influence of teachers' interests, personalities and life experiences in intercultural languages teaching. *Teachers and Teaching, 20*(3), 375–390. https://doi.org/10.1080/13540602.2013.848525

Plews, J. L., Breckenridge, Y., & Cambre, M. C. (2010). Mexican English teachers' experiences of international professional development in Canada: A narrative analysis. *Electronic Journal of Foreign Language Teaching, 7*(1), 5–20. Retrieved from https://e-flt.nus.edu.sg/v7n12010/plews.pdf

Plews, J. L., Breckenridge, Y., Cambre, M. C., & Fernandes, G. M. de F. (2014). Mexican English teachers' experiences of international professional development in Canada: A narrative sequel. *Electronic Journal of Foreign Language Teaching, 11*(1), 52–75. Retrieved from http://e-flt.nus.edu.sg/v11n12014/plews.pdf

Risager, K. (2012). Linguaculture and transnationality: The cultural dimensions of language. In J. Jackson (Ed.), *The Routledge handbook of language and intercultural communication* (pp. 101–115). Abington, UK: Routledge.

Root, E., & Ngampornchai, A. (2012). 'I came back as a new human being': Student descriptions of intercultural competence acquired through education abroad experiences. *Journal of Studies in International Education, 17*(5), 513–532.

Ryan, P. (2012). The English as a foreign or international language classroom. In J. Jackson (Ed.), *The Routledge handbook of language and intercultural communication* (pp. 422–433). Abington, UK: Routledge.

Sercu, L. (2004a). Intercultural communicative competence in foreign language education. Integrating theory and practice. In K. van Esch & O. S. John (Eds.), *New insights into foreign language learning and teaching* (pp. 115–130). Frankfurt: Peter Lang.

Sercu, L. (2004b). Researching the acquisition of intercultural communicative competence in a foreign language. Setting the agenda for a research area. In K. van Esch & O. S. John (Eds.), *New insights into foreign language learning and teaching* (pp. 131–151). Frankfurt: Peter Lang.

Shaules, J. (2015). *The intercultural mind. Connecting culture, cognition and global living*. Boston: Intercultural Press.

Smolcic, E., & Katunich, J. (2017). Teachers crossing borders: A review of the research into cultural immersion field experience for teachers. *Teaching and Teacher Education, 62*, 47–59. https://doi.org/10.1016/j.tate.2016.11.002

Spitzberg, B. H., & Changnon, G. (2009). Conceptualizing intercultural competence. In D. K. Deardorff (Ed.), *The Sage handbook of intercultural competence* (pp. 2–52). Thousand Oaks, CA: Sage.

Stake, R. (1995). *The art of case study research*. Thousand Oaks, CA: Sage.

Triandis, H. C. (1995). *Individualism and collectivism*. Boulder, CO: Westview.

Vande Berg, M., Paige, R. M., & Lou, K. H. (2012). Student learning abroad, paradigms and assumptions. In M. Vande Berg, R. M. Paige, & K. H. Lou

(Eds.), *Student learning abroad: What our students are learning, what they're not, and what we can do about it* (pp. 3–28). Sterling, VA: Stylus.

Vatalaro, A., Szente, J., & Levin, J. (2015). Transformative learning of preservice teachers during study abroad in Reggio Emilia, Italy: A case study. *Journal of the Scholarship of Teaching and Learning, 15*(2), 42–55.

Vogt, K. (2016). Teaching practicums abroad: Increasing the professionalization of preservice foreign language teachers. In D. M. Velliaris & D. Coleman-George (Eds.), *Handbook of research on study abroad programs and outward mobility* (pp. 540–577). Hershey, PA: Information Science Reference.

Wernicke, M. (2010). Study abroad as professional development for FSL teachers. *Canadian Journal of Applied Linguistics, 13*(1), 4–18.

Wernicke, M. (2016). Hierarchies of authenticity in study abroad: French from Canada versus French from France? *Canadian Journal of Applied Linguistics, 19*(2), 1–21.

Wicke, R. E. (2007). Deutsch um die Ecke: Ein kanadisches Projekt und seine Folgen. In C. Lorey, J. L. Plews, & C. L. Rieger (Eds.), *Intercultural literacies and German in the classroom* (pp. 141–159). Tübingen: Narr.

Witte, A. (2011). On the teachability and learnability of intercultural competence: Developing facets of the 'Inter'. In A. Witte & T. Harden (Eds.), *Intercultural competence: Concepts, challenges, evaluations* (Vol. 10, pp. 89–108). Bern: Peter Lang.

Adopt a Class: Engagement and Reflection During the Year Abroad

Elizabeth A. Andersen and Sophie Stewart

Introduction

The Adopt a Class project run by Routes into Languages (2017a) links secondary school pupils with university students of modern languages during their year abroad. The aim of the project is to promote the increased uptake of languages and student mobility across England and Wales. While evidence already points to the positive reception of this scheme in secondary schools (Shervill, 2012), of particular interest in this chapter is the impact that involvement in the scheme has on the university students (see also Hampton, 2016). It considers how students are challenged by and benefit from the process of defining, relaying, and adapting their experiences abroad in order to communicate effectively with the school pupils. The chapter explores the extent to which participation in the Adopt a Class project, as a paid extracurricular activity, provides a valuable

---

E. A. Andersen (✉) • S. Stewart
Newcastle University, Newcastle upon Tyne, UK
e-mail: elizabeth.andersen@ncl.ac.uk

opportunity for students' self-reflection upon their own cultural learning as well as their professional and personal development.

Context: Modern Languages in the UK

The UK has faced a sharp decline in the number of young people studying modern foreign languages (MFLs) at the level of General Certificate of Secondary Education (GCSE), ordinarily taken by pupils between the ages of 14 and 16. According to the *Language Trends 2014/15* report (Board & Tinsley, 2015), the total number of MFL entries at GCSE level fell from a peak of 76 per cent of pupils in 2002 to a low of 40 per cent of pupils in 2011. The attrition sharply accelerated in 2004 following the introduction of a government policy making the study of MFL optional at GCSE level. Some—albeit scant—ground has been recovered since the introduction of the school performance measure, the English Baccalaureate (EBacc) (Department of Education, 2017) in 2012 (the EBacc allows people to see how many pupils achieve a grade C or above in the core academic subjects at key stage four in any government-funded school). To qualify for the EBacc, a pupil must study a language (classical or modern) at GCSE level. However, even with the pressure of the EBacc, total MFL entries in 2014 still equated to less than half (49 per cent) of all pupils.

The decline of MFL at GCSE level has had further implications for the uptake of languages at higher levels. According, again, to the *Language Trends 2014/15* report (Board & Tinsley, 2015), at Advanced Level (normally studied between the ages of 16 and 18) a drop of 60 per cent occurred in numbers studying French and German between 1996 and 2014. There has been a 28 per cent fall in MFL study at A Level across all languages. Inevitably, the decline in languages at school level has had negative repercussions for higher education institutions (HEIs). Between 1998 and 2014 the number of universities offering degrees in languages fell from 93 to 56. The alarming drop in the number of MFL students led to the inclusion of MFL within the Roberts Review into Strategic and Vulnerable Subjects (Higher Education Funding Council for England, 2005), alongside science, technology, engineering, and mathematics. This in turn led to the inception of the Routes into Languages programme.

The Routes into Languages Programme

The Routes into Languages programme was established in 2006 with funding from the Higher Education Funding Council for England (Hefce). Following the recommendation of the *Languages Review* (Department for Education and Skills, 2007), additional funding from the Department of Children, Schools and Families (now the Department for Education) was awarded to the programme; this led to a growth in the number of regional consortia to a total of 10 across England and Wales, with 67 HEIs involved. The primary aim of the Routes programme is for universities to work collaboratively in partnership with schools and colleges to enthuse and encourage young people to study languages. The first phase of work ran from 2007 to 2012. Certain activities such as school visits from Student Language Ambassadors (SLAs) and 'Why Study Languages?' presentations are common to all, but each consortium developed their own particular activities, from employability conferences to cultural festivals. Sustained interventions such as the Adopt a Class scheme engage learners over longer periods.

Further to the confirmation of an additional £3.1 million funding from Hefce in May 2013, the second phase of work began in August 2013, finishing in July 2016. It saw a continuation of those activities judged most effective thus far with the additional twin foci of increasing participation in work and study abroad and promoting careers and employability for students of languages through new partnerships with organisations such as Third Year Abroad and the UK Higher Education International Unit.

The Role of the Student Language Ambassador

The concept of the SLA is at the centre of the Routes into Languages programme. Employed in teams across institutions within each regional consortia, as current students of modern languages or those who have direct experience of studying abroad (e.g., ERASMUS and international exchange students), the SLAs are trained to promote MFL to pupils at key decision points ahead of GCSE and A Level option choices. Being close in age and with recent experience of the GCSE and A Level exam systems, the SLAs represent accessible role models for the school pupils they work with, whether in school delivering 'Why Study Languages?' presentations or supporting outreach events on university campuses.

In the majority of consortia, SLAs are paid for their work but in all cases, they stand to gain a great deal regarding their future employability upon graduation through the training they receive and the transferable skills they develop through the role. According to a survey of SLAs, many reported improved communication, presentation, and organisation skills, as well as a boost to overall confidence. In the context of the North East Consortium, the SLA model was developed at an early stage to include a formal application, presentation, and interview process for students wishing to join the team. Particular to Newcastle University was the development of a team of Senior Ambassadors who support the Project Manager in the coordination of a programme of regional school visits (see Andersen & O'Rourke Magee, 2013, pp. 352–353).

The Adopt a Class Project

The Adopt a Class initiative was first developed by Routes into Languages Cymru [Wales] in 2010. The success of the scheme was recognised through the prestigious European Language Label Award in 2012 (see Al-Amri, 2012). Further to this success, the scheme has been taken up by nearly all the other regional consortia; it was piloted in the North East Consortium in the academic year 2014/15.

In keeping with the additional focus on student mobility in Phase 2 of the Routes programme, the aim of Adopt a Class is to highlight the opportunities open to students of modern languages during their year abroad with the intention of encouraging young people to continue with their language studies after the age of 14. The efforts of the Adopt a Class scheme are directed at the year in which pupils make the key decision whether to take a language or languages at GCSE. The Project Manager matches the SLA with a local school (see Appendix A for notes for schoolteachers). The SLA visits the class prior to the year abroad when pupils are in Year Eight (aged 12–13); the student keeps in regular contact with their class of pupils (now in Year Nine, aged 13–14) during their time abroad, revisiting them upon their return home post year abroad, at which point pupils are in Year Ten (aged 14–15) and studying towards GCSE qualifications. Communication between the student and the class during the year abroad can take various forms, including emailing, blogging, video-conferencing, sending postcards, and utilising other resources in the target language. This contact with the foreign country, or, indeed, countries, brings the language and culture alive for the pupils and demonstrates to them the relevance of learning a language, through the mediation and communication of a near-contemporary role model who serves to bolster the efforts of the class teacher in this respect.

Both the university students and the schoolteachers sign an agreement outlining the anticipated commitment and agreed timescales for the project prior to the start of the academic year. The SLAs receive additional training in the form of a briefing and supporting documents (including links to pre-existing Adopt a Class blogs) to equip them with relevant ideas and strategies (see Appendix B for notes for students). Upon successful completion of a post–year abroad visit to their partner school, students are paid £100 in recognition of their commitment to the project.

The Routes North East Consortium Pilot of 2014/15

The Three Case Study Participants

In order to explore the impact of the Adopt a Class scheme, three partnerships involving students Fraser, Geoffrey, and Josephine (pseudonyms) formed the focus of this study, as outlined in Table 1. They are representative of the three main pathways open to students on their year abroad, that is, as an ERASMUS exchange student, as a language teaching assistant, and as a work experience intern. Data were collected by means of pre- and post-interviews before and after the year abroad with both students and schoolteachers, together with email contact between the project manager and the students during the year abroad. These particular students were selected for the case studies because of the diversity

Table 1 Summary profile of the students' educational background and their engagement with the project

Name	Fraser	Geoffrey	Josephine
University	Newcastle University	Newcastle University	Northumbria University
Languages studied	French and Spanish (with Catalan)	French, German, and Spanish (with Dutch)	French and Spanish
Residence abroad activity	Studying as an ERASMUS student in Semester 1 in Paris and in Semester 2 in Barcelona	Semester 1 volunteering as an English teacher in Lima and Semester 2 working as an intern in PR in Berlin	Semester 1 working as a teaching assistant in Réunion and Semester 2 working as an au pair and in other casual jobs across Spain
Partner school	Independent (private) boys' school in the city of Newcastle	State secondary school with academy status in Gateshead	State secondary school with academy status in Hartlepool
Primary method of communication	Weekly Skype sessions with associated tasks facilitated by the teacher	Emails to the class via the teacher with photos	Dedicated multilingual blog posts about various aspects of life abroad
Main focus of communication	To develop pupils' language skills through speaking and listening exercises	To showcase benefits of the year abroad, for example, cultural insight and exposure to authentic language	To attempt cross-cultural mediation by exploring differences in daily life while living abroad

of their experiences as well as the variety of communication channels they employed with their school classes. Furthermore, each of them had strong regional connections, having grown up or attended school in the North East, and viewed the Adopt a Class scheme as a natural continuation of their work as SLAs with Routes North East during their year abroad. Geoffrey and Fraser joined the Newcastle University Routes team in their first year of study and both were promoted to the position of Senior Ambassador the following year. Meanwhile, Josephine joined the team at Northumbria University in her second year of study.

The three case studies along with follow-up interviews with the contact teachers also reveal many of the operational challenges of the project, chiefly in the coordination of pre- and post-project visits and the maintenance of regular and sustained communication between the university students and the schoolteachers.

The Research Considerations

In considering the impact of participation in the Adopt a Class scheme on the three case study students, we were mindful of 'the multiple variables that can impact on the language and (inter)cultural learning, identity expansion and "whole person development" of participants' (Jackson, 2012, p. 452) during the year abroad. Research on the development of models of intercultural communicative competence and the processes involved in language and intercultural learning (see Byram & Dervin, 2008; Byram & Feng, 2006; Coleman, 2007; Dufon & Chrurchill, 2006; Jackson, 2008, 2010, 2012; Kinginger, 2009; Risager, 2012) as well as on the importance of social networks (Coleman, 2015; Isabelli-García, 2006; Mitchell, Tracy-Ventura, & McManus, 2017) helps to contextualise the manner in which the students structured the interaction with their adopted class. As Pellegrino Aveni (2005, p. 147) notes, '[t]he balance learners gain between the culture from which they come and the culture into which they enter gives them greater insight into their own self-construction between the two worlds'. In their interaction with their adopted classes, the three case study students found themselves 'existing in a third space in between two cultures' (Hampton, 2015, p. 225), as they sought to mediate their experiences of living in another cultural context. We had recourse to the L2 Motivational Self System as developed by Dörnyei (2005) in order to interpret both the students' self-projection and the particular nature of the role they adopted in their engagement with their classes (see Andersen & O'Rourke Magee, 2013; Hampton, 2016).

L2 Motivational Self System

Within the L2 Motivational Self System, the SLAs embody for the school pupils 'possible selves' as 'visions of the self in a future state; they represent the individuals' ideas of what they *might* become' (Dörnyei & Ushioda, 2011, p. 80). The L2 Motivational Self System identifies three main elements in the motivation to learn a foreign language: the vision of the learner as an accomplished L2 speaker, the social pressure exerted on the learner by those in positions of authority, and the positive experience of the learning process. Within this model, the SLAs function as powerful representatives of Ideal L2 Selves. As near-contemporaries, the SLAs can anchor the school pupils' vision of their Ideal L2 Self in a sense of realistic expectations. In 2011, SQW (2011), a leading sustainable economic and social development consulting firm, was appointed to evaluate the first phase of the Routes into Languages project. In their final report, SQW commented on the impact of the Student Ambassadors as follows:

> As we have found throughout the evaluation to date, student ambassadors are by far the most cited successful element of Routes. The reasons for this [are]: young people listen to ambassadors because of who they are (young, 'cool') and because of who they are not (teachers or parents). This gives the ambassadors a credibility that other potential role models often lack. (p. 42)

Having chosen to read for a degree in modern languages and then to promote languages in outreach work through the Routes programme, the SLAs are committed and convinced linguists. Furthermore, besides functioning as aspirant Ideal Selves, they are effective in communicating the messages associated with Dörnyei's 'Ought-to Self'. As trained SLAs, the students fully understand and identify with the key messages about the value of modern languages that those leading the Routes project seek to convey, namely, enhanced communication and social skills, intercultural knowledge and expertise, employability, and personal development. In the debriefing interviews we held with the SLAs on their return to Newcastle, the students all expressed their passionate commitment to passing on these key messages, responding to questions about their motivation to participate in the scheme as follows:

For me, projects like these are always fulfilling, being able to share your passion with kids and see them take an interest in learning about new languages and cultures is what it is all about. (Fraser)

Similar to other Routes work, a sense of satisfaction, knowing that I could be inspiring pupils to continue with their language studies. (Geoffrey)

I mostly hoped to be able to inspire the class, I knew I would be doing something cool and interesting and I thought the kids would enjoy hearing about it, and make them realise that they could do the same thing if they want to. (Josephine)

Self-organised Learning Environments (SOLE)

At Newcastle University, the research of SOLE Central, a research flagship in the School of Education, Communication and Language Sciences (Dolan et al., 2013; Newcastle University, 2017), provides another lens through which to examine the self-projection of the SLAs and their impact on the adopted classes. Within the context of 'self-organised learning environments', Professor Sugata Mitra (Clark, Hall, Leat, & Mitra, 2011) developed the concept of a cloud of 'Skype Grannies'. These were volunteers of all ages and, despite the name, both male and female, who skyped into learning centres across India. The term 'Granny' was used to signal the kind of relationship that these volunteers would have with the children, that is, it would be informal, provide unconditional encouragement, and express appreciation of the children's efforts. Learning would take place *naturally* through conversation rather than through direct and planned teaching. The initial objective was for the children to become confident and more fluent in English.[1]

In a project that took the concept of Skype Grannies into schools in the North East of England (Thomas et al., n.d.), the decision was taken to rename the Grannies as Skype Seniors in order to promote a better gender balance among the volunteers. This small-scale exploratory research and development project had the following aims:

- To explore the potential impact that these new voices in the classroom would have on student engagement
- To examine the technical infrastructure required to support the project
- To explore the motivations and experiences of the 'Seniors'

In their analysis of the data generated by the Skype Seniors project, the SOLE team drew on the work of the sociologist Basil Bernstein, in particular his ideas on the balance of power and control in the pedagogical relationship between pupil and teacher. Bernstein (1975, p. 90) distinguishes between two types of framing in the classroom—strong and weak: 'In a strongly-framed pedagogical relationship the power that the pupil has over "what, when and how he receives his knowledge"' is reduced, whereas it is increased correspondingly in a relationship that is 'weakly framed'. At the end of the year-long exploratory research in selected schools in the North East of England, the SOLE project team concluded: 'In relation to the impact on curriculum, pedagogy and student engagement [...] Skype Seniors act as a powerful catalyst which fuels the imagination of some teachers and assists them in moving their teaching in the direction of their values constructs' (Thomas et al., n.d.). At the same time, it was noted that the examination targets set by the state control of education were an inhibiting factor in the development of the relationship with the Skype Seniors. In our pilot study of the Adopt a Class scheme, we found Bernstein's concept of strong and weak framing helpful in analysing the choice and the consequent impact of the channel of communication adopted in the three case studies.

Student Language Ambassadors as Online Buddies

The main aims and objectives of the Adopt a Class project reflect the overarching goal of the Routes into Languages programme, which is to stimulate and foster interest in languages among school pupils with a view to increasing the language uptake from GCSE onwards. This project, however, has the additional objectives of providing pupils with direct access to authentic experience of aspects of life in another country, as well as increasing their awareness of student mobility and of future opportunities made accessible through a command of languages. The SLAs act as genuine and relevant role models, introducing a new voice into the classroom. In this regard, they have an analogous role to the Skype Grannies and Skype Seniors, although they function more as 'older siblings', or 'buddies'. Whereas the SLAs had communicated more generalised messages about modern languages in their teamwork as Routes Ambassadors while in Newcastle, for the Adopt a Class project they were required to reflect critically on their individual responses to their new environment in order to mediate their personal intercultural experience. The manner in which they conveyed this experience was negotiated with the schoolteacher who decided how 'strong' or 'weak' the framing of their contribution should be.

The Three Student Case Studies and Follow-Up Teacher Interviews

Case Study 1: Fraser and the Independent Boys' School in Newcastle

Preparation Pre–year Abroad

Fraser already had an existing connection with his school through outreach visits in his first two years as a Routes Ambassador. In Spring 2014 he met the Year Eight pupils who were to become his adopted Year Nine French class. Prior to the start of his year abroad in September 2014, Fraser had email correspondence with the Newcastle teacher in which the teacher mapped out clearly the place, nature, and function of Fraser's input into language lessons. The intention was to integrate Fraser's contribution in a strong framework. Language acquisition was to be the primary focus with a particular emphasis on the development of vocabulary and oral proficiency.

Interaction During the Period of the Year Abroad

To launch the relationship with the class, Fraser made an introductory video about his life in Paris. This was in French with a summary in English. A regular rhythm was then established with weekly Skype sessions

(Mondays, 11:00–11:15) in which he and the pupils spoke mainly in French. In advance of the Skype sessions, the teacher provided vocabulary lists and set pupils questions to ask Fraser. Fraser reported that, as far as possible, he made a conscious effort to keep the language uncomplicated and to speak slowly. On occasion, he used video, as in an end-of-year clip featuring himself at the Eiffel Tower, and PowerPoint, as for example in *Les Aventures de Fraser à Paris* in which he took the class on a tour of selected monuments. He incorporated cultural information (e.g., Christmas traditions in France, French film and television) and introduced pupils to different environments (e.g., his flat, the buildings he was taught in at university). As time progressed, he began to develop his own language exercises and homework tasks under the supervision of the teacher. The relationship with the class lasted three months. Fraser had intended to continue the link when he moved to Barcelona for the second part of his year abroad, but conflicting timetables prevented the continuation of the relationship.

Post–year Abroad Meeting

Fraser visited his adopted (now Year Ten) class in February 2016. This was later than anticipated because of the difficulty of finding a mutually convenient time in their timetables. The teacher deemed the project to have been highly successful and issued an invitation to Fraser to return two years later to share his experiences of working life post graduation. This future visit is intended to coincide with another key point of transition, that is, when the pupils would be opting for those subjects that they would take to A Level.

Impact on Fraser

Fraser reported that participating in the Adopt a Class project had 'a huge impact' on his decision to consider teaching as a potential career. The sense of success he enjoyed led to his decision to take a credit-bearing module offered in the final year of the Modern Languages degree programme at Newcastle: 'Communicating and Teaching Languages for Undergraduate Ambassadors'. This module combines university-led input that focusses on the areas of language policy, pedagogy, professionalism, and reflection with a 60-hour in-school placement that allows students to gain first-hand experience of the teaching profession.[2]

Fraser and the Newcastle teacher clearly developed a harmonious and productive working relationship. Fraser enjoyed the 'strong' framing the Newcastle teacher had provided, to the extent that he voluntarily started devising his own languages exercises for the class. He had a clear sense of his function as a role model, seeking to communicate his personal experiences of life in Paris as an ERASMUS student.

Case Study 2: Geoffrey and the State Secondary School with Academy Status in GATESHEAD

Preparation Pre–year Abroad

Geoffrey was unable to visit the Year Eight German class he was to adopt prior to his year abroad because of timetable incompatibility. He reported that preparatory emails between the Gateshead teacher and himself were 'relaxed' in tone, with the teacher indicating that he would like Geoffrey to concentrate on his experience of adjusting to life abroad. Geoffrey understood that the teacher wanted the interaction with the class to focus mainly on the 'experience of taking languages further', on the opportunities and cultural insight that the year abroad would bring. Communication was to be by email to the teacher who would then share the messages with the class.

Interaction During the Period of the Year Abroad

The first correspondence Geoffrey had with the adopted Year Nine class was an email he sent from Peru, where he was a volunteer English assistant teacher, introducing himself and the concept of the year abroad, together with photos reflecting his first impressions of life in Peru. This was written in German with an English translation. Subsequent emails followed a similar pattern, in which he recorded his experiences. Geoffrey described his relationship with the class in terms of being a pen pal. The class shared photos with Geoffrey and a photo of Geoffrey formed part of a dedicated wall display in the classroom. By the time Geoffrey moved into the second half of his year abroad, which he spent in Berlin as an intern in a public relations firm, pupils were being encouraged by the teacher to write individual replies to Geoffrey in German. Geoffrey said that he made a conscious decision to showcase 'authentic' German rather than 'textbook' German in his email correspondence. The language he used was fairly complex for Year Nine pupils but was accessible to them through the teacher's mediation.

Post–year Abroad Meeting

Geoffrey visited his adopted (now Year Ten) class in December 2015. At this meeting Geoffrey shared with the pupils more of the cultural experiences he had enjoyed in Berlin (music, film festivals, and so forth). He explicitly encouraged them to consider continued study of languages at A Level. He reported that the relationship with the pupils was very positive and friendly: 'It felt like the kids were almost my friends.' Following the visit, Geoffrey received a handwritten card signed by all the pupils and the teacher thanking him.

Impact on Geoffrey

On his post–year abroad visit, Geoffrey was delighted to learn that the overwhelming majority of the class had opted to continue with German to GCSE, feeling that his effort may have contributed to this. He had identified strongly with the pupils, as he had himself attended a state comprehensive school and sixth-form college in the North East of England. Geoffrey saw involvement in the Adopt a Class project as 'giving something back' to local schools. He expressed his satisfaction with having been able to maintain a connection with the Routes programme during his year abroad and saw it as a natural continuation of this work that, like Fraser, he would take the module 'Communicating and Teaching Languages for Undergraduate Ambassadors' as part of a range of options in his final year. Geoffrey's contact with the Gateshead school had been 'weakly' framed by the Teacher with regard to the curriculum. Geoffrey used the space he had been given with the class to focus primarily on the communication of his cultural experiences, functioning strongly as a charismatic L2 Ideal Self.

Case Study 3: Josephine and the State Secondary School with Academy Status in Hartlepool

Preparation Pre–year Abroad

Josephine had hoped to visit the Year Eight class she was to adopt before she set off on her year abroad to French-speaking Réunion Island, a French Department in the Indian Ocean. However, the school was unable to organise this before her departure. Josephine set up a blog to record her experiences during her year abroad. She established this as her principal channel of communication with her adopted class and in doing so consciously shaped the blog 'to be instructive and educational' rather than simply a personal record of her experiences and impressions.

Interaction During the Period of the Year Abroad

Josephine communicated with her adopted class via blogposts. She received some email feedback from the Hartlepool teacher. This response was limited because the original teacher who had introduced the Adopt a Class project into the school went on maternity leave and the replacement teacher did not engage with the same commitment. Josephine wrote a total of five blogposts in a mixture of French and English, with a further one in Spanish during the second part of the year abroad which she spent in Spain. All of these were intended to give a picture of her daily existence, covering her day-to-day activities, her work as a teaching assistant, what she ate, how she moved around the island, and so forth. In addition, she created a video in English to showcase differences in school life between the UK and Réunion. She had planned to set up a letter exchange between the pupils she was teaching in Réunion and her adopted class, but this was not taken up by the North East school because of the break in communications caused by the change in personnel there.

Post–year Abroad Meeting

As part of her normal Routes work as an Ambassador, Josephine undertook a general school visit to the school in February 2016. She had arranged to meet with her (now Year Ten) adopted class as part of this. However, the teacher did not prioritise the session, making it an optional lunchtime session. No pupils turned up to meet Josephine. Nonetheless, she did pass on letters written by pupils in the Réunion school to the teacher in the hope that a letter exchange might be established.

Impact on Josephine

Despite the disappointing response from the school, Josephine felt that maintaining the blog enabled her to reflect on her year abroad experiences through writing for a specific target audience. She made a conscious attempt at cross-cultural mediation through her UK–Réunion letter-writing initiative. She said that she would not otherwise have done this outside the context of the Adopt a Class scheme. Josephine remained positive about her involvement with the project, although she regretted the missed opportunities for interaction and dialogue because of the disruption in the continuity of the relationship with the original teacher and the lack of commitment on the part of the substitute teacher. Josephine's immediate plans for her future are to take up a further British Council Assistantship post graduation.

What emerges clearly from Josephine's case study is the strong and independent motivation on her part to act as an L2 Ideal Self role model. However, the management of the vicissitudes in the staffing of the school prevented any 'framing' of Josephine's contributions.

Follow-Up Interviews with the Contact Teachers

Once the project had been completed, we conducted follow-up interviews with the contact teachers in the schools. The interviews were loosely structured around their expectations of the project, the extent to which these had been realised, how strongly or weakly the students' contributions had been framed in the curriculum and what impact the students had had on the class. Finally, we asked how the Adopt a Class project could be improved.

Follow-Up Interview with the Newcastle Teacher

The Newcastle teacher was keen that his pupils see Languages as a 'real subject, not just something they do with their teacher in the classroom'. Through engagement with Fraser he had wanted to give his pupils insight into a life using languages that was not too distant from their own experience. The Newcastle teacher highlighted how advantageous it had been that Fraser had already met and worked with the class as part of his regular Routes Ambassador role. The class had remembered Fraser because of his charismatic enthusiasm. As the class had met Fraser at three different stages in the course of his degree, they had gained a clearer view of what a degree in modern languages entails and an insight into some of the excitement of the year abroad. The Newcastle teacher felt that this had helped the class to make a much more informed choice about whether to continue with MFL at GCSE.

The Newcastle teacher had appreciated the contact with Fraser before the year abroad started, as it had allowed him to plan how Fraser's Skype presence might be used most advantageously in lessons. In advance of the lessons he had advised Fraser via email on what subjects to prepare and how he would integrate Fraser's contribution into the lesson to facilitate a lively interaction with the class. The Newcastle teacher reported how the pupils, as they had already met Fraser, were not anxious about having to speak to a stranger; indeed the prospect of seeing Fraser on screen had apparently created excited anticipation. The Newcastle teacher had not used Skype in the classroom before and was impressed by how 'focussed' the pupils became and how earnestly they engaged with the requirement to speak French. He was certain that the Adopt a Class project will remain in the memory of the class for some time and was convinced that it had been a 'positive experience' for all concerned.

Regarding possible improvements to the project, the Newcastle teacher reiterated how valuable it had been that the class already knew Fraser before the project began and thought that additional pre–year abroad visits would have brought further benefit. With hindsight, he thought he could have developed an entire mini-project on 'Life in Paris' as seen through Fraser's eyes. He stressed the value of the post–year abroad visit as a 'great way to round off the experience'.

Follow-Up Interview with the State Academy Gateshead Teacher

The Gateshead teacher had been motivated to engage with the Adopt a Class project by an anxiety about a lack of interest in languages among his pupils: 'To the kids languages don't really mean anything, they're like a code to learn to get a certain mark but that's all.' He hoped that through interaction with a university student the pupils would understand more readily the purpose and value of learning a language. He was looking for an 'inspirational role model'. Geoffrey proved to be just that with the result that the Gateshead teacher noted greater engagement with languages and an articulated awareness among pupils of the possible usefulness of German in the future. His hope that the pupils might use more German was not fully realised. Initially, the pupils had been reluctant to engage in German as Geoffrey was a stranger to them and the first contacts with Geoffrey were during that period of his year spent in Peru when, according to the Gateshead teacher, Geoffrey used English predominantly to communicate with them. Pressure on the curriculum because of controlled assessments had also reduced the time available for developing contact in the target language.

The Gateshead teacher had seen the dialogue with Geoffrey as a way of making classroom tasks more 'realistic'. For example, one activity introducing the topic of 'family and relationships' required the pupils to write a letter to Geoffrey about themselves. When working on German musical culture, pupils had, inspired by Geoffrey, independently downloaded and listened to German music from the Internet. Ahead of Geoffrey's post–year abroad visit to the school, pupils spent time eagerly preparing questions to ask him, although these were mostly in English rather than in German.

The Gateshead teacher reported a greater degree both of engagement with language learning and of curiosity about German culture. Geoffrey proved to be a 'very confident and engaging role model' who was successful in convincing the students of the potential advantage of learning languages.

The pupils enjoyed Geoffrey's post–year abroad visit so much that plans were under way for another visit before the end of the current academic year. An unexpected outcome was a renewed interest and increased correspondence in an existing pen-pal scheme set up with a school in Germany, as reported by parents at a parents' evening. The Gateshead teacher reported that his school had been criticised in an Ofsted inspection[3] for not challenging the pupils sufficiently. He felt that the engagement with Geoffrey had provided such a challenge to which the pupils very readily rose.

Regarding possible improvements to the Adopt a Class project, the Gateshead teacher commented that it would have been very beneficial had it been possible for the class to have met Geoffrey before he set off on his year abroad. He was inclined to move to a stronger framing of the student's contribution, introducing some form of organised team-teaching exercises, although he recognised the requirement that would bring for careful forward planning.

Follow-Up Interview with the Hartlepool Teacher

Unfortunately, the lack of commitment to the Adopt a Class project on the part of the school precluded a post–year abroad interview on the impact of the project.

Conclusion and Recommendations

From the cases described, it is clear that the three students had quite different experiences in their engagement with the Adopt a Class project. This is no doubt due as much to differences in the personality of both students and teaching staff as to other external factors such as timetable issues and teacher/school commitment. What does emerge consistently is the strong engagement on the part of all three students, their willingness to invest considerable time and energy in mediating their experiences during the year abroad, as well as their clear sense of the value of what they achieved. They had a keen sense of their potential influence as role models, as defined in Dörnyei's L2 Motivational Self System. The different ways in which their voices were articulated, especially regarding the strength of the framing of the students' interaction with the class, reveals the inherent flexibility and versatility of the project. This protean quality releases energy and stimulates creativity. However, the difficulties and frustrations encountered by Josephine demonstrate at the same time the vulnerability of the project to the vicissitudes of daily life in a school. Of the three case studies, Fraser's experience was the most strongly framed, with this university student functioning as a virtual language teaching assistant. Geoffrey, on the other hand, was less constrained by the framing of a lesson plan. There was evidence of his identity as a charismatic role model inspiring the pupils to independent action (e.g., downloading German music, renewed engagement with pen pals). Josephine's voice was the most weakly framed with the result that there was no tangible evidence of her impact on the school pupils.

The Adopt a Class scheme has proved to be a highly versatile and successful project that has been taken up across the Routes into Languages consortia. It is inexpensive—all three students in the case studies said that, although the £100 was welcome, they would have engaged in the project without the financial incentive—and it reaches a significant number of pupils, providing sustained intervention. The London Consortium has developed the sustained nature of the intervention further by holding Adopt a Class conferences (see Routes into Languages, 2017b).

The Adopt a Class model introduces a new voice into the classroom, additional linguistic input, a positive role model, and a vicarious experience of aspects of the year abroad. The activity of the SLAs may serve as an aid to recruitment to modern languages at GCSE and eventually to degrees in modern languages. For the students, the interaction with the school class serves as a stimulus to reflect critically on their experience of the year abroad. They are given a 'third space' (video, blog, vlog, email, Skype, and so forth) in which to articulate this creatively in an informal rather than an academic format, resulting in a more purposeful development of the students' linguistic and cultural awareness.

As is evident from the current three case studies, the Adopt a Class project releases energy and creativity, it enthuses and excites, and it has multiple benefits. However, there are challenges, the biggest of which is that demand from schools currently outstrips the supply of SLAs. This has been partly met by Global Graduates (2015) 'Inspire a class' scheme in which students are invited to post vlogs of their experiences abroad, but this scheme lacks the continuity of sustained intervention and interaction characteristic of the Adopt a Class model. Managing the expectations of both teachers and students can be problematic, not least in synchronising the school timetable with the work/study commitments of the student. The project is vulnerable to the vicissitudes of life, thus communication issues may arise as a result of changes in staffing at school. Nonetheless, the benefits of the Adopt a Class scheme far outweigh adverse administrative circumstances.

Typically, the year abroad in a UK context may be spent as a student at an exchange university, or as a British Council language teaching assistant, or on a work placement. The North East Consortium project demonstrates that the Adopt a Class model is suitable for all three activities. There could, however, be an especially strong alignment with the British Council language teaching assistant scheme, with the opportunities it provides for partnering school classes as part of the exercise.

For the future development of the project a careful balance needs to be struck between the 'strong framing' (Bernstein, 1975) of the project and the creative energy that the students bring to it. Universities in the UK spend considerable time preparing their students for the year abroad. However, this preparation is generally to do with practical matters (health and safety, insurance, visas, banking arrangements, and so forth) and academic requirements (essays, projects, dissertations, and so forth). What the Adopt a Class project requires for it to fulfil its potential is an explicit grounding in concepts of intercultural knowledge and competence, of transnational agency, coupled with pedagogic instruction in the dynamics of a Year Nine class group.

Summary of recommendations for a successful 'Adopt a Class' scheme
• Embed the scheme in the HEI's year abroad offer.
• Incorporate sessions into the preparation of the year abroad on intercultural knowledge and competence; transnational agency; effective virtual communication with Year Nine pupils.
• Where possible, draw on the expertise of MFL staff in the HEI's School of Education.
• Foster strong and reliable contacts between the project leader and the contact schoolteachers.
• Discuss with the schoolteachers the balance between strong and weak framing of the students' contributions.
• Create an event to celebrate the achievements of the project.

Appendix A: Adopt a Class—How It Works

Notes for Teachers

Reasons for Starting the Scheme

- A decrease of school exchanges and trips abroad
- Decrease of Foreign Language Assistants (FLAs) in schools

Aims of the Scheme

- Raise awareness amongst young people of student mobility opportunities.
- Bring a foreign language and culture to the classroom.
- Enthuse young people about studying languages.
- Support teachers in promoting MFL as an option in KS3.

Timeline

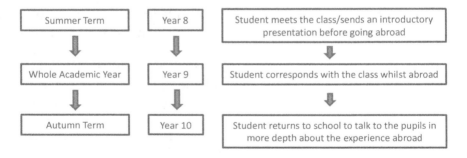

Example of Blogs

http://www.girlinrouen.blogspot.co.uk/
http://euroanticsfr.wordpress.com/

What Happens Next?

- You will receive notification of your pairing.
- You will arrange either with the student to visit the school or for them to send a presentation via email if this is not possible.
- You and the student will each receive a contract which you will need to sign and send back outlining the anticipated commitment from each of you.

Appendix B: Adopt a Class—How It Works

Notes for Students

Blogs and Diaries

It is important to bear in mind that many of the pupils (aged 13–14) will not have been abroad and will have had little to no exposure of foreign language or culture in its original context. It is really important to remember the target audience and to consider carefully what information you plan to share (this should be discussed with the teacher beforehand). Here are some ideas as to what you could discuss:

- What you ate for breakfast/lunch/dinner (elaborate—different from the usual?)
- What you will be doing that day (please keep stories of parties very brief!)
- Who you've met/new friends (from different parts of the world?)
- Interesting places you've visited/plan to visit
- Films/music/gigs/events you've seen/attended in the local area (include reviews?)
- Tips, for example, how to use public transport, tips you've picked up along the way

Include sections in the target language in order to challenge the pupils. Pupils like to see pictures of what you're discussing as it makes the experience come alive for them. Please ensure that these are appropriate at all times. Video blogs are also great!

Please also bear in mind that you should not interact directly with the pupils and so all communication should be between you and the teacher.

Resources

You may want to discuss with the teacher certain topics/themes which are being studied in order to select the correct type of resource. Here are some ideas of resources which you could send back to your class:

- Train/travel tickets and information
- Menus
- Newspaper/magazine cuttings (based on topics discussed with the teacher?)
- Postcards
- Local maps and tourist information

You can read about the success of the scheme in other consortia across England and Wales and access existing Adopt a Class blogs for inspiration. https://routeslanguageblog.wordpress.com/2013/05/03/find-out-more-about-adopt-a-class/

Notes

1. The role of the Skype Grannies has evolved further. They now provide 'big questions' that lead children to embark on intellectual adventures by engaging and connecting with information and mentoring online. In 2013, Professor Mitra won the TED prize (£1 million) to build a 'School in the Cloud', a series of learning laboratories across India and the UK where children can engage with a global community interested in experimenting with self-organised learning (see Newcastle University, 2017).
2. This module was established between 2010 and 2012 as a Routes into Languages legacy project, at a time when it was not clear whether there would be a second phase of funding for the Routes project.
3. Ofsted is the Office for Standards in Education, Children's Services and Skills. It inspects and regulates services that care for children and young people, and services providing education and skills for learners of all ages.

Bibliography

Al-Amri, M. (2012). *Adopt a class wins European language label.* Retrieved from http://routesintolanguagescymru.co.uk/adopt-a-class-wins-european-language-label/

Andersen, E., & O'Rourke Magee, R. (2013). Student ambassadors for languages in the UK context: From the extracurricular to the curricular. In J. L. Plews & B. Schmenk (Eds.), *Traditions and transitions: Curricula for German studies* (pp. 349–371). Waterloo, ON: Wilfrid Laurier University Press.

Bernstein, B. (1975). *Class, codes and control volume 3: Towards a theory of educational transmission* (2nd ed.). London: Routledge & Kegan Paul.

Board, K., & Tinsley, T. (2015). Language trends 2014/15. The state of language learning in primary and secondary schools in England. Retrieved from https://www.educationdevelopmenttrust.com/en-GB/our-research-library/2015/r-language-trends-2015

Byram, M., & Dervin, F. (Eds.). (2008). *Students, staff and academic mobility in higher education.* Newcastle upon Tyne: Cambridge Scholars.

Byram, M., & Feng, A. (Eds.). (2006). *Living and studying abroad. Research and practice.* Clevedon, UK: Multilingual Matters.

Clark, J., Hall, I., Leat, D., & Mitra, S. (2011). *Developing the potential of retired Skype mediators ('Skype Grannies').* Retrieved from http://www.ncl.ac.uk/ecls/research/project/3956

Coleman, J. A. (2007). A new framework for study abroad research. In C. Way, G. Soriano, D. Limon, & C. Amador (Eds.), *Enhancing the ERASMUS experience: Papers on student mobility* (pp. 37–46). Granada: Atrio.

Coleman, J. A. (2015). Social circles during year abroad: What students do and who with. In R. Mitchell, N. Tracy-Ventura, & K. McManus (Eds.), *Social interaction, identity and language learning during year abroad* (pp. 33–52). EuroSLA Monographs Series, Vol. 4. Retrieved from http://www.eurosla.org/eurosla-monograph-series-2/social-interaction-identity-and-language-learning-during-residence-abroad/

Department for Education and Skills. (2007). *Languages review.* Consultation Report. December 2006. Retrieved from https://www.education.gov.uk/consultations/downloadableDocs/6869-DfES-Language%20Review.pdf

Department of Education. (2017). Policy paper. *English baccalaureate (EBacc).* Retrieved from https://www.gov.uk/government/publications/english-baccalaureate-ebacc/english-baccalaureate-ebacc

Dolan, P., Leat, D., Mazzoli Smith, L., Mitra, S., Todd, L., & Wall, K. (2013). Self-organised learning environments (SOLEs) in an English school: An example of transformative pedagogy? *Online Educational Research Journal,* *3*(11). ISSN 2044-0294.

Dörnyei, Z. (2005). *The Psychology of the language learner: Individual differences in second language acquisition.* Mahwah, NJ: Lawrence Erlbaum.

Dörnyei, Z., & Ushioda, E. (Eds.). (2011). *Teaching and researching motivation.* Harlow: Pearson Education.

Dufon, M. A., & Churchill, E. (Eds.). (2006). *Language learners in study abroad contexts.* Clevedon: Multilingual Matters.

Global Graduates. (2015). Inspire a class! Retrieved from https://globalgraduates.com/articles/we-need-you-to-inspire-a-class

Hampton, C. (2015). Meeting in the virtual middle: Blending online and human resources to generate a year abroad community. In R. Mitchell, N. Tracy-Ventura, & K. McManus (Eds.), *Social interaction, identity and language learning during year abroad* (pp. 223–239). EuroSLA Monographs Series, Vol. 4. Retrieved from http://www.eurosla.org/eurosla-monograph-series-2/social-interaction-identity-and-language-learning-during-residence-abroad/

Hampton, C. (2016). Cultural discovery as a post-year abroad agent of change for UK modern language students. *Comparative and International Education, 45*(2), Article 3. Retrieved from https://ir.lib.uwo.ca/cie-eci/vol45/iss2/3/

Higher Education Funding Council for England. (2005). *Strategically important and vulnerable subjects.* Final report of the 2005 advisory group [Roberts Review]. Retrieved from http://www.hefce.ac.uk/pubs/hefce/2005/05_24

Isabelli-García, C. (2006). Study abroad social networks, motivation and attitudes: Implications for second language acquisition. In M. DuFon & E. Churchill (Eds.), *Language learners in study abroad contexts* (pp. 231–258). Clevedon, UK: Multilingual Matters.

Jackson, J. (2008). *Language, identity, and study abroad: Sociocultural perspectives.* London: Equinox.

Jackson, J. (2010). *Intercultural journeys: From study to year abroad.* Basingstoke, UK: Palgrave Macmillan.

Jackson, J. (2012). Education abroad. In J. Jackson (Ed.), *The Routledge handbook of language and intercultural communication* (pp. 449–463). Oxford: Routledge.

Kinginger, C. (2009). *Language learning and study abroad: A critical reading of research.* New York: Palgrave Macmillan.

Mitchell, R. F., Tracy-Ventura, N., & McManus, K. (2017). *Anglophone students abroad: Identity, social relationships and language learning.* New York: Routledge.

Newcastle University. (2017). *Sole Central*. Retrieved from http://www.ncl.ac.uk/solecentral/

Pellegrino Aveni, V. A. (2005). *Study abroad and second language use: Constructing the self*. Cambridge: Cambridge University Press.

Risager, K. (2012). Linguaculture and transnationality: The cultural dimensions of language. In J. Jackson (Ed.), *The Routledge handbook of language and intercultural communication* (pp. 101–115). Oxford: Routledge.

Routes into Languages. (2017a). Retrieved from https://www.routesintolanguages.ac.uk/

Routes into Languages. (2017b). London. Retrieved from https://routesintolanguages.ac.uk/activities/london

Shervill, S. (2012). Adopt a class—A route into languages. Retrieved from https://globalgraduates.com/articles/adopt-a-class-routes-into-languages

SQW. (2011). *Evaluation of routes into languages*. Final Report, 31 May 2011. Retrieved from http://www.sqw.co.uk/files/5013/8694/8185/10.pdf

Thomas, U., Leat, D., Comber, R., Finnigan, S., McHugh, A., Olivier, P., & Vincent-Lopez, P. (n.d.). *New voices in the classroom: An exploration of the impact of Skype seniors on curriculum and pedagogy*. Unpublished manuscript.

Second Language Speaking and Intercultural Friendship Formation in Study Abroad: Experiences and Perspectives of International Students in the USA

Rebecca K. Smith

Introduction

When language learners study abroad (SA), it is often assumed that their immersion in a host environment will inevitably lead to frequent interactions, new relationships or friendships, and rapid linguistic and intercultural development. This may be especially true regarding international students who enrol in foreign universities for extended periods, such as the 1,078,822 international students who were registered for higher education in the USA during the 2016/17 school year (Institute of International Education, 2017). However, as decades of research have indicated, participating in a SA programme does not automatically result in high levels of second language (L2) use outside of the classroom or

---

R. K. Smith (✉)
Lone Star College - Tomball, Tomball, TX, USA
e-mail: rebecca.k.smith@lonestar.edu

© The Authors(s) 2018
J. L. Plews, K. Misfeldt (eds.), *Second Language Study Abroad*,
https://doi.org/10.1007/978-3-319-77134-2_11

exceptional language gains (Kinginger, 2009). The same can be said of intercultural learning (Jackson, 2009). Because the quantity and quality of L2 interaction while studying abroad may have significant implications for both linguistic and intercultural outcomes, this chapter contributes to the body of SA research by investigating levels of L2 speaking in addition to how international and domestic students interact at an American university. By understanding if and how intercultural connections are formed, as well as any potential barriers to interaction, it may be possible to better assist SA participants in obtaining the maximum benefit from their experiences in a host country.

Context: Study Abroad in the USA and Global Citizenship

The issue of intercultural interaction in education has risen to the forefront in recent years, largely driven by surging populations of international students around the globe and the interconnectedness of an increasingly mobile global population. As these students have arrived on campuses to begin SA programmes in ever-increasing numbers, many scholars (e.g., Jackson, 2010; Ranta & Meckelborg, 2013; Tanaka, 2007; Zhang & Zhou, 2010) in the fields of applied linguistics and intercultural studies have become aware of the need to investigate how international and domestic students interact in educational settings. A primary goal of international study is for students to learn to function as global citizens by developing relationships across cultural boundaries, which will benefit both individuals and societies as students complete their programmes and either return to their homelands or remain as immigrants in the host country. As such, it is important to know if and how intercultural connections are being made, as well as to understand any potential barriers that could impede them.

The issue of intercultural communication is also relevant to the linguistic and intercultural development of students who are studying internationally. Those individuals who arrive for studies in a host country often hope to improve their L2 skills as they pursue other goals, such as obtaining a degree from a university. Many who study in the USA enrol in classes of English as a Second Language (ESL), either as a programme requirement or simply due to a desire to enhance their experiences. As valuable as classroom instruction may be to these L2 learners, they also have the opportunity while studying abroad to interact regularly with other speakers of the target language. These L2 interactions can be important to learners' linguistic development, providing rich and meaningful contexts for using the L2 and potentially leading to greater gains in language development. Many international students also have a desire to broaden their perspectives through intercultural interactions and hope to do so by forming relationships with local students while studying in the host country. As such, SA directors and instructors may be interested in finding ways to optimize learners' opportunities to have beneficial L2 interactions throughout the course of their SA experiences. If programmes successfully support students in these endeavours, they will be more likely to experience sustained interest and recruitment of new students in future years.

Literature Review: Second Language Interaction in Study Abroad

The idea that frequent L2 interactions impact SA participants' ultimate language development as well as intercultural awareness has been widely assumed due to its common-sense appeal. Early research did indicate that studying in an immersive setting can lead to L2 proficiency gains for many learners (Carroll, 1967). Additionally, some studies have suggested that SA participants may achieve greater gains than their counterparts in traditional foreign language classrooms, especially within the realms of oral fluency and vocabulary acquisition (e.g., Freed, 1995; Keppie, Lindberg, & Thomason, 2016; Segalowitz & Freed, 2004). These positive findings also coincide with Pérez-Vidal's (2014) edited volume, which contains several studies conducted with Spanish/Catalan learners of English in conjunction with the Barcelona Study Abroad and Language Acquisition project. The findings of these studies indicate that SA leads to improvements in many areas and has an advantage as opposed to traditional classroom instruction.

Gains were observed in areas such as fluency, oral accuracy, listening, and cultural awareness, though not in pronunciation.

There is also evidence that the amount of time spent speaking in the L2 on SA may directly impact proficiency levels. Initial research on the topic did not reveal a convincing connection between levels of out-of-class L2 use and proficiency (Freed, Segalowitz, & Dewey, 2004; Spada, 1986), but a more recent study using a longer study time and larger sample size demonstrated that there may be a significant positive correlation (Baker-Smemoe, Cundick, Evans, Henrichsen, & Dewey, 2012). Findings from other studies (Hernández, 2010; Segalowitz & Freed, 2004) have also suggested that learners' increased L2 usage on SA, as compared with learners in traditional language classrooms, may be connected to greater gains in speaking proficiency.

However, it is important to note that SA participants do not necessarily receive more L2 input than other learners might in some at-home language programmes, such as intensive immersion programmes (Freed et al., 2004). Many factors impact the level of L2 interactions, and those who travel abroad may frequently use their native or first language (L1) with friends or classmates. Research regarding time spent using the L1 as opposed to the target language is still tenuous; some studies have indicated that SA participants report using the L2 more than the L1 (Freed et al., 2004; cf. Ranta & Meckelborg, 2013), while others have found the opposite to be true (Trentman, 2013a). Additionally, participants at low proficiency levels in the L2 may experience fewer L2 gains from a SA experience (DeKeyser, 2010; Pérez-Vidal, 2014). Clearly, no two SA programmes are identical, and many variables—ranging from programme design (Bown, Dewey, & Belnap, 2015; Jackson, 2009) to the number of L1 speakers in the locale (Schwieter & Ferreira, 2016; Trentman, 2013b), individual goals and motivations (Hernández, 2010; Isabelli-García, 2006), positive or negative experiences (Tanaka, 2007; Ward & Masgoret, 2004), or social media (Mitchell, Tracy-Ventura, & McManus, 2017)—could impact the degree to which learners use their L1 and L2 while on SA.

Additionally, some research has indicated that the quality of L2 interactions may be more significant than the quantity. For example, a learner who regularly interacts in short conversations with new people may repeat the same common introductory topics, while repeated interactions with the same interlocutor may lead to more in-depth conversations on a variety of topics and allow for a wider range of vocabulary and grammatical structures. Since the formation of friendships often facilitates these types of advanced conversations, relationship formation may impact the quality of L2 interactions. A large-scale study of over 100 language learners participating in SA programmes in six different countries found that factors relating to the types of relationships learners formed with native speakers were more significantly related to proficiency gains than the amount of out-of-class L2 usage (Baker-Smemoe, Dewey, Bown, & Martinsen, 2014). For example, statistical analyses revealed that learners' social dispersion, or the number of social groups to which they belong, and the intensity, or closeness, of their relationships were significantly related to language development. This seems to indicate that simply using the target language outside of class is not sufficient to drive substantial linguistic gains. Instead, participation in many groups and the formation of close relationships may be necessary, as these enable learners to participate in frequent, meaningful L2 interactions.

Similar findings are reported in Isabelli-García's (2006) study involving qualitative data gathered from interviews and diary entries provided by four students on SA in Argentina. In this case, learners' success in developing strong social relationships while living in the host country was related to their ultimate language gains over the course of the SA, perhaps because the relationships provided increased opportunities for in-depth conversations in the L2. Mitchell et al. (2017) similarly reported, in a study of British students in France, Mexico, and Spain, that the formation of extensive L2 social networks was essential for significant linguistic gains while on SA. No participant in that study made high gains without either a single intensive network or multiple diverse networks, often including socializing in the L2 online. The formation of social networks created extensive opportunities for meaningful engagement in the L2. These results are supported by other studies finding a positive correlation between intercultural friendships and learners' L2 development as well as their general satisfaction with SA experiences (e.g., Rohrlich & Martin, 1991).

Developing intercultural relationships or friendships is not always an easy task, however. While research has shown that SA participants generally want to befriend native speakers of the target language, they often encounter difficulties such as intercultural differences, large co-national populations in the host country, low L2 proficiency, and poor relationships with host families (Bataller, 2010; DeKeyser, 2010; Gareis, Merkin, & Goldman, 2011; Trentman, 2013b). Many learners form no or few close friendships with host nationals while on SA; for example, one study at a university in New York City reported that 24 per cent of learners did not form friendships with native speakers (Gareis et al., 2011). Research regarding participant interactions has offered some insights into this lack of intercultural friendships. For instance, studies have found that some L2 learners struggled to bond with native-speaker students because they felt that their relationships were superficial and pursued merely for academic purposes (e.g., Bown et al., 2015; Trice & Elliott, 1993). In other cases, it was found that some learners gravitated towards other L2 speakers since they were more easily able to understand and support each other, causing them to group together rather than reach out to the host community (Carnine, 2016; Gareis et al., 2011). Clearly, merely ensuring that learners are in close spatial proximity to native speakers of the target language, such as by placing them with host families or enrolling them in classes with domestic students, is not always sufficient to facilitate frequent meaningful interactions or relationship development.

To better understand the complex sociocultural factors that impact individual SA experiences, Jackson (2009, 2010) used ethnographic research to investigate the language development and intercultural competence of Chinese students from Hong Kong learning English on a short-term SA in the UK. Other researchers have indicated that learners' perceptions of their own and the host community's cultural identities may impact motivation and L2 use while on SA (Isabelli-García, 2006; Kinginger, 2013), and Jackson expands on this by closely examining participants' levels of ethnocentrism or ethnorelativism and the ways in which this measure of cultural competency interacts with L2 use and overall SA experiences. Individuals who are more ethnocentric generally deny or minimize cultural differences, or insist that one group is superior. They may have more negative feelings towards the host culture or be less open to learning about cultural differences, potentially leading to less L2 interaction. In contrast, those who have progressed to ethnorelativism tend to acknowledge and accept differences in cultures, recognizing the role they play in individual and group identities, which leads to greater acceptance of L2 interactions and relationships. While Jackson found that most learners moved towards ethnorelativism over time, it is possible for a student to regress and end the programme with more negative views regarding the host community (2009). Further, while intercultural competence does affect patterns of L2 use, gains in L2 proficiency do not necessary correlate with increased cultural development (Jackson, 2010).

In sum, previous research has established that while SA can be highly beneficial for both linguistic and cultural development, some SA participants do not necessarily have high levels of L2 interaction throughout their time in the host country and are not always successful at forming intercultural relationships with native L2 speakers. Many theories have been developed to explain differences in SA experiences, including the amount of L2 input, the social networks developed with L2 speakers, and participants' levels of intercultural competency. In light of the continued increase in international student numbers worldwide, and especially in the USA, and given the fact that a core aim of international education is to develop and consolidate global citizenship and understanding, further exploration into participants' own perspectives on these key components of SA is necessary. As such, this study examines patterns of L2 speaking, intercultural friendship formation, and participant reflections on their experiences in order to better understand the underlying factors that could either inhibit or facilitate successful interaction and the formation of intercultural relationships in an immersive environment.

Methodology

A mixed-methods approach was chosen for this study in order to examine the ways in which SA participants used the L2 outside of class and to gain insight into their perspectives on intercultural interaction. Quantitative data gathered from a repeated questionnaire include information about L2 speaking and types of intercultural relationships formed, as these can be measured and numerically reported. Qualitative data regarding participants' experiences with intercultural interaction, which cannot be easily encapsulated and measured, were gathered through written journal entries.

Both types of analysis are useful for this study since the qualitative analysis provides vital information on factors such as motivations, challenges, and facilitators that may explain differences in the measured frequency of L2 speaking and success in forming relationships for each participant.

Programme and Participants

This study was undertaken with 32 participants, all of whom were international students at a medium-sized private university in central New York State. This number represents approximately 0.8 per cent of international students enrolled at this institution on average in a given year. The participants were degree-seeking students who were required to complete a series of for-credit ESL classes to supplement their regular coursework. The purpose of the ESL programme was to provide additional support in academic English and to satisfy a general education writing requirement. During the semester in which the current study was conducted, the participating students were enrolled in an upper-intermediate writing class, the third in a sequence of six core ESL courses; they had been assigned to this particular level due to their scores on an English placement exam taken upon arrival in the USA immediately prior to the start of the semester. This course focussed heavily on reading, writing, and critical thinking in order to equip the students with skills needed for success in their other university classes. As international students, the participants were fully immersed in the university community—taking a full schedule of classes, living in dormitories alongside domestic and other international students, and participating in university and community activities, such as student clubs, athletics, and seasonal festivals.

As shown in Table 1, the participants' ages ranged from 18 to 30, but the vast majority (88 per cent) were between 18 and 20 years old. There was a nearly even split between male and female participants, with 47 per cent male and 53 per cent female; this gender division differs slightly from that of the university as a whole, in which 56 per cent of international students were male and 44 per cent were female. While all of the participants were in their first semester at the university and most were freshmen, four had prior university experience: two were undergraduate transfer students from another US university, and two were graduate students. Additionally, most participants had entered the USA immediately before the semester, but a total of nine had spent time in the USA prior to entering university. Eight of these had been high school exchange students, and one was a refugee who had been in the USA for 10 years. Twenty-six participants were Chinese, two were South Korean, and there was one participant from each of Brazil, France, Iran, and Iraq. This demographic pattern, with a large majority of Chinese students, reflects the overall population of international students at the university as well as general trends among international students throughout the USA in recent years; in the 2016/17 academic year, Chinese students made up 32.5 per cent of the international student population and were by far the largest national group studying in the USA (Institute of International Education, 2017). Each participant was assigned a number and a pseudonym, as indicated in Table 1; the numbers are used in the discussion of quantitative results below, while both numbers and pseudonyms are used in reporting the qualitative findings.

Data Collection

To gather a range of information regarding the participants' L2 spoken interaction and intercultural relationships, a survey was administered halfway through the semester (week 7) and again at the end of the semester (week 15). The survey, consisting of a background information profile as well as a series of items related to language use, was adapted from the Language Contact Profile (see Appendix A), which has been used successfully by researchers in a variety of language learning environments (e.g., Baker-Smemoe et al., 2012; Freed et al., 2004). Further survey items (see questions 14–17 in the adapted Language Contact Profile) were added to ascertain the types of relationships that students formed and thus to obtain more quantitative data with which to enable an evaluation of how participants interacted with native English speakers. (Because this study was designed to explore how international students interacted with domestic students, the survey questions asked specifically about friendships with native English speakers. As a result, intercultural friendships

Table 1 Demographic information of participants

	Pseudonym	Gender	Age	Country of origin
1	Ji-min	F	19	South Korea
2	Liufang	F	18	China
3	Wangjie	M	20	China
4	Linqin	F	18	China
5	Mingzhu	F	20	China
6	Chenglei	M	18	China
7	Guozhi	M	18	China
8	Jingfei	F	19	China
9	Biyu	F	18	China
10	Seo-yun	F	20	South Korea
11	Wangyan	F	19	China
12	Liwei	M	20	China
13	Nasim	M	23	Iraq
14	Quinfan	M	20	China
15	Meifeng	F	18	China
16	Hualing	F	18	China
17	Jinhai	M	19	China
18	Lina	F	19	China
19	Lijing	F	18	China
20	Zhangwei	M	19	China
21	Zhangjun	M	19	China
22	Huidai	F	22	China
23	Shen	M	18	China
24	Tengfei	M	19	China
25	Daiyu	F	18	China
26	Camille	F	18	France
27	Yanlin	M	18	China
28	Jiang	M	18	China
29	Jianjun	M	20	China
30	Sahar	F	30	Iran
31	Mariana	F	28	Brazil
32	Xueqin	M	18	China

with non-native English speakers are not represented in this analysis. Given the reality of our global and multilingual world, further research in this area should explore SA participants' intercultural relationships with both fluent and native speakers.)

Descriptive statistics were used to analyse the quantitative data, providing information on participants' use of spoken English as opposed to their native or other languages, as well as their success in forming relationships with native English speakers. Taken as a whole, the results of this survey allow for an understanding of the quantity and general quality of L2 interaction in which the participants engaged across the semester. It must be noted that the data regarding amounts of language use are self-reported estimates that may be either over- or underestimated and should not be used to draw conclusions regarding actual time spent using the L2. Nevertheless, they do provide useful insight into the participants' own perceptions and allow for comparisons between learners.

Qualitative data were gathered through free-writing exercises in which the learners were encouraged to reflect on their language development and intercultural interactions and experiences as international students. The exercises took the form of ten journal entries written in English on a near-weekly basis in response to targeted writing prompts (see Appendix B). The exercises were in fact also part of their coursework, aimed specifically at providing both writing practice and a way for participants to process their linguistic and general experiences as they adjusted to attending a university while living in a new culture. The journal entries were analysed qualitatively, based on the coding procedures outlined by Corbin and Strauss (2008). This analysis offers useful insight into the participants' experiences and attitudes, allowing for a greater understanding of how various factors may have shaped certain patterns of L2 intercultural interaction throughout the semester.

Results and Discussion

The quantitative results are presented below, followed by the qualitative. Frequency of L2 speaking is discussed first, with analysis of responses to two survey items; the first asked participants to indicate how many days per week they spoke English outside of class, and the second asked for an estimate of the percentage of total speaking, on an average day, that was in English, a native language, or another language. Results are also presented from a survey item in which participants indicated whether they had formed various types of relationships with native English speakers. The subsequent qualitative analysis presents insight into factors that may have affected levels of L2 usage and participants' success in forming intercultural relationships. These factors include motivations for L2 use, positive and negative intercultural experiences, challenges faced, and facilitators of L2 interactions.

Quantitative Analysis: L2 Speaking and Intercultural Relationship Formation

Target Language Speaking

Analysis of the survey data revealed that most participants reported speaking the L2 outside of class on a daily basis, as displayed in Fig. 1.

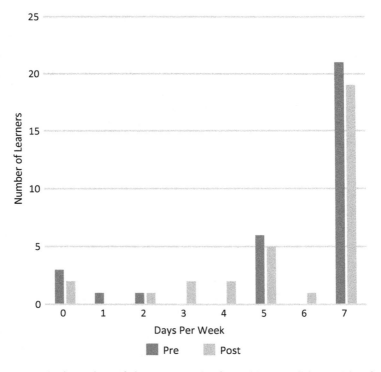

Fig. 1 Reported number of days per week of speaking English outside of class. Note: *Pre* refers to the results from the initial survey, and *Post* to those from the final survey

When the initial survey was administered midway through the semester, 21 out of the 32 students (65 per cent) indicated speaking English outside of class every day; at the end of the semester, this number had decreased slightly to 19 participants (59 per cent). Furthermore, an even greater majority reported speaking in the L2 outside of class at least 5 days per week—27 participants (84 per cent) in the first survey and 25 (78 per cent) in the second. Despite frequent L2 usage among the majority, a substantial minority—35 per cent initially, and 41 per cent by the end of the semester—did not have daily out-of-class L2 speaking. Moreover, three (nine per cent) indicated that they used English outside of class zero days per week mid-semester, and two (6 per cent) said the same at the end of the term.

There are a few differences with regards to gender, age, and nationality. Males reported speaking English daily at slightly higher rates than females. Of the 15 male participants, 11 (73 per cent) indicated that they spoke English outside of class 7 days per week in the initial survey, with ten (67 per cent) reporting the same in the final survey. In comparison, ten out of 17 female participants (59 per cent) initially and nine out of 17 (53 per cent) in the second survey gave the same response. Additionally, two females and one male reported speaking English zero days per week when the survey was first given, and those numbers changed only slightly to one female and one male by the end of the semester.

With regards to age and nationality, all three of the participants who reported never speaking English outside of class, at either point in the semester, were 18 years old and were Chinese. However, there was little difference in the percentages of younger and older students reporting 7 days per week of speaking English out of class, with 64 per cent of the 14 18-year-olds and 67 per cent of the 18 older students giving this response in the first survey; in the second survey, the results were 57 per cent for the younger group and 61 per cent for the older group. Only two participants were over the age of 23, and each of these students reported using English outside of class at least 5 days per week on both iterations of the survey. However, these two students—S31, aged 28, and S30, aged 30—were Brazilian and Iranian, respectively. Since these two were from minority groups among the university-wide body of international students, their nationalities, in addition to their ages, could have led them to speak English more often.

Out of the six non-Chinese participants, only two reported speaking English fewer than 5 days per week on either of the surveys: S13, from Iraq, reported 2 days per week initially and 7 finally, and S10, from South Korea, reported 5 days per week initially and 3 finally. S13 was a refugee who lived off-campus with his family, which could explain his low initial response. As a whole, the majority of both Chinese and non-Chinese students reported using English outside of class at least 5 days per week: 85 per cent of Chinese students mid-semester and 77 per cent at the end of the semester, compared with 83 per cent of non-Chinese students at both points in the semester. As such, although Chinese students likely had more opportunities to interact with co-nationals in their native language, it appears that participants of all nationalities were speaking English to some extent outside of class on a daily or near-daily basis.

Additional insight is gained from the participants' estimates of the average percentage of their daily speaking, both in and out of class, that was in English. These self-reported percentages do not provide information about the actual amount of time that English was spoken by the participants, but they do provide a general understanding of how frequently they used English in comparison with their native or other languages. The percentages reported varied widely, as displayed in Fig. 2. On the initial survey, one participant (S1), a 19-year-old South Korean woman, reported almost never using English to speak with others, only 0.1 per cent of her speaking, while another (S32), an 18-year-old Chinese man, reported using it almost exclusively (98 per cent). On the final survey, the range in numbers was slightly less extreme, with S1's reported percentage at eight per cent and S32's at 90 per cent.

Although there were a few high percentages—three participants reported using English for at least 70 per cent of their speaking at both points in the semester—the majority indicated that they did not speak English as their primary language for all tasks in and out of class on an average day, and there was a general decline over time. The overall mean percentage was below 50 per cent in both surveys (40.1 per cent initially, decreasing slightly to 37.3 per cent finally), and only seven participants (22 per cent) reported using English for more than 50 per cent of their speaking in both the initial and the final survey. These results indicate that while the participants may have spoken in English on a daily basis,

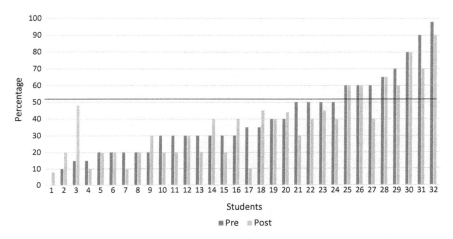

Fig. 2 Reported percentages of English speaking on an average day. Note: *Pre* refers to the results from the initial survey, and *Post* to those from the final survey

most were not using it as their primary language. Additionally, while eight participants did have a substantial increase over time in the percentage they reported, there was a general trend of reporting constant or lower percentages of English speaking at the end of the semester. As a whole, only 25 per cent of learners indicated using a higher percentage of English for their speaking at the end of the semester than in the middle, while 28 per cent remained constant and 47 per cent indicated a lower percentage. Even among those who reported speaking English more than 50 per cent of the time, four out of seven reported a decrease.

Notably, of the seven learners who reported using English for more than 50 per cent of their speaking at both points in the semester, three were non-Chinese. Since there were only six non-Chinese participants included in the study, this means that half (50 per cent) of the non-Chinese learners reported using English more often than another language, while only four out of 26 Chinese nationals (15 per cent) reported similarly high rates of English usage. Additionally, out of the four participants who were neither Chinese nor Korean, only one reported using English less than 50 per cent of the time. On average, non-Chinese participants indicated that they used English for 48 per cent of their speaking in the initial survey and 43 per cent of their speaking in the final survey. These results are higher than those reported by the Chinese participants, who had a mean of 38 per cent on the initial survey and 36 per cent on the final survey. However, the percentage of English speaking decreased more for the non-Chinese than for the Chinese participants, with average decreases of five and two per cent, respectively.

Since there were many opportunities for interacting with native English speakers in this immersion context, it is not surprising that 65 per cent of participants reported speaking in English 7 days per week even at the beginning of the study. However, the fact that a substantial minority reported never speaking the L2 outside of class, or speaking it only a few days per week, suggests that not all participants took full advantage of those opportunities. Additionally, since only 22 per cent of participants reported using the L2 for the majority of their speaking on an average day throughout the research period, most used other languages more frequently; this corresponds with Trentman's (2013a) finding that American SA participants learning Arabic in Egypt used the L2 less often than their native language. This result may lend support to the notion that when learners have access to speakers of their native language while on SA, as was particularly the case for the Chinese in this study, they are not forced to use the target language as frequently and may therefore spend less time using it than is often assumed (see also Freed et al., 2004; Schwieter & Ferreira, 2016). It is also possible that L2 interactions were not a primary motivator for every participant, as some may have believed that their academic language skills were sufficient and were focussed more on their degree path than on linguistic or cultural development.

It is also noteworthy that overall English speaking decreased throughout the course of the study. Participants may have been more enthusiastic about interacting in the L2 earlier in the semester, when the SA experience was still relatively fresh. Additionally, since friendships and social groups are often established early in the semester in a college setting, as students are first introduced in dormitories and classrooms, participants may have initially had more frequent social interactions with new L2 interlocutors. As social circles solidified over time, participants may have devoted less effort to seeking out opportunities to interact with native L2 speakers, particularly if they had been discouraged by early attempts.

This may have been especially true for participants who had access to large groups of co-nationals and could have become content with the intracultural relationships they had formed, therefore reducing their motivation to interact with native L2 speakers; a similar pattern was found with Chinese SA participants in France in a study by Carnine (2016). Busy schedules at the end of the semester, when the final survey was administered, could also have caused the learners to report lower percentages of spoken English, since they may have had less time for socializing in general, and since it has been suggested that engagement in cultural and social activities may be an important factor in target language usage for SA participants (Hernández, 2010).

Relationships with Native Speakers

Survey data regarding participants' intercultural relationships provide additional information regarding socialization patterns. In the survey, participants indicated whether they knew native English speakers that they would describe as acquaintances, friends, or close friends. The understanding of these terms inevitably varies between cultures and individuals, as requirements for a friendship or relationship at any level will differ according to social norms and individual preferences. Brief definitions of each term were provided in the survey: acquaintances were described as people 'that you see occasionally but don't know well', friends as those 'that you know well but don't see often', and close friends as 'friends that you see often'. Further interpretation of the terms was left to individual participants, meaning that the data cannot be extrapolated to describe the exact nature of any relationship that was reported. The data do reveal, however, how the participants viewed their intercultural relationships.

As displayed in Table 2, when the survey was first administered midsemester, 25 participants (78 per cent) reported having native English-speaking acquaintances, 20 (63 per cent) reported having friends, and 14 (44 per cent) reported having close friends. By the end of the semester, the number of participants in each of these categories had increased, with 29 (90 per cent) reporting acquaintances, 24 (75 per cent) reporting

Table 2 Reported relationships with native speakers

	Acquaintances	Friends	Close friends	Any type	All types
Pre	25 (78%)	20 (63%)	14 (44%)	30 (94%)	12 (38%)
Post	29 (90%)	24 (75%)	17 (53%)	32 (100%)	15 (47%)

Note: *Pre* refers to the results from the initial survey, and *Post* to those from the final survey. Each category (*Acquaintances*, *Friends*, and *Close Friends*) refers to the number and percentage of students who reported having at least one relationship of the indicated type. *Any Type* includes participants who reported having at least one acquaintance, friend, or close friend, and *All Types* includes those who reported having at least one of each type of relationship

friends, and 17 (53 per cent) reporting close friends. Additionally, all 32 participants reported having at least one close friend, friend, or acquaintance by the end of the semester. However, this does not mean that all had formed relationships at each level; in the first iteration of the survey, only 12 (38 per cent) reported having at least one relationship in each of the three categories, with that number increasing to 15 (47 per cent) in the second iteration.

It is encouraging to see that the reported numbers of relationships with native English speakers increased from the initial survey to the final survey, indicating that many participants were regularly using the L2 in social settings and were successful in developing intercultural relationships throughout the course of the semester. The development of a friendship is often a slow process that can require numerous repeated encounters with the same individual before it becomes strong and lasting, so it is logical that more friendships would be reported after a longer time in the host country. It should be noted that participants were less likely to have established relationships with native L2 speakers at closer social levels than at more distant levels. While two participants reported having friends or close friends but no acquaintances, in general, far more students reported having acquaintances than close friends. Significantly, only a few participants (22 per cent initially and 10 per cent finally) reported no native English-speaking acquaintances, while about half of the participants reported having no close friendships at either stage in the data collection (56 per cent and 47 per cent, respectively) and one quarter (25 per cent) reported still having no friendships with native speakers by the end of the study.

As mentioned previously, while each participant likely understands the terms 'acquaintance', 'friend', and 'close friend' differently, this means that substantial minorities of participants did not feel that they had developed true friendships with native L2 speakers during their first semester abroad. This finding aligns with previous research indicating that many SA participants struggle to form intercultural friendships, despite a desire to do so (Ward & Masgoret, 2004), and it closely mirrors a finding from Gareis et al. (2011) that 24 per cent of learners at a New York City university did not form friendships with native L2 speakers while studying abroad. Since close friendships can be expected to provide a rich environment for high-quality conversations and greater intercultural learning, the students without these types of relationships could be at a disadvantage regarding linguistic and cultural growth.

Qualitative Analysis: Participant Perspectives

Qualitative analysis of the participants' SA experiences as reflected in journal entries helps explain their intercultural interactions and patterns of L2 usage. It is clear from the journal entries that most participants wanted to have significant interactions with native or fluent English speakers while on SA. For example, participants make comments such as 'I think it is super necessary and helpful for us to make more American friends' (Guozhi, S7) and 'Making more American friends can be my goal and my wish in this semester' (Biyu, S9). However, as the quantitative data reveal, not all participants were successful in establishing intercultural friendships or speaking regularly in the L2. Although there are certainly complex factors that shaped each participant's experience, the qualitative data revealed common motivations for intercultural interaction, positive and negative experiences, typical challenges, and facilitators of intercultural communication.

Motivations

From the journal entries, it appears that many participants had linguistic motivations for intercultural interaction; many shared a desire to meet Americans in order to improve their English skills. For example, learners write that having American friends would provide 'more chance to speak English' (Liufang, S2), the opportunity to improve 'oral English speaking' (Biyu, S9), and the ability to 'improve my English speaking, learn other slang words, and learn American style gestures' (Liwei, S12). The learners wanted to develop their skills and believed that interacting in English would allow them to do so. Tengfei (S24) shares that even though his schedule is so busy that he often does not have time to socialize, he is able to speak with friends in the dining hall. He says that in that setting 'each of us know we have time to talk unlike just greeting when we meet', providing him with the opportunity to develop his speaking skills beyond the level of superficial greetings or small talk. Similarly, Chenglei (S6) writes about the advantages of having American friends by stating, 'I can also practice my English speaking and study how to communicate with others.' It appears that these participants valued intercultural interactions and friendships for the practical purpose of being able to develop their language skills.

Additionally, some participants had psychological and sociocultural motivations for interacting in the L2, indicating that developing intercultural relationships could help them adapt to their new social environment and fit in with their fellow students. Some write that they feel like outsiders and believe that gaining American friends might allow them to feel more comfortable. Liufang (S2) expresses this sentiment when she writes, 'As an international student, the most dominantly emotional challenge is that I always feel different.' She goes on to say that she hopes to befriend some of her native-speaker classmates so she would not feel so different as the only international student in some of her classes. Others also write about how forming intercultural relationships could help them adapt, such as Daiyu (S25), who says that having more friends would help to 'give me the sense of belonging', and Biyu (S9), who explains, 'I think I can fit in the new life in the USA by making more American friends. Many things here are different from China, so having someone can help you fit in must be a happy thing.' It thus seems that many of the participants wanted to integrate into their new host environment and felt that forming intercultural friendships would help them navigate the unfamiliar setting and ultimately feel less like outsiders at the university.

Many participants also demonstrated a motivation to expand their cultural knowledge and awareness, seemingly recognizing the value of cross-cultural interaction for the sake of increasing intercultural understanding. Several journal entries discussed the idea that interacting with people from around the world can 'expand the vision and widen the horizon', as Lijing (S19) states. For example, Meifeng (S15) writes that, although it can be difficult to build intercultural relationships, she wants to have 'more American friends and friends from other countries' because 'it seems important for to know more about the people around the world. Communicating with diverse people can open my eyes'. Although these comments, and others like them, are vague in their mention of expanded horizons and broadened perspectives, they nevertheless indicate an appreciation of the cultural knowledge that can be gained through cross-cultural interaction.

Other participants were more specific, describing favourable elements of American culture that they had noticed since beginning their international studies. Wangyan (S11), for instance, describes how her experiences interacting with friends in the USA have taught her to 'always have positive attitude in any situation'. Several others indicated a perception of general politeness and friendliness, such as when Ji-min (S1) writes, 'One thing I admire about American culture is that people are just so nice to each other even though they do not know who they are. People here say hi to anyone and to everyone. They are really friendly.' Additionally, Liwei (S12) says that 'I was surprised that American holds the door for the next person. I noticed that is the basic manner because the most Americans hold the door when they leave. It means that Americans caring other people even if they do not know each other.'

Though practices such as greeting strangers on campus or holding doors may be common social rituals for members of the host culture in this study, the participants interpreted them through a lens of intercultural awareness and concluded that they represented positive cultural traits. Some participants indicate that this perceived friendliness helped to facilitate the formation of intercultural relationships. For example, Tengfei (S24) writes, 'I have to say get friends here is not that difficult. … Most of them are more friendly and warmer.' From entries such as these, it appears that many recognized the cultural benefits that can come from intercultural interaction in general, and some offered examples of specific lessons they had gained through their personal experiences. These participants appear to have achieved a high degree of intercultural awareness, with the ability to critique their own and other cultures. This is reflected in an entry from Yanlin (S27), which states, 'It is important to make friends with people from different cultures. It helps me to realize the real world instead of the world I imagined. … The part of culture that I think is better than my country could help me to find out the solution or just wrongness in my culture.' This quote suggests that the participant is moving from the realm of speculation about culture towards actual knowledge, which could facilitate problem-solving and more effective and empathetic (inter)cultural encounters.

Experiences

While participants had compelling motivations to interact in the L2, their experiences in interacting across cultural boundaries varied extensively. For some, formal language learning and linguistic challenges hindered successful intercultural encounters; many report that they had a difficult time communicating with fluent L2 speakers because they lacked casual, as opposed to academic, vocabulary and structures, and they struggled to understand rapid, natural speech. For instance, Tengfei (S24) says, 'When I first met my roommate, he said "what's up", I was frozen when I heard it. What does the "what's up" mean? I have never learned it in high school class, how should I respond? That is embarrassing right?' Although all the participants had studied academic English for years, prior learning for many had likely focussed on grammar, reading, writing, and examinations rather than authentic communication, creating difficulties in their attempts to interact. Similarly, Chenglei (S6) says that one of the main reasons why 'it is difficult for me to make friends with Americans' was the 'language problem which I often cannot completely understand their meaning if they talk too fast or use some words that I do not know.'

In these instances in which participants found that they did not understand or know how to respond, some reported feelings of anxiety or embarrassment. As Huidai (S22) writes, 'Language is also an impediment for me. Since my oral English is not good enough, I cannot completely understand conversations that include a large number of slangs and idioms. When I chatting with my roommate, I feel extremely jittery because I cannot completely understand what she exactly talking about.' Guozhi (S7) also writes about his struggles to converse in casual conversations, stating, 'I found that there are still many obstacles when I talking with an American, especially with those … who speak so fast that I even can't understand what he or she was talking about. When meeting those trouble, I felt super upset and embarrassed.' These reports of embarrassment and difficulty communicating did decrease as the semester progressed, but it is clear that a lack of linguistic knowledge and skills impacted participants' attempts to interact with and befriend native speakers. Some may have been able to overcome this challenge as their oral and speaking skills improved over time, but others may have been intimidated and less likely to engage in intercultural interaction.

In contrast to these negative experiences, many positive intercultural encounters were reported, particularly towards the latter half of the semester. Several participants mention that fluent L2 speakers were kind and encouraging as they attempted to communicate in English and that their skills improved over time. For instance, Liufang (S2) writes that she intends to 'try to talk with American students' more often since she recognizes that 'they never pick my grammar mistake' when she speaks with them. Huidai (S22) also writes about having supportive conversation partners that help her improve her linguistic and pragmatic skills, stating, 'I always try to talks with my roommates and my dorm neighbours. I always ask them about the slangs and idioms I don't know and discuss about the culture difference I have met.' As a result of these types of positive interactions, many students appeared to gain confidence over time. As Mariana (S31) explains, 'During these past few weeks I could get more used to the language, so the conversations are better. I am able to understand people a little bit more than what I used to.'

Additionally, many participants report that through their L2 interactions, they began to better understand the host culture and to develop a sense of belonging. Tengfei (S24) writes, 'I have a great American roommate, and his friends and other Americans all treat me really good. They taught me a lot of things about American culture.' Shen (S23) expresses a similar sentiment when he states, 'Making lots of local American friends bring me lots of joy and make me have far more understanding about American culture.' Because of these positive encounters, some participants indicate that they were adjusting to the new environment. As Huidai (S22) explains, 'By the process of conquering setbacks ... I have courage to chat with my roommates and ask questions in classes. I could see that I make visible progress in not only study but also adaptation.'

This sense of adaptation and belonging was often mentioned in connection with friendship, indicating that the participants who were successful in establishing intercultural relationships were also likely to feel comfortable in the host culture. Linqin (S4) writes, 'Comparing to the beginning of the semester, I really get used to live here and make friends here. ... I am so thankful for them, my dear friends and people who say "Hi" to me, people who hold the door for me and people who answer my question.' Similarly, Daiyu (S25) explains that 'I met some American friends here, and some of them from other country like Spain and Mexico. ... I made friends here by being myself. I feel good here to be surrounded by people and this gives me the sense of belonging.' A third example comes from Wangjie (S3), who reports significant increases in levels of L2 speaking over the course of the study. This student describes feeling nervous initially, but making an effort to 'talk to [Americans] frequently'. He goes on to say that 'soon, we became friends and I got to fit into this culture fast. Things went on really well.' These journal entries illustrate that many participants experienced successful intercultural interactions, with regard to the development of both linguistic and intercultural competencies, throughout the SA experience.

Challenges

One challenge that may have impacted participants' degree of success in interacting in the L2 relates to differences in social practices, reflected in their reports of struggling to understand common patterns of behaviour in the host environment, particularly with regard to initiating and maintaining friendships. Many seem unsure of how to find friends at the university. For instance, Huidai (S22) writes, 'The way we making friends is completely different. American are more prone to make friends through clubs, parties or other social activities, but we more like the traditional ways. For example, new friends are usually introduced by our old friends.' Jinhai (S17) agrees, stating, 'Americans enjoy holding parties with their friends, while we Chinese tend to stay in our room, playing video game and connecting with friends online.' These comments highlight a specific challenge for SA participants in the USA—navigating the party culture that is a major aspect of socialization on many college campuses but that is quite foreign to many SA participants. As Linqin (S4) writes, 'Another thing making me confused is that why people always like parties. … They seem not fun at all.'

Significantly, a few learners from each class describe feeling that they had not made friends because they did not attend enough parties. Near the start of the semester, Jingfei (S8) writes, 'Last Friday night when I'm about to sleep, the people live next to my room ask me to play outside, and I said I'm too sleepy to go. He seems kind of do not understand me why I need to go to sleep that early on Friday night and I do disappointed him.' Later on in the semester, this same participant writes that she had struggled to befriend Americans, writing, 'They have invited us several times to parties, and we said no because it was our time to sleep. In my hometown, I don't think people will not become friend if they miss some parties.' Although this participant wanted to make friends, she felt that her decision to follow her custom of going to bed relatively early instead of attending parties made it difficult for her to connect with others in her dormitory, thus hindering her attempts to establish lasting intercultural relationships. While there are surely individual differences among the participants, it is apparent that many viewed these distinct social patterns—such as meeting spontaneously at parties versus being formally introduced—as deeply entrenched and incompatible cultural practices. A lack of willingness to be flexible or adapt to the host culture in this regard may have influenced participants' success in forming relationships and using the L2 while studying abroad.

Furthermore, the journal entries reveal that a lack of common interests or shared knowledge of popular culture may have inhibited the development of close and meaningful intercultural friendships. Some participants describe challenging encounters and attribute their difficulties interacting with American peers to having different interests and little shared knowledge in areas such as music, television, religion, and politics. As Wangjie (S3) explains, 'It is pretty hard to be real friends with American kids. I think that's because the culture is just so different that we don't have enough common topics.' Humour also proved to be a challenge. Huidai (S22) states, 'Since the remarkable culture difference, I cannot understand the punch line of my roommate's joke. ... We treat things differently, we joke differently, so it's difficult for us to get along.' The vastly different socialization histories and cultural backgrounds of these participants and their interlocutors appear to have presented a substantial challenge for many; without sufficient interest from all parties, it is difficult to have meaningful conversations that lead to the formation of close relationships.

The journals also provide insight into negative impressions that many participants have regarding American culture, which could have affected their willingness to form friendships. One common theme was that many felt their interactions with Americans seemed superficial; they were confused by Americans treating them as friends upon first meeting but not having a close or lasting friendship follow from those initial interactions. Jingfei (S8) writes, 'When we moved in the first time, people said hello all the time and acted very friendly to us. However, a month later, most of them were tired of being as friendly as we met the first time. We just pass by each other as if we were invisible. I don't know what happened.' Others explain that they were accustomed to fewer friendly interactions between strangers or acquaintances in their home countries but that they took the relationships they did form there more seriously, as opposed to the wide but shallow networks of friendships they observed among their American peers. Camille (S26) summarizes this sentiment, stating, 'It's very superficial, when you meet someone you can have fun with him or her, but that's all. ... That's why you can say that in one hand it's easy to make friend with American people ... but it's the American definition of "friends". So if you want to make good or deep friends like in France, it's not so easy.' This dissatisfaction with 'superficial' intercultural friendships coincides with similar findings from Zhang and Zhou (2010) and Carbaugh (2005), indicating that perceptions of cultural and social differences have a significant effect on relationship formation. Many participants seem to have been disappointed when the types of friendships they may have anticipated early on did not materialize, and this frustration could have made it difficult to pursue further relationships.

In addition to misunderstandings of social practices and insufficient knowledge of how to respond appropriately in the host culture, negative stereotypes impeded successful intercultural interactions for some participants. For these participants, negative perspectives and lack of cultural understanding appear to have contributed to a perspective of cultural difference as a deep rift preventing the establishment of successful relationships. This is reflected in a journal entry from Wangyan (S11), who bluntly writes that the main reason why she has few American friends is because 'we are too different when we think to become a close friend'. Jingfei (S8) took a similarly rigid approach, referencing the idea of divergent worldviews between cultures when she states, 'There are a plenty of differences that make us think in different ways. We are forming our thinking pattern according to the environment since we were born.' These types of inflexible perspectives indicate that, for some participants, cultural differences were seen as insurmountable obstacles and were offered as an explanation for unsuccessful attempts to socialize, despite the fact that it was perhaps an unwillingness to compromise, rather than the presence of difference, that prevented more positive outcomes.

Aside from these challenges related to social and cultural differences, it is important to consider the impact that co-national friendships can have on intercultural interaction. Even though many participants wrote about their desires to form relationships with Americans, a few mentioned that it was easier to form friendships with those from a shared cultural and linguistic background and that doing so helped them manage the unique challenges of SA, such as culture shock, loneliness, and homesickness. Mingzhu (S5) writes, 'Before I came to America, I am afraid of being alone. However, I made a lot of Chinese friends there.' This learner goes on to explain that she 'really want[ed] to have more American friends', but that she often spent time with people from her home country because it was easier to form relationships without having to overcome 'the language problems [that] make us have some difficulties in communication'. Mariana (S31) has a similar opinion, saying that making friends 'is very important, because it is very common to feel lonely. They will need a friend to share their frustrations and joys. Having friends from their hometown is also very helpful. Although this may not help they practice their English, sometimes is good to have someone to share the difficulties without the language barrier.' For these students, having friends from the same background seemed to be helpful because it provided support and an escape from the stress of communicating in the L2.

A few other participants also explained that they appreciated having friends who understood their perspective and interests. Wangjie (S3) writes about the benefits of being able to form close friendships with classmates who shared his background: 'We can often find common hobbies and we like to hang out after classes.' Huidai (S22) explains that having friends from the same background could be especially beneficial when dealing with stress or difficult challenges. She says that it is important to 'try your best to communicate with local students' to learn about the culture and to practise speaking, but she also says that international students 'should make friends from your own country. Those friends would help you when you feel nostalgia, homesick, and upset about the culture difference. Their suggestions and consolations might more suitable for you since they know you better.' From these examples, it seems that co-national friendships, established based on pre-existing socialization patterns from the home country, may offer emotional benefits to participants. As Mitchell et al. (2017) found, these L1 networks are normal for SA participants and can be helpful for counteracting homesickness and culture shock. However, they may also pose a challenge by reducing the frequency of cross-cultural interactions. Participants should be careful not to restrict themselves to L1 interactions, as this will affect the SA experience by removing or limiting the incentive to interact interculturally in addition to potentially hindering the flexibility, openness, and self-questioning needed for successful intercultural friendships.

Facilitation

Throughout the journal entries, there is evidence to support the use of several facilitators in SA programmes. One important topic that was referenced by many participants is participation in clubs and other student activities on campus. Students describe activities as diverse as on-campus festivals, conversation groups, geology and other special-interest clubs, and intramural sports. These activities provided opportunities for participants to interact in the L2. Chenglei (S6) writes that 'participating activities is really helpful, which helps you orientate the campus and make friends quickly', and Lina (S18) says that 'at these activities, it is easy to meet people who have the same interest as I do and it is easy to make friends'. A few also mention that engaging in group activities was beneficial emotionally, as it provides 'relief from the homesick' feelings (Xueqin, S32) and helps students to 'deceive loneliness while they are not totally comfortable in their new city' (Mariana, S31). Engaging in these types of extracurricular activities seems to provide multiple benefits, allowing participants to interact in the L2, form intercultural relationships, and be exposed to new cultural elements of the host country. Teachers and programme directors can facilitate this involvement by providing incentives to participate, informing students of various activities, and encouraging them to interact outside their own groups of co-national students. As Zhang and Zhou (2010) mention, it is also important for programmes to encourage domestic students to become involved in activities with international students in order to facilitate friendship formation. Especially if participants join a team or club and regularly interact with the same group of people, they may be able to move beyond superficial small talk and more easily engage in conversations on higher-level topics.

Additionally, living arrangements may have affected participants' L2 interactions. While nearly all lived in campus dormitories during the semester of this study, some were paired with roommates of differing nationalities, while others had roommates who shared their native language and culture. As was mentioned previously, many participants had positive experiences interacting in the L2 with roommates who were

American or from other cultural backgrounds, reporting that their roommates were friendly, welcoming, and willing to help teach slang or various elements of language and culture. In some instances, these roommate arrangements helped participants meet many local students. This was the case for Lijing (S19), who says that 'my roommate is excellent. ... I meet lots of fantastic friends. We drove to [a local amusement park] and enjoyed our trip.' Not all arrangements were as successful—of course, there will always be individual differences, and even roommates of the same nationality will often have conflicts—but it stands to reason that if SA participants live in close quarters with other students who do not share their native language, they will have additional opportunities to speak in the L2 and form friendships with host nationals, which could lead to deep and rich L2 conversations. This is in accordance with research from Carnine (2015), who found that living alongside host nationals was a key factor in meeting and befriending native speakers of the target language.

Another factor that proved to have a substantial impact on many participants was interaction with supportive professors and teaching assistants (TAs). Several described feelings of gratitude and encouragement due to the positive interactions they had with these teachers and role models from various disciplines across the university. For some, it was helpful simply to know that their professors were aware of them and available to provide additional assistance when needed. Daiyu (S25), says, 'It's a little bit hard for me to process and remember the information from my lecture. But my TAs helped me a lot, they comfort me with very helpful information,' and Jinhai (S17) writes, 'As a student who learn English as a second language, we would always misunderstand or miss something in class. Keeping communication with instructors can solve this problem.' Having access to professors and TAs is important for all students, but particularly so for those from different cultural and linguistic backgrounds.

In addition, participants were positively affected when professors actively strove to include L2 students in the classroom. Lina (S18) explains that 'all my teachers are nice and patient. Because I am quiet in the class, they will ask if I have any question or idea.' Similarly, Seo-yun (S10) describes what she calls her 'greatest motivation' for speaking in

English. She says, 'I don't want to say something wrong in class. So, I rather not talk. ... [My professor] said he liked when I spoke up in class. I felt so thankful. It also encourages me a lot. Since then, I do not hesitate to speak up in class, rather it is right or wrong. I am eager to participate in class now.' These examples demonstrate the powerful influence that teachers can have on SA participants. Professors and other mentors who interact with international students should be trained regarding the particular needs of this population so they can provide encouragement and help all students achieve success.

Within the realm of the language classroom, instructors working with SA participants can also facilitate successful L2 engagement by teaching social norms and pragmatics in addition to cultural awareness. As described previously, many participants were frustrated by not understanding how to approach native English speakers or establish friendships. Some felt unsure of how to proceed beyond small talk, or felt that their interlocutors' friendliness was insincere due to sociocultural differences in relationship styles. Furthermore, while the students in this study were enrolled in academic English courses, it was important for them to learn common phrases or casual language that would benefit their L2 interactions, such as greetings, introductions, or polite refusals. Biyu (S9) mentions how useful it is to learn that 'American people use the euphemism for rejecting others, like "I'd like to … but …" while in China, people normally just reject more directly.' Incorporating pragmatic aspects of language in addition to cultural instruction could lead to smoother interactions and fewer breakdowns in communication. This is consistent with research from Mitchell et al. (2017), which indicates that SA participants often struggle to understand cultural and social differences and could benefit from opportunities for cultural learning and guided reflection. As Jackson (2009) describes, incorporating instruction on the host culture and intercultural awareness into the language classroom can guide participants towards a greater understanding of those they meet while on SA and an enhanced ability to be self-critical and recognize areas in which they can improve with regards to intercultural interaction.

Conclusion and Recommendations

The results of this study confirm earlier research (Bown et al., 2015; Gareis et al., 2011; Trentman, 2013a) suggesting that not all SA participants are immersed in the L2 and develop close cross-cultural friendships, as is commonly assumed. While some participants did report high levels of L2 speaking and most spoke English on a daily basis, the findings from the group as a whole indicated that the majority of their spoken language was in the L1 rather than the L2. It is also noteworthy that overall spoken English usage decreased throughout the course of the semester. There are several possible reasons for this observed decline. While it might be speculated that this was due to a higher propensity to over-report earlier in the semester and the effect of declining motivation levels due to increasingly busy academic schedules, analysis shows that some learners, who were motivated to reach out and interact with native speakers initially, later became discouraged if their efforts did not result in meaningful relationships or if they struggled with adapting to the expectations and customs of the new social and cultural context. Alternatively, participants could have developed co-national friendships early in the semester due to the relative ease or sociocultural familiarity of interacting within their own linguistic and cultural group, and therefore had fewer incentives to spend time with native speakers of the target language. To better understand the impact of co-national friendships on SA, further research should explore the positive or negative effects of these relationships on L2 outcomes and intercultural relationship formation.

It is also important to recognize that while 75 per cent of participants reported having developed friendships and 53 per cent reported close friendships with native speakers of the target language by the end of the semester, many did not—25 per cent had no friendships, and 47 per cent had no close friendships with native speakers. This lack of intercultural friendships provides an explanation for the low levels of L2 speaking that many participants reported and indicates that they may not have had many opportunities for the high-quality communicative interactions that are facilitated by close relationships. The qualitative data provide some insight into the reasons why some participants struggled to develop intercultural relationships, despite their general awareness of the benefits of L2 interaction and a desire for greater cultural understanding. While specific language issues were listed (e.g., difficulty understanding rapid L2 speech, lacking the skills to engage in casual conversations, and low levels of speaking proficiency), the difficulty of navigating unfamiliar social customs related to initiating and maintaining relationships presented the greatest obstacle. Additionally, some participants struggled to process the new culture, even believing that cultural differences were insurmountable, leading to a lack of effort in establishing relationships. While some learners expressed thoughtful cultural reflections and shifted towards ethnorelativism, several did not progress past a lack of cultural knowledge or negative stereotyping of the host culture and did not seek to develop the flexibility required to view interactions and customs differently and so lead to mutual understanding.

In order to more fully access the benefits of L2 interaction, there are many challenges to overcome. As such, it would be worthwhile to explore techniques for assisting learners to move beyond initial interactions and achieve the development of close intercultural relationships to optimize the SA experience. Since many SA participants struggle with social language and pragmatics, instructors can integrate instruction on these topics in their L2 courses, both prior to and during the SA programme. This can include the teaching of common idioms and slang, as well as social rituals such as casual greetings and ways to continue a conversation. Even learners with extensive backgrounds in the L2 often have difficulty navigating informal social interactions when they first arrive in a new culture, so explicit training may be useful in helping them confidently meet and speak with new L2 interlocutors. Students can also be provided with resources such as websites and online videos to learn more about social aspects of the L2.

It is also important to teach both the host culture and cultural awareness in the classroom, as recommended by Jackson (2009). When students are exposed to elements of culture such as art, humour, music, politics, history, and common values, they may be able to develop a more nuanced understanding of the host culture and cultural differences. Additionally, by teaching students about common challenges of intercultural interaction and encouraging them to reflect about their own and other cultures, they may increase in intercultural competency, which will better equip them for forming relationships with host nationals.

Instructors or programme directors can also provide a space for students to ask questions or discuss any concerns they have had regarding intercultural experiences. This debriefing time can be regularly scheduled throughout the SA programme and will allow students to process difficult experiences, receive guidance on how to navigate particular aspects of the host culture, share their successful interactions, and receive support from their peers. It will also allow instructors to receive feedback on what additional pragmatic or cultural training the students might need.

While it is expected that SA participants will want to interact with others from their same L1 background, instructors should ensure that they understand the importance of expanding their social circles and also developing relationships with native speakers or other fluent speakers of the target language who do not share their linguistic and cultural heritage. While students may occasionally enjoy chatting in their native language and escaping from the intense immersion experience, they should be aware that over-reliance on L1 relationships may hinder their success in interacting in the L2 and that the development of intercultural relationships will allow for higher-quality L2 interactions and will likely lead to higher L2 gains.

To assist students in interacting with local speakers, instructors can create incentives for participation in campus or community events. For example, assignments could be given to select a club or team to attend regularly throughout the semester; students would then be able to reflect on their experiences in writing assignments or report orally to the class. When festivals or other events occur on campus, instructors can provide background information to their SA participants and then assign them to attend the event, perhaps with a worksheet or survey to complete in response. This may provide helpful encouragement and scaffolding for students who might otherwise be too intimidated to attend a new event on their own.

Finally, it is important to note that SA participants will likely have better success in intercultural interactions if domestic students are also interested in interacting and have received instruction in (inter)cultural awareness. In many universities in the USA, where international students make up a substantial portion of the student body, it is virtually impossible for domestic students to avoid encountering international peers. By organizing events such as intercultural focus groups, cultural celebrations, or presentations about the different cultures represented on campus, international and domestic students will have frequent opportunities to socialize and to learn more about each other, facilitating better relationships for all.

Summary of recommendations for increasing L2 interaction that might facilitate intercultural friendships

- Include pragmatic instruction in the L2 classroom prior to and during SA.
- Provide instruction on the host culture and cultural awareness in the L2 classroom.
- Organize debriefing sessions for learners to discuss questions or concerns about social and cultural practices that they have encountered.
- Emphasize the importance of forming L2 social networks rather than restricting interactions to co-national networks.
- Incentivize learners to attend campus or community events and join clubs or teams.
- Provide intercultural competency training to domestic students as well as structured opportunities for domestic and international students to interact.

Appendix A: Language Contact Profile

<u>Language Contact Profile</u>

Part 1: Background Information

1. Gender: Male / Female
2. Age: _____
3. What country were you born in?
   _____
4. What is your native language?
   _____
5. At which of these levels have you studied English in the past? (Check all that apply.)
   - ____ 1. Elementary school
   - ____ 2. Junior high (middle) school
   - ____ 3. High school
   - ____ 4. University/college
6. <u>Besides your native language and English,</u> how many other languages do you speak? (For this study, it doesn't matter how well you speak them.) (Circle one)

   None   *One*   *Two*   *Three or more*

7. If you speak languages other than English and your native language, which languages do you speak?
   _____
8. How long have you been in the United States? (Circle one)

   Less than 4 months   5-8 months   9-12 months   1-2 years   More than 2 years

9. a. Have you ever lived in another English-speaking country? Yes / No

   b. If yes, how long did you live there? (Circle one)

   Less than 4 months   5-8 months   9-12 months   1-2 years   More than 2 years

10. What year are you in school? (Circle one)

    Freshman   Sophomore   Junior   Senior   Graduate   Other

11. What is your major?
    _____

12. Which situation best describes your living situation while studying at [university]?
    a. I live with only native English-speaking roommates.
    b. I live with some native English-speaking roommates.
    c. I live with only non-native English-speaking roommates.
    d. I live with my own family and we mostly speak in my native language.
    e. I live alone.

13. How many native English speakers do you know that you would describe as:

   a. close friends that you see often _____
   b. friends that you know well but don't see often _____
   c. acquaintances that you see occasionally but don't know well
   _____

14. If you have friends who are native English speakers, how did you meet them? (Check all that apply)

   ____ 1. roommates or lived in the same dormitory
   ____ 2. classmates
   ____ 3. in the same major
   ____ 4. in a club or extracurricular group (e.g., sports team, music group, etc.)
   ____ 5. through other friends
   ____ 6. other: _____

15. How often do you participate in extracurricular activities at [university](clubs, sports, university activities, etc.)? *This question refers to participating on a team or club, not attending sports or other events.* (Circle one)

   a. never
   b. less than once a month
   c. once a month
   d. 2-3 times a month
   e. once a week
   f. 2-3 times a week
   g. daily

16. If you do participate in extracurricular activities, which ones do you participate in?
   _____
   _____

Part 2: Language Contact Profile

1. How many days per week do you speak your native language outside of class? _____

2. How many days per week do you speak English outside of class? _____

3. On an average day, what percentage of your speaking is in English, your native language, or another language? (The percentages should add up to 100.)

English:	_____	%
My native language:	_____	%
Another language:	_____	%
Total:	**100%**	

For the following items, please specify:
(i) How many *days per week* you typically use English in the situation indicated, and
(ii) on average how many *hours per day* you did so.

Circle the appropriate numbers.

Outside of class, how often do you speak *in English* to:

a. teacher(s) or teaching assistants
   Typically, how many *days per week?*   0   1   2   3   4   5   6   7
   On those days, typically how many *hours per day?*   0-1   1-2   2-3   3-4   4-5   more than 5

b. roommates who do not share your native language
   Typically, how many *days per week?*   0   1   2   3   4   5   6   7
   On those days, typically how many *hours per day?*   0-1   1-2   2-3   3-4   4-5   more than 5

c. friends who do not share your native language
   Typically, how many *days per week?*   0   1   2   3   4   5   6   7
   On those days, typically how many *hours per day?*   0-1   1-2   2-3   3-4   4-5   more than 5

d. classmates who do not share your native language
   Typically, how many *days per week?*   0   1   2   3   4   5   6   7
   On those days, typically how many *hours per day?*   0-1   1-2   2-3   3-4   4-5   more than 5

How often do you:

a. try deliberately to use things you were taught in the classroom (grammar, vocabulary, expressions) with native or fluent speakers of English outside the classroom?
   Typically, how many *days per week?*   0   1   2   3   4   5   6   7
   On those days, typically how many *hours per day?*   0-1   1-2   2-3   3-4   4-5   more than 5

b. read e-mail or Internet web pages *in English?*
   Typically, how many *days per week?*   0   1   2   3   4   5   6   7
   On those days, typically how many *hours per day?*   0-1   1-2   2-3   3-4   4-5   more than 5

c. read newspapers, magazines, or novels, or listen to movies, TV, or music *in English?*
   Typically, how many *days per week?*   0   1   2   3   4   5   6   7
   On those days, typically how many *hours per day?*   0-1   1-2   2-3   3-4   4-5   more than 5

d. read newspapers, magazines, or novels, or listen to movies, TV, or music *in your native language?*
   Typically, how many *days per week?*   0   1   2   3   4   5   6   7
   On those days, typically how many *hours per day?*   0-1   1-2   2-3   3-4   4-5   more than 5

e. read e-mail or Internet web pages *in your native language*
   Typically, how many *days per week?*   0   1   2   3   4   5   6   7
   On those days, typically how many *hours per day?*   0-1   1-2   2-3   3-4   4-5   more than 5

Appendix B: Writing Prompts

On a regular basis, the learners were given a series of questions as a prompt for their weekly journal assignment. The instructions for each journal were as follows:

> This journal is a space for you to write freely, without worrying about grammar or the rules of academic writing. This will allow you to practice writing quickly and fluently. For this week's journal assignment, please respond to any or all of the questions listed below. You should write at least 20 sentences and try to write for about 10–20 minutes. This assignment will be graded for completion.

The ten writing prompts used throughout the semester are listed below:

1. What are the biggest differences between your culture and American culture? What things have been most surprising to you or most difficult to adjust to since you arrived in the USA? What do you admire about American culture, and what do you not like?
2. How is your semester going so far? What have been the best or worst parts? Do you like your classes? Which are interesting or challenging for you? How do you feel about [course]? Do you have any suggestions or questions?
3. If you had 2 weeks to travel anywhere in the world, where would you go? What are your reasons? (Try to use modals in your writing!) Do you enjoy travelling? Why or why not? What are the advantages or disadvantages of travelling?
4. Are there any differences between relationships (families, friends, dating, etc.) in your culture and in American culture? Is it easy or difficult to make friends with Americans? Explain your answer. Do you wish you had more American friends? Do you think it is important to have friends from different cultures?
5. Now that we are getting towards the middle of the semester, how are things going for you? Do you have any comments or feedback about [course]? (You can share positive or negative comments that you have so that we can continue making the class as good for you as possible.)

What advice would you give to new students starting out at [university]? What are the essential tips to follow if you want to have a good experience as an international student here?
6. What different types of motivation are there? What do you think is your greatest motivation for school, for learning English, or for something else that you are pursuing? Explain. What types of motivation are not as important for you? Explain your answer.
7. In class this week, we talked about how languages can merge and adapt when there are large groups of people who speak different languages coming into contact with each other. For example, Spanglish has developed in the USA due to the contact between English speakers and Spanish speakers. Aside from linguistic changes, in what other ways are societies impacted by contact between different cultural groups? Try to think of different aspects of society that might be impacted either positively or negatively.
8. For your homework this week, you are reading about some of the effects that emotions can have on us. In light of this topic, please answer the following questions: even if we do not have emotional personalities, all of us have to deal with difficult challenges. What are some of the emotional challenges that you currently face or have faced as an international student at [university]? Do you have any strategies for helping yourself overcome the challenges you have encountered this semester? If so, what are they? If not, do you have any ideas about something that might be useful in the future?
9. In class this week, we talked about life sentences and the prison system in the USA, and we discussed the point that this is a very controversial issue. We have also discussed other controversial topics throughout the semester, such as poverty, caring for the elderly, video game violence, and immigration. What makes these kinds of topics so controversial? Do you think you generally agree with your American colleagues on these or other controversial topics? What are some of the biggest differences or similarities between how you (or people from your culture, in general) and Americans usually think about these or other topics?
10. Now that you have nearly completed one semester at [university], how do you think your thoughts or feelings about being here have

changed? (e.g., Has it been easier or more difficult than you had expected? Have your interactions with other [university] students affected your perceptions of US culture?) Do you think that being in an English class [course] has been useful to you for (a) improving your language skills and (b) learning more about American culture? Explain your answers for each of these areas.

Bibliography

Baker-Smemoe, W., Cundick, D. K., Evans, N., Henrichsen, L., & Dewey, D. P. (2012). Relationship between reported out-of-class English use and proficiency gains in English. *Applied Language Learning, 22*, 21–45.

Baker-Smemoe, W., Dewey, D. P., Bown, J., & Martinsen, R. A. (2014). Variables affecting L2 gains during study abroad. *Foreign Language Annals, 47*(3), 464–486.

Bataller, R. (2010). Making a request for a service in Spanish: Pragmatic development in the study abroad setting. *Foreign Language Annals, 43*(1), 160–175.

Bown, J., Dewey, D. P., & Belnap, R. K. (2015). Student interactions during study abroad in Jordan. In R. Mitchell, N. Tracy-Ventura, & K. McManus (Eds.), *Social interaction, identity and language learning during residence abroad* (pp. 199–222). EuroSLA Monographs Series 4. Retrieved from http://www.eurosla.org/eurosla-monograph-series-2/social-interaction-identity-and-language-learning-during-residence-abroad/

Carbaugh, D. (2005). *Cultures in conversation*. New York: Psychology Press.

Carnine, J. (2015). The impact on national identity of transnational relationships during international student mobility. *Journal of International Mobility, 3*, 11–30.

Carnine, J. (2016). The social networks of Chinese students studying in France. *Journal of Chinese Overseas, 12*(1), 68–95.

Carroll, J. B. (1967). Foreign language proficiency levels attained by language majors near graduation from college. *Foreign Language Annals, 1*(2), 131–151.

Corbin, J., & Strauss, A. (2008). *Basics of qualitative research* (3rd ed.). London: Sage.

DeKeyser, R. (2010). Monitoring processes in Spanish as a second language during a study abroad program. *Foreign Language Annals, 43*, 80–92.

Freed, B. F. (1995). What makes us think that students who study abroad become fluent? In B. F. Freed (Ed.), *Second language acquisition in a study abroad context* (pp. 123–148). Philadelphia: Benjamins.

Freed, B. F., Segalowitz, N., & Dewey, D. P. (2004). Context of learning and second language fluency in French: Comparing regular classroom, study abroad, and intensive domestic immersion programs. *Studies in Second Language Acquisition, 26,* 275–301.

Gareis, E., Merkin, R., & Goldman, J. (2011). Intercultural friendship: Linking communication variables and friendship success. *Journal of Intercultural Communication Research, 40*(2), 153–171.

Hernández, T. A. (2010). Promoting speaking proficiency through motivation and interaction: The study abroad and classroom learning contexts. *Foreign Language Annals, 43*(4), 650–670.

Institute of International Education. (2017). *Open doors report on international educational exchange.* Retrieved from http://iiebooks.org/opdoreonined.html

Isabelli-García, C. (2006). Study abroad social networks, motivation and attitudes: Implications for second language acquisition. In E. Churchill & M. A. DuFon (Eds.), *Language learners in study abroad contexts* (pp. 231–258). Buffalo, NY: Multilingual Matters.

Jackson, J. (2009). Intercultural learning on short-term sojourns. *Intercultural Education, 20,* 59–71.

Jackson, J. (2010). *Intercultural journeys: From study to residence abroad.* Basingstoke: Palgrave Macmillan.

Keppie, C., Lindberg, R., & Thomason, S. (2016). The benefits of study abroad on the fluency of learners of French as a second language. *Canadian Journal of Applied Linguistics, Special Issue, 19*(2), 44–63.

Kinginger, C. (2009). *Language learning and study abroad: A critical reading of research.* New York: Palgrave Macmillan.

Kinginger, C. (2013). Identity and language learning in study abroad. *Foreign Language Annals, 46*(3), 339–358.

Mitchell, R., Tracy-Ventura, N., & McManus, K. (2017). *Anglophone students abroad: Identity, social relationships and language learning.* New York: Routledge.

Pérez-Vidal, C. (Ed.). (2014). *Language acquisition in study abroad and formal instruction contexts.* Philadelphia: Benjamins.

Ranta, L., & Meckelborg, A. (2013). How much exposure to English do international graduate students really get? Measuring language use in a naturalistic setting. *Canadian Modern Language Review, 69*(1), 1–33.

Rohrlich, B. F., & Martin, J. N. (1991). Host country and reentry adjustment of student sojourners. *International Journal of Intercultural Relations, 15,* 163–182.

Schwieter, J. W., & Ferreira, A. (2016). On the interrelated nature of study abroad learners' language contact, perceptions of culture, and personal outcomes. *Canadian Journal of Applied Linguistics, Special Issue, 19*(2), 151–173.

Segalowitz, N., & Freed, B. F. (2004). Context, contact, and cognition in oral fluency acquisition: Learning Spanish in at home and study abroad contexts. *Studies in Second Language Acquisition, 26*(2), 173–199.

Spada, N. (1986). The interaction between type of contact and type of instruction: Some effects on the L2 proficiency of adult learners. *Studies in Second Language Acquisition, 8*(2), 181–199.

Tanaka, K. (2007). Japanese students' contact with English outside the classroom during study abroad. *New Zealand Studies in Applied Linguistics, 13*, 36–54.

Trentman, E. (2013a). Arabic and English during study abroad in Cairo, Egypt: Issues of access and use. *Modern Language Journal, 97*(2), 457–473.

Trentman, E. (2013b). Imagined communities and language learning during study abroad: Arabic learners in Egypt. *Foreign Language Annals, 46*(4), 545–564.

Trice, A. D., & Elliott, J. (1993). Japanese students in America: College friendship patterns. *Journal of Instructional Psychology, 20*, 262–264.

Ward, C., & Masgoret, A. (2004). *The experiences of international students in New Zealand: Report on the results of the national study*. New Zealand: International Policy and Development Unit, Ministry of Education. Retrieved from http://www.educationcounts.govt.nz/publications/international/14700

Zhang, Z., & Zhou, G. (2010). Understanding Chinese international students at a Canadian university: Perspectives, expectations, and experiences. *Canadian and International Education, 39*(3), 43–58.

Gender as a Cultural and Social Construct in Language Learning During Study Abroad

Mar Galindo

Introduction: Gender and Study Abroad[1]

The field of study abroad (SA) has been widely explored in the last couple of decades.[2] It is much more than a language learning experience: it may involve academic advancement, personal growth, improved socialisation, future job contacts, the acquisition of cultural knowledge, or a heightened perspective of the world (Shirley, 2006, p. 6; Twombly, Salisbury, Tumanut, & Klute, 2012, p. ix). Nonetheless, language remains one of the central motivators and, indeed, numerous studies in the field of applied linguistics have explored the benefits of education abroad for language learning by looking at different aspects: length of the stay, language skills development, communicative, pragmatic, and conversational competence, and fluency (e.g., Dewey, 2007; Kinginger, 2009b; Pérez-Vidal, 2014; Trentman, 2013a, 2013b). An excellent sum-

M. Galindo (✉)
University of Alicante, Alicante, Spain
e-mail: Mar.Galindo@ua.es

mary of the main findings can be found in Dewey (2007). He addresses the general indicators of the linguistic benefits of SA (the impact of the amount of time spent, significant gains in the four skills, grammatical development, oral proficiency), cross-context comparisons between abroad and at-home learners (in terms of oral proficiency and fluency, communication strategies, vocabulary development), nature of the SA experience (homestay, use of the target language, classroom instruction), and predictors of gains during SA, where he includes—besides age, prior language learning, and aptitude—gender.

Together with this *linguistic* approach, there is another perspective adopted more recently to account for what the sojourner experiences when living in a foreign country, having to face a new language and culture. This *social, intercultural* approach has shed light on the lived dimensions of SA,[3] involving not only language skills but also issues of *identity*. Identity is a complex category with several possible dimensions or components (e.g., gender, nationality, ethnicity, culture, first and second languages, class, 'foreigner' status, and so forth); this article focusses on one specific component: *gender*.

This choice is not random. Although SA involves a wide range of characteristics, possibilities, and effects, there is one aspect that garners 100 per cent agreement across advisors, programme administrators, teachers, and researchers: two thirds of students going abroad are female. Figures are consistent across geographic location and time. The two to one female-to-male ratio has stayed remarkably stagnant (Redden, 2008). Although the number of students going abroad is increasing by 12 per cent each year (Sood, 2012), the proportion of male and female participants remains stable: out of 100 students going abroad, 65 are female. This proportion is found across most data sources, including: official SA statistics such as those collected and published by UNESCO, international education associations such as NAFSA: Association of International Educators, Asociación de Programas Universitarios Norteamericanos en España (or the Association of American Programs in Spain), and the *Open Doors* reports published by the Institute of International Education (IIE, 2016); academic newspapers such as *The Chronicle for Higher Education*; SA handbooks or research reviews such as Lewin's (2009) *The Handbook of Practice and Research in Study Abroad* or

Twombly et al.'s (2012) *Study Abroad in a New Global Century*; doctoral dissertations (Bufmack, 2013; Shirley, 2006); and international mobility offices in colleges and universities (Adkins, 2004). 'Gender gap' (Bown, Dewey, & Belnap, 2015; Bryant & Soria, 2015; Bufmack, 2013; Redden, 2008; Salisbury, Umbach, Paulsen, & Pascarella, 2009), 'gender disparity' (Shirley, 2006), 'gender imbalance' (Adkins, 2004; Redden, 2008), 'disproportional representation' (Redden, 2008), 'domain of women' (Twombly et al., 2012), and 'feminized activity' (Kinginger, 2009b) are, accordingly, all terms used to refer to this often observed disproportion or inequality in SA participation.

SA was conceived in the mid twentieth century as a way for young middle-class women to become more eligible for marriage or just a pastime for wealthy young ladies (the so-called *Grand Tour*, Gore, 2005; Kinginger, 2009b), which explains the historical predominance of female students in SA programmes. However, the stated purpose of the SA experience nowadays is very different (Salisbury et al., 2009; Twombly et al., 2012, pp. 13–26), involving issues of global competency and global understanding, and yet the proportion of participants by gender has not changed. Furthermore, SA programmes are marketed ever more towards women in general (Shirley, 2006). This female supremacy in SA thus raises two initial questions: (1) What are the reasons for the current *gender gap* in SA? (2) To what extent can gender influence the SA experience? In other words, the conclusive figures on female participation in SA make it necessary to explore, first, why female students decide to go abroad to learn foreign languages much more often than their male counterparts. I will address this question about the gender gap in the following section on context. Second, the overwhelming presence of women in SA programmes also draws attention to the issue of whether and how gender can affect their learning (and life) experiences abroad. I will thus review the research on SA as a possibly gendered experience in a third section. Following this, I will focus on how a feminist poststructuralist approach to gender and SA can fulfil the needs of the field. I will close by summarising the main conclusions and presenting some implications and recommendations for programme design, teaching, learning, and researching in SA.

Context: The Gender Gap in SA or Why More Women Go on Study Abroad

During the last two decades, international education has experienced a huge growth all across the globe. Its benefits for college and university students—proficiency in a foreign language, emotional maturity, empathy, experiential learning, better preparedness to live and succeed in a globalising world, greater understanding of cultural diversity—are well documented (Bryant & Soria, 2015; Salisbury et al., 2009; Twombly et al., 2012) and yet, by and large, enrolment in SA programmes has been marked by a predominance of female students. For example, in their study of 2772 full-time freshmen at 19 institutions, Salisbury et al. (2009) explored their probability of planning to SA. The results showed that males were approximately eight percentage points less likely to intend to study abroad than females. As Shirley (2006, p. 2) states, this gender gap would not be an issue if it accurately reflected university enrolments, but it does not. Twombly et al. (2012, p. 37) notice that the typical sojourner is white, female, young, single, financially comfortable, and without disability. Several researchers have sought to understand this disproportion or imbalance between men and women, providing a range of expectations for it. In the following, I review some of this work.

One of the reasons for the female dominance of SA enrolment may be women's preference for learning second languages (L2s). For some time, researchers (e.g., Burstall, 1977; Kobayashi, 2002) have indicated that women show a more positive attitude towards foreign languages. Prada (1993) found that female learners show more positive attitudes and motivation than their male counterparts. Similarly, Schmidt, Boraie, and Kassagby (1996) found females were better foreign language learners because they were more intrinsically motivated, whereas males expressed more extrinsic motivation. Meanwhile, female learners seem to experience more anxiety in the language classroom than male students (Campbell, 1999; Dewaele & McIntyre, 2014). Even a difference in learning contexts does not alter the dominance of female students in language learning. Roquet, Llopis, and Pérez-Vidal (2016) hypothesised that content and language integrated learning (CLIL) programmes may blur the differences between female and male learners, since male students might feel more motivated to learn both the language and the subject matter. Their research focussed on the influence of the gender variable on the level of English competence attained by Catalan/Spanish bilingual learners of English as a third language in a formal instruction (FI) context versus a FI + CLIL context. Data showed, however, that the CLIL approach did not erase gender differences: female participants outperformed their male peers not only in the FI context but also in the CLIL one. Similar findings can be read in Lasagabaster (2008), whose female CLIL students outperformed their male counterparts in almost all the English tests and in overall proficiency. In conclusion, contrary to expectations, results to date indicate that female learners perform better in both the traditional FI context and the CLIL context.

In his study about the gender gap in SA, Shirley (2006) found three significant differences between genders. First, women were more likely to state that their parents and other relatives were a strongly positive influence on their decision to go abroad than did men. Second, more women felt that a scheduling conflict with an internship or job as well as the overall cost of the programme were obstacles to SA than did men. Finally, men more strongly felt studying abroad delayed their potential point of graduation than did women.

The first difference is also found in several studies, such as King and Sondhi (2016), where female students were more likely to be sensitive to the encouragement of their families than men. Going further, King and Sondhi (2016, p. 18) suggest that 'it is the mother who is the dominant figure in guiding the children's educational pathways abroad'. The authors reported a relationship between gender, SA, and parents' social class and education in India (p. 19), where significantly more female students came from highly educated parental backgrounds than males. The relevance of these factors was also highlighted in Salisbury et al. (2009). Following the sociological theory of human capital (including social, cultural, and financial capital), the authors linked the decision to study abroad to students' socioeconomic backgrounds: 'predisposition to study abroad reveals a complex interplay between socioeconomic status, social and cultural capital accumulated before college, and social and cultural capital gained during the freshman year' (Salisbury et al., 2009, p. 137). Interestingly, this study refers to the role that the field of specialty plays in the decision to go abroad. Historically, SA was aimed at majors in art, art history, foreign languages, general humanities, history, and political science, that is, majors primarily in 'female-dominated' fields (King & Sondhi, 2016, p. 18; Redden, 2008; Shirley, 2006, pp. 1–3; Twombly et al., 2012, p. 37). Nowadays, this trend is changing. SA programmes for students in the so-called STEM disciplines—science, technology, engineering, maths—have increased in the last ten years. In their research, Salisbury et al. (2009) found no statistically significant differences in intentions to go abroad between arts and humanities majors and students in business, education, or science, technology, engineering, and maths, although the gender gap was still there. Moreover, according to the IIE's *Open Doors 2016* report, the top five major fields of study for American students abroad are STEM specialisations, business, social sciences, foreign languages and international studies, and fine and applied arts.

The second significant difference reported by Shirley (2006, p. 39) alluded to the obstacles women had to face concerning a scheduling conflict with an internship or job and overall cost of the programme:

> Regarding the impact of conflicting with a job or internship, 65 per cent of female respondents agreed or strongly agreed that this could be a significant barrier discouraging students from studying abroad. Meanwhile, only 49 per cent of male respondents agreed or strongly agreed that a job opportunity was a potential barrier. Likewise, only 14 per cent of females disagreed or strongly disagreed that job/internship opportunities were potential barriers to studying abroad while 28 per cent of males disagreed or strongly disagreed that job and internship opportunities pose significant barriers.

Thirdly, it seems men are less inclined to go abroad because they have more rigid schedules within their courses of study (Shirley, 2006). Experts agree that curricular restrictions in education and STEM majors tend to truncate participation in SA programmes (Salisbury et al., 2009; Twombly et al., 2012, pp. 62–63), linking again participation in international sojourns with field of specialty, since STEM degrees are perceived to have more rigid schedules than other options. However, Twombly et al. (2012, p. 50) think this argument is not enough to account for the gender gap:

While rates of SA participation by women coincide with their representation in certain majors to some extent, this fact does not sufficiently explain why rates remain higher even for women in male-dominated fields such as business and engineering.

Redden also notes this phenomenon in her article (2008, para. 16): 'Even in a field where men substantially outnumber women—engineering—SA's particular appeal to female students shines through, in this case all the more dramatically.' However, the rise of short-term SA programmes, like summer programmes, ideal for curricularly-restricted students such as STEM undergraduates, do not show a shift in the gender imbalance (Redden, 2008, para. 23). Redden adds further reasons:

> differing maturity and risk-taking levels among 18- to 21-year-old men and women; a sense that females, concerned about safety, are more inclined to attend a college-sanctioned study abroad program than travel on their own; and, again, varying study abroad participation rates in male versus female-dominated fields.

She (Redden, 2008, para. 31) also mentions age and motherhood as motivators for women to go abroad more often than men. Kinginger (2009b, p. 24) discusses these reasons when talking about SA from Japan:

> most women find little occasion to develop English-language skills at work. In combination with ideology in which ageing for women is expected to be accompanied primarily by family accomplishments such as child-rearing and caring for the elderly, this situation has encouraged a population of both career-oriented and non-elite single adult Japanese women to study English abroad for personal reasons, combining language education with the realization of desire for travel and experience of Western culture.

Beyond these differences, Shirley (2006) found limited differences among males and females regarding studying abroad in their thoughts on the perceived barriers, perceived benefits, influential people, promotional factors, influential reasons, academic rigour, and likelihood to repeat their experience. The example of the Japanese female sojourners mentioned by Kinginger (2009b) adds another reason for the gender gap:

certain contexts—that is, either departing or destination locations—may involve different gendered practices, varying the participation in SA by gender. Specific home cultural contexts where women are more subjected to sexism in daily life tend to favour their participation in SA programmes, according to Kobayashi (2002) and Boey (2014), who referred to the aforementioned case of Japanese young women: 'many Japanese female students [...] view the opportunity to study overseas as a ticket out of their home country' (Boey, 2014, p. 2); '[Japanese women] adopt liberated gender subject positions linked to their sojourns away from Japan' (Block, 2014, p. 221). Japan is, thus, a telling example of how gender operates differently when motivations to go abroad arise. An exception to this trend is King and Sondhi's (2016) study of Indian and UK international students, whose motivations for studying abroad were rather similar, despite their background differences.

As for destination countries where gender plays a differentiating role, Russia has been widely researched in the field of SA, starting with the large-scale study carried out by Brecht, Davidson, and Gingsberg (1995), in which 658 American students took part. The study showed that men were more likely than women to make significant gains in oral skills:

> one might hypothesise that men and women spend their time differently in-country, and that, therefore, the difference in acquisition might be due to a difference in time-on-task. On the other hand, one might imagine a difference between the interactions of American men and women with Russian men and women as a reflection of the two cultural differences involved: American and Russian, as well as male and female. (Brecht et al., 1995, p. 57)

In reviewing this research, Polanyi (1995) dealt specifically with the differences experienced by male and female sojourners in Moscow. She discovered that men had access to a wider variety of communicative situations and were considered as competent participants, while women rarely participated in such social interactions (with the exception of unwanted interactions with Russian men). Similar results were reported in Twombly's (1995) work about American female students in Costa Rica, where catcalling and difficulty in making female friends marked their SA experience. Both studies are significant examples of how women encountered difficulties in making friends in the host culture and were often subjected to sexist behaviour. Equally, Pellegrino Aveni (2005) found that female students felt uncomfortable in their conversations with Russian males, which limited their access to interaction opportunities.

Mathews (2000) also explored the benefits obtained by women from interacting in Russian with Russian speakers. She found that developing relationships with individuals was much more important for females than for males. Finally, Davidson (2010), who replicated the study by Brecht et al. (1995), did not find any correlation with gender and L2 gains in the experiences of 1881 American students in Russia. He attributed this to changes in society as well as to special training on the part of female sojourners, which included training in self-management and strategy selection in the form of 'both linguistically supported and unsheltered activities in tandem with improved metacognitive learner and instructor preparation in self-managed learning, learning strategies, and "identity competence"' (Davidson, 2010, p. 20).

Another documented context that seems to favour men over female participants: Arab countries. Bown et al.'s (2015) study of 82 American sojourners learning Arabic in Amman (Jordan) shows that the student distribution by gender did not follow the typical pattern, as there were 32 females (not even 40 per cent) versus 52 males. As a result of their experience in Jordan, a social environment that gave male students more opportunities for communication, men were overall better equipped to handle more linguistically complex functions (Bown et al., 2015, p. 207).

Similar figures are found in Smith and Bown (2013) in their study of the same context and participants: 52 American students (20 females and 32 males) in Amman, Jordan. Although from a quantitative perspective the data showed that male and female students did not differ in their tasks (ability to complete the two hour a day speaking assignment, the amount of time spent speaking alone, per cent of time spent finding speaking partners, satisfaction with speaking experiences, engagement during conversations with Arabs, their final Oral Proficiency Interview (OPI) score), Smith and Bown (2013, para. 5) note that from a qualitative perspective, the journals showed that female students speak more in private, such as in a home, while male students speak more in public. This correlation was attributed to both the increased number of men in public and sexual harassment (defined as everything from groping to catcalling), which was expressed by every girl on the program.

Similar results are found in Trentman's (2013a) study of 18 American and European sojourners (13 females, 5 males) at the American University in Cairo. The dominant gender roles in Egyptian society made it difficult for female students to interact with locals (Trentman, 2013a, p. 458); women reported being harassed on the street, no matter how conservatively they were dressed (p. 467). Likewise, Ishmael (2010) concluded that female SA participants in Arab countries felt their social opportunities were limited in comparison to their male counterparts. In fact, in a similarly Middle-Eastern context, as early as 1980, F. Schumann reported her difficulties as a female learner of Farsi in Iran, where her language learning opportunities were limited because of her gender.

Despite these disadvantages, women seem to adapt better to the SA situation. Rohrlich and Martin's (1991) study on host country and reentry adjustment of student sojourners found that gender is critical when dealing with SA conditions—namely: housing, coursework, food, climate, language, health, sufficient money, homesickness, interaction with new people, unfamiliar currency, adjustment to new customs, extracurricular travel while abroad, and local transportation. The authors state that 'Women were more realistic about their ability to deal with the intercultural experience than were men' (p. 44). Furthermore, echoing the words of Gore (2005), women can gain respect for having chosen to SA.

In summary, studies exploring different areas of language learning agree on the existence of a female-oriented culture of foreign languages. Women seem more inclined to study both second and foreign languages and, consequently, outperform their male counterparts, thus turning SA into a women's phenomenon. Since SA is a context where issues of identity may arise, there are reasons to assert that gender plays a definitive role in the experience, as we have seen. However, since SA involves a larger number of benefits beyond language learning (Twombly et al. 2012, pp. 67–87), men should be appropriately challenged to take part in the experience.

The majority of students strongly agree that the international experience offers them many personal and professional benefits, for example, 'new views on everything from politics and international affairs to food and fashion' (Bufmack, 2013, p. 1), which men would risk losing by not attending SA programmes. Therefore, a large number of educational institutions are starting to promote marketing campaigns targeting men, especially for short-term programmes that easily fit their schedule. Correspondingly, Salisbury et al. (2009, p. 118) conclude:

> The long-standing gap between the proportions of men and women who participate in study abroad is replicated in our study of intent to study abroad. This suggests that efforts to boost male participation may need to include an examination of the ways in which each gender is socialized before college toward activities that might enhance their educational experience during college.

Experts suggest that faculty members and educators should encourage male students to go abroad, and that this can be supported by men who have already been abroad and can provide testimonies to their male peers. However, the goal is not only to get them abroad, but also to get them engaged with their SA programmes by encouraging other male students to go abroad and by helping programme designers and administrators to improve programmes abroad.

Gender as a Factor in the Learning Outcomes of International Education: Recent Advances in Study Abroad Research

For a long time, both applied linguistics and second language acquisition (SLA) were equally *gender blind* (Pavlenko, Blackledge, Piller, & Teutsch-Dwyer, 2001). Linguists have ignored their participants' gender for decades, giving the impression that gender does not affect the process of learning languages. But, in the light of recent research, we know it does: a couple of excellent examples of works explaining the relationship between gender and language learning are Pavlenko et al.'s (2001) book

Multilingualism, Second Language Learning and Gender and Norton and Pavlenko's (2004a, 2004b) co-edited volume *Gender and English Language Learners*. These books attest that an applied linguistics explanation of language learning may turn out to be incomplete (Vanderick, 2000), especially in the case of education abroad. As Kinginger maintains, student sojourners abroad may encounter challenges not only to their language skills, but also to their identities (2015, p. 6). They experience affective, behavioural, and cognitive effects of their sojourn in different ways, depending on a number of variables, including gender (Zhou, Jindal-Snape, Topping, & Todman, 2008). Kinginger (2009b, p. 183) elaborates, 'When students go abroad, they may encounter different ways of performing gender, and they may find that their gender influences the ways they are positioned in interactions in unfamiliar ways.' Indeed, in her study on gender and SA in Australia, Boey (2014, p. 2) notes the same pervasiveness of *gender blindness* in research on international education and SA.

As mentioned above, language learning in the context of a residence abroad experience is especially subjected to gendered practices, affecting the sojourner's identity and access to local social networks: 'We can see the highly context-sensitive nature of the gendered practices and the corresponding outcomes of language learning and language contact' (Shi, 2006, p. 2). Likewise, Pavlenko (2001) maintains that gendered identities are social and cultural constructs, in the context of speech communities. From this perspective, Kinginger (2009b, pp. 184–196) reviews some studies exploring the role of gender during SA. In the following, I discuss some of these and others.

Several studies, as mentioned in Bown et al. (2015, p. 200), have reported that extensive contact with native speakers may not lead to L2 proficiency. Rather, it is the type of interaction that leads to language development. Moreover, learners' engagement in those interactions is primarily influenced by their linguistic goals and perceived threats to their identities. As in the studies noted above, American female students in Jordan had qualitatively different speaking experiences from men: they were advised to avoid conversations with unfamiliar men and had a hard time trying to find female interlocutors. Also, conversation topics were very limited; 'girly, fluffy stuff'; 'weddings and makeup', as reported by some students (Bown et al., 2015, p. 208). Also in the Middle East, Trentman (2013b, p. 556) reports that seven of the female sojourners in her study complained that 'their Egyptian roommates were not interested in serious topics and that they felt frustrated with culturally imposed gender restrictions'.

Taking these studies as a whole, we can see that in the field of SA gender has mainly been explored in terms of American women's perception of sexism and harassment while abroad (Bown et al., 2015; Brecht et al., 1995; Kinginger & Whitworth, 2005; Kline, 1998; Polanyi, 1995; Talburt & Stewart, 1999; Trentman, 2015; Twombly, 1995): Kinginger (2009b, p. 184) asserts that 'American women abroad perceive that they are positioned as sexual objects or as lesser participants in social interaction'; and Block (2014, p. 190) concludes that 'there can be little doubt that sexual harassment can be a defining factor of the SA experience'. There is even a specific section on sexual harassment in Kinginger's (2009a, pp. 66–70) guidebook to contemporary SA and foreign language learning as well as Block's (2014, p. 145) chapter on SA in his *Second language identities*. A comprehensive summary of these works can be found in Trentman (2015, pp. 265–266). She reviews different reports on SA in various locations, and all of them show how American female sojourners accounted for their gendered limited access to local social networks and felt alienated from their environment. Some of them refused to behave in ways that might lessen their exposure to catcalls and sexual harassment only because that would conflict with their individual rights. In addition, girls reported difficulties in making friends with local women. The reasons included competition for local men, undeniable differences between the lives of local and American women, and negative or uninterested attitudes towards SA students (Trentman, 2015, p. 265).

A notable exception to this treatment of sexual harassment behaviours abroad is Patron's (2007) research of French sojourners in Australia, where the absence of sexual harassment from the locals, interpreted as a lack of interest, provoked negative reactions among female participants.

As Kinginger points out (2009a, p. 67), the reported experiences of harassment are found in student journals and interviews, but do not take into account local people's viewpoints, like those of local women (Kinginger, 2015). An excellent exception to this trend is Goldoni's doctoral study (2009), where he included the host institution director's perspective to account for the possible reasons behind the reported experiences of sexual harassment.

Definitely, sexism is a turning point for women pursuing international education. In describing this situation, Kinginger (2009a, pp. 69–70) calls for a broader picture for researching and understanding this kind of intercultural conflict:

> The perception of sexual harassment is a very obvious problem for our students when they go abroad. For those who feel harassed, the experience can severely curtail engagement in local activities and social networks and thereby limit language learning. This fact is particularly distressing in light of the feminised nature of SA, with its majority of female participants. Even for males who do not see themselves as victims of sexual harassment, the experience of observing their female classmate's difficulties can cement negative attitudes toward the host community. [...] If we consider ways in which these activities are interpreted by local people, including representatives of host institutions and the presumed victims of sexual harassment, we may find that we are in the presence not of inexplicably appalling behavior, but of a 'rich point' worthy of further investigation. Instead of rushing to the conclusion that the rest of the world is wrong about gender relations, and we are right, it might be better to consider 1) how our students' behavior is interpreted in the contexts they frequent, and 2) what purposes are served locally and how people might feel that they are benefitting by the activities we call sexual harassment.

Kinginger illustrates her reflection with examples from American students abroad (mainly in France). Elsewhere, in Australia, Boey (2014, p. 3) summarises similar reports on difficulties experienced by female SA students. These include racism, discrimination, disrespect, loneliness, stereotypical and sexist assumptions, disappointment, and lack of support, contrasting the personal growth, confidence, and independence achieved by others. Compared to their male counterparts, female sojourners had greater difficulties making friends and poorer levels of interaction and integration into the local community. The overall experience is significantly less satisfying for them.

A different point of view on gender and SA is provided by Siegal (1996). She focusses on a case study of a white American woman learning Japanese in Japan, and how her perception of the target society and her views on the L2 and culture influenced her sociolinguistic competence. Mary, the learner, had to acquire Japanese pragmatics, including how to speak like a Japanese woman, a path travelled only with difficulty because of the strong context-dependency of Japanese. Far from recurring cases of sexual harassment, Siegal's study brings another perspective on the relationship between identity and SA. Researching in the other direction, Morita (2009) explores the experiences of a male Japanese doctoral student (Kota) who was studying at a Canadian university. Using a community of practice perspective and adopting a social constructivist view on identity and gender, she suggests that differences in language, culture, and gender impacted Kota's participation and socialisation in significant ways by limiting his participation both outside and inside the classroom.

Specifically in the case of Asian and African women, the outcomes of SA are very much differentiated by gender. For them, returning home after the overseas experience means facing a strong gender-biased context. The reverse culture shock is especially traumatic in Asian and African countries where the traditional values of marriage and motherhood conflict with the professional interests of internationally educated women, as Boey (2014, p. 4) maintains: 'It is somewhat difficult to establish a positive connection between the benefits of overseas higher education and the individual female graduate in terms of empowerment, improved mobility and greater gender equity when they return home.' King and Sondhi (2016) also illustrate how the cycle of SA and return is played out differently by gender. In the case of Indian sojourners, young men feel the labour market pressure, marriage, family responsibilities, and care duties towards their parents. Males are expected 'to return to an advantageous position in the home-country labour market and are under pressure to secure well-paid jobs in order to prepare a stable platform for marriage' (p. 7) as a result of 'the patrifocal ideology of the Indian family' (p. 21). It seems marriage pressure applies not only to female students, but also to male sojourners, depending on the context. In the case of Indian women returning home, sojourners experience discrimination in the local labour market and lack of gender equity (p. 7). Indian women are more unsettled: 'Overall, the women's "narratives of return" reveal a greater struggle to fit back into home spaces' (p. 24). The discrimination they face in the labour market pushes them to look for new ways of staying or moving abroad, or makes them succumb to the expectation to get married soon and consequently lose the freedom they experienced while abroad.

As anticipated earlier, such restrictions affecting gendered practices also during SA are context dependent. In the aforementioned study, King and Sondhi (2016) compared the commonalities and differences of UK and Indian international students' experiences of social interaction in and out of class. They noted that 'Gendered contrasts in experiences of studying abroad are quite evident in the Indian sample, but largely absent from the British students' narratives' (p. 2). UK participants were in countries where the 'performances' of gender in student-inhabited spaces were broadly similar to their own (Australia, Ireland, USA, and so forth). On the contrary, Indian sojourners found performances of masculinity and femininity in their SA that made them feel out of place in terms of gendered expected behaviour (p. 26).

Finally, another dimension of SA concerning gender and identity are the experiences of lesbian, gay, bisexual, transgender, questioning, or queer (LGBTQQ) students. Bryant and Soria (2015, p. 92) remark that 'this group may face safety, discrimination, and prejudicial concerns abroad as they experience different cultural norms about sexual orientation and gender identity'. Their study shows that LGBTQQ students were more likely to enrol in a SA programme, especially, again, in the case of female participants, who were more likely to SA than men (p. 101).

In short, reasons to pursue an international education, opportunities to interact with locals while abroad, speaking experiences, access to social networks, perceptions of sexual harassment, levels of integration in the host country, respect for individual rights and even reverse culture shock and the returning process are all mediated by gender, affecting men and women in different ways. In a study that is not specifically about gender, Doerr (2015, p. 374) recounts an American college student's (Sophie) experience in Paris: 'When asked what she learned the most, she mentioned learning how to act French. French women swing their arms and strut, she explained, whereas American women walk slouched over. She said she had learned to look French in terms of attire and behavior.' Here, it is worth recalling Kinginger and Whitworth's (2005, p. 5) explanation of how new gender ideologies and performances may conflict with the old ones. Negotiating female gendered identities can both confirm the dominant narrative of negative experiences abroad as well as provide avenues of resistance (Trentman, 2015, p. 266). Consequently, SA research needs a suitable theoretical framework beyond the standard approaches of applied linguistics to explore how gendered practices are shaping residence abroad experiences and language learning outcomes, beyond the observation of sexism in host cultures (Kinginger, 2009b, p. 192).

A Feminist Poststructural Approach to Gender and Study Abroad

From applied linguistics we know that men and women may learn languages in different ways according to their attitudes, motivations, beliefs, and learning strategies and styles. However, researchers often fail to account for the reasons behind those differences and the extent to which issues of gender and gender identity can shape the learning process, especially in contexts where learners are dealing with a new culture. Therefore, Pavlenko et al. (2001, p. 3) have proposed 'a more context-sensitive approach which treats gender as a system of social relations and discursive practices whose meaning varies across speech communities'. It is clear that we need to have a deeper approach, since 'gender both structures and influences the world of the learner and learner experience; therefore, learning needs to be contextualized to women's personal, social, mental and emotional milieux' (Sen & Samdup, 2009, p. 165). This contextualising approach is especially suitable in SA research, where the learner's gender identities and understandings of gender may be confronted with different customs and conceptions concerning gender and the target culture; this may affect language learning in particular, as well as the overall experience of being abroad.

A good example of the necessity of this perspective emerges from Smith and Bown's (2013) study of 52 American students spending a semester in Jordan. Quantitatively, both male and female participants showed the same progress according to their ability to complete the assignments, the time devoted to speak, their satisfaction with speaking experiences, engagement during conversation with Arabs, and their final OPI score. However, qualitatively, the researchers showed that female sojourners spoke more in private, such as in the home, whereas male students spoke more in public. According to the students, this was due to both the greater number of men in public and the sexual harassment of women, a point made by every single female student participating in the programme. Smith and Bown's study clearly shows that gender can mediate speaking opportunities for international students. We know from the SA literature that this is not only the case in the Middle East context. Therefore, SA experts would benefit from a theoretical framework considering how issues of gender overlap with new identities during residence abroad.

In the introduction to this chapter, I noted the separation assumed in sociopsychological approaches to language learning between social and individual or psychological factors. According to Pavlenko (2002), this dichotomy creates a further problem, since many individual factors are socially constructed. Therefore, she argues for a theory of social identity that can integrate the learner and the learning context: 'A strong explanatory theory of social contexts in SLA needs to consider the issues of power and domination in the relationships between majority and minority groups, as well as to find ways of relating the social to the linguistic' (pp. 281–282). Together with Pavlenko, I argue that poststructuralism provides a suitable framework to account for language learning. It can be conceived as 'an attempt to investigate and to theorise the role of language in construction and reproduction of social relations, and the role of social dynamics in the processes of additional language learning and use' (Pavlenko, 2002, p. 282), as conceived by Norton (2000). In SA literature, this social approach has proved valuable in studies such as Jackson (2008) or Diao (2014, p. 1), who consider gender as a crucial dimension of social differences that can be constructed and indexed through language. Diao analyses how gender is constructed and indexed through language as three American students (one female, two males) learn to use Mandarin affective sentence-final particles (a feature of women's language), with their Chinese roommates in a college dorm in China. In the case of the female participant, the theme of gender recurred frequently in her interactions with her Chinese roommate; gender was a dimension along which they arranged their linguistic and discursive practices (Diao, 2014, p. 11). Their male counterparts also discussed gender-related topics (women, heterosexual masculinity, policing sexuality); for example, how to speak and act 'like a man' in the host language and culture. Diao (p. 18) concludes her study indicating that gender appears to be equally present for men and women when they are overseas and engage in L2 practices.

Diao's (2014) research is a good example of how a poststructuralist theory of SLA understands language acquisition as language socialisation, with L2 users as agents with multiple and dynamic identities. In SA research, a poststructuralist approach provides a frame of reference to look at language as a site of identity construction and negotiation. As Diao (p. 3) states, 'it remains unclear how the students actually interact with the local people and to what extent they appropriate local ways of performing identities such as gender'. In the case of foreign language learners—L2 users—their access to linguistic resources in the L2 is mediated by their race, ethnicity, class, and gender. Their identity is not unitary and stable, but multiple and dynamic. Different factors may play different roles in different contexts, or all factors might play varying roles at varying times. Since SA is a feminised activity, a poststructural approach needs to be a feminist one, by keeping in mind how issues of gender are shaping identity while abroad. Thus feminism would be not only a theoretical framework to account for the sojourners' experiences, but also a driving force to implement programme interventions that address issues of gender construction and socialisation while abroad.

In this regard, the study by King and Sondhi (2016) is an excellent example of a feminist poststructuralist approach to gender and SA. These researchers use Judith Butler's feminist theories (1993, 1999) to account for the construction of gender identity displayed by Indian and UK sojourners. Specifically, they apply the Butlerian concept of *matrix of intelligibility* that constructs a coherent gender identity discourse, which varies across space and time regarding what is acceptable or expected and what is not (King & Sondhi, 2016, p. 21). Thus, Indian and UK participants' performance abroad can be viewed as 'intelligible' in the new language and culture. King and Sondhi show how Indian international students resisted following certain patterns of (heterosexual) masculinity and femininity of the host culture (Canada), which affected their L2 interactions and their identity abroad. As the authors explain:

> performances of Indian masculinity did not always fit into the 'Western' and, specifically, 'white Canadian' narratives of heterosexual masculinity. [...] Young male migrants from 'sexually conservative' countries have expressed and experienced similar dissonance when faced with an environment where having extra-marital sex and/or multiple sexual partners was not only accepted but encouraged. (King & Sondhi, 2016, p. 22)

Another example of this poststructuralist approach to SA can be found in Block's book *Second language identities* (2014), in which some feminist theory (again, by Judith Butler) can be read to account for issues of identity (including gender) in L2 learning and SA.

A poststructuralist approach thus contributes to a deeper understanding of SA experiences, emphasising the local and sociohistorically situated nature of language learning activity (Plews, 2015, p. 282). In this regard, an excellent study about gendered identities negotiated by female international students is Trentman (2015). She analysed the narratives of 54 American learners of Arabic (32 female, 22 male) in Egypt and identified six gendered identities female participants had to confront. (1) *Traditional good girls*: the traditional Egyptian woman does not stay late or have male friends, according to students' perception. Female sojourners performing this stereotype limited their chances for interaction and felt a tension with their will to interact and practise the language. (2) *Loose foreign women*: when ignoring the role of traditional good girls, American students were considered, as Western women in Egypt, overly sexually liberal, as Trentman's students recognise.

In general, the students reported a great deal of difficulty negotiating the tensions between the *traditional good girl* and *loose foreign women* identities. They were often uncertain which identity they were expected to perform, or even which one they wanted to perform, if they felt that there was a conflict between this performance and their own sense of identity or their interactional goals. (Trentman, 2015, p. 270)

(3) *Targets of sexual harassment*: female participants, as foreign women in Egypt, were subjected to all kinds of harassment, this being a major challenge for them. Initial frustration was followed, in some cases, with developing some coping strategies, including the limiting of their access to local social networks. (4) *Female interlocutors*: there were opportunities for American women to engage in informal encounters with Egyptian women. (5) *Guests of the family*: it was easier for female students to enter Egyptian family life than for their male counterparts, for example, by participating in a homestay experience in Alexandria. (6) *Romantic partners*: some female sojourners dated Egyptian males (while the reverse was highly unlikely).

As a result, American females reported serious limitations on their ability to engage with some local social networks as a result of gendered experiences. Yet the multiple ways in which female gender could be performed in this context meant that some female students were also able to actively negotiate gendered identities that helped rather than hindered their access to Egyptian social networks (Trentman, 2015, p. 274). In this case, programme intervention seems vital to help students overcome gender stereotypes as well as to provide them with sufficient tools to improve social interactions.

As Trentman's (2015) study shows, poststructuralist theories considering identity not as a fixed category, but rather as a dynamic, multiple, temporal, cultural, socially constructed, and context-related variable prove valuable for applied linguistics to explore how sojourners negotiate their identities in ways that are advantageous for their language learning goals. As SA is an especially salient context for identity negotiation, the contribution of feminist theory can doubtless help us to understand how gender shapes the experience.

Conclusion and Recommendations: Implications for SA Research and Programme Design from a Gender Perspective

In this chapter I have reviewed available and current research on language and gender, especially in the field of SA. We know that learning a language abroad may imply the negotiation of one's identity, affected by new, place-specific gendered practices conflicting with prior ones. Since most students going abroad are young women, and due to the female nature of language learning discussed above, it is time to call for a new turn in applied linguistics: a gendered, feminist turn. In the studies mentioned in the previous sections, the salience of gendered identities abroad and their impact in the students' lives was noteworthy, especially those related to perceptions of discrimination and sexual harassment. However, the gendered practices abroad go further than sexism. In their study, Kinginger and Whitworth (2005, p. 1) highlight the need for a subtler account of gendered practices during SA rather than the emphasis on sexism or harassment. In this sense, Siegal's study of European women learning Japanese in Japan (1996) presents a different perspective, by focussing on the acquisition of sociolinguistic competence (use of honorifics, mainly) and issues of gender and power (and their subsequent conflicts, when not used appropriately). Her conclusion is that we need to explore learners' identities in addition to their linguistic performance when investigating language acquisition during SA.

Therefore, the connection between feminist theory and language research, present in sociolinguistic approaches to gender and language, cannot be absent in applied linguistics. We need more studies grounded on feminist poststructuralist theory in line with Shi (2006) or Block (2014). The poststructuralist approach to SLA that I encourage follows Pavlenko's formulation (2002, p. 283), which conceives of language as symbolic capital and the site of identity construction, and the L2 user as agent whose multiple identities are dynamic and fluid. Once again, I concur with Trentman (2015, p. 278) when she says that

Further research is needed to show the extent to which study abroad programs can influence students' ability to negotiate identities advantageous to gaining entrance to social networks and language learning. Future research should also investigate other types of gendered and non-gendered identities [...] and particularly the intersections between them. [...] research can help positively transform these experiences for both study abroad students and locals, rather than reinforcing the negative and distressing experiences reported in much of the current study abroad literature.

By reviewing different studies on gender and SA, I have underscored how the sojourner's gender affects their experience abroad in various ways. Those SA programmes taking place in countries where gendered practices are far and distant from those of the home culture are often testimonies of difficulties in dealing with new identities, which result in affective, behavioural, and cognitive experiences of acceptance, resistance, avoidance, or reflections about the target society and the new role performed by the sojourner.

Thus, a qualitative approach seems appropriate to obtain valuable data on how social factors are shaping the students' experience in a given context, as in Patron (2007). Accordingly, at the beginning of their edited volume on SA research, Mitchell, Tracy-Ventura, and McManus (2015), make a case for applying this methodology:

> Given the social dislocation inevitably attaching to the experience of study/residence abroad, it is not surprising that qualitative research traditions investigating its impact on sojourners' personality, identity and intercultural awareness has flourished strongly in this particular domain [...]. This research has highlighted sojourners' growth as practical problem-solvers, and their increasing ease with diversity and self-discovery. At the same time, this research tradition has documented contradictions and troubles concerning the evolution of identity and creation of new relationships (*for example, with respect to gender*). (p. 8; emphasis added)

In short, the cultural, social, ethnic, and linguistic backgrounds of international students have been recognised as influencing the motivations, expectations, experiences, and outcomes of international students studying abroad (Boey, 2014, p. 1; King & Sondhi, 2016).

Among them, gender seems to be a conclusive factor in understanding the attitudes and perceptions of international students pursuing higher education abroad. With the help of feminist theories, a poststructural approach to language as a site for identity construction and gender as a dynamic variable can contribute to the advance of SA as a field of research.

SA programmes are typically framed as invaluable opportunities for students to be immersed in a target language and culture. However, the anticipated gains in L2 communicative competence are affected by a great number of variables, with gender and, broadly, identity being two of the main variables affecting the language learning process: 'the SA experience may, in the end, be primarily about frustration at the inability to develop TL[target language]-mediated subject positions, as women feel threatened by male TL speakers and in some cases come to avoid going out' (Block, 2014, p. 176). Among those gendered practices, sexual harassment has been described in the current chapter. In studies such as Polanyi's (1995), friendship with local women helped the sojourners to develop strategies to cope with sexual harassment, so programme design should guarantee opportunities to meet local people and encourage these exchanges in order to get foreign students into local communities of practice (Twombly, 1995). Furthermore, the introduction of ethnographic work as part of the students' tasks abroad may have a positive impact on their experience. A good example of these practices comes from SA in Costa Rica. In Twombly's (1995) study there, female students reported being sexually harassed, but the researcher also pointed out their inability or even unwillingness to engage with local women as equals. Some years afterwards, Anderson (2003) presented a more positive experience of American students in the same context after some pedagogical changes in programme design were made, which included pre-programme training about the host country and anthropological tools to interpret their experience abroad as critical evaluators not only of the target culture but also of their position as SA students there. As Block (2014, p. 187) suggests, the result of further engagement with the local would favour the emergence of target-language-mediated subject positions, especially through participation in activities involving local people, such as sports.

Concerning programme intervention, another successful experience is found in Dewey et al. (2014). In their study of 118 American students from six SA programmes (Cairo, Madrid, Mérida [Mexico], Moscow, Nanjing, and Paris), researchers found that females typically reported using the language less in class than males. However, according to their data, gender played a minimal role in predicting language use in their study, seemingly because programme design that required students to talk to native speakers outside of class and use the target language a certain amount of time per day may have counteracted the effects that gender may have had initially. In general, their research shows the potential of programme interventions to improve the quality of the SA experience.

Thus, pre-programme training and programme interventions prove to be necessary to develop strategies to face difficulties in accessing the target language. Kinginger (2015, p. 12) advises that 'it is incumbent upon educators to develop explicit pedagogical strategies to assist students in developing awareness of the identity-related challenges involved in language learning'. This would include LGBTQQ students who may glean many positive outcomes from studying abroad, as Bryant and Soria (2015) suggest. Trentman (2013a, pp. 458, 468) points out that these pedagogical and programmatic interventions must be informed by an understanding of the particular context. She advocates the need to connect pedagogical interventions to the local context, pre-departure training, and postsojourn reflection with the help of ethnographic methods. Programmes can work to help students engage with the host community by sharing activities of mutual interest, even with the use of technology to develop relationships prior to arrival and to continue after the stay (Trentman, 2013a, p. 470):

> Expanding the period of study to predeparture and postsojourn, including local as well as study abroad student perspectives, examining language ideologies within the local and global contexts, and evaluating pedagogical interventions in the study are also crucial to improving the study abroad experience. By pursuing this agenda, future research can move from documenting the ways in which study abroad often fails to result in language and cultural learning to pushing for well-developed practices that promote improvement in these areas.

Similarly, Kinginger (2009b, p. 218) believes that researchers from sending and receiving societies might work together to gather data on student perceptions and use these data as a basis for productive interchange and conflict resolution.

Finally, since SA research and practice have historically ignored or obscured an undeniable gender gap, pedagogical decisions should be made to incorporate male students into the experience. Short-term programmes, like summer courses abroad, together with STEM syllabi specifically marketed to men, may be among the priorities of SA stakeholders, advisors, and programme administrators.

Summary of recommendations for programme design from a gender perspective
• Help the sojourners develop strategies to cope with sexual harassment, especially in pre-programme advisory sessions. • Include pre-programme training about the host country and anthropological tools to interpret their experience abroad as critical evaluators not only of the target culture but also of their position as SA students there. • Use technology to develop relationships prior to arrival and after the SA period. • Connect pedagogical interventions to the local context, pre-departure training, and postsojourn reflection with the help of ethnographic methods. • Introduce ethnographic work as part of the students' tasks abroad in order to engage with local people. • Favour opportunities to meet local people and encourage friendship with local women, so that SA students can get into local communities of practice.

Notes

1. This chapter is part of the research project 'The role of gender in language learning during study abroad: Researching students' experiences in CIEE Alicante' (CIEE1-16I), funded by Council on International Educational Exchange Alicante in co-operation with the University of Alicante. The author would like to thank the reviewers for their valuable feedback.
2. *The International Research Foundation for English Language Education* (TIRF, 2017) has in its webpage different reference lists about language

learning. One of them is 'Study abroad and language learning: Selected references'. It is updated regularly and includes more than a hundred titles on this topic, providing an excellent overview of SA research.
3. This distinction corresponds, *mutatis mutandis*, to the two main branches in applied linguistics research: the syntactic and psycholinguistic aspects of L2 learning, on the one hand, and the social dimension, on the other (Pavlenko, 2002, p. 277; see also Block, 2003). I return to this dichotomy in the section on a feminist poststructural approach to gender and SA.

Bibliography

Adkins, M. K. (2004). *Why are more women studying abroad than men? Investigation of the gender imbalance at SIT Study Abroad.* Capstone Collection, Paper 124. Retrieved from http://digitalcollections.sit.edu/capstones/124

Anderson, A. (2003). Women and cultural learning in Costa Rica: Reading the context. *Frontiers: The Interdisciplinary Journal of Study Abroad, 9*, 21–55.

Block, D. (2003). *The social turn in second language acquisition.* Edinburgh, UK: Edinburgh University Press.

Block, D. (2014). *Second language identities.* London: Bloomsbury.

Boey, J. (2014). How does gender matter in the context of the international higher education experience? *IEAA (International Education Association of Australia) Research Digest, 6*, 1–7.

Bown, J., Dewey, D. P., & Belnap, R. K. (2015). Student interactions during study abroad in Jordan. In R. Mitchell, N. Tracy-Ventura, & K. McManus (Eds.), *Social interaction, identity and language learning during residence abroad* (pp. 199–222). EuroSLA Monographs Series 4. Retrieved from http://www.eurosla.org/eurosla-monograph-series-2/social-interaction-identity-and-language-learning-during-residence-abroad/

Brecht, R., Davidson, D. E., & Gingsberg, R. B. (1995). Predictors of foreign language gain during study abroad. In B. Freed (Ed.), *Second language acquisition in a study abroad context* (pp. 37–66). Amsterdam: Benjamins.

Bryant, K. M., & Soria, K. M. (2015). College students' sexual orientation, gender identity, and participation in study abroad. *Frontiers: The Interdisciplinary Journal of Study Abroad, 25*, 91–106.

Bufmack, J. (2013). *Understanding the value of a study abroad experience and closing the gender gap.* All Regis University Theses, Paper 582. Retrieved from https://epublications.regis.edu/cgi/viewcontent.cgi?referer=https://www.google.com.mx/&httpsredir=1&article=1582&context=theses

Burstall, C. (1977). Primary French in the balance. *Foreign Language Annals, 10*(3), 245–331.

Butler, J. (1993). *Bodies that matter: On the discursive limits of sex.* New York: Routledge.

Butler, J. (1999). *Gender trouble. Feminism and the subversion of identity.* New York: Routledge.

Campbell, C. M. (1999). Language anxiety in men and women: Dealing with gender difference in the language classroom. In D. J. Young (Ed.), *Affect in foreign language and second language learning: A practical guide to creating a low-anxiety classroom atmosphere* (pp. 19–41). Boston: McGraw Hill.

Davidson, D. E. (2010). Study abroad: When, how long, and with what results? New data from the Russian front. *Foreign Language Annals, 43,* 6–26.

Dewaele, J., & McIntyre, P. D. (2014). The two faces of Janus? Anxiety and enjoyment in the foreign language classroom. *Studies in Second Language Learning and Teaching, 4*(2), 237–274.

Dewey, D. P. (2007). Language learning during study abroad: What we know and what we have yet to learn. *Japanese Language and Literature, 41*(2), Study Abroad for Advanced Skills, 245–269.

Dewey, D. P., Bown, J., Baker, W., Martinsen, R. A., Gold, C., & Eggett, D. (2014). Language use in six study abroad programs: An exploratory analysis of possible predictors. *Language Learning, 64*(1), 36–71.

Diao, W. (2014). Peer socialization into gendered L2 Mandarin practices in a study abroad context: Talk in the dorm. *Applied Linguistics, 35*(1), 1–23.

Doerr, N. M. (2015). Learner subjects in study abroad: Discourse of immersion, hierarchy of experience and their subversion through situated learning. *Discourse: Studies in the Cultural Politics of Education, 36*(3), 369–382.

Goldoni, F. (2009). *Ethnographic interpretation of study abroad as a cultural immersion event.* PhD dissertation, University of Georgia. Retrieved from https://getd.libs.uga.edu/pdfs/goldoni_federica_200908_phd.pdf

Gore, J. E. (2005). *Dominant beliefs and alternative voices: Discourse, belief, and gender in American study abroad.* New York: Routledge.

Institute of International Education. (2016). *Open Doors 2016.* Report on International Educational Exchange. Retrieved from https://www.iie.org/WhyIIE/Announcements/2016-11-14-Open-Doors-Data

Ishmael, A. (2010). *Studying abroad in the Arab-speaking world: Gender perspectives.* Paper presented at the Georgetown University Roundtable on Languages and Linguistics, Washington, DC.

Jackson, J. (2008). *Language, identity and study abroad: Sociocultural perspectives.* London: Equinox.

King, R., & Sondhi, G. (2016). *Gendering international student migration: A comparison of UK and Indian students' motivations and experiences of studying abroad.* Working Paper No. 84. University of Sussex. Retrieved from https://www.sussex.ac.uk/webteam/gateway/file.php?name=mwp84.pdf&site=252

Kinginger, C. (2009a). *Contemporary study abroad and foreign language learning: An activist's guidebook for language educators.* University Park, PA: CALPER Publications.

Kinginger, C. (2009b). *Language learning and study abroad. A critical reading of research.* New York: Palgrave Macmillan.

Kinginger, C. (2015). Student mobility and identity-related language learning. *Intercultural Education, 26,* 6–15.

Kinginger, C., & Whitworth, K. F. (2005). Gender and emotional investment in language learning during study abroad. *CALPER Working Papers Series, 2,* 1–18.

Kline, R. (1998). Literacy and language learning in a study abroad context. *Frontiers: The Interdisciplinary Journal of Study Abroad, 10,* 19–42.

Kobayashi, Y. (2002). The role of gender in foreign language learning attitudes: Japanese female students' attitudes towards English learning. *Gender and Education, 14*(2), 181–197.

Lasagabaster, D. (2008). Foreign language competence in content and language integrated courses. *Open Applied Linguistics Journal, 1*(1), 30–41.

Lewin, R. (2009). *The handbook of practice and research in study abroad: Higher education and the quest for global citizenship.* New York, NY: Routledge.

Mathews, S. A. (2000). *Russian second language acquisition during study abroad: Gender differences in student behavior.* Unpublished doctoral dissertation, Bryn Mawr College, Bryn Mawr, PA.

Mitchell, R., Tracy-Ventura, N., & McManus, K. (Eds.). (2015). *Social interaction, identity and language learning during residence abroad.* EuroSLA Monographs Series 4. Retrieved from http://www.eurosla.org/eurosla-monograph-series-2/socialinteraction-identity-and-language-learning-during-residence-abroad/

Morita, N. (2009). Language, culture, gender, and academic socialization. *Language and Education, 23*(5), 443–460.

Norton, B. (2000). *Identity and language learning: Gender, ethnicity, and educational change.* London: Longman.

Norton, B., & Pavlenko, A. (2004a). Gender and English language learners: Challenges and possibilities. In B. Norton & A. Pavlenko (Eds.), *Gender and English language learners* (pp. 1–14). TESOL Case Studies in TESOL Practice Series. Alexandria, VA: TESOL.

Norton, B., & Pavlenko, A. (Eds.). (2004b). *Gender and English language learners*. Alexandria, VA: TESOL.

Patron, M. (2007). *Culture and identity in study abroad contexts: After Australia, French without France*. Oxford: Peter Lang.

Pavlenko, A. (2001). 'How do I become a woman in an American vein?': Transformations of gender performance in second language socialization. In A. Pavlenko, A. Blackledge, I. Piller, & M. Teutsch-Dwyer (Eds.), *Multilingualism, second language learning and gender* (pp. 133–174). New York: Mouton de Gruyter.

Pavlenko, A. (2002). Poststructuralist approaches to the study of social factors in second language learning and use. In V. Cook (Ed.), *Portraits of the L2 user* (pp. 277–302). Clevedon, UK: Multilingual Matters.

Pavlenko, A., Blackledge, A., Piller, I., & Teutsch-Dwyer, M. (2001). *Multilingualism, second language learning and gender*. New York: Mouton de Gruyter.

Pellegrino Aveni, V. (2005). *Study abroad and second language use: Constructing the self*. Cambridge: Cambridge University Press.

Pérez-Vidal, C. (Ed.). (2014). *Language acquisition in study abroad and formal instruction contexts*. Philadelphia: Benjamins.

Plews, J. L. (2015). Intercultural identity-alignment in second language study abroad, or the more-or-less Canadians. In R. Mitchell, N. Tracy-Ventura, & K. McManus (Eds.), *Social interaction, identity and language learning during residence abroad* (pp. 281–304). EuroSLA Monographs Series 4. Retrieved from http://www.eurosla.org/eurosla-monograph-series-2/social-interaction-identity-and-language-learning-duringresidence-abroad/

Polanyi, L. (1995). Language learning and living abroad: Stories from the field. In B. Freed (Ed.), *Second language acquisition in a study abroad context* (pp. 271–291). Philadelphia: Benjamins.

de Prada, E. (1993). *Aspectos psicolingüísticos del aprendizaje de una lengua extranjera*. Santiago de Compostela: Servicio de Publicaciones de la Universidad e Intercambio Científico.

Redden, E. (2008, December 8). Women abroad and men at home. *Inside Higher Ed*. Retrieved from https://www.insidehighered.com/news/2008/12/04/genderabroad

Rohrlich, B. F., & Martin, J. N. (1991). Host country and reentry adjustment of student sojourners. *International Journal of Intercultural Relations, 15*(2), 163–182.

Roquet, H., Llopis, J., & Pérez-Vidal, C. (2016). Does gender have an impact on the potential benefits learners may achieve in two contexts compared: Formal instruction and formal instruction + content and language integrated learning? *International Journal of Bilingual Education and Bilingualism, 19*(4), 1–17.

Salisbury, M. H., Umbach, P. D., Paulsen, M. B., & Pascarella, E. T. (2009). Going global: Understanding the choice process of the intent to study abroad. *Research in Higher Education, 50*(2), 119–143.

Schmidt, R., Boraie, D., & Kassagby, O. (1996). Foreign language motivation: International structure and external connections. In R. L. Oxford (Ed.), *Language learning motivation: Pathways to the new century* (pp. 9–20). Honolulu, HI: Second Language Teaching & Curriculum Center, University of Hawaiʻi at Mānoa.

Schumann, F. (1980). Diary of a language learner: A further analysis. In R. Scarcella & S. Krashen (Eds.), *Research in second language acquisition* (pp. 51–57). Cambridge, MA: Newbury House.

Sen, R. S., & Samdup, P. E. (2009). Revisiting gender in open and distance learning—an independent variable or a mediated reality? *Open Learning, 24*(2), 165–185.

Shi, X. (2006). Gender, identity and intercultural transformation in second language socialisation. *Language and Intercultural Communication, 6*(1), 2–17.

Shirley, S. W. (2006). *The gender gap in post-secondary study abroad. Understanding and marketing to male students*. Unpublished doctoral dissertation, University of North Dakota, Grand Forks, ND.

Siegal, M. (1996). The role of learner subjectivity in second language sociolinguistic competency: Western women learning Japanese. *Applied Linguistics, 17*, 356–382.

Smith, A., & Bown, J. (2013). Study abroad, gender, and the speaking experience. How gender mediates speaking opportunities for students studying abroad in the Middle East. *Journal of Undergraduate Research*. Retrieved from http://jur.byu.edu/?p=4445

Sood, S. (2012, September 26). The statistics of studying abroad. Retrieved from http://www.bbc.com/travel/story/20120926-the-statistics-of-studying-abroad

Talburt, S., & Stewart, M. A. (1999). What's the subject of study abroad? Race, gender and 'living culture'. *Modern Language Journal, 83*(2), 163–175.
The International Research Foundation for English Language Education (TIRF). (2017). Study abroad and language learning: Selected references. Monterey, CA. Retrieved from http://www.tirfonline.org/resources/references/
Trentman, E. (2013a). Arabic and English during study abroad in Cairo, Egypt: Issues of access and use. *Modern Language Journal, 97*(2), 457–473.
Trentman, E. (2013b). Imagined communities and language learning during study abroad: Arabic learners in Egypt. *Foreign Language Annals, 46*(4), 545–564.
Trentman, E. (2015). Negotiating gendered identities and access to social networks during study abroad in Egypt. In R. Mitchell, N. Tracy-Ventura, & K. McManus (Eds.). *Social interaction, identity and language learning during residence abroad* (pp. 263–280). EuroSLA Monographs Series 4. Retrieved from http://www.eurosla.org/eurosla-monograph-series-2/social-interaction-identity-and-language-learning-during-residence-abroad/
Twombly, S. B. (1995). Piropos and friendship: Gender and culture clash in study abroad. *Frontiers: The Interdisciplinary Journal of Study Abroad, 1*, 1–27.
Twombly, S. B., Salisbury, M. H., Tumanut, S. D., & Klute, P. (2012). *Study abroad in a new global century: Renewing the promise, refining the purpose.* ASHE Higher Education Report: Vol. 38, No. 4, Jossey-Bass Higher and Adult Education Series. San Francisco, CA: Wiley.
Vanderick, S. (2000). The need for more research on female language learners in the classroom. *Temple University Working Papers in Applied Linguistics, 7*, 11–25.
Zhou, Y., Jindal-Snape, D., Topping, K., & Todman, J. (2008). Theoretical models of culture shock and adaptation in international students in higher education. *Studies in Higher Education, 33*(1), 63–75.

Index[1]

A

Abbott, A., 184
Abuamsha, K., 55
ACTFL, *see* American Council on the Teaching of Foreign Languages
Adopt a Class project, 11, 299–322
Africa, 29, 90
AFS New Zealand, 259–260, 272, 275
Akande, Y., 170
Alexandria, 51, 52, 391
Alred, G., 28
Altman Dautoff, D., 186
Alturó, N., 251n3
American Council on the Teaching of Foreign Languages (ACTFL), 51, 73, 78n2
Amman, 52, 54–57, 379
Anderson, A., 394
Andon, N., 128, 133
Anya, U., 91, 95
Arabic study, at Brigham Young University, 49–78
   lessons, 60–70
   programme development history, 50–60
Argentina, 35, 181, 260, 331
Australia, 175, 268, 382–384, 386
Austria, 29, 203
Awareness of teaching and learning, 125–158
   CSSG, 129–131
   innovative teaching approaches, 132–136
   recommendations, 155–158
   research project, 136–155

---

[1] Note: Page numbers followed by 'n' refer to notes.

B

Barkhuizen, G., 10, 129, 196
Beckles, Sir H., 85
Belgium, 29, 203, 260
Belnap, L., 63
Belnap, R. K., 8, 53, 63
Bennett, M., 264
Benson, P., 10, 196, 197, 203, 205, 209, 210, 213–217, 225
Bernstein, B., 308
Biggs, J., 28
Bird, M., 59
Biyu, 345, 346, 357
Block, D., 128, 129, 158, 196, 383, 392, 394
Bloom, B., 168
Bodycott, P., 10, 196
Boey, J., 378, 382, 384, 385
Boraie, D., 374
Bown, J., 2, 6, 54, 58, 63, 379, 382, 388
Brazil, 290, 335
Brecht, R., 378, 379
Brigham Young University (BYU), 50
British Academy, 26
British Council, 30, 37, 319
British Council Assistantship, 314
Brockington, J. L., 6
Brower, H. H., 264, 265, 277, 280, 282, 285
Brown, J., 10, 196
Brubaker, C., 6
Bryant, K. M., 386, 395
Bucholtz, M., 216
Butler, J., 389
Byram, M., 28, 35, 258, 262, 265, 269, 286
BYU, *see* Brigham Young University

C

Cairo, 52–55, 67, 380, 395
Camille, 352
Canada, 2, 7, 29, 130, 131, 136, 137, 139, 140, 143, 145, 156, 166, 260, 390
Canadian Summer School in Germany (CSSG), 129–133, 135, 136
Carbaugh, D., 353
Caribbean, 7, 9, 29
  context, study abroad in, 83–114
Carnine, J., 343, 356
CASA, *see* Center for Arabic Study Abroad
Causal relationship, 225
CEFR, *see* Common European Framework of Reference for Languages
Center for Arabic Study Abroad (CASA), 69
Chameleon complex, 168
Changnon, G., 261
Chenglei, 346, 348, 355
Chile, 260
China, 7, 260, 268, 270, 272, 278, 279, 346, 357, 389
Churchill, E., 243
CLIL, *see* Content and language integrated learning
Coleman, J. A., 28, 33, 85
Collentine, J., 126
Comanaru, R. S., 5
Common European Framework of Reference for Languages (CEFR), 227, 248
Community service learning (CSL), 165–189

Comp, D., 3
Connective learning, 186, 187
Content and language integrated learning (CLIL), 374, 375
Cook, V., 128
Corbin, J., 337
Corder, D., 258
Cornell University, 64
Cotteral, S. l., 128
Course development, 9, 99
Craig, I., 86, 111, 113, 114
Critical Pedagogy, 89, 97, 98, 105
Cross-cultural interaction, 347
Crozet, C., 276
CSL, *see* Community service learning
CSSG, *see* Canadian Summer School in Germany
Cultural awareness, 357
Cultural identities, 332
Cultural immersion, 263–267
Cultural integration, 186
Cultural intelligence, 264, 265, 269, 278, 280, 282, 283, 287–290
Curriculum design, 28, 40, 42, 60
Curriculum integration, 40, 84, 88, 93, 94, 103, 115n1
Cushner, K., 4

D

Daiyu, 350, 356
Damascus, 52
Daniels, H., 28
Data collection, 225, 229, 335–337
Davidson, D. E., 378, 379
Davis, J. M., 64
'Day for Others' programme, 173
Deardorff, D. K., 200, 263, 284
DeKeyser, R. M., 126, 127

Denmark, 7, 10, 203, 230–232, 235, 236, 240, 247, 248
Developmental factor, 229
Dewaele, J. M., 5
Dewey, D. P., 2, 53, 63, 68, 372, 394
Dewey, J., 87
de Wit, H., 169
Diao, W., 389
Dick-Forde, E., 115n3
Dissonance factor, 284–285
Do for Smile@East Japan Project, 173, 175–184
Doerr, N. M., 386
Doidge, N., 278
Domestic L2 curricula, 226–231
Dörnyei, Z., 28, 305
Drama pedagogy, 128, 132–134, 142–144, 148, 155
Driscoll, P., 263, 266, 282
Du Bois, J. W., 230
Duff, P., 267

E

East, M., 266
EBacc, *see* English Baccalaureate
Eckerth, J., 128
ECTS, *see* European Credit Transfer and Accumulation System
Egypt, 7, 51, 52, 66, 342, 390, 391
Ehrman, M., 53
England, 7, 175, 204
Engle, J., 6, 49, 66, 100, 169
English as Second Language (ESL), 128, 129, 329, 334
English Baccalaureate (EBacc), 300
ERASMUS, 10, 25, 29, 36–38, 195–218, 223–251, 251n2, 303, 311

ERASMUS (*Cont.*)
   immersion, 226–231
   research design, 228–231
ESL, *see* English as Second Language
Estonia, 203
Ethnorelativism, 332, 333, 359
European Commission, 25, 199, 200, 227
European Credit Transfer and Accumulation System (ECTS), 204
European Union, 26
   Online Linguistic Support, 36
Even, S., 132, 133
Experiential learning, 8, 28, 33, 34, 41, 42, 84, 169, 171–173, 202, 374
Experiential Learning Cycle, 87

F

Faraco, M., 5
Female interlocutors, 391
Female students, 373–375, 377–380, 382, 385, 388, 391, 394
Feminism, 389
Fez, 52
Finland, 203
Follow-up interviews
   Gateshead teacher, 316–317
   Hartlepool teacher, 317
   Newcastle teacher, 314–316
Foreign language, 226
Formal learning, 32, 33, 40, 42
Former Yugoslav Republic of Macedonia, 218n2
France, 7, 29, 35, 204, 260, 268, 275, 276, 331, 335, 343, 352, 384

G

Gareis, E., 181, 345
Garrett, P., 128
GCSE, *see* General Certificate of Secondary Education
Gender, 11, 13, 270, 371–396
   balance, 307
   blindness, 381, 382
   feminist poststructural approach, 387–391
   gap, 373–381
   imbalance, 377
   learning outcomes and, 381–387
   SA research and programme design, 392–396
   and study abroad, 371–373
Gender and English Language Learners, 382
General Certificate of Secondary Education (GCSE), 300, 308
Generalitat de Catalunya, 227
Geoffrey and the State Secondary School case study, 311–312
Germany, 7, 9, 29, 129, 131, 136, 138, 204, 260, 268, 272–274, 280, 281, 317
Gingerich, O., 97
Gingsberg, R. B., 378
Gladding, S., 3
Global citizenship, 328–329
Global Graduates, 318
Globalized infotainment, 27
Goldoni, F., 383
Gore, J. E., 380
Grünzweig, W., 187
Guozhi, 345, 349

H

Hall, K., 216
Hall, S., 96
Handbook of Practice and Research in Study Abroad, 3
Harrison, J. K., 264, 265, 277, 280, 282, 285
Harvey, S., 258, 260, 261, 265, 267, 269, 270, 279, 286, 287
Hawkey, R., 128
Healey, M., 28
HEIs, *see* Higher education institutions
Higher education, 4, 26, 61, 89, 195, 198, 200, 202, 327, 385, 394
Higher Education Funding Council for England (Hefce), 301
Higher education institutions (HEIs), 300
Holliday, A., 201
Holmes, P., 279, 283
Houghton, S., 269
Huidai, 349–352, 354
Hungary, 204

I

ICC, *see* Intercultural communicative competence
Iceland, 204, 218n2
Identity, 10, 37, 62, 70, 130, 133, 195–218, 262–264, 278, 280, 282–284, 288–290, 318, 333, 372, 379, 380, 382, 385–387
IEREST, *see* Intercultural Education Resources for ERASMUS Students and their Teachers
ILEP, *see* International Languages Exchanges and Pathways
Imagined identities, 247
Immersion for Languages' course, 86–94
Immersion programmes, 53, 64, 129, 330
 See also Language and culture immersion experiences (LCIEs)
Informal learning, 28, 33, 35
In-sojourn, 236–246
Institutional collaboration, strengthening, 55–57
Institutionalized commercial rhetoric, 27
Intercultural awareness, 347
Intercultural communication, 328, 345
Intercultural communicative competence (ICC), 10, 12, 35, 257–291, 305
Intercultural Development Inventory, 115n1
Intercultural Education Resources for ERASMUS Students and their Teachers (IEREST), 28, 36, 195–218
Intercultural friendships, 9, 180–182, 186, 188, 327–362
Interculturality, 2–4, 6, 7, 9–14, 28, 29, 31, 35–39, 49, 68, 84–88, 93, 94, 96, 100, 103, 105, 106, 126, 135, 138, 155–157, 165, 167, 168, 171, 172, 180, 183, 380
Intercultural knowledge and expertise, 288, 306
Intercultural learning, 195–218

Intercultural relationship, 338–345
International education
  learning outcomes, 381
International Languages Exchanges
  and Pathways (ILEP), 259, 270
International service learning (ISL),
  167, 169, 172, 184–187, 189
International students, 11, 130,
  131, 136, 327–362, 378,
  386, 388, 390
  See also specific entries
Iran, 335
Iraq, 335
Isabelli-García, C., 2, 181, 182, 331
Ishmael, A., 380
Italy, 7, 10, 29, 227
ISL, *see* International service-learning
Itin, C., 173

J

Jackson, J., 6, 28, 167, 196, 200,
  211, 250, 264, 270, 279, 283,
  332, 357, 359
Japan, 7, 9, 165–189, 260, 377,
  378, 385
Jenkins, A., 28
Jerusalem, 52
Ji-min, 347
Jingfei, 351–353
Jinhai, 356
Jones, M., 263, 284
Jordan, 7, 52, 64, 66, 67
  study abroad reading assignment
    instructions, 74–78
Josephine and the State Secondary
  School case study, 313–314

K

Kassagby, O., 374
Kiely, R., 167–170
Kim, Y. Y., 88
King, R., 375, 378, 385, 386, 389
Kinginger, C., 3, 100, 182, 283,
  377, 382–384, 387, 392,
  395, 396
Klute, P., 5
Kobayashi, Y., 378
Kolb, A., 28
Kolb, C., 4
Kolb, D. A., 28, 34, 87, 201, 202
Kramsch, H. C., 276, 281
Krathwohl, D., 168
Kubota, R., 225, 251n1

L

L1 speaking/interactions, in study
  abroad, 354
L2 Ideal Self, 306, 314
L2 identity, 2–7, 195–218, 231, 390
L2 learning, 223–224, 250
L2 Motivational Self System, 305,
  306, 317
L2 proficiency, 248
L2 speakers, 306, 332, 333, 344, 348
L2 speaking/interaction, in study
  abroad, 6, 33, 83–114,
  327–362
Lafford, B., 126
Language and culture immersion
  experiences (LCIEs), 258–260,
  263, 265, 267, 268, 270, 272,
  275–277, 280, 282, 284–290
Language awareness, 125–158, 262

Language learning, 239, 382, 397n2
Language Learning and Study Abroad, 3
Language requirement, 10
Language teachers, 10, 257–291
Language teaching assistant, 303, 318, 319
Language Trends 2014/15 report, 300
LARA, *see* Learning and Residence Abroad
Lasagabaster, D., 375
Latin America, 29
LCIEs, *see* Language and culture immersion experiences
Lear, D., 184
Learning and Residence Abroad (LARA), 31
Learning support, 12, 13, 28, 33–39
Lesbian, gay, bisexual, transgender, questioning, or queer (LGBTQQ), 386, 395
Levant, 66
Levin, J., 263
Lewin, R., 3
LGBTQQ, *see* Lesbian, gay, bisexual, transgender, questioning, or queer
Liddicoat, A., 276
Liechtenstein, 218n2
Lifelong Learning Programme, 200
Lijing, 347, 356
Lina, 355, 356
Lingard, R., 251n1
Linguistic self-concept, 207–210, 236
Linqin, 350, 351
Lithuania, 204
Liufang, 349
Liwei, 347
Llopis, J., 374
Local affordances, taking advantage of, 52–53
Long, S. O., 170, 187
Longitudinality, 229
Loose foreign women, 390
Lou, K. H., 4, 28, 167, 282, 286
Lutterman-Aguila, A., 97

M

McManus, K., 87, 223, 393
Majdoubeh, Ahmad, 52
Malaysia, 175
Male students, 374, 375, 379–381, 388, 396
Mariana, 349, 354
Martin, J. N., 380
Marx, H., 266, 279, 282, 284–286
Masia, B., 168
Mathews, S. A., 379
Matrix of intelligibility, 389
Maximizing Study Abroad, 6
Meier, G., 28, 39
Meifeng, 347
Meiji Gakuin University (MGU) Volunteer Center, 172–174
Mentoring, 285–286
Meta-pedagogical awareness, 128, 129, 155
Mexico, 93, 184, 331, 350
Mezirow, J., 263
MGU, *see* Meiji Gakuin University
Middle East Studies/Arabic (MESA), 51
Middlebury College, 64
Mingzhu, 353

Minnesota Model of curriculum
  integration, 115n1
Misfeldt, K. F., 6, 134
Mitchell, M., 182, 223
Mitchell, R., 87, 95, 331, 354,
  357, 393
Modern foreign languages
  (MFLs), 300
Modern languages, 299, 309, 318
  and cultures, 8, 25–42, 156
  in UK, 300
Morita, N., 385
Morocco, 7, 52, 64, 66
Moss, D. M., 266, 279, 282,
  284–286
Motivations and challenges,
  180–183, 186, 187, 206, 264,
  271, 272, 275, 278, 280, 281,
  285, 308, 334, 345–348, 393
Müller, M., 265
Muñoz, C., 128
Murphy-Lejeune, E., 227, 243,
  247, 250

N

Nakano, K., 170
National Middle East Language
  Resource Center (NMELRC),
  53, 54
Netherlands, the, 204
New Caledonia, 260
New Zealand, 7, 10, 175, 184,
  258–260, 266–268, 270, 272,
  274–276, 282, 283, 286, 290
Newton, J., 262
Nicaragua, 167, 186
NMELRC, *see* National Middle East
  Language Resource Center

Non-essentialist perspective, of
  culture, 196–198, 201
Norton, B., 382, 388
Norway, 218n2
Nowitzki, W., 262
Nunan, D., 146

O

Ogden, A., 100
O'Neill, G., 283
Online buddies, 308
OPI, *see* Oral Proficiency Interview
Oraga Otsuchi, 177
Oral Proficiency Interview (OPI), 65

P

Paige, R. M., 4, 6, 28, 167, 200,
  264, 278, 282
Parker, B., 186
Parker, L., 28, 33
Parkinson, D., 55, 57
Participant perspectives, 345–357
Passarelli, A. M., 28
Patron, M., 383, 393
Pavlenko, A., 381, 382, 387, 388
Payrató, N., 251n3
Pedagogy
  critical, 89, 97, 98, 105
  drama, 128, 132–134, 142–144,
    148, 155
  framework for Caribbean
    sojourners, 94–98
  in practice, 98–100
Peiser, G., 263, 284
Pellegrino Aveni, V. A., 305, 379
Pérez-Vidal, C., 126, 329, 374
Perry, A. M., 85

Peru, 7, 311, 316
Philippines, 175
Piller, I., 115n3
Plater, W. M., 170, 171
Plews, J. L., 2, 6, 115n3, 286, 288
Polanyi, L., 378
Portugal, 204, 227
Postcolonial students, from Caribbean, 84, 96, 97, 100, 103–106
Postcolonial Theory, 96
Postcolonialism, 97
Poststructuralism, 388
Prada, E. de, 374
Pre-departure preparation, 10, 87, 88, 101
Pre-departure requirements, 248
Pre-departure training, 395
Pre-sojourn, 231–236
Prior, M. T., 238
Programme assessment, 5, 8, 30–33, 37, 38
Programme culture, 35, 60–64
Programme evaluation, 64–66, 101
Punnett, B. J., 115n3
Purdy, R. W., 170

Q

Qasid Institute (QI), 55

R

Ramírez, G. B., 166
Reading development, 53–55, 68–70
Redden, E., 377
Rhodes, G., 3
Rinehart, N., 187

Rizvi, F., 251n1
Robinson, J., 115n3
Rohrlich, B. F., 380
Roquet, H., 374
Roskvist, A., 258
Routes into Languages programme, 11, 301–303
　Adopt a Class initiative, 302, 303
　SLAs, 301, 302
Routes North East Consortium Pilot of 2014/15, 303–309
　L2 Motivational Self System, 306
　research considerations, 305
　Self-organised Learning Environments, 307, 308
　Three Case Study Participants, 303
Rowe, J. E., 263
Ryan, C., 61

S

SA experience, 225, 226, 230, 247, 249
SA from the Caribbean context, 7, 9, 29, 83–114
SA participants, 2–7, 11–13, 38, 115n1, 266, 328–331, 333, 336, 342, 343, 345, 351, 354, 356–358, 380
SA participation, 373, 377
SA pedagogy, 2–15, 87, 95, 106
SA programming, 2–7, 85, 86, 90, 93, 95, 97, 103, 127, 129, 134, 137, 139, 141, 149, 154–156, 195, 199, 216, 229, 261, 266, 268, 291, 327, 328, 330, 331, 355, 359, 360, 373, 374, 376, 393–395

SA research, 2–7, 28, 84, 103, 125–127, 140, 156, 170, 246, 261, 266, 270, 277, 328, 387, 389
SA social imaginary, 224
Salisbury, M. H., 5, 374–376, 381
Samoa, 260
Sanz, C., 3, 126
Schewe, M., 132
Schmenk, B., 265
Schmidt, R., 128, 374
School of Modern Language and Cultures, Durham, 28
Schumann, F., 380
Second language learning, *see* L2 learning
Second language acquisition, 308, 381
Secondary education, 27
Self-organised Learning Environments (SOLE), 307, 308
Seo-yun, 356
Sercu, L., 281
Sexism, 384
Sexual harassment
  behaviours abroad, 383
  targets, 391
Shaules, J., 263, 278, 279, 286
Shearn, S., 262
Shen, 350
Shi, X., 392
Shirley, S. W., 374–377
Short-term study abroad, 9, 84, 90, 93, 129–131, 259, 332, 377
Siegal, M., 385
Sinicrope, C., 64
Situated Learning, 94
Skarin, R., 115n3
Skehan, P., 135
Smith, A., 379, 388

Social interaction, 35
Social Learning analytical framework, 94
Sojourn, 131, 169, 170, 182, 185, 196, 258, 267, 268, 270, 271, 279, 286, 290
Sojourner, 9, 196, 266, 372, 377–380, 382–386, 388–390
  non-traditional, 83–114
Sondhi, G., 375, 378, 385, 386, 389
Soria, K. M., 386, 395
Spain, 7, 9–11, 29, 35, 83, 89–94, 100, 105, 204, 260, 313, 331, 350
Speaking and writing appointments, institutionalising, 57–58
Speaking partners, 55, 57–60, 63, 66–68, 379
Spitzberg, B. H., 261
Stacey, K., 258
Stake, R., 268
Steffen, P., 54, 63
Stephenson, S., 3
Strategy for Outward Mobility, 25–26
Strauss, A., 337
Strongly-framed pedagogical relationship, 308
Student engagement, 7, 52, 62, 94, 98, 165–189, 308
Student Language Ambassadors, 11, 301, 308
  role of, 301–302
Student's Guide for Maximizing Study Abroad, 111
Student-centred second language study, 83–114
Students' Imagined Identities, 231

Study abroad, 301, 327–362,
  371–396
  gender gap in, 374
  in USA, 328–329
  See also specific entries
Switzerland, 218n2
Szente, J., 263

T

Taillefer, G. F., 51
Taiwan, 175
Takahashi, K., 115n3
Target language, 227
Target language speaking, 338–345
Task-based language teaching
  (TBLT), 9, 128, 132,
  134–136, 144–148, 150,
  151, 155
Teaching assistants (TAs), 356
Tendenko, 177
Tengfei, 346–348, 350
Thomae, M., 263
Thompson, G., 6
Three Student Case Studies,
  309–311
Tracy-Ventura, N., 87, 223, 393
Traditional good girls, 390
Transformational learning, 167–172
Transformative learning, 258, 263,
  265, 266, 269, 277–280, 282,
  285–288, 290
Trentman, E., 66, 342, 380, 383,
  390–392, 395
Triandis, H. C., 281
Tschirner, E., 6, 126
Tumanut, S. D., 5

Turkey, 218n2
Twombly, S. B., 5, 373, 374, 376, 378

U

UCML, *see* University Council of
  Modern Languages
UIMP, *see* Universidad Internacional
  Menéndez Pelayo
United States, 7
Universidad Autónoma de Yucatán
  (Mexico), 93
Universidad Internacional Menéndez
  Pelayo (UIMP), 83, 85, 87, 88,
  91–93, 99, 107–110
  Spanish Language and Culture
    Course, 91
University Council of Modern
  Languages (UCML), 26, 39
University of the West Indies (UWI),
  83, 89–95, 98, 100, 101, 104,
  105, 107
Urlaub, P., 203
USA, 166, 175, 328–329
Ushioda, E., 28
UWI, *see* University of the West Indies

V

Vande Berg, M., 3, 4, 6, 28, 39, 167,
  200, 282
Vatalaro, A., 263, 279
Virtual Learning Environment
  (VLE), 37
Vogt, K., 266
Volunteer work, 174, 181, 185,
  187, 188

W

Wales, 10
Wangjie, 350, 352, 354
Wangyan, 347, 353
Wanner, D., 4
Wanpaku-Hiroba, 175
Watanabe, Y., 64
Wernicke, M., 266, 290
Wessel, N., 184
Whiteley, P., 85
Whitworth, K. F., 387, 392
Wiedenhoeft, M. D., 6
Willis Allen, H., 28
Willis, J., 134
Wingate, U., 133
Witte, A., 263, 284
Wong, E. D., 94, 95

Y

Yanlin, 348
Yates, E., 262
Year Abroad, 299–320
Year-long study abroad, at Durham University, 25–42
    history and development, 30–33
    institutional context, 28–30
Young, R., 128

Z

Zarate, G., 28
Zemach-Bersin, T., 27
Zhang, Z., 353, 355
Zhou, G., 353, 355
Zlotkowski, E., 173

CPSIA information can be obtained
at www.ICGtesting.com
Printed in the USA
LVHW04*1243280518
578630LV00001B/4/P